CIVIL-MILITARY RELATIONS

———— ■ ————

Latin America in Global Perspective

The fundamental purpose of this multivolume series is to broaden conceptual perspectives for the study of Latin America. This effort responds to a perception of need. Latin America cannot be understood in isolation from other parts of the world. This has always been so; it is especially true in the contemporary era.

Accordingly, the goal of this series is to demonstrate the desirability and the feasibility of analyzing Latin America in comparative perspective, in conjunction with other regions, and in global perspective, in the context of worldwide processes. A subsidiary purpose is to establish a bridge between Latin American "area studies" and mainstream social science disciplines, to the mutual benefit of both. Ultimately, the intent is to explore and emphasize intellectual challenges posed by dynamic changes within Latin America and in its relation to the international arena.

The present volume examines the relationship between regional integration schemes in the Americas and in the Pacific Rim, thus promoting the comparative analysis of Latin America and East Asia within a global perspective. The series thus far includes:

Civil-Military Relations: Building Democracy and Regional Security in Latin America, Southern Asia, and Central Europe, edited by David R. Mares;

Latin America in Comparative Perspective: New Approaches to Methods and Analysis, edited by Peter H. Smith;

EnGENDERing Wealth and Well-Being: Empowerment for Global Change, edited by Rae Lesser Blumberg, Cathy A. Rakowski, Irene Tinker, and Michael Monteón;

Cooperation or Rivalry? Regional Integration in the Americas and the Pacific Rim, edited by Shoji Nishijima and Peter H. Smith;

Institutional Design in New Democracies: Eastern Europe and Latin America, edited by Arend Lijphart and Carlos H. Waisman; and

Latin American Environmental Policy in International Perspective, edited by Gordon J. MacDonald, Daniel L. Nielson, and Marc A. Stern.

This series results from a multiyear research program organized by the Center for Iberian and Latin American Studies (CILAS) at the University of California, San Diego. Principal funding has come from the Andrew W. Mellon Foundation.

CIVIL-MILITARY RELATIONS

■

Building Democracy and Regional Security in Latin America, Southern Asia, and Central Europe

edited by

David R. Mares

WestviewPress

A Division of HarperCollins*Publishers*

Latin America in Global Perspective

Copyright © 1998 by Westview Press, A Division of HarperCollins Publishers, Inc., except for Chapter 2, which is © by Rebecca L. Schiff.

Published in 1998 in the United States of America by Westview Press, 5500 Central Avenue, Boulder, Colorado 80301-2877, and in the United Kingdom by Westview Press, 12 Hid's Copse Road, Cumnor Hill, Oxford OX2 9JJ

Library of Congress Cataloging-in-Publication Data
Civil-military relations : building democracy and regional security in
    Latin America, Southern Asia, and Central Europe / edited by David
    R. Mares.
        p.   cm. — (Latin America in global perspective)
    Includes bibliographical references and index.
    ISBN 0-8133-2421-1 (hardcover)
    1. Civil-military relations—Latin America.   2. Civil-military
relations—Asia.   3. Civilian-military relations—Europe, Eastern.
I. Mares, David R.   II. Series.
JL956.C58C58   1998
322'.5—dc21   98-9524
                                                                    CIP

The paper used in this publication meets the requirements of the American National Standard for Permanence of Paper for Printed Library Materials Z39.48-1984.

10   9   8   7   6   5   4   3   2   1

Contents

Acknowledgments   ix
List of Acronyms   xi

1 Civil-Military Relations, Democracy, and
   the Regional Neighborhood, *David R. Mares*   1

Part One   **Conceptions of Civil-Military Relations and Democracy**   25

2 Concordance Theory: The Cases of India and Pakistan,
   Rebecca L. Schiff   27

3 Civil-Military Relations in Indonesia: The Case of
   ABRI's Dual Function, *J. Soedjati Djiwandono*   45

4 Civil-Military Relations in Venezuela,
   Gisela Gómez Sucre and María Dolores Cornett   59

Part Two   **Civilian-Dominated Relationships**   77

5 From Confrontation to Cooperation: Democratic Governance
   and Argentine Foreign Relations, *David Pion-Berlin*   79

6 Civil-Military Relations in the Czech and Slovak Republics,
   Thomas S. Szayna   101

7 The Restructuring of Civil-Military Relations in Poland
   Since 1989, *Mark Kramer*   132

Part Three   **Civil-Military Partnerships**   163

8 Civil-Military Relations in Chile's Geopolitical Transition,
   Francisco Rojas and Claudio Fuentes   165

 9 Changing Patterns of Civil-Military Relations and
    Thailand's Regional Outlook, *Surachart Bamrungsuk*   187

10 The Interplay of Internal War and Democratization
    in Guatemala Since 1982, *Caesar D. Sereseres*   206

11 Democratization and International Integration: The Role of
    the Armed Forces in Brazil's Grand Strategy,
    Thomaz Guedes da Costa   223

12 Conclusion: Civil-Military Relations, Democracy, and
    Regional Security in Comparative Perspective, *David R. Mares*   238

About the Editor and Contributors   259
Index   263

Acknowledgments

I am grateful to multiple organizations for funding this book. The book began as part of the project "Latin America in Comparative Perspective" sponsored by the Center for Iberian and Latin American Studies of the University of California, San Diego, and supported by a grant from the Andrew W. Mellon Foundation. Additional start-up funding was provided by the Institute on Global Conflict and Cooperation of the University of California. The Pacific Rim Research Program of the University of California provided major funding for authors' research and for a conference held at the University of California, San Diego, in November 1995.

As editor, I would like to thank my research assistant Risa Brooks, Ph.D. candidate in the Department of Political Science at the University of California, San Diego, for the time, energy, and intellectual resources that she contributed to the project. Many chapters, mine included, benefited from her attention. Patricia Rosas also deserves special thanks for tireless and exceptional editing; the coherence of the book is in no small measure due to her skill. Peter Smith, colleague and series editor, and two Westview Press editors, Barbara Ellington and Karl Yambert, provided encouragement through the editing process. I am also grateful to conference participants for stimulating comments and to chapter authors for working together.

I especially thank Alejandro, Gabriel, and Jane for accepting the intrusion of this project into our family life.

David R. Mares

Acronyms

ABRI	Armed Forces of the Republic of Indonesia
AD	Democratic Action (Acción Democrática, Venezuela)
ASV	Association of Slovak Soldiers
BJP	Bharatiya Janata Party (India)
CACIF	Coordinating Committee of Agricultural, Commercial, Industrial, and Financial Associations
CACM	Central American Common Market
CEFTA	Central European Free Trade Agreement
CEM	Center for Military Studies (Centro de Estudios Militares, Guatemala)
CERJ	Council of Ethnic Communities
CFE	Conventional Forces in Europe
CONAVIGUA	War-Widows Association of Guatemala
COPEI	Social Christian Party (Venezuela)
CPSU	Communist Party
CUC	Committee for Campesino Unity (Comité de Campesinos Unidos, Guatemala)
DCG	Christian Democratic Party of Guatemala (Democracia Cristiana Guatemalteca)
DPR	House of Representatives (Indonesia)
EC	European Community
EGP	Guerrilla Army of the Poor (Ejército Guerrillero de los Pobres, Guatemala)
EU	European Union
FAR	Rebel Armed Forces (Fuerzas Armadas Rebeldes, Guatemala)
FDNG	Democratic Front of the New Guatemala (Frente Democrático de la Nueva Guatemala)
FSLN	Sandinista National Liberation Front (Frente Sandinista de Liberación Nacional, Nicaragua)
GAM	Mutual Support Group (Grupo de Apoyo Mutuo, Guatemala)
GDP	gross domestic product
GNP	gross national product
HZDS	Movement for a Democratic Slovakia

IAEDEN	National Institute for Advanced Defense Studies (Instituto Avanzado de Estudios de la Defensa Nacional, Venezuela)
IPM	Instituto de Prevision Militar (Guatemala)
IUPFAN	Polytechnic Institute of the Armed Forces (Venezuela)
KOK	State Defense Committee (Poland)
MAS	Solidarity Action Movement (Movimiento de Acción Solidario, Guatemala)
MINUGUA	United Nations Observer Mission
MLN	National Liberation Movement (Movimiento de Liberación Nacional, Guatemala)
MPR	Consultative Assembly (Indonesia)
MR-13	13th of November Revolutionary Movement (Movimiento Revolucionario 13 de Noviembre, Guatemala)
NACC	North Atlantic Cooperation Council
NAFTA	North American Free Trade Agreement
NATO	North Atlantic Treaty Organization
NGO	nongovernmental organization
NU	Muslim Scholars' Association (Indonesia)
OECD	Organization for Economic Cooperation and Development
ORPA	Revolutionary Organization of the People in Arms (Organización Revolucionario del Pueblo en Armas, Guatemala)
OSCE	Organization on Security and Cooperation in Europe
PDI	Indonesian Democratic Party
PfP	Partnership for Peace (NATO program)
PID	Partido Institucional Democrático
PR	Revolutionary Party (Partido Revolucionario, Guatemala)
PRC	People's Republic of China
PSD	Social Democratic Party (Partido Social Demócrata, Guatemala)
PSL	Polish Peasants' Party
PZPR	Polish United Workers' Party
R&D	research and development
RN	National Renewal Party (Renovación Nacional, Chile)
SDL	Party of the Democratic Left (Poland)
SNS	Slovak National Party
TNI	Indonesian National Army
UCN	Nacional Centrist Union (Unión del Centro Nacional, Guatemala)
UDI	Independent Democratic Union (Unión Demócrata Independiente, Chile)
UN	United Nations
URD	Unión República Democrática (Chile)

URNG	Guatemalan National Revolutionary Union (Unión Revolucionaria Nacional de Guatemala)
WEU	Western European Union
WSI	Military Information Services (Poland)
ZRS	Association of Workers of Slovakia

CHAPTER ONE

———————— ◼ ————————

Civil-Military Relations, Democracy, and the Regional Neighborhood

David R. Mares

The end of the Cold War produced dramatic changes in both domestic and international politics. Democracy has blossomed, but the economic and political adjustments of the transition have led to severe internal tensions. The possibilities of a great-power war seem remote; regional-level armed confrontations continue unabated. At present the most severe conflicts are occurring largely in the Balkans and among the new states of the former Soviet Union. Elsewhere—Latin America, Southern Asia, and Central Europe—historical animosities, arms races, and domestic instabilities suggest that the future of regional interactions remains uncertain.

The authors of this volume contend that the dynamics of the domestic civil-military relationship determine the likelihood of conflict or cooperation at the regional level. In that arena, international and domestic challenges and opportunities shape a state's foreign policy preferences. The economic and military interests of civilians and the military are key to determining the degree to which regional relations will be conflictive or cooperative. This chapter proposes a framework that postulates which civilian and military interests are most important in determining policy preferences. It demonstrates how these interests produce variation in the pattern of domestic civil-military relations, and it suggests hypotheses relating patterns of civil-military relations to the consolidation of democracy[1] and to cooperation in regional relations.[2] The framework uses insights from the study of grand strategy, historical sociology, interest group politics, and organizational theory. The grand-strategy perspective[3] suggests the importance of distinguishing among (1) identification of threats (economic, political, and military at both domestic and international levels); (2) elaboration of strategies to counter the identified threats; and (3) implementation of doctrines for each strategy. Historical sociology focuses our attention on the domestic social and economic bases of government,[4] whereas interest-group politics disaggregates these bases into more specific political actors.[5] Organizational theory examines how the military's degree of professionalism, need for autonomy and resources, as well as desire for growth, affect the perception of threat and the options for response.[6]

An important assumption made here is that overt military challenges to fundamental national security assets are unlikely to dominate regional relations. Authors in the realist school contend that territorial and resource disputes will continue into the future, but the authors in this volume maintain that those conflicts will play a secondary role to disputes related to the domestic political and organizational interests of civilian politicians and military officers.

We have also accepted the premise that the civil-military relationship and its potential implications for domestic and regional relations is best studied by undertaking theoretically informed, structured, and focused comparisons within and across regions. To accomplish this, we examine southern Asia (Thailand, Indonesia, India, and Pakistan) and Latin America (Argentina, Brazil, Chile, Venezuela, and Guatemala). These cases offer a range of potential causal variables identified in the social-science literature, such as region, type of government, military power, and culture. The addition of three Central European cases (Poland and the Czech and Slovak Republics) helps us evaluate whether unique regional factors are important determinants of behavior. Countries selected also have varied experiences with democratic institutions. India and Venezuela are long-standing democracies; Thailand, Argentina, Brazil, and Chile have recently redemocratized; and Indonesia and Guatemala are suffering a problematic transition toward democracy. The confluence of the end of the Cold War, global economic restructuring, and worldwide political liberalization has affected each country differently.

This introduction begins by developing a typology of civil-military relations and examining the determinants of where a relationship falls in the typology, using as variables political culture and constitutive rules of political interaction. Next I analyze the dynamics of the civil-military relationship by focusing on civilian and military interests as they relate to the potential sources of threat and possible policy responses. The chapter concludes with hypotheses on how civil-military relations influence the consolidation of democracy and produce cooperative or competitive regional relations.

CIVIL-MILITARY RELATIONS:
A FRAMEWORK FOR ANALYSIS

The determinants of the civil-military relationship are found in both the political culture of a society and the constitutive rules that arise out of the struggles among its principal political forces to create a governmental structure. Political culture influences but does not determine the construction of the civil-military relationship. Constitutive rules not only affect the role that the military plays in national politics but also influence the mechanisms of control that will permit the dominant coalition to delegate tasks to its subordinate partner.

Political Culture

Political culture comprises "a people's predominant beliefs, attitudes, values, ideals, sentiments, and evaluations about the political system of its country, and the role of the self in that system."[7] Political culture is the product of inherited ideas and historical experience, but at any particular moment, it acts as a causal factor.[8] Political culture changes very slowly, generally only when there has been a fundamental failure in the old pattern. Some countries studied in this book have experienced such dramatic events—Venezuela in the late 1950s, Argentina in the early 1980s, Central Europe in 1989—so we should see important changes in their political cultures at these moments.

Although political culture consists of cognitive, affective, and evaluative components,[9] only the first is relevant to our purpose. To identify the "proper" relationship between state and society and to examine the use of state power to confront threats, a focus on beliefs, values, and ideals is sufficient. The affective and evaluative aspects of political culture build on the cognitive and are secondary in identifying threats to the political system.

The cases discussed here present four ideal-type political cultures: liberal, corporatist, militarist, and patrimonialist (see Table 1.1). A liberal political culture is individualist. Society exists for the benefit of its members. The state is subordinated to society. The government exists to defend the individual and not the reverse. Sovereignty rests in the people. There is no "state" but only a "government," which guides a bureaucratic apparatus, and that government expresses the will of the dominant social forces through the mechanism of free elections that effectively represent the people. The military is part of the governmental apparatus, and as such, it is subordinated to the will of the people via the civilian government.[10]

In an organic-corporatist political culture, people speak of the nation in anthropomorphic terms. The nation defines the context in which society exists.[11] Sovereignty is inherent in the "state." Citizens are an agglomeration of groups and not of individuals; individuals define themselves and act in accordance with the group to which they belong. Because the nation is the "parent" of the citizen, each corporatist group has a responsibility for the nation's defense, but each group expects to be nurtured in return. The military establishment is understood to be the people in arms and therefore has a special responsibility to defend the state. In corporatist states, military participation in politics is facilitated by constitutional clauses that permit fairly easy declarations of states of emergency.[12]

In a militarist political culture, the armed forces are seen as the vanguard in a process of national modernization. The state is organic: It either grows or it dies. Individualism represents a threat to the nation because it subordinates the national good to personal good. In an anarchic world, the military is the repository

TABLE 1.1 Models of State–Society Relations and the Role of the Military in Each

Model	"State"	Basis of Sovereignty	Elements Relationship Government to People	How Popular Will Expressed	Role of Military
Liberal	Does not exist	The people	Subordinate	Directly/ individually	Subordinate
Organic corporatist	Society exists only in its context	Inherent in state	Dominant	In corporate groups	Special defense responsibility
Militarist	Society exists only in its context	Inherent in state	Dominant	Through military	Vanguard
Neopatrimonialist	Embodied in leader	Embodied in leader	Dominant	Through intra-elite competition	Part of the elite

of the national vision, and there are historical moments in which it has the moral obligation to assume leadership. The organizational and professional qualities of the military are favorably contrasted with those of politicians and leaders of principal social organizations, who are viewed as entrenched political and economic forces that defend their own interests and thus impede development.[13] The national defense depends on military capacity, and this justifies disproportionate expenditures on technological and industrial innovations.

A neopatrimonial political culture is hierarchical and looks to the personal leader for its cues. The political community is thus defined largely by reach of the ruler's authority. The people are politically quiescent because they do not believe that they are legitimate actors in the political struggle for influence. Yet the leader's decisions are not made in a vacuum. The ruler's power depends upon his ability to secure the support of a "winning coalition" among the political elite. The elite recognize the legitimacy of the ruler and compete among themselves for his favor. The bargain involves an exchange of tribute and loyalty from the elite in return for benefits generated by the power of the government (e.g., office holding and largesse). In this type of political culture, the military is perceived as one more group of elites who wish to gain favor with the leader and whom the leader wishes to include in his coalition.[14]

Societies may be dominated by one political culture, as is the case with liberalism in the United States. However, influential groups in society may represent distinct political subcultures,[15] or a hybrid variant of the primary types may predominate. Political culture can change. As chapters in this volume indicate, in Argentina and, to a lesser degree, Brazil, the civil-rights horrors and economic disasters of the bureaucratic-authoritarian governments of the 1970s and 1980s fundamentally changed each country's political culture by delegitimizing military rule and state power, and pushing these societies in the direction of liberalism.[16] Dramatic economic growth seems to be contributing to changes in Thai political culture, and liberalism appears to be flourishing in a post–Cold War Czech Republic that faces significant new opportunities for integration into the West European economic and security systems. At the same time, there seems to be less change in political culture in the more isolated Slovak Republic and perhaps in Indonesia.

Constitutive Rules of Politics

In addition to a society's political culture, the *constitutive rules of politics* are critical to the shaping of a country's civil-military relationship. These rules have a fundamental impact on how the philosophic vision embodied in political culture is translated into the reality of politics. By establishing precedents and constitutional guarantees, these rules lend legitimacy to certain themes while denying it to others. They also affect, directly and indirectly, who can participate in the domestic political game as well as how.[17] Independent of whether a regime is or is not democratic, its institutional order can be inclusionary or exclusionary. It is the former only when all groups in society can legitimately participate in the political process. Liberal democracies have excluded slaves and women from the political process and used legislation to keep labor from organizing and expressing itself in effective ways. In contrast, authoritarian regimes can be inclusive, as was the case with the Peruvian military government from 1968 to about 1973.[18] During periods of great social, political, or economic change, political culture and constitutive rules determine whether civilians support the military's demand for the restriction of the political rights of those who question the path on which the nation finds itself. Restrictions imply an increase in the police power of the state, which directly affects the position of the military in society.

These determinants produce four ideal-type relationships. In two, "civilian-dominant" or "military-dominant," one side controls the other and has the power to identify the primary threats confronting the country and the appropriate response to those threats. In a third type, a "pact among equals," the two sides share equally in determining threat and policy. In the final type, civilian actors and the military have separate but parallel spheres of action.

TYPOLOGY OF CIVIL-MILITARY RELATIONS

Each of the four types of civil-military relationship has its own dynamic and thus produces different results concerning threat identification and the role of civilians and the military in responding to those threats.

In a *dominant-subordinate relationship,* the dominant partner identifies and responds to threat, and this action is based on that partner's interests and perceptions. The complexity of foreign policy making, however, often requires a degree of involvement by the subordinate partner. For example, a civilian government with no expertise in military affairs must seek information from the leadership of the armed forces, and a military government needs the input of the business community if it is to successfully design foreign economic policy.[19] Thus, much turns on the delegation of tasks to the subordinate partner. A principal-agent framework helps describe the bargaining dynamics in this unequal relationship. Each agent (that is, the group to which the dominant partner—the principal—has delegated power) has its own interests so that even with the best intentions, the results of the delegation may fall far short of the principal's expectations.

To ensure that implementation conforms with the expectations of the principal, a delicate oversight system must be developed that gives the agent freedom to act efficiently, but not to the degree that the principal is left "out of the loop."[20] An additional problem is posed by the need to attain consensus within the principal. When the parties constituting the principal disagree over appropriate policies, that impedes oversight and by default the agent gains greater autonomy. Further complication is introduced when members of the agent disagree, making implementation policy impossible regardless of how well or how poorly it fits the designs of the principal.[21]

As we have seen, the idea that civilians are the principals and should control the military, who are their agents, is embodied in the liberal model (although it is also present in communist political culture).[22] The Venezuelan case from 1958 to at least 1993, Argentina especially after 1990, and the Czech Republic and Poland after the end of the Cold War are examples. In a militarist political culture, the military establishment is the agent that loyally interprets the needs of an anthropomorphic state. In turn, the military is the principal with respect to society and its representatives. Civilian cabinet members of military regimes, "puppet rulers" dependent on the military, or "official" labor unions and business groups all become "agents." Brazil, Argentina, Guatemala, and Thailand have all experienced military domination.

A personalist dictatorship headed by a military leader does not represent military domination of the polity, however. What matters in the relationship is not from where the leader comes, but the relationship between civilian forces in society and the military as an institution. When the political leadership comprises members drawn from the armed forces and who remain dependent on them, the government can be viewed analytically as military-dominant. When that leadership is made up of individuals who have retired or have taken a leave of absence from the armed forces, or whose ability to remain in power does not depend on them, the military can be viewed as being subordinate to political power. Chile's General Pinochet and Indonesia's General Soeharto are examples of military officers whose power comes from political control and not from hierarchical authority within the military institution. These generals see themselves as the loyal interpreters of an organic state, with the military relegated to agent status along with the rest of society.

A *pact among equals* can be found in an organic state-society relationship, where the state is the principal and both politicians and military officers are its agents. Since the state cannot articulate its policy preferences, they must be interpreted, which provides an opportunity for either a negotiation between equals or for one group to attempt to impose its interpretation on the other. The revolutionary junta in Venezuela from 1945 to 1948 exemplifies this arrangement despite the efforts of civilians from the Acción Democrática party to introduce a liberal model. Since 1989 Chile's new democracy, with a constitution written under military dictatorship and an army that periodically undertakes military maneuvers to remind the civilian government of its presence, also appears to be a pact among equals. In contrast, the Indonesian concept of *Dwifungsi* formally embodies a pact among equals, but the reality is that General Soeharto has institutionalized a one-man rule.

In a pact among equals, principal-agent theory must be replaced by an analysis of the dynamics of the negotiation process between the partners, whose resources are never equal. Civilians, who in a corporatist political culture cannot appeal to the legitimacy of civilian domination, find that their greatest resource is the unity among the active political forces in civil society. By presenting a united political front and taking advantage of the fundamental role that the private sector plays in a capitalist economy, the tool with which the military attempts to negotiate (its control of coercive power) is neutralized or at least significantly diminished. For its part, the professionalism that ensures the military's prestige in a corporatist political culture is undermined by the daily requirements of exercising authority. Because their professionalism may be compromised in the entanglements of governing, corporatist military officers prefer to leave civilians in charge of the workings of government, except for matters of military security, where officers prefer to take a leading role. That preference widens the space in which civilians can negotiate. Even the coups d'état typical of twentieth-century Latin America before the Brazilian coup of 1964 are instances of civilian domination because the armed forces intervened only when asked by civilians, to whom they quickly returned control of the polity.[23] Yet in pacts among equals, there is always the temptation for one of the parties to impose its vision on the other. In Venezuela between 1945 and 1948, the military defected from the partnership, whereas in contemporary Chile, the center-left civilian coalition seeks to do so.

A *parallel-spheres-of-action* pattern is distinguished from the pact among equals by its separation of tasks, whereby civilians and the military each have an autonomous sphere of action. The military legitimately monopolizes every issue related to security. Politicians, in turn, are charged with developing the national wealth. This scenario is stable only under the stringent conditions of a growing economy and internal and external peace, indicating that each side is fulfilling its appointed role. Given that military power depends ultimately on the wealth of the nation, the parallel pattern of civil-military relations is inherently unstable. Defense budgets demand resources, and agreement over the armed-forces budget can be ruined when civilians mishandle economic development. Civilians, for their part, are tempted to meddle in security questions because these are not easily separated from social, political, or economic issues. In exclusionary regimes, for example, the state may rely on police power to defend the existing order when domestic opposition cannot be controlled by other means. Even inclusive regimes may respond to sudden popular uprisings against policy by calling in the army to restore order. Each of these scenarios represents a breakdown of the parallel pattern. The most striking example of a successful parallel-spheres-of-action relationship is found in the Chilean dictatorship between 1977 and 1981.

Only in liberal and exclusionary-militarist regimes do we find unique patterns of civil-military relations (see Table 1.2). In both inclusive and exclusive liberal political cultures, the ideal of separation of society and state leads to "objective" control, in which civilians respect the professional needs of the military and the military accepts its subordination to political institutions.[24] In a militarist political culture, exclusion of members of the polity can be justified by the belief in the military's intrinsic leadership role.

Each of the other potential combinations of political culture and constitutive rules is compatible with multiple patterns of civil-military relations. For example,

TABLE 1.2   Determinants of Civil-Military Relations

Political Culture	Constitutive Rules	Civil-Military Relationship
Liberal	Inclusive	Civilians dominant
Liberal	Exclusive	Civilians dominant
Corporatist	Inclusive	All types
Corporatist	Exclusive	All types
Militarist	Inclusive	Military dominant; Pact among equals
Militarist	Exclusive	Military dominant
Neopatrimonial	Inclusive	All types
Neopatrimonial	Exclusive	All types

when a militarist political culture combines with inclusive rules, civilian groups may participate in politics through paramilitary organizations. In this case, the civil-military relationship may be characterized as a pact among equals. Alternatively, civilians may be content to let the military lead. Since corporatist and patrimonial political cultures are compatible with military leadership, whether or not they combine with either inclusive or exclusive constitutive rules to produce any of the four ideal types of civil-military relationships depends on the bargains made during the process of negotiating the constitutive rules. If civilians dominate the military, however, it is via "subjective" control. In this case, the military defends particular politicians rather than institutions and politicians politicize the military institution, rather than allow it to professionalize autonomously, in efforts to command loyalty.

THE POLITICS OF THREAT IDENTIFICATION

As we have seen, political culture and constitutive rules delimit the expression of civilian and military interests. Those interests shape the perception of threat, and threat perception orients a nation's grand strategy.

Civilian Determinants

In the civil-military relationship, two factors determine civilian interests. The terms of exchange among the relevant partners in the governing coalition are fundamental in tracing the range of acceptable threats from which the political leadership will draw in addressing its domestic and international needs.[25] Any argument about civilian threat perception must focus on the particular interests of the major domestic political forces, the bargains made among them to achieve a winning coalition, and the interests of the political leaders who make the actual decisions about civilian threat perception. Social coalition analysis is useful for analyzing policy within both democratic and authoritarian governments; the difference between the two lies more in the size of the coalition and the ability of the opposition to influence it.

Economic and development-policy analysts find class useful in distinguishing among domestic contenders. Because material interests also drive foreign policy, using the classifications of labor, business, and agriculture is helpful in analyzing the civilian side of the civil-military relationship.[26] Without claiming that these groups are homogeneous, one can still draw useful conclusions about the self-interests of their resulting coalitions.

Whatever endangers the governing social coalition is identified as a threat to "national security." Civilian threat perception, therefore, depends on the nature of the political bargains supporting the regime. The more inclusive the polity, the less likely it is that domestic issues will be identified as threats; exclusion, to the contrary, heightens the perception of domestic threats. External threat perception will depend on how economic competition and political tolerance by the potential foreign adversary affect the governing coalition (see Table 1.3).

The *agrarian/industrial coalition* is most likely to exist in an outward-oriented, primary-product economy, with some "natural" import substitution stimulating an incipient industrial structure.[27] The main threats to such a coalition are domestic and come from either independent unionization or an alliance between "nationalist" industrialists pushing vigorous import substitution and industrial labor unions. For this coalition, foreign powers are perceived as a threat under two conditions. First, given the historical absence of free trade in agricultural markets,[28] developing-country agricultural producers are likely to worry when foreign powers compete directly in the same international agricultural markets. Second, if foreign powers were favorable to labor movements and/or import-substitution-industrialization (ISI) development strategies that would also be viewed as a threat. The progressive integration of a country into a competitive world market challenges sovereignty and autonomy in a way that cannot be identified with any one country, so transnational economic forces are seen as allies because they purchase and/or distribute the country's exports and supply intermediate and capital goods, as well as items for conspicuous consumption.

The industrialists in the *industrial/labor coalition,* unlike those in the agrarian/industrial alliance, support an import-substitution model in the intermediate- and capital-goods markets (as opposed to consumer-goods markets). Labor, for its part, seeks high wages, socioeconomic benefits, and cheap food. Because of their opposing beliefs, a renewed ascendancy of the agrarian/industrial coalition represents the chief domestic threat to the industrial/labor coalition. However, this coalition's evaluation of foreign-power threat matches that of the agrarian/industrial coalition: A foreign power could threaten economically if it opposed the coalition's import-substitution-industrialization policies by, among other tactics, restricting foreign investment in the country or reducing its imports of the protected manufactures. A political threat would also arise if foreign powers actively favored the agrarian/industry coalition.

TABLE 1.3   Domestic Determinants of Civilian Perceptions of Threat

Character of Governing Coalition	Potential Threat		
	Foreign Powers	Transnational Economic Forces	Domestic Rivals
Agriculture/ industry	Varies by economic structure and political coalition	Ally	Labor, peasants, and national industry
Industry/ agriculture	Varies by economic structure and political coalition	Threat	Labor and peasants
Industry/labor	Varies by economic structure and political coalition	Threat	Agriculture and mining
Industry/ agriculture/ labor	Varies by economic structure and political coalition	Varies by terms of national coalition	None

The industrial/labor coalition is based on an economic development strategy that seeks to modify, if not isolate, the effect of international market forces on the national economy. As a result, transnational economic forces, whether corporations or impersonal price signals, are threats. Nevertheless, because the international economic threat tends to be implicit, it can be manipulated at some cost in the short run, and is determinant only in the longer run, domestic political threats take precedence in the view of the industrial/labor coalition.

In the *industrial/agrarian coalition,* industry leads, with agriculture subordinate and labor excluded. This alliance corresponds to an economy with an outward-oriented industry and a noncompetitive agricultural sector, such as is found in East Asia, but not as yet in Latin America. The bargain underpinning this coalition is sustained by subsidies and selected protection for industrial exporters, subsidies and extensive protection for the agriculture sector producing for the domestic market, and the absence of an independently organized labor force. Labor organization and agricultural producers who are competitive internationally are the primary domestic threats because they prefer an open national economy. Once again, if either domestic rival develops significant political power, domestic issues will become the focus of the coalition's threat perception.

Foreign powers pose a threat when they are internationally competitive and are motivated to advocate liberal international economic policies.[29] A great power will have influence over the international economic order, and the industrial/agricultural coalition will feel pressure to respond to its wishes. If the international economy moves increasingly toward managed trade in the manufactures produced by developing countries (as in the contemporary era), market share becomes increasingly competitive and regulated.[30] Under these circumstances, if two developing nations have export-oriented manufacturing economies, perceptions of threat may arise. Threat perception will also increase when a foreign power seeks to gain more domestic influence for unionized labor and/or internationally competitive agriculture. Transnational forces are important threats to the basically mercantilist worldview of the industrial/agricultural coalition. Because industry is outward-oriented, this coalition must deal with transnational forces to a greater extent than a coalition that supports import-substitution industrialization.

The *industrial/agrarian/labor coalition,* the broadest alliance, can range from a Swedish-style social democracy to a U.S.-style New Deal policy set. What is important is that all of the major domestic social forces participate; hence these governing coalitions are found only in stable democracies. Its inclusive nature renders domestic rivals less threatening.

The contemporary democracy and foreign-policy literature suggests that civilians do not view other democracies and liberal transnational economic forces as threats. Foreign powers can be seen as threats when they are not practicing democracy, and transnational economic forces can become threatening when they ignore or distort market signals.[31]

Unfortunately, the history of democratic foreign policy is not so simple. Athens subjugated neighboring democratic *poli* and the United States carried out an aggressive foreign policy against democratically elected Allende. These cases illustrate that when democracies perceive that democratic politics in regions considered fundamental to their security is leading either to political bargains disruptive of their own domestic political bargains (socialism in Chile) or undermining the "necessary" balance of power (control of sea lanes for Athens), the content of policy and not its democratic character will be key to threat identification.

A more fruitful approach to understanding foreign policy in democratic nations incorporates the terms on which the domestic political coalition is built. For example, if labor is included in the coalition via compensation for adjusting to international market fluctuations, transnational economic forces are unlikely to be identified as "threatening."[32] But if the coalition was created when labor worked in internationally competitive industries and thus benefited from transnational market forces, compensation measures may not have been built into the terms of alliance between capital and labor. Once labor's price becomes increasingly noncompetitive, labor at least will begin to perceive a threat from the international market. Whether the coalition itself adopts such a view depends on the speed at which noncompetitiveness is occurring as well as the relative weight of labor, and other losers, in the coalition.[33]

Military Determinants

We also need to understand the determinants of military perceptions of threat. Most of the theoretical work concerning military perceptions is bifurcated. Analysts focusing on great powers examine military doctrine during periods in which the identity of the enemy and possible allies is relatively clear. As a result, they can skirt the other two issues in grand strategy (identification of threat and possible responses) and focus on the issue of how to militarily confront the enemy. Analysts focusing on developing countries tend to downplay external threats and focus on internal politics when discussing military threat assessment.

In most developing countries, however, the role of the military in threat identification is more problematic than either approach suggests. Unless the civil-military relationship completely excludes the military from the threat identification, the armed forces will be a lesser or greater participant in threat identification. These militaries are confronted with the issue not only of how to fight, but more importantly, against whom to prepare. At times the chief threat has been identified as deriving from great powers, neighbors, transnational forces, and internal subversives. We need, therefore, to think systematically about how the military interprets threat and evaluates potential responses, including its own.

One could begin with the theoretical orientation of the military toward the question. Many analysts have demonstrated that geopolitical thinking dominates the South American military.[34] But geopolitical thinking has been too diffuse to help us understand threat identification. There has been a proliferation of competing "schools" and consequent identification of key areas to examine for relevant threats, but even the relevant threats that a school might identify have been defined in terms that are often contradictory: the lack of national integration, the lack of regional integration, or the local military balance.[35] We need to understand why different schools and different threats arise. In short, geopolitics takes us back where we began.

Threat identification by the military depends fundamentally on its relationship to the government and the resulting institutional incentives. If the military dominates the polity or is identified with preserving a particular political faction, it will identify threats in a fashion similar to our analysis of civilian threat perception in the previous section. But if the military aspires to a Western style professionalization, the institutional incentives guiding its behavior will differ dramatically. In this case an organizational focus promises to be more helpful for understanding military threat identification. Many studies have profitably utilized organizational logic to explain how great power militaries formulate and modify military doctrine in response to threat.[36] The identity of the threat undoubtedly affects the military organization's growth, autonomy, and response to uncertainty. Consequently, if the military is confronted with a variety of potential threats, we should see some organizational bias introduced into the prioritization of threats by a professional military.

Organizational theory begins with the assumption that uncertainty impedes an organization from reaching its goals; consequently, it must be reduced.[37] Uncertainty arises from the behavior of individuals within the organization and the environment within which the organization secures resources and pursues goals. (In our study, this environment has both international and domestic arenas.) To deal with uncertainty, organizations develop standard operating procedures (SOP).

These SOPs interpret demands and opportunities in the environment and suggest appropriate responses from an organization's repertoire of procedures, thus safe-guarding organizational autonomy. In addition, SOPs constrain the behavior of individuals within the organization so that they select a standard rather than idio-syncratic response.

The need to reduce uncertainty and defend institutional autonomy and re-sources becomes a lens to interpret the world, much the same way as the civilian leadership's political coalition colors their view of the world. This process, not pe-culiar to military organizations, is the consequence of professionalization in any organization. Thus the military-bias argument is that the military identifies threat based on how they perceive its impacts on those organizational factors.[38]

The impact of identifying a great power as a military threat is variable in the case of resource acquisition and negative across the other two organizational de-terminants (see Table 1.4). In terms of resource acquisition, the firepower gap be-tween a great power and the middle or small power is too large to be successfully breached via regular military buildups. A request for such an enormous increase in military resources might bring some additional resources but could not help but provoke civilian concern about the military budget and consequently a closer evaluation of such requests. The negative influence on institutional autonomy is not limited to increased scrutiny of military budgets by the government. Swiss neutrality is based on a deterrence that relies on geographical peculiarities and an army based on reservists.[39] Unless the military were already composed of re-servists, such a manpower strategy would have significant implications for both institutional autonomy and doctrinal simplification.[40]

In the post–Second World War period, Cuba, Vietnam, and Afghanistan, small states defeating a great power, illustrate these points. In each case, defense was un-dertaken by a nonconventional military. In the Afghan case, it was completely guerrilla organized. The Cuban and Vietnamese militaries (the latter also bene-fited enormously from the Viet Cong guerrilla action) were heavily politicized and part of a mass-based revolutionary government. But the move to a guerrilla or popular army response to great-power threat would dramatically undermine the institutional autonomy of an existing regular army because guerrilla and pop-ular armies fight best when the *political* side of the war is of paramount concern. And because guerrilla and popular armies operate in very different ways than professional troops, significant changes in military doctrine must be undertaken as well.[41]

Vietnam, Cuba, and Hungary illustrate another concern of middle- or small-power military institutions whose nations are caught in regional hegemonies. It was massive outside military aid, not just a willingness to die for national sover-eignty, that allowed Vietnam to design military attrition strategies to politically defeat the French and the United States. Cuba also combined fundamental mili-tary aid from outside the region with a willingness to fight; the result was a U.S. political decision not to pay the costs of a military engagement. Hungary in 1956,

TABLE 1.4   Domestic Determinants of Military Perceptions of Threat

Organizational Determinants	Relationship to Geopolitical Target			
	Great Power	Transnational	Neighbor	Domestic
Resource acquisition	Variable	Variable	Positive	Positive
Institutional autonomy	Negative	Negative	Positive	Variable by stage
Doctrinal simplification	Negative	Negative	Positive	Negative

on the other hand, was caught in a regional hegemony. The Hungarians were willing to die for national sovereignty and offered neutrality to the Soviets. But the Soviets perceived regional hegemony as necessary to their security. When no great power was willing to side with Hungary against the Soviet Union, the Hungarian Revolution was crushed.[42]

The identification of a neighbor as a threat has a positive impact on each of the organizational determinants. Middle- and small-power neighbors constitute a reasonable military foe for a developing country's military. To the degree that historical rivalries, territorial disputes, and geopolitical thinking abound, seemingly reasonable arguments can be advanced for subregional balancing. Formulating a response to the local balance of power should have a positive effect on resource acquisition, at least in the absence of comprehensive subregional arms control agreements. Institutional autonomy should also be positively affected initially because the task appears a reasonable one for the military. Only in the event of a military defeat by the neighbor would institutional autonomy be negatively affected as civilians rush to discover the "cause" of defeat.[43] Doctrinal simplification would be positively affected if offensive strategies were chosen,[44] but even with defensive strategies the impact would be positive relative to the doctrinal implications of any of the other potential threats.

Transnational forces are largely irrelevant to the military as an institution. When they do affect organizational interests, their impact is likely to be negative, although somewhat contingent in terms of resource acquisition. On the one hand, these forces cannot be fought with arms. On the other hand, there may exist important linkages between certain transnational forces and the quality and quantity of arms supplies and, therefore, resource acquisition. These linkages could either serve to block supplies (as transnational corporations attempt to do with respect to nuclear weapons components) or serve as alternative sources of supply (as in the case of Chile and Argentina in the 1970s) or as a market conduit for arms exports (Brazil). Institutional autonomy would probably be adversely affected by the identification of transnational forces as a threat because the creation of domestic industries to supplant international flows would most likely be costly and inefficient, thereby drawing the attention of the government's budget managers. Finally, the impact on doctrinal simplification would be negative if the military were involved in the response because they would need to develop management skills and the switch in weaponry may require recasting doctrine.

Our last potential threat to national security comes from within the country itself. Domestic rivals can be political (revolutionary movements of the left or right wing) or criminal (e.g., drug cartels) in character. The impact of this threat identification on resource allocation for the military should be positive. The government will seek to protect itself, and although it may attempt to address the social causes of the unrest, the government can be expected to attempt a military containment of the subversives until long-term sociopolitical solutions can be implemented. It has been amply demonstrated that the impact on institutional autonomy, however, will vary according to the stages of the battle against subversives.[45] Under civilian rule, fighting fellow citizens has a negative impact on institutional autonomy. If the military responds by overthrowing the government and creating a military regime, the initial impact on institutional autonomy will be favorable, but soon the demands of governing the sociopolitical and economic complexities that a modern state represents will erode institutional autonomy. The impact on doctrinal simplification is clearly negative. A military can never develop doctrines to defeat an enemy that can appeal to the government's own rules. These organizational interests help us understand why Latin American militaries prefer, at least in the initial stages of subversion, to see domestic threats as police rather than military questions.[46]

In summary, the military of a developing country is likely to confront multiple sources of threat. Organizational factors will have greatest impact on the military's perceptions concerning grand strategy when institutional interests are under threat, when the interests at stake are fundamental, and/or when the demands of sound strategy and organizational interests conflict. The power of organizational interests on decisionmaking is further heightened by the psychological ability to see the necessary as possible.[47] Until the perceptions of threat derived from organizational bias are demonstrated to have negative consequences for the military as an institution, they will remain in force.

These organizational interests suggest that the professional military prefers to avoid internal and economic threats and to focus on the subregional balance of power. The question of whether their next preference is internal security or a great power depends on the degree of subversion and the willingness of another great power to supply resources at low cost to institutional autonomy and doctrinal simplification. If outside aid is channeled through the military and in accordance with its doctrine, the professional military will become a willing ally in great-power politics, so long as playing this role does not undermine its ability to play regional balance of power games. If outsiders demand too much control for these resources, professional militaries will reluctantly find themselves drawn into internal policing.

CIVIL-MILITARY RELATIONS, DEMOCRACY, AND REGIONAL INTERACTIONS

We have now come full circle, examining the cultural and institutional determinants of the civil-military relationship and the determinants of civilian and military perceptions of threat and response. What remains is to develop hypotheses about the effect of the civil-military relationship on the likelihood of the consolidation of democracy and the creation of cooperative regional economic and military relations.

The hypotheses are derived from the core argument of this book: Political culture and constitutive rules set the structural context within which civil-military relations play themselves out over long periods. But the structure of the relationship itself is not determinant of the policies adopted. The particular interests of governing coalitions and military organizations interact within the context of the relationship, and it is in that interaction that the specific national responses to the challenges and opportunities presented by democratization and regional relations develop.

Democracy

In this study, we conceive of the consolidation of democracy as defined by Mainwaring, O'Donnell, and Valenzuela: "The new authorities respect all human and democratic rights of citizenship, commit themselves to an electoral process which local oppositions view as fair, and govern following constitutional procedures that correspond to the broad outlines of democratic practice."[48] The specific way in which these functions and guarantees are offered varies over time and place.[49] In particular, those constitutional procedures are in many ways the result of bargaining among the major forces in civil society and the military. Democracy is a complex compromise: Constitutions vary in the safeguards used to defend civil, property, and religious rights and in the specifics of due process which, in turn, protect those safeguards.[50] The consolidation of democracy is a never ending task, with the democratic process continually facing new challenges as a result of social, political, and economic change.[51]

Democratic consolidation requires values that sustain democratic politics as "a permanent value and not just as a temporary tactic" and the "creation of governmental institutions that have increased strength, autonomy, and legitimacy." For most analysts, a reduction in military autonomy and prerogatives is also fundamental to the consolidation of democracy. If the military controlled one part of the state (that pertaining to the force of arms and intelligence functions), a government could find itself captive to this group when sectors of the civilian opposition threaten to knock on the barracks' door. Although such a situation is a fundamental threat to democracy, if the military has its own working definition of democracy, even short of fundamentally altering existing political structures, a military response substitutes the use of military force for the ballot box.[52]

Notice that this particular threat from the military to democracy assumes that civilian sectors would appeal to the military, that the military would want to listen and would be willing to act. As Rebecca Schiff points out in Chapter Two, concordance among the military and the civilian elite on democratic politics can help consolidate democracy even in the absence of civilian control. A pacted civil-military relationship is sufficient for the consolidation of democracy as long as the civilian sector allied with the military is willing to accept the outcome of the democratic game (assuming that the nonallied civilian sector is itself willing to abide by the democratic rules of the game in its efforts to institute change). That is to say, that democracy is accepted as a value, not merely a political tactic. A military with its own definition of democracy, or willing to listen to knocks, is a threat; this military is best dealt with by putting it under civilian control.

The question is whether the military can stay out of politics or would be drawn into politics to safeguard its professional interests. Stepan's work demonstrated the reality of such interventions by professional militaries. But if civilians are willing to accept democracy as a value, it is difficult to see how a professional military would be drawn into politics. And if civilians, especially powerful corporate groups, do not accept the rules of the democratic game,[53] it is difficult to see how democracy could be consolidated whether or not the military intervenes.

The analysis presented here leads to a hypothesis that the chief threat to democratic consolidation after the Cold War does not arise from a professional military. A professional military's initial preference is to eschew the politics of governing. Whether that preference can guide its behavior depends on the terms of the civil-military relationship. In a civilian-dominant relationship in which the military has no legitimate role in defending the political system, the military is likely to let civilians deal with threats to internal stability according to civilian interests. But in a civilian-dominant relationship in which the military has a legitimate role in defending the political system, a professional military will find itself drawn into the political battles if the civilians' own battles threaten the stability of the system. The chief threat, therefore, to democratic consolidation is found in civilian battles over exclusionary politics, or from a national political culture that idealizes the military's commitment to the nation as well as the beneficial implications of their professionalization (militarism).

We should expect, therefore, that inclusionary political systems with civilian-dominated civil-military relations and a liberal political culture will be the most likely to consolidate democracy. But inclusionary polities with corporatist political cultures could be supportive of democracy if civilians do not push their policy disagreements to the point of destabilizing the polity. In addition, since a professional military will be reluctant to identify threats from internal sources, it may use the legitimacy of its role in a corporatist political culture to help keep civilians from undermining the democratic process by identifying domestic opposition groups as threats.

We can thus see that professionalization of the military can have positive payoffs for democratic consolidation even in the absence of a liberal political culture. There is a potential trade-off, however, between the beneficial implications of a professional military for democracy and the negative implications for cooperative regional relations.

Regional Security Relations

From the analysis in this introduction, we can hypothesize that the key to cooperative regional security relations is to keep the professional military from having a major role in the identification of threat, the selection of appropriate responses, or even in the elaboration of military doctrines (specifically what weapons to buy and whether they will defend by attacking the enemy or waiting for him to invade). The organizational tendency of professional militaries is to prepare to defend the nation against neighbors. Preparation means focusing on the local balance of power and thus regional cooperation will be hindered by competitive arms buildups. In addition, because professional militaries prefer offensive strategies,[54] confidence-building measures will be difficult to implement.

But civilian domination per se is not a guarantee of cooperative regional relations. Exclusionary civilian governments, even of a liberal stripe, will tend to look to international factors to explain why a domestic opposition mobilizes among the excluded. If regional states vary in whom they include in the legitimate political process, civilian regimes of exclusionary states will have an opportunity to engage in diversionary tactics as they seek to retain exclusionary politics.

We can thus hypothesize that the civil-military relationships most conducive to regional cooperation will be those in which either inclusionary civilians dominate or in which the pacted or parallel relationships force a nonprofessional military to look inward (see Table 1.5).

Although military-dominated polities may rarely fight external wars,[55] their militarized foreign policies will tend to create tense regional relations and thus hinder cooperation. The civil-military relationship most dangerous for regional relations is likely to be a parallel relationship in which the professional military is given carte blanche on security matters.

Regional Economic Relations

Cooperative regional economic relations may be based on either economic liberalization (at least within the context of the region) or state-managed integration (as in the Latin American schemes of the 1960s and 1970s). In the contemporary period, state-managed integration has been heavily discredited, so the integration schemes are now based on economic liberalization. Unlike democracy, economic liberalization is a path toward something but is not valued for itself. This fact makes economic liberalism in a country continually problematic. Civilian members of the governing coalition will color their support of economic liberalization by how the process affects their particular constituencies. This bias is true whether we are speaking of a democratic or nondemocratic regime, since every regime needs to have the support of some members of society to govern.

Civilian-dominated democratic or authoritarian regimes thus may find themselves inhibiting economic liberalization as its domestic costs to their constituencies

20

TABLE 1.5   The Civil-Military Relationship and Regional Relations: Hypotheses

Characteristics of the Civil-Military Relationship	Tendency of Regional Security Policy	Determinant
Civilian dominant with professional military and inclusionary politics	*Cooperative*	Civilians do not fear neighbors
Civilian dominant with nonprofessional military and inclusionary politics	*Cooperative*	Civilians fear outside support for excluded group
Civilian dominant with professional military and exclusionary politics	Competitive	Civilians do not fear neighbors
Civilian dominant with nonprofessional military and exclusionary politics	Competitive	Civilians fear outside support for excluded group
Pacted with professional military and inclusionary politics	Competitive	Professional military focuses on neighbors
Pacted with professional military and exclusionary politics	Competitive	Both civilians and military focus on neighbors
Pacted with nonprofessional military and inclusionary politics	*Cooperative*	Nonprofessional military focuses internally and civilians do not fear neighbors
Pacted with nonprofessional military and exclusionary politics	Competitive	Civilians fear outside support for excluded group
Parallel with professional military and inclusionary politics	Competitive	Professional military focuses on neighbors
Parallel with professional military and exclusionary politics	Competitive	Professional military focuses on neighbors
Parallel with nonprofessional military and inclusionary politics	*Cooperative*	Military in charge of security and inward looking
Parallel with nonprofessional military and exclusionary politics	Competitive	Military in charge of security and fears outside support for excluded group
Military dominant[a] with professional military	Competitive	Professional military focuses on neighbors
Military dominant with nonprofessional military	Competitive	Military fears outside support for excluded group

[a]Military domination requires exclusionary politics.

rise or stimulating it as benefits rise. The greatest defenders of economic liberalization may be a professionalized military in civilian-dominated, pacted, or parallel
civil-military relationships. If a professional military takes the lead in defending economic liberalization, however, regional economic interdependence may not increase
since, in a developing country, the professional military's prime threat is its neighbor.

ORGANIZATION OF THE BOOK

We start our empirical analyses with a foundational moment: the historical period in which the latest institutional version of civil-military relations was created. For our two Central European countries, this is the construction of democratic politics after the end of the Cold War. In Latin America and Southern Asia,
it varies by historical experience: For India, Malaysia, and Thailand, it is the moment of independence; for Indonesia, the end of democratic politics in the 1960s;
for the Latin American countries, it is the return of democracy (Venezuela 1958,
Argentina 1984, Brazil 1987, Chile 1989–1990, and Guatemala the mid-1980s).

The body of the book is divided into two sections. The first considers the relationship between the type of civil-military relations and democracy in India, Indonesia, and Venezuela. A second section focuses on the impact of civil-military
relations and democracy on regional relations. This latter section is divided into
two subsections. The first subsection examines those countries in which civilians
dominate the relationship (Argentina, Czechoslovakia, the Czech Republic, Slovakia, and Poland). A second grouping deals with countries having a civil-military
relationship best characterized as a pact among equals (Brazil, Chile, Thailand,
and Guatemala). Although no country analyzed currently has a military-dominated or parallel civil-military relationship, some of the analyses cover periods
when these patterns reigned (Thailand, Argentina, and Guatemala).

In the concluding chapter to this book, I return to the hypotheses offered in
this introduction and evaluate the comparative evidence.

NOTES

I would like to thank the Pacific Rim Research Program and the Institute on Global Conflict and Cooperation, both of the University of California, as well as the Center for Iberian
and Latin American Studies of the University of California, San Diego, for supporting this
project. This chapter benefited from comments received at presentations at the Instituto de
Altos Estudios de la Defensa Nacional in Caracas in March 1995 and at a conference on
"Civil-Military Relations" at UCSD in November 1995. I would especially like to thank
Risa Brooks, Brian Loveman, and particularly Peter Smith for comments, as well as Adrian
Bonilla and Fernando Bustamante for their insights into civil-military relationships. I am
responsible for all views presented here.

1. Following Scott Mainwaring, Guillermo O'Donnell, and J. Samuel Valenzuela, we define "consolidation of democracy" as the following: "the new authorities respect all human

and democratic rights of citizenship, commit themselves to an electoral process which local oppositions view as fair, and govern following constitutional procedures that correspond to the broad outlines of democratic practice." "Introduction" in Mainwaring, O'Donnell, and Valenzuela, eds., *Issues in Democratic Consolidation* (Notre Dame, Ind.: University of Notre Dame Press, 1992), p. 3.

2. "Cooperation in regional relations" is defined by whether economic relations are interdependent and whether military defenses lean toward confidence-building measures or balance of power.

3. Peter Paret, *Understanding War* (Princeton: Princeton University Press, 1992); Edward Luttwak, *The Grand Strategy of the Roman Empire* (Baltimore: Johns Hopkins University Press, 1976); Paul Kennedy, ed., *Grand Strategies in War and Peace* (New Haven: Yale University Press, 1991); B. H. Liddell Hart, *Strategy* (New York: Praeger, 1954), pp. 366–372.

4. Barrington Moore, *Social Origins of Dictatorship and Democracy* (Boston: Beacon Press, 1967); Immanuel Wallerstein, *The Modern World System* (New York: Academic Press, 1974); Perry Anderson, *Lineages of the Absolutist State* (London: NLB, 1974).

5. I. M. Destler and John S. Odell, *Antiprotectionism: Changing Forces in United States Trade Politics* (Washington, D.C.: Institute for International Economics, 1987); Helen V. Milner, *Resisting Protectionism* (Princeton: Princeton University Press, 1988).

6. David Mares and Walter Powell, "Cooperative Security Regimes: Preventing International Conflict" in Robert Kahn and Mayer Zald, eds., *Organizations and Nation-States* (San Francisco: Jossey Bass, 1990).

7. Larry Diamond, "Introduction: Political Culture and Democracy" in Larry Diamond, ed., *Political Culture and Democracy in Developing Countries* [textbook edition] (Boulder: Lynne Rienner, 1994), pp. 7–8.

8. Richard J. Ellis and Dennis J. Coyle, "Introduction" in Coyle and Ellis, eds., *Politics, Policy, and Culture* (Boulder: Westview, 1994), pp. 2–3; Diamond, "Introduction," p. 9.

9. Diamond, "Introduction," p. 8.

10. Michael W. Doyle, "Liberalism and World Politics," *American Political Science Review* 80, no. 4 (December 1980):1151–1169.

11. Alfred Stepan distinguishes between organic-statism as a normative approach to politics and corporatism as a mode of interest representation. *The State and Society* (Princeton: Princeton University Press, 1978), pp. 46–47. Because the correlation between the two is very strong, we can conflate them when distinguishing between ideal liberal and militarist types of political culture. On corporatism, see Philippe Schmitter, "Still the Century of Corporatism?" in Frederick B. Pike and Thomas Stritch, eds., *The New Corporatism: Social-Political Structures in the Iberian World* (Notre Dame, Ind.: University of Notre Dame Press, 1974), pp. 85–131.

12. See the analysis in Brian Loveman, *The Constitution of Tyranny* (Pittsburgh: University of Pittsburgh Press, 1993).

13. V. R. Berghahn, *Militarism* (Cambridge: Cambridge University Press, 1981); Alfred Vagts, *A History of Militarism*, rev. ed. (New York: Free Press, 1959).

14. My characterization of this political culture draws from Lloyd I. Rudolph and Susanne Hoeber Rudolph, "Authority and Power in Bureaucratic and Patrimonial Administration," *World Politics* 31, no. 2 (January 1979):216–227; Harold Crouch, "Patrimonialism and Military Rule in Indonesia," *World Politics* 31, no. 4 (July 1979):572–573; and Fernando Uricoechea, *The Patrimonial Foundations of the Brazilian Bureaucratic State* (Berkeley: University of California Press, 1980), pp. 2–3.

15. Diamond, "Introduction," p. 8.

16. For a discussion of change in the political culture of other Latin American countries, see John A. Booth and Mitchell A. Seligson, "Paths to Democracy and the Political Culture of Costa Rica, Mexico, and Nicaragua" in Diamond, ed., *Political Culture*, pp. 99–130.

17. Douglass C. North, *Institutions, Institutional Change, and Economic Performance* (Cambridge: Cambridge University Press, 1990).

18. Stepan, *The State and Society;* Cynthia McClintock and Abraham F. Lowenthal, eds., *The Peruvian Experiment Reconsidered* (Princeton: Princeton University Press, 1983).

19. Stepan analyzes the possible negative consequences of this situation on civilian control of the military as it relates to democratization in *Rethinking Military Politics* (Princeton: Princeton University Press, 1988), pp. 128–146.

20. D. Roderick Kiewiet and Matthew D. McCubbins, *The Logic of Delegation* (Chicago: University of Chicago Press, 1991), pp. 24–37.

21. Deborah D. Avant, "The Institutional Sources of Military Doctrine: Hegemons in Peripheral Wars," *International Studies Quarterly* 37, no. 4 (December 1993):409–430.

22. Samuel Huntington, *The Soldier and the State* (Cambridge: Harvard University Press, 1967).

23. Alfred Stepan, *The Military in Politics* (Princeton: Princeton University Press, 1971), pp. 57–66.

24. The distinction between objective and subjective control is developed in Huntington, *The Soldier and the State.*

25. Peter A. Gourevitch, *Politics in Hard Times* (Ithaca: Cornell University Press, 1986), pp. 54–60.

26. Moore, *Social Origins of Dictatorship and Democracy*; Ronald Rogowski, *Commerce and Coalitions* (Princeton: Princeton University Press, 1989); Gourevitch, *Politics in Hard Times.*

27. For an introduction to the fundamental policy clashes between primary product exporters and inward-oriented industrialists, see Ian Little, Tibor Scitovsky, and Maurice Scott, *Industry and Trade in Some Developing Countries* (London: Oxford University Press for the Development Centre of the Organization for Economic Cooperation and Development, 1970).

28. T. K. Warley, "Western Trade in Agricultural Products," in Andrew Shonfield, ed., *Politics and Trade,* vol. 1, *International Economic Relations of the Western World* (London: Oxford University Press, 1976).

29. Rogowski, *Commerce and Coalitions.*

30. David Yoffie, *Power and Protection* (New York: Columbia University Press, 1983); Vinod Aggarwal, *Liberal Protectionism* (Berkeley: University of California Press, 1985); David R. Mares, *Penetrating the International Market* (New York: Columbia University Press, 1987).

31. Doyle, "Liberalism and World Politics"; John M. Owen, "How Liberalism Produces the Democratic Peace," *International Security* 19, no. 2 (Fall 1994):87–125.

32. See the analysis in Peter J. Katzenstein, *Small States in World Markets* (Ithaca: Cornell University Press, 1985).

33. Katzenstein, *Small States in World Markets.*

34. For an introduction, see John Child, "Geopolitical Thinking in Latin America," *Latin American Research Review* 14, no. 2 (1979):89–112; Howard Taylor Pittman, "La geopolítica en los paises del ABC. Una comparación," *Revista Chilena de Geopolítica* 3, no. 1 (December 1986):53–103.

35. Jack Child, *Geopolitics and Conflict in South America* (New York: Praeger, 1985).

36. Barry S. Posen, *The Sources of Military Doctrine* (Ithaca: Cornell University Press, 1984); Jack Snyder, *The Ideology of the Offense* (Ithaca: Cornell University Press, 1984); Avant, "The Institutional Sources of Military Doctrine."

37. W. Richard Scott, *Organizations* (Englewood Cliffs, N.J.: Prentice-Hall, 1981).

38. Gregory W. Fischer and Patrick D. Larkey, "Organizational Theory and Military Threat Assessment," *Research and Public Policy Analysis and Management* 2 (1981):223–224.

39. For a theoretical and historical discussion of various non-nuclear responses to security threats, including those by countries with fewer standard military resources, see John J. Mearsheimer, *Conventional Deterrence* (Ithaca: Cornell University Press, 1983); Adam Roberts, *Nations in Arms,* vol. 18 in *Studies in International Security* (London: Chatto and Windus for the International Institute for Strategic Studies, 1976).

40. Joshua Cohen, *Civil-Military Relations* (Ithaca: Cornell University Press, 1985; Snyder, *Ideology of the Offensive,* pp. 54–55.

41. Roberts, *Nations in Arms,* pp. 15–37.

42. Paul E. Zinner, *Revolution in Hungary* (New York: Columbia University Press, 1962); Zbigniew K. Brezinski, *The Soviet Bloc* (Cambridge: Harvard University Press, 1967), pp. 210–229.

43. Posen, *Sources of Military Doctrine.*

44. Posen, *Sources of Military Doctrine.*

45. The pioneering studies are Stepan, *The Military in Politics* and Luigi Einaudi, *The Peruvian Military,* Monograph #RN-6048-RC (Santa Monica, Calif.: RAND Corporation, May 1969).

46. Stepan, *The Military in Politics.*

47. Snyder, *Ideology of the Offensive.*

48. Mainwaring, O'Donnell, and Valenzuela, eds., *Issues in Democratic Consolidation,* p. 3.

49. See the discussion of ancient and modern democracies in Josiah Ober and Charles Hedrick, eds., *Demokratia* (Princeton: Princeton University Press, 1996).

50. Rhoda Rabkin, "The Aylwin Government and Tutelary Democracy: A Concept in Search of a Case?" *World Affairs* 33, no. 4 (Winter 1992/1993):119–194. For example, in the United States, due process allows for the appeal by the defense for a conviction, but not by the prosecution for an acquittal, whereas European legal systems allow both sides to appeal. "All Things Considered," Public Radio International, February, 1997.

51. In contrast, Giuseppe DiPalma describes democratic consolidation as not necessarily requiring institutional strength and legitimacy, the consent of the governed being sufficient to bring about democratic consolidation. In addition, he argues that consolidation better represents a process that begins immediately after the agreement to democratize. For DiPalma, institutionalization, habituation, and socialization are better terms for the lengthy process. Giuseppe DiPalma, *To Craft Democracies* (Berkeley: University of California Press, 1990), p. 137–153.

52. Stepan, *Rethinking Military Politics,* pp. xiv–xv; 128–45; citations are from page 129; J. Samuel Valenzuela, "Democratic Consolidation in Post-Transnational Settings: Notion, Process, and Facilitating Conditions," in Mainwaring et al., *Issues in Democratic Consolidation,* pp. 87–93; 137.

53. DiPalma, *To Craft Democracies,* p. 155.

54. Posen, *The Sources of Military Doctrine,* pp. 41–59.

55. Stanislav Andreski, "On the Peaceful Disposition of Military Dictatorships," *Journal of Strategic Studies* 3 (1980).

PART ONE

———— ■ ————

Conceptions of Civil-Military Relations and Democracy

Conceptualizing the range of civil-military relationships constitutes a fundamental step in evaluating their impact on the consolidation of democracy. The introduction presented a theoretical argument that the range is broad and the links between a civil-military relationship and democracy varied. Part One of this volume examines the empirical experience of four of the most intriguing cases in this volume: India, Pakistan, Indonesia, and Venezuela.

Rebecca Schiff begins this section by investigating the Indian and Pakistani cases. She organizes her analysis around the concept of a concordance between civilians and the military as an alternative to civilian control of the military. This form of pacted relationship has been successful in guaranteeing democratic politics even as the Indian polity increasingly strains against the centrifugal forces of caste and ethnicity. In contrast, the Pakistani civil-military relationship produced military rule in the face of domestic civil strife.

J. Soedjati Djiwandono's analysis of Indonesia explores the possibilities of creating a democratic polity in which the military has a legitimate role as partner. Although critical of the way in which the current civil-military relationship constitutes a barrier to democratization, Djiwandono believes that the cultural and historical characteristics of Indonesia require the military's participation in politics. Hence his analysis focuses on the conditions under which *Dwifungsi* (the military's dual function) can support democratic consolidation.

Venezuela is one of Latin America's longest-standing democracies. Gisela Gómez Sucre and María Dolores Cornett demonstrate that the country has a civilian-dominant civil-military relationship. Nevertheless, in 1992 there were two major coup attempts. The chapter thus investigates how such military insubordination could occur under civilian dominance. In many ways, the Venezuela case compels us to recognize that democrats should be ever vigilant in defending democracy, in both civil society and the military.

CHAPTER TWO

— ■ —

Concordance Theory:
The Cases of India and Pakistan

Rebecca L. Schiff

More nations today are engaged in the process of realigning and reorganizing their militaries than at any point since World War II. Civil-military relations have reemerged as a vital topic of study for students of international relations, comparative politics, and military sociology. A major conclusion of current civil-military relations theory is that militaries should remain physically and ideologically separated from political institutions. The theory describes the separation of civilian and military institutions found in the United States and other Western countries, and it prescribes such a separation as the best deterrent to domestic military intervention for Western states and non-Western nations.

The alternative theory proposed in this chapter argues that three partners—the military, the political elites, and the citizenry—should aim for a cooperative relationship that may or may not involve separation but does not require it. This concordance theory sees a high level of integration between the military and other parts of society as one of several types of civil-military relationship. Because all such relationships reflect specific institutional and cultural conditions shared by the three partners, no single type is seen as leading necessarily to domestic military intervention. Concordance does not preclude the separation of civilian institutions and control of the military; but under certain cultural conditions, civilian institutions or the very idea of "civil" may be inappropriate.[1] Therefore, the specific type of civil-military relationship adopted is less important than the ability of the three partners involved to agree on four indicators: the social composition of the officer corps, the political decisionmaking process, recruitment method, and military style. Concordance theory achieves two goals: First, it explains the institutional and cultural conditions that affect relations among the military, the political elites, and society; second, it predicts that if the three partners agree on the four indicators, domestic military intervention is less likely to occur.

Concordance theory resolves two problems found in the current theory of separation. First, the prevailing theory is derived largely but not exclusively from the experience of the United States, and it assumes that to prevent domestic military intervention U.S. or Western-style institutional separation should be applied to all nations. I argue, however, that the U.S. case is grounded in a particular historical and cultural experience—and may not be applicable to other nations. Concordance theory, by contrast, considers the unique historical and cultural experiences of nations and the various other possibilities for civil-military relations, which may be different from the U.S. and Western example. Moreover, concordance theory shows that democratizing countries need not adopt the traditional Western model of civil-military relations in order to achieve democracy, for there exists a model of a working democracy in which civil-military relations take a different form, specifically India. India's successful civil-military relations are contrasted to the Pakistani case, where "discordance" led to domestic military interventions, civil war, and the eventual partition of Pakistan.

Second, the prevailing theory argues for the separation of civil and military institutions. Institutional analysis is the theory's centerpiece. Yet this method of analysis fails to take into account the cultural and historical conditions that may encourage or discourage civil-military institutional separation. Concordance moves beyond institutional analysis by addressing issues relevant to a nation's culture. Current international events demonstrate that ethnic orientations and issues of multicultural diversity are causes of the domestic unrest now found throughout the world, and most significantly in South Asia. Concordance theory operationalizes the specific institutional *and* cultural indicators mentioned above and explains the empirical conditions under which the military, the government, and the society may agree on separate, integrated, or other forms of civil-military relations in order to prevent domestic military intervention.

Both the current theory of civil-military separation and the new theory of concordance proposed here are descriptive as well as prescriptive. Separation theory describes the separation of civil and military institutions that is found in the United States and other Western nations. It prescribes separation as the best deterrent to domestic military intervention for nations throughout the world. By contrast, concordance theory describes a concordance among the military, the political elites, and the citizenry found in a wide range of cultures (including the U.S., where there has long been substantial agreement among all sectors of the society about the role of the armed forces). It prescribes this theory as a deterrent to domestic military intervention that flexibly applies to cultures different from each other and from the United States.

The case studies discussed in this chapter, India and Pakistan, challenge separation theory and illustrate the merits of concordance theory. Relative to its military, India's civil institutions have been in decline for several years, and yet the armed forces have not intervened. The Indian case demonstrates how *different* historical and cultural experiences encourage similar positive relationships among the military, the political elites, and the citizenry without necessarily embracing U.S. or Western civil-military separation. Pakistan, by contrast, reflects early crises in all four of the concordance indicators: officer corps composition, decisionmaking process, recruitment method, and military style. Pakistan's state of discordance led to domestic military intervention in 1958, the failed military dictatorship of Ayub Khan throughout the 1960s, and civil war that resulted in the creation of Bangladesh in 1971.

The first part of this chapter briefly discusses and critiques the current civil-military relations theory. The second part introduces concordance theory. The third and fourth parts apply concordance theory to India and Pakistan respectively. Whereas the major portion of the chapter discusses Indian and Pakistani civil-military relations, the final section addresses some of the regional concerns of this book by offering a brief analysis of concordance theory within the context of regional challenges to South Asia, including Chinese influence and its impact on nuclear proliferation.

CIVIL-MILITARY RELATIONS THEORY

The separation between civilian and military institutions is the centerpiece of the current civil-military relations literature, which enjoyed theoretical ascendancy in the 1950s and 1960s. During this period many nations underwent significant transformations involving domestic military interventions, such as coup, blackmail, and "supplantment."[2] Some scholars viewed the armed forces as a potential contributor to positive domestic political development. Most, however, warned of domestic coercion and dominance by the military.[3] Because of these potential threats to democracy, the U.S. theoretical and empirical approach, which emphasized the separation between "civil" and "military" institutions, was devised to influence civil-military relations abroad. That theory postulates an institutional separation: Detaching the professional military from political ambitions and specific political causes leaves it no reason to intervene in the sphere of civilian institutions. The professional military is prepared to advise civilians and defend the nation from foreign incursions, but the armed forces are not involved in political decisionmaking. Civil-military separation requires a distinct set of civilian institutions that maintain political control over the armed forces.[4]

The first major critique of separation theory is that it is historically and culturally bound to the U.S. case. More specifically, the separation of the U.S. military from civilian institutions is based upon a particular standard of professionalism. That standard highlights military insularity, political neutrality, and conservative defense planning.[5] Because the U.S. standard of military professionalism subsequently became the model, it consequently was exported to nations that had standards, histories, and cultures of professionalism quite different from the Western norm.

Even with respect to U.S. military professionalism, historical and cultural issues have always played an important role. For example, in 1951, Louis Smith wrote the following about civilian dominance of the U.S. military:

> Civil dominance, regardless of how securely grounded it may be in the constitution and in the statutes, is not self implementing. Like any other principle, it must be cherished in the public mind if it is to prevail. Like any other policy, it requires translation into effective leadership. . . . every system of military power and of civil-military relations operates at a given time and in terms of the conditions and opinions of that time.[6]

Simply because they happen to work well in the United States, civil institutions will not arise naturally in another nation nor can they be superimposed on its culture. Smith understood that the constitutional process and the public mind, which harbors particular political and cultural values, must work hand in hand to create an effective relationship between political institutions, the military, and the citizenry. Civilian control prevails in U.S. political culture because the conditions for implementing that type of control are embedded there.[7] Civilian control is not necessarily applicable to other political cultures.

The second major criticism is the institutional emphasis of separation theory. Although institutional analysis is a vital aspect of civil-military relations, the literature that points to the separation of civil and military institutions neglects cultural and historical issues.[8] As noted, the very idea of U.S. institutional separation is grounded in a particular historical experience; and institutional separation is a norm that is embedded within prevailing theory. Institutional separation is not the only possible form of civil-military relationship, but it is the one that occurs in the United States and other Western states. Depending upon the culture, history, and politics of a particular nation, civil-military relations may involve separation, integration, or a variety of other forms. Although civilian and military institutions are important elements in civil-military relations, the literature fails to consider the important influence of civilian society and culture.

Cultural factors include the values, attitudes, and symbols informing not only the nation's view of its military but also the military's own view of that role. As the Indian case study shows, these factors have tremendous influence on the absence or prevalence of domestic military intervention. The literature refers to civilian and military institutions. Yet these institutions must often contend with disparate societal forces. For example, characteristics of the general population may influence the role and purpose of the military. When the army recruits its soldiers, it must draw from existing civilian sectors with distinctive cultural norms and values. How does the background of these soldiers affect recruitment patterns and military service? How do communities view the military? And how does this affect their support for or opposition to the armed forces? Cultural considerations, absent from separation theory, are important factors affecting civil-military relations.

Consequently, there are two types of cases that reveal the shortcomings of separation theory of civil-military separation: those contradicting predictions of intervention and those contradicting predictions of nonintervention. In this chapter, India and Pakistan provide examples of both.

CONCORDANCE THEORY

Current civil-military relations theory emphasizes the separation of civil and military institutions and the authority of the civil sphere over the military to prevent domestic military intervention. By contrast, the theory of concordance highlights dialogue, accommodation, and shared values or objectives among the military, the political elites, and society. Concordance theory accomplishes two goals. First, it explains which institutional and cultural conditions—involving separation, integration, or some alternative—prevent or promote domestic military intervention. Second, it predicts that when agreement on the four indicators prevails among the three partners, domestic military intervention is less likely to occur. The central argument, therefore, is that if the military, the political elites, and the society achieve concordance on the four indicators, then domestic intervention is less probable.

Concordance theory explains the specific conditions determining the military's role in the domestic sphere that includes the government and society. Concordance does not require a particular form of government, set of institutions, or decisionmaking process. But it usually takes place in the context of active agreement, whether established by legislation, decree, or constitution, or based on long-standing historical and cultural values. In contrast to the prevailing theory, which emphasizes the separation of civil and military institutions, concordance encourages cooperation and involvement among the military, political institutions, and society at large. In other words, concordance does not assume that separate civil and military spheres are required to prevent domestic military intervention. Rather, it may be avoided if the military cooperates with the political elites and the citizenry. Cooperation and agreement on the four specific indicators may result in a range of civil-military patterns, including separation, the removal of civil-military boundaries, and other variations.

Military, Political Leadership, and the Citizenry

Concordance theory views the military, the political leadership, and the citizenry as partners and predicts that when they agree about the role of the armed forces by achieving a mutual accommodation, domestic military intervention is less likely to occur in a particular state.

The first partner—the military—can be defined quite simply. It encompasses the armed forces and the personnel who represent the military. The officers and the enlisted personnel are usually those most dedicated to the armed forces. The second partner—the political leadership—can best be defined in terms of function. The exact nature of governmental institutions and the methods of their selection are less important when determining concordance than is identifying the elites who represent the government and have direct influence over the composition and support of the armed forces. Thus, cabinets, presidents, prime ministers, party leaders, parliaments, and monarchs are all possible forms of governmental elites.

The third partner—the citizenry—is by corollary even more heterogeneous and is also best defined by function. How do the citizens interact with the military? And is there agreement among the citizens themselves over the role of the military in society? The current civil-military relations literature does not consider the citizenry but relies instead on political institutions as the main "civil" component of analysis. Although the relationship of civil institutions to the military is indeed important, it only partially reflects the story of civil-military relations. By contrast, concordance considers the citizenry as an important partner of the military and the political elites. Thus, concordance is not restricted to an institutional analysis but incorporates additional elements of society that affect the role and function of the armed forces.

On what levels can the government and the citizenry affect the military's role in a nation? It is argued here that there are four indicators of concordance: the social composition of the officer corps, the political decisionmaking process, the recruitment method, and the military style. In the past, the first three have been discussed in the context of theories emphasizing the separation of political institutions from the military. Concordance borrows important concepts of civil-military relations from the current literature but places them in a wider historical and cultural context that allows richer theoretical conclusions and enables better evaluation of empirical case studies. The four indicators are important elements of concordance because they reflect specific conditions that influence agreement or disagreement among the three partners. Thus, depending on particular cultural and historical conditions, the indicators will determine whether relations among the military, the government, and the society take the form of separation, integration, or some other alternative. The crucial point, therefore, is the cultural and historical context that shapes the relationship among the partners and the indicators.

The Officer Corps Composition

Composition of the officer corps is a primary indicator of concordance. Most modern militaries have an officer corps that is in charge of broad institutional and day-to-day functioning of the armed forces; these are the career soldiers who dedicate their lives to soldiering and to the development of the military and the definition of its relationship to the rest of society. The officer is distinguished from the rank-and-file soldier, and as leaders of the armed forces, the officer corps can provide not only the critical links between the citizenry and the military but also between the military and the government.

A particular composition of the officer corps exists in all modern militaries. In democratic societies, the officer corps usually represents the various constituencies of the nation. Broad representation, however, is not a requisite for concordance, since it is conceivable that the society and the military could agree on a less broadly representative corps. For example, Stephen P. Cohen notes that during the British colonial period in India the "very fact that the army was drawn from particular castes and classes sets these classes well apart" from the "mass of Indian peasantry."[9] This example affirms that particular historical and cultural traditions prevail in nations and that those traditions can affect agreement or disagreement over the composition of the officer corps.

Political Decisionmaking Process

The political decisionmaking process involves the institutional organs of society that determine important factors for the military, such as budget, materials, size, and structure. That process does not imply a particular form of government—democratic, authoritarian, or any other. Rather it refers to the specific channels that determine the needs and allocations of the military. For example, budgets, materials, size, and structure are issues decided by open parliaments, closed cabinets, special committees, and political elites and may involve the participation of military officers. Often the military makes its needs known through a governmental channel or agency that takes into consideration both military and societal resources and requirements. In many countries there is a close partnership or in some instances a collusion between the military and industry, which is known as the "military-industrial complex." Such a partnership may have the support of the citizenry, which may be persuaded that external threat conditions facing a nation warrant a close relationship between the military and industry. Also, the domestic economy may play a role as the business sector and citizens stand to gain from the creation of new industry and employment. The critical issue is that agreement occurs among the political elites, the military, and the citizenry over the political process that best meets the needs and requirements of the armed forces.

Recruitment Method

The third indicator of concordance is recruitment method. Recruitment is the enlistment of citizens into the armed forces, and the method of recruitment may be either coercive or persuasive.[10] Coercive recruitment refers to the forcible conscription of people and supplies for military purposes. Demands are made upon the citizenry, through conscription and taxation, to supply the needs and obligations of the military. Such demands are often harsh because citizens are forced to cooperate against their will. Consequently, this form of recruitment usually does not allow concordance between the military and the citizenry.

Persuasive recruitment can take the form either of voluntary or involuntary enlistment. Persuasion is based on "beliefs": The population believes that the sacrifice of military service is worthwhile for the sake of security, patriotism or any other national cause. The government is not forced to coerce its people into military service when they "willingly offer themselves" by volunteering or accepting the need for enlistment.[11] Persuasive recruitment implies an agreement among the political leadership, the military, and the citizenry over the requirements and composition of the armed forces.

Military Style

The final indicator of concordance is military style. This refers to the external manifestations of the military and the inner mental constructions associated with it: what it looks like, what ethos drives it, and what people think about it. Why is style so important? Style is about the drawing of social boundaries or their elimination. It is the mode by which members of particular elites relate to each other as peers and differentiate themselves from the members of other elites and the members of nonelite groups. It is important because it reflects how something appears; and appearance stands as a symbol that, by the nature and force it conveys, connotes a type of power or authority. Military style deals directly with the human and cultural elements of the armed forces. How the military looks, the overt and subtle signals it conveys, the rituals it displays—these are all part of a deep and nuanced relationship among soldiers, citizens, and the polity.

Military style is not separate from the other indicators of concordance. To the contrary, it manifests itself within, among, and throughout the substance of the other variables. It is usually part of the historical development associated with military traditions and symbols: The uniform, for example, has always been one important symbol of respectability, professionalism, separateness, or cohesiveness—depending upon the character of the nation and its armed forces. Other military symbols and rituals include military parades and marches, military music, social traditions, and ceremonies that capture the meaning of belonging to the armed forces. Symbols and rituals may be found in the officer corps, in the methods used to induct soldiers, and in the institutional processes that determine the needs and requirements of the military.

A CASE OF CONCORDANCE: INDIA

This chapter offers a new conceptual framework for examining civil-military relations, different from the assumption in the prevailing literature, which argues that the military should remain separate from civilian political institutions. Although concordance theory incorporates what is of value in that literature, it does not assume that the separation between civil and military institutions is necessarily the most desirable theoretical and empirical scenario. Institutional civil-military separation may be one form concordance takes, since in some countries separation is precisely what is agreed upon by the military, the political elites, and the citizenry. As a conceptual framework, however, concordance does not limit itself to one civil-military scenario based on separation. Concordance explains the institutional and cultural conditions that affect the distinctive relationships among the three partners. Furthermore, concordance has predictive power: If the military, the political elites, and the citizenry agree on the four indicators, domestic military intervention is less likely to occur.

Nations without a history of Western civil institutions, or nations that incorporate both Western and indigenous values into their political systems, are less likely to benefit from a conceptual approach that emphasizes a Western-style separation of civil institutions and the military. Concordance theory, by contrast, does not superimpose predetermined values upon a nation. In the Indian case, domestic military intervention has never occurred. Concordance has been achieved among the military, the political elites, and the society in politically and culturally distinctive ways.

At first glance, India does not appear to be a case that challenges the theory of civil control. The Indian armed forces still betray the influence of the many decades of British rule. The legacy of British professionalism and the related subordination of the Indian armed forces to civil institutional control are often put forth as major reasons for the prevention of domestic military intervention in India and as examples supporting separation theory of "civilian control." Why should we concern ourselves with concordance theory, then, if civilian control provides an adequate explanation of civil-military relations in India?

Despite the traditional separation between civil and military institutions, the Indian political system over the past ten years has undergone significant changes that have greatly weakened the central government. Many of these changes were prompted by domestic social violence, as well as by economic problems resulting from the post–Cold War environment. It is argued here that the military has adapted to these political transformations, despite their impact on the civilian government. A major reason for this adjustment is that Indian political development is not limited strictly to an institutional relationship with a strong political center. Since independence, the military, as an institution and in conjunction with civilian authorities, has groomed Indian soldiers to adapt to the changing and often conflict-filled political and cultural landscape of Indian society. This process has nurtured agreement among the military, the political elites, and the citizenry about the role and function of the armed forces in India; and it is this long-term concordance that has enabled the military to meet the challenges of critical stages in Indian state-building.

To demonstrate the agreement that has been achieved among the military, the political elites, and the citizenry of India on the question of the military's role, it is necessary to examine the four indicators of concordance. These reveal a substantial evolution since independence, and they are sharply contrasted to the subsequent Pakistani case.

For many years after independence, the Indian officer corps was considered the "last outpost of the British Raj,"[12] as the corps preserved the style and selective recruitment of the British. The British sepoy armies were divided into regiments covering the three provincial presidencies: Bengal, Madras, and Bombay. All had contained a mixture of religious groups (Hindu and Muslim) and caste (from the high Brahmin to the lower caste groups); however, Hindu Brahmins had predominated. Moreover, the Bengali Army was drawn mostly from a narrower population than the other two. After the mutiny of 1857–1858, the British retained this selective recruitment policy but especially favored individuals from the Punjabi Sikh community.

In the wake of independence, this profile of the officer corps initially did not change much. The recruits to the officer corps remained largely Hindu Brahmins and Punjabi Sikhs (the latter constituted about a third of the cadets). Aside from the high proportion of recruits from Punjab, another 15 percent came from Delhi. Other regions, such as Madya Pradesh and Kerala, supplied less than 5 percent.[13]

Since the 1980s, however, the corps has been drawn more from the middle class and reflects a greater diversity of regions and castes. This change, it is true, has reflected both conscious recruitment practices and socioeconomic factors. For example, many of the wealthier Indian families have declined to send their sons to cadet school, and the military pay scale, lagging behind inflationary trends, has persuaded many potential officers to seek more lucrative jobs elsewhere. Nonetheless, it is unquestionable that the officer corps has now become significantly more representative of Indian society than it was during the early years of statehood. The British historical legacy and the Indian socioeconomic and cultural reality thus became the cornerstone of the ethnic and social composition of the officer corps.[14]

Within the military's rank and file, recruitment is both voluntary and persuasive. As in other democratic nations, many of India's less wealthy citizens are motivated by patriotism, loyalty, monetary remuneration, and quality living conditions. Furthermore, the Indian military is an internationally respected institution that has performed well during wartime. Past successes have given the armed forces prestige and a meaningful role and function in Indian society. Thus, recruits are often persuaded to join the military for nationalistic and personal reasons.

Although in the past Hindus and Sikhs provided a disproportionate number of recruits, since independence the ranks have been diversified by caste and region. For example, in a Mahar or Dogra regiment, one can find recruits from different geographical areas and caste backgrounds. As recruitment continues to broaden the societal base of the corps and the ranks, the likelihood of ethnic or religious cliques diminishes. In recruitment, the government and the military clearly have been sensitive to establishing positive links between the armed forces and the general population.[15]

With respect to the political decisionmaking process, the Congress Party and a respected military tradition emerged during the early development of Indian state-building. A three-tier committee system was established that remains in place to the present. This consisted of the Defense Committee of the Cabinet

(DCC), the Defense Minister's Committee, and the Chief of Staff Committee (CSC). In matters of security, the prime minister's council delegated its authority to the DCC and what is now called the Political Affairs Committee (PAC). The result is that the civilian component of the three-tier system has been the major partner in military affairs; and the armed forces have responded professionally.

Despite this professional attitude, the Indian political center relative to the armed forces has weakened significantly. This weakening of civilian institutions resulted from (1) the political center's failure to control Hindu-Muslim violence; (2) the challenge of preserving a secular state; (3) India's post–Cold War economic conditions; and (4) increased government scandal and corruption. The religious-ethnic turmoil that the central government now confronts has even brought about growing involvement of the Indian military in aiding civilian authorities to quell domestic violence and terrorism. One important Indian scholar summarizes the situation as "the disintegration of India's dominant political institutions."[16]

Why has the Indian military not intervened in politics under such circumstances? Civilian control over the military obviously cannot be the sole explanation, for the theory of civilian control looks only at institutional mechanisms shaping the relationship between the civilian government and the armed forces. The concordance about the role and function of the armed forces that arose among the military, the political elites, and the citizenry during the tremendous political and social changes since independence must be taken into account as well. Despite civilian institutional weakness, the military remains adaptive to the current decisionmaking process that often utilizes the military for civilian purposes. A diverse officer corps and a broad rank-and-file recruitment policy undergird this political situation. In other words, the role and function of the armed forces and its noninterventionist history reveal a distinctive historical and societal concordance in India.

Civil control theory concerns only the institutional mechanisms controlling the relationship between the civilian government and the armed forces. Both India and Pakistan, however, have undergone tremendous political and social changes since independence. Thinking about Indian civil-military relations in terms of concordance on the role and function of the armed forces among the military, the political elites, and the citizenry captures a more accurate description of Indian civil-military relations. The composition of the officer corps, the military's recruitment method, and military style, in conjunction with the political decisionmaking process, are essential to an understanding of Indian civil-military relations. They draw attention to the importance of specific cultural and institutional contexts, such as religion, caste, language, and domestic conflicts—not to mention the integration of a British legacy into these indigenous societies.

For example, despite more egalitarian trends in recruitment, the Indian martial tradition is still heavily influenced by British military history. Indian military style often exhibits the British "brusqueness" and swagger-stick manner; and of course

English is the language used within the corps. Soldiers live and train in secluded British-inspired cantonments. Yet despite this British influence, the Indian army is a true example of the integration between British and native India. An illustration of this integration is the military uniform. Since the 1800s Indian uniforms have been characterized by "native costume and European fashion." One such uniform is the infantry's prim and well-kept British khaki, highlighted by a native Sikh turban. The uniform and general style of the officer corps and rank and file symbolize a successful bridge between British colonial presence and Indian independence.[17]

The Indian case demonstrates how the theory of separation of civil-military relations fails to explain a particular example of relationships between the military, the political elites, and the society. The historical and cultural conditions found in India are distinctive and bear significantly on the way in which the military views its role in that nation. India integrated British colonial history into its rich native culture. Although strong civil institutions are important political constructions, they alone do not explain the complexity of Indian civil-military relations, especially because those institutions have been greatly weakened and the military has refrained from the interventionist fate of Pakistan.

A CASE OF DISCORDANCE: PAKISTAN

Pakistan's domestic military interventions are an anomaly because the country's early history embraced the British-Indian tradition of parliamentary government. The founders of Pakistan had intended to establish civilian control over the military—a principle and practice that was not foreign to the British-trained soldiers. In fact, a large proportion of the Pakistani officer corps had been trained at Sandhurst or the Indian Military Academy.[18] On the issue of civilian control, Stephen Cohen states: "By the end of the Raj the role of the military had been limited and elaborate administrative and fiscal mechanisms were devised to control it."[19] Pakistan's founder Mohammed Ali Jinnah followed this prescription for civilian control over the military and made clear to his officer corps that it was the civilians who "make national policy" while the armed forces remain the "servants of the people."[20] The professional Pakistani military had intended to follow the tradition of civilian law and order as well as professional military insularity.

Civilian institutions and military professionalism were well established in Pakistan. The events which led to domestic military intervention were the result of weak political leadership and an even weaker political decisionmaking process. Edward Feit claims that Pakistan's early political problems were due to the fact that "[no] real leader emerged who had the prestige, power, or determination to forge a unity among power contenders."[21] Contrary to the profound and stable Indian founders, Mahatma Gandhi and Jawaharlal Nehru—Pakistan suffered leadership setbacks with the assassinations of Ali Jinnah and his successor, Liaquat Ali Khan. Despite Pakistan's inheritance of civil parliamentary institutions, subsequent "shifting governments" provided no effective mechanism for political stabilization and direction for the armed forces.[22]

The focus on political process, rather than civil institutions, is important because the Pakistani armed forces did not want to challenge the legality and form of parliamentary institutions—a tradition which they inherited from British India. Even after he had seized power in 1958, General Khan was "concerned about the legality of [his] initial action and the subsequent acts that [he] and [his] subordinates commit[ed] under the rubric of martial law."[23] This was not a situation of rogue officers determined to seize power because of their disagreement with the concept of civil institutional control. Rather this was a situation where ten years of political vacuum forced professionally trained generals to enter politics; and as a result of their exposure to the concept and reality of civilian control in British India, they remained concerned about the institutional viability of the state. Khan's Basic Democracies were established to create a more effective political process and to enable the military to have a more secure role and mission. Although these political processes also failed to establish a healthier relationship between the military and society, it does not diminish the fact that civilian institutions per se were not the point of contention; rather, it was the civilians' inability to construct an effective political decisionmaking process that would protect the military's long-held professional ethic.

By addressing the additional three indicators of concordance (the social composition of the officer corps, the recruitment method, and military style), we can show further discordance between the military, the political elites, and the citizenry during the regime of Ayub Khan (1958–1969).

In newly created Pakistan, Punjabi Muslims constituted about 60 percent of the sepoys and officers. The rest of the corps was divided among members from the Northwest Frontier, Sind, Baluchistan, and Azad Kashmir.[24] Bengalis were conspicuously absent in the configuration of the Pakistani officer corps. During World War II, no regular Bengali Muslim army units were formed. In contrast to the Punjabi Muslims, who were considered a "martial" class, by the 1850s, Bengali officers had developed a reputation quite antithetical to the martial spirit.[25]

The Bengali nonmartial reputation would stick to the eastern Bengali population during the creation of the Pakistani nation, military, and officer corps. From the start, the eastern wing of Pakistan would consistently receive far less attention in budget allocations, political representation and social status. For example, between 1950 and 1969 Pakistani defense expenditures were approximately 56 percent of the federal budget. "Significant is the fact that out of the total defense expenditure, barely 10 percent was used in East Pakistan, where large revenue collections were made through taxes."[26] With respect to officer recruitment, by 1967 only 5 percent of the army officers came from East Pakistan. In the navy and air force the total numbers hovered around 10 percent.[27] Although recruitment of Bengali officers gradually increased, there existed a "considerable distaste for the quality of Bengali officers and other ranks."[28] Thus, in the officer corps discrimination against Bengalis points to discordance between the military and a large sector of Pakistani society.

Recruitment among the rank and file also reflected a disproportionately small number of Bengali soldiers. The recruitment method appeared both voluntary and persuasive, which according to concordance theory should encourage partnership among the political elites, the military, and society at large. Whereas many from West Pakistan were encouraged to join the ranks, significant discrimination occurred with respect to East Pakistan. This fact was instrumental in the events that led to domestic strife, the imposition of martial law in East Pakistan, and, ultimately, to civil war.

A lack of cooperation and agreement among the military, political leadership, and the citizenry is also evident in the area of military recruitment. The Pakistani military is organized along British lines, composed of an army, air force, and navy. As one of the most "central institutions" in Pakistan, citizenship is largely determined by participation in the military. Soldiers volunteer for seven years and may enroll for a maximum of eighteen years of service. Similar to the British-inspired Indian military, the Pakistani ranks live in military cantonments that provide well-furnished facilities for military training and extracurricular activities such as sports and education.[29]

Feit argues that in the early years, the British-influenced cantonment system "enhanced the esprit de corps of the army" and that the ready supply of recruits "always therefore exceeded demand."[30] That ready recruitment supply, however, was mainly from West Pakistan and most predominantly drawn from the Punjab. The Eastern Bengali sector, although comprising 60 percent of Pakistan's population, provided only three battalions (three thousand men) in an army of three hundred thousand.[31] Furthermore, the Bengalis constituted the only single-class units in the Pakistani army, whereas the West Pakistani Muslims were combined in different units.[32] As a result of this overt discrimination, and other social and political disparities directed against East Pakistanis, the Bengalis felt threatened by their lack of representation in one of Pakistan's most vital institutions.[33]

A disproportionate officer corps composition and discriminatory recruitment of the rank and file are also relevant to the final indicator of concordance: military style. As mentioned above, military style directly expresses the human and cultural elements involved in the armed forces. It is often part of the historical evolution associated with military traditions and symbols. One important military tradition of the British-Indian and Pakistani militaries is the theory of "martial races." That theory, developed in the late nineteenth and early twentieth centuries, argued that "some Indian peoples were warlike by tradition and others were not."[34] For example, the Punjabi Muslims and Sikhs became part of the an established warrior class, and that status gave these select groups social and political privileges that were denied to other groups.[35] As the martial races tradition became more culturally entrenched in British India, it affected the recruitment of soldiers, because those who were considered part of the privileged elite were more actively recruited into the prestigious British-Indian military.

During its post-independence period, the Indian army, in contrast to the Pakistani military, tried to de-mythologize the concept of martial races developed under British rule. One way this was accomplished was by gradually recruiting officers and soldiers from wide sectors of the Indian population, thereby preventing the alienation or domination of any one group.[36] This broad recruitment process has helped India avoid domestic military intervention. In Pakistan, the mythology of the martial races remained embedded in the armed forces, thereby fostering discrimination among the so-called nonmartial groups, such as the Bengalis.[37]

The culture of military traditions, inherited from British colonial rule, continued in Pakistan. This was reflected in the recruitment of the officers and rank-and-file soldiers. In the case of the East Bengalis, this overt form of discrimination, coupled with additional political and social grievances, led to civil war, the downfall of Ayub Khan, and the eventual creation of Bangladesh in 1971.

SOUTH ASIA'S REGIONAL CHALLENGE

This chapter has focused on the development of concordance with respect to India's civil-military relations and Pakistan's early yet significant state of discordance which led to domestic military intervention. On a regional level discordance is far more prevalent, and India operates in a South Asian environment where domestic military interventions are not uncommon—Pakistan, Bangladesh, and Sri Lanka being examples. Moreover, the influence of China in the region should not be overlooked, since Indian defense policy is often a reaction to the role of China and the presence of its conventional and nuclear forces.[38] The proliferation of nuclear weapons, in particular, threatens a delicate balance in a highly volatile region where China exerts enormous influence on neighboring states including Pakistan. An argument can be made that India's domestic concordance between the military, the political elites, and the citizenry contributes to the preservation of regional stability, because India has chosen to both maintain its regional strength vis-à-vis China and Pakistan, while continuing to search for a peaceful solution to the nuclear issue. In other words, the domestic partnering among military and societal actors is extended to regional partnering among India's allies and adversaries.

U.S. foreign policy makers have often neglected to understand the influence of China on South Asian politics. India, however, has not failed to comprehend the growing threat of China and its overt support of Pakistan. Although China's nuclear capability is superior to that of India and Pakistan, India views the continued growth of its arsenal and its undeclared ambiguity as being critical to maintaining a qualitative advantage in the region. Therefore, India has chosen not to sign the Nuclear Non-Proliferation Treaty (NPT) because the treaty divides the world into nuclear haves and have-nots: those who have detonated a nuclear device before 1967 and those who have not detonated such a device. India's detonation did not take place until 1974. Thus, signing the NPT would effectively diminish its standing among the nuclear weapon states.

Nevertheless, India has chosen to maintain a delicate balance between protecting its undeclared nuclear capability and attempting to achieve agreements with the United States and other major powers on a "comprehensive test ban and a verifiable, global ban on the production of fissile materials for nuclear weapons."[39] India, therefore, has struggled to maintain its military capability in the face of China and Pakistan while trying to promote a peaceful approach to regional proliferation. This delicate balance may be attributed largely to India's continuing domestic partnership between the military, the political elites, and society at large. Despite the Congress Party's decline over the years, it has remained steadfast in helping to preserve delicate regional agreements with respect to nuclear proliferation, and the military has abided by these efforts. The noted Indian opposition party Bharatiya Janata Party (BJP) has recently rejected the nuclear test ban treaty and is pushing for an overt nuclear weapons test and an open declaration of India's capability. Such a move might result in a detrimental withdrawal of U.S. economic support.[40] Nevertheless, for now, India remains committed to achieving international reciprocity on nuclear arms, while maintaining its domestic concordance over the role of the armed forces.

Therefore, in the case of South Asia, having at least one major nation with a long-standing domestic concordance may help preserve a regional balance on nuclear arms. India's insistence on maintaining an ambiguous yet flexible approach to nuclear proliferation can be considered part of a well-established internal relationship between the military, the political elites, and Indian society. Although India experiences many levels of political and social flux, the underlying civil-military agreement among the three major partners enables India to protect its regional interests while encouraging peaceful resolutions to outstanding issues of proliferation.

CONCLUSION

This chapter challenges some basic assumptions of the prevailing theory about why military intervention in internal politics does or does not occur. That theory, which posits a dichotomous power relationship between the civil and military spheres, suggests that military intervention in domestic politics is prevented if civilian institutions are in control and maintain a check over a professional military. Conversely, it holds that military intervention in internal politics is more likely to take place if civilian institutions do not exist or are greatly weakened.

As the Indian example has demonstrated, active and enduring agreement among the military, the political elites, and the citizenry in a country may offer a better explanation of why military intervention in domestic politics has not occurred there. This concordance arises from cultural and institutional factors and relates particularly to the composition of the officer corps, the political decision-making process, the method of recruiting the rank and file, and military style. Pakistan, by contrast, reflects a nation where cultural and institutional discordance resulted in domestic military intervention, civil war, and the country's eventual partition. Concordance, as opposed to civil control over the military offers a better explanation for predicting domestic military intervention. Moreover, on an interstate level, at least in South Asia, one major country characterized by a long-standing domestic concordance, India, may also support a regional concordance on issues of international security.

NOTES

This chapter was previously published as "Civil-Military Relations: A Theory of Concordance," *Armed Forces and Society,* vol. 22:1 (1995). Reprinted by permission of Transaction Publishers. Copyright © 1995 by Rebecca L. Schiff; all rights reserved.

1. See Rebecca L. Schiff, "Civil-Military Relations Reconsidered: Israel as an 'Uncivil' State," *Security Studies* 1, no. 4 (Summer 1992); Rebecca L. Schiff, "Civil-Military Relations Reconsidered: A Theory of Concordance," *Armed Forces and Society* 1 (Fall 1995):7–24.

2. For a discussion of various forms of domestic military intervention, see Samuel Finer, *The Man on Horseback* (Boulder: Westview Press, 1988), 78–79.

3. See, for example, the work of Lucian Pye and Guy Pauker in contrast to that of Morris Janowitz and Samuel Huntington; Lucian Pye, "Armies in the Process of Political Modernization," in J. J. Johnson, ed., *The Role of the Military in Underdeveloped Countries* (New Haven: Princeton University Press, 1968), 69; Guy Pauker, "Southeast Asia as a Problem Area in the Next Decade," *World Politics* 11 (1959); Morris Janowitz, *The Military in the Political Development of New Nations* (Chicago: University of Chicago Press, 1964); and Samuel Huntington, *Political Order in Changing Societies* (New Haven: Yale University Press, 1968), 222.

4. See, for example, Samuel Huntington, *The Soldier and the State* (Cambridge: Harvard University Press, 1957), 72–93, 83–85.

5. Ibid., 83–85, 96–97.

6. Louis Smith, *American Democracy and Military Power* (Chicago: University of Chicago Press, 1951), 11, 32.

7. Political culture is defined as "that elusive notion that encompasses the attitudes, dispositions, orientations, expressive symbols and values defining the situation in which political actions take place." Myron Weiner, "Political Culture in Foreign Area Studies," in Richard J. Samuels and Myron Weiner, eds., *The Political Culture of Foreign Area and International Studies* (Washington, D.C.: Brasseys, 1992), 4.

8. This thesis agrees with Clifford Geertz's idea that culture is found in a particular context that is to be uniquely understood and described—and not superimposed upon another culture: "As interworked systems of construable signs . . . culture is not a power, something to which social events, behaviors, institutions, or processes can be casually attributed; it is a context, something within which they can be intelligibly—that is, thickly—described." Clifford Geertz, *The Interpretation of Cultures* (New York: Basic Books, 1973), 14.

9. Stephen P. Cohen, *The Indian Army* (Berkeley: University of California Press, 1971), 50, 51, 62.

10. These two forms of recruitment are borrowed from Samuel Finer's "extraction coercion-persuasion cycle" in "State and Nation-Building in Europe: The Role of the Military," in *The Formation of National States in Western Europe* (Princeton: Princeton University Press, 1975), 95–96.

11. Ibid., 95–96.

12. Cohen, *The Indian Army,* 182; "The Military in India and Pakistan: Contrasting Cases," paper presented to the University of Chicago South Asia and Middle East workshop, February 1993, 15.

13. Cohen, *The Indian Army,* 183.

14. Pradeep P. Barua, "Ethnic Conflict in the Military of Developing Nations: A Comparative Analysis of India and Nigeria," *Armed Forces and Society* 19 (Summer 1992):131–132.

15. Cohen, *The Indian Army,* 188–189.

16. Sumit Ganguly, "From the Defense of Nation to Aid to the Civil: The Army in Contemporary India," *Journal of Asian and African Studies* 26, nos. 1–2 (1991):22; Atul Kohli, "State-Society Relations in India's Changing Democracy," in Atul Kohli, ed., *India's Democracy* (Princeton: Princeton University Press, 1990), 306.

17. Richard Knotel, Herbert Knotel, and Herbert Sieg, *Uniforms of the World* (New York: Exeter Books, 1980), 276–277.

18. Stephen P. Cohen, *The Pakistan Army* (Berkeley: University of California Press, 1984), 53.

19. Ibid., 117.

20. Ibid., 117; Cohen cites Mohammed Ali Jinnah, address to the Staff College, June 14, 1948, reprinted in several editions of Jinnah's speeches and the official history of the Staff College, 1905–1980.

21. Edward Feit, *The Armed Bureaucrats* (Boston: Houghton Mifflin, 1973).

22. Feit, *The Armed Bureaucrats,* 64

23. Cohen, *The Pakistan Army,* 120.

24. Ibid., 42, 52.

25. Brig. Gen. John Jacob, *Tracts on the Native Army of India: Its Organization and Discipline* (London: Smith Elder, 1858), 106; Cohen, *The Indian Army,* 34.

26. Shelton U. Kodikara, "Bangladesh," in Shelton U. Kodikara, ed., *External Compulsions of South Asian Politics* (New Delhi: Sage 1993), 127.

27. Ibid., 128.

28. Cohen, *The Pakistan Army,* 43.

29. Ibid., 66.

30. Feit, *The Armed Bureaucrats,* 66.

31. Ibid., 66–67.

32. Cohen, *The Pakistan Army,* 43.

33. Ibid., 40–41.

34. David Omissi, "Martial Races: Ethnicity and Security in Colonial India, 1858–1939," *War and Society* 9, no. 1 (May 1991):7.

35. Ibid., 8.

36. Barua, "Ethnic Conflict in the Military of Developing Nations," 131–132.

37. Cohen, *The Pakistan Army,* 43.

38. Brahma Chellaney, "Regional Proliferation: Issues and Challenges," in *Nuclear Proliferation in South Asia* (Boulder: Westview, 1991), 308.

39. *Arms Control Today* (July/August 1994):27.

40. Miriam Jordan, "Indian Opposition Party Would Assert Nuclear Capability If It Gains Power," *Wall Street Journal,* April 2, 1996, A10.

CHAPTER THREE

———— ∎ ————

Civil-Military Relations in Indonesia: The Case of ABRI's Dual Function

J. Soedjati Djiwandono

The civil-military relationship in Indonesia is best characterized by the concept of *Dwifungsi*, or "the dual function," of the Armed Forces of the Republic of Indonesia (ABRI). The armed forces are not merely a state apparatus for national defense and security; they constitute a sociopolitical force that interacts with civil society. This chapter explores the development and evolution of the doctrine of *Dwifungsi* and its implications for democracy in Indonesia. In an era when countries from all regions of the world are democratizing, this chapter questions the conventional wisdom regarding the relationship between particular configurations of civil-military relations and democracy. Is the consolidation of democracy contingent on civilian dominance in civil-military relations, to use David Mares's terminology, or can it proceed when the military plays an active political role in politics? Specifically, is ABRI's dual function antithetical to Indonesian democracy or not?

This chapter's first section reviews the historical development of the Indonesian polity, from the postindependence experiment with parliamentary democracy through the establishment of the New Order under President Soeharto. The second section discusses the genesis of ABRI's dual-function doctrine, as well as criticisms of the concept. The final section discusses ABRI's dual function and its implications for Indonesian democracy.

IN SEARCH OF INDONESIAN DEMOCRACY

In its relatively brief history, Indonesia has experienced numerous changes in its system of government and in its approach to democracy. In the initial months following the country's proclamation of independence on August 17, 1945, Indonesia had a presidential system of government, which was subsequently transformed into a parliamentary system under the same constitution. For more than a decade, the parliamentary system of government persisted. Nevertheless, the experiment with parliamentary democracy was doomed by the population's growing disillusionment with the system. There were countless reasons for this dissatisfaction, both internal and external in nature. In short, the decade of parliamentary government was regarded as a dismal failure.

Frustration with "Western liberal democracy," or what in Indonesia has always been regarded as the failure of "liberal democracy," ultimately led to the initiation of "Guided Democracy" under President Sukarno in 1959 (what is now termed the "Old Order" in Indonesia). The period of Guided Democracy was characterized by the strengthening of presidential powers, including a dramatic increase in legislative and other prerogatives enjoyed by that office. Eventually, Guided Democracy was discredited and abandoned with the fall of President Sukarno, its principal sponsor. Since the 1960s, the country has been experimenting with what has been designated as "*Pancasila* Democracy" in the "New Order" of General, now President, Soeharto. The term *Pancasila* literally means "five principles." These principles constitute the state ideology of the Republic of Indonesia as embodied in the Preamble of the 1945 Constitution, and they consist of a belief in God, national unity, humanity, democracy, and social justice.

In fact, the great divide in Indonesia's half century of independence is that between the period of the Old Order under President Sukarno and that of the New Order under Soeharto. The epoch-making event that divided the two periods was the abortive communist coup of 1965. It marked the only time in the half-century history of Indonesian independence that a change in the national leadership had taken place, albeit in a less-than-peaceful way.

It is important to note that, differences aside, President Sukarno's Guided Democracy and the *Pancasila* Democracy of the New Order exhibit a common antipathy toward traditional concepts of democracy. Both regimes bitterly criticized Western or liberal democracy for its "individualism" and "unbridled individual liberties," which, they argued, are contrary to Indonesian culture and identity, characterized by the "family spirit" or the "family principle" and the spirit of *gotong-royong,* or mutual cooperation. The terms "Western democracy" and "liberal democracy," and even the word "liberal," have thus acquired a negative connotation. Both regimes attributed the failure of Western, liberal, parliamentary democracy in Indonesia in the postindependence period on the system itself, rather than on the practitioners of democracy, the political parties and their leaders at the time.

In other ways, the regime of General Soeharto represented an effort to break with the past regime. In the state address in which he laid out the goals of the New Order, General Soeharto stated, among other things, that "the ideological foundation of the New Order is none other than *Pancasila;* the basis of the State of the New Order is none other than the 1945 Constitution; and the basis of its mental attitude is the pure dedication to the interests of the people at large." He defined the New Order as a total correction of all forms of deviation perpetrated during the Order that was then in power, which is now called the Old Order. Deviations from Pancasila and the 1945 Constitution . . . had wide and deep consequences. . . . Human rights were almost gone, for everything was determined by the will of the authority. Legal guarantees and protection hardly existed. . . . The principle of the people's sovereignty became vague; what existed was the "sovereignty" of the leaders. . . . The wealth of the State was used for personal interests. . . . The system of "guided economy" in practice became "a license system" that benefited only a few close to the authority.[1]

In sum, Soeharto criticized Sukarno's regime as corrupt and aspiring to absolutism because power was held, not by the supreme governing body (People's Consultative Assembly and the House of Representatives) but by the "Great Leader of the Revolution," President Sukarno himself.

Despite the aspirations of the new regime, many of the same criticisms leveled against the Old Order can be applied to *Pancasila* Democracy under the New Order. For example, the powers of the presidency have continued to increase unchecked by legislative accountability. The president has been able to dominate legislative institutions such as the People's Consultative Assembly (MPR) and the House of Representatives (DPR).[2] This is due in part to the fact that the majority of the MPR members are appointed by the president himself and that all candidates for the DPR and MPR undergo "special screening" as a condition for nomination well before the general election or before their appointment.

Recent demonstrations by Indonesia's youth, particularly university students, and workers attest to the inefficacy of legislative institutions relative to the almost absolute power of the executive. The lack of legislative autonomy is complicated by the absence of an independent judiciary. Moreover, restrictions on freedom of speech and freedom of assembly remain firmly in place. Recently, an emerging independent trade union was banned, and its leader sentenced to prison. In short, the political system seems to have been ossified, which makes communication almost impossible, except as a one-way process from top to bottom.

Perhaps it is in recognition of such a situation that openness has been encouraged by government leaders over the past few years; there have, in fact, been indications of growing openness in the regime. The trade union leader referred to previously was suddenly released and a magazine recently won a court case against the Information Minister over restrictions on publishing licenses. Moreover, for some time a newly formed independent journalists' alliance has continued to exist, albeit without official recognition. At one point the alliance's publication was banned and three of its leaders were arrested, brought to trial, and sentenced to prison. Nevertheless, the publication has continued to survive, and no action seems to have been taken by the government against it. At the same time, the Indonesian Democratic Party (PDI), in some cases even the government party Golkar (Functional Group) at the provincial and district levels, and the Muslim Scholars' Association (NU) seem to have succeeded in averting, or at least minimizing, government intervention particularly in the election of their leadership. Nonetheless, it is difficult to determine the limits to the regime's openness.[3]

In sum, at the present stage, democracy in Indonesia is limited. This is not to say that there has been no progress. In fact, although throughout the regime of President Sukarno there was only one general election (in 1955), since 1971 there has been a general election every five years. This progress has occurred primarily at the formal level, for the holding of general elections has not helped state institutions to perform their proper functions. Instead, the political system has become more a situation of one-man rule, with the increasing concentration of power in the hands of the presidency. What is needed is reform on all levels of the political system so that state institutions function as stipulated by the constitution. Such reform should include the development of mechanisms to control the executive and a system of accountability; the establishment of judicial review and an independent court of law; and a mechanism for a peaceful change of national leaders, that is, a system of succession. In other words, a revitalization of the existing system is in order.

THE GENESIS OF *DWIFUNGSI*

The military roles embodied in the concept of *Dwifungsi* emerged in the postindependence period, as a result of both the sociopolitical role assumed by the military and the crystallization of an ideology supporting such a role. The sociopolitical role of the armed services was initiated when many military personnel were required to fill the vacant managerial posts left by foreign, particularly Dutch, companies that had been nationalized as a form of reprisal against the Dutch refusal to negotiate over West Irian. As a result of such initiatives, during the parliamentary period of the 1950s the role of ABRI in the nonmilitary fields was to some extent sanctioned by legislation.[4]

The origin of *Dwifungsi* is also grounded in the evolution of an ideology based on hostility toward the type of civilian supremacy over the armed services usually associated with liberal democracy. During the period of parliamentary democracy in the postindependence period of the 1950s, ABRI was resistant to efforts to limit it to defense and security roles by keeping it outside the political and economic arenas and away from the process of political decisionmaking. ABRI resented what it perceived as efforts to manipulate and exploit it by the ideological political parties of the time. Exclusion from the political arena was anathema to the armed services, which had taken part in the struggle for national independence, not as professional soldiers, but as an integral part of the entire Indonesian population engaged in a national independence movement. The perception was that, as a result of its role in the independence movement, ABRI was entitled to take part in the nation's effort to give content to that independence. From this perspective, the doctrine of *Dwifungsi* is fundamentally a formulation, an affirmation, and an institutionalization of the role ABRI has played since the beginning of the republic.

Nevertheless, it was during the Guided Democracy period that the dual-function concept began to be formulated into a concrete doctrine. The first articulation of the doctrine of *Dwifungsi* was by General Abdul Haris Nasution. As Chief of Staff of the Army, in an extemporaneous speech at a graduation ceremony at the military academy at Magelang, a town in central Java, Nasution asserted that the position of the Indonesian National Army (TNI)[5] was not like that of an army in a Western country, in which the military was solely an "instrument of the government." Neither was it like that of various Latin American armies which monopolized political power. Rather the TNI was one of the forces of the people's struggle and was equal to the other social forces with which it had fought shoulder to shoulder.[6] Later on, a prominent lawyer at the University of Indonesia called this concept the army's "middle way."

Moreover, Nasution shared President Sukarno's growing disenchantment with parliamentary democracy. In fact, the Indonesian armed forces' disappointment with the parliamentary system had been building steadily throughout the parliamentary period. This was evident in the "October 17, 1952 Affair," when there was a demonstration in front of the presidential palace demanding the dissolution of Parliament. The demonstration was rumored to have been masterminded by the Indonesian armed forces at least partly as an expression of their dissatisfaction with the political system.[7] At the same time, the armed forces had recently succeeded in restoring their authority after crushing a regional rebellion in West Sumatra and North Sulewesi, while demonstrating their capacity to play a crucial sociopolitical role in filling many of the managerial posts left vacant by the Dutch. As a result, President Sukarno's efforts to develop a new political "concept," the culmination of which was embodied in the principles of "guided democracy," enjoyed the support of ABRI leadership, which viewed it as an opportunity to put into practice Nasution's "middle way."[8] Ultimately, with the support of ABRI, Sukarno issued the presidential decree of July 5, 1959, that dissolved the Constituent Assembly and reinstalled the 1945 Constitution, on the basis of which President Sukarno would no longer act simply as a ceremonial head of state but as an executive president. President Sukarno then had the opportunity to put into effect his concept of "Guided Democracy," premised on ABRI's playing an enhanced role in the political arena. In short, the implementation of Guided Democracy represented a convergence of interests between President Sukarno and the leadership of ABRI.

Although ABRI's dual function has its roots in the period of Guided Democracy, it is within the New Order regime under President Soeharto that *Dwifungsi* as a doctrine has been given its constitutional and legal basis. The 1965 abortive communist coup attempt was a turning point for ABRI's dual role, not only because it was an epoch-making event that served as the great divide in the recent history of Indonesia between the Old and New Orders, but also because it initiated a deepening of the entrenchment of ABRI's role as a sociopolitical force in the polity. The legitimacy of the dual function originated in the esteem ABRI earned as a result of its role in the crisis; it had protected the nation from the devastation of a communist coup attempt.

ABRI's claim to the dual function originates in its historical role in the development of the independent Indonesian state. In short,

> ABRI was born out of the people, raised by the people, for the people, and forms an inseparable part of the people . . . as a logical consequence of the Proclamation of Independence of the Indonesian nation on 17 August 1945, when the whole people were struggling to assert, defend, and preserve their independence in order to realize their ideals as a nation. . . . It is of these struggling people that a part later became ABRI.[9]

In his first state address as acting president on August 16, 1967, General Soeharto's comments outlined the aspirations of the New Order and conveyed a similar sentiment:

> The role contributed by ABRI to political developments and state affairs can easily be understood if we look back at the birth and history of its growth. ABRI was born simultaneously with the outbreak of the physical Revolution. . . . ABRI is an armed force that was born and grew to give birth to independence. ABRI is not a mere mercenary armed force, it also gives content to independence; ABRI has also the right and obligation to take part in determining State policy and the running of government.[10]

Such a historical claim, however, has engendered a problem largely overlooked in the debate about the legitimacy of *Dwifungsi*. The dual function may be justified for the original independence fighters, who subsequently constituted the core of Indonesia's armed forces. But the historical justification may be dubious for the post-1945 generations of ABRI members, for whom *Dwifungsi* is not founded on personal experience.[11]

Nevertheless, it may be argued that now *Dwifungsi* should be viewed in terms of the constitutive rules which regulate Indonesian politics. The dual function has, in fact, been legally entrenched in a long series of legislative initiatives. The codification of the dual role is evident in legislation related to defense and security, that associated with elections and political parties, and legislation that addresses the relationship between society and the armed forces. For example, law No. 20/1982 describes ABRI as a "dynamizer" and "stabilizer" that "together with other social forces assumes the duty and responsibility of securing and bringing to fruition the struggle of the nation based on freedom and raising the welfare of the whole Indonesian people."[12]

Yet, although the historical explanation of *Dwifungsi* would be incomplete without taking into consideration the institutionalization of the concept, it is also essential to recognize that the evolution of the constitutive rules based on *Dwifungsi* have occurred within a particular ideological climate. It is important in this context to explore how ABRI itself perceives its role. In ideological terms, *Dwifungsi* is said to stem from the principles of *Pancasila; Pancasila* implies that in addition to being a defense and security force, the members of ABRI also constitute a social force: "The two [roles] are a realization of its function as an Indonesian citizen, fighter, and soldier with responsibility for the maintenance of national security and the realization of a just and prosperous society, materially and spiritually, on the basis of *Pancasila* and the 1945 Constitution."[13]

ABRI's dual function is also reflected in its relationship with other social forces in society. ABRI views itself as a partner or participant in civilian politics, neither dominant or subordinate to it: "Cooperation between ABRI and existing [forces] in society needs to be promoted and fostered. ABRI always wants and tries to uphold democracy on the basis of *Pancasila* and the 1945 Constitution and does not wish for militaristic, dictatorial, and authoritarian methods. In this case, ABRI as principal supporter of the New Order must try to set an example in carrying out *Pancasila* Democracy, refraining from always having its way."

The basis of the cooperative relationship between ABRI and the rest of the population is reflected in the 1945 Constitution and, in particular, in Article 30. It states that "every citizen shall have the right and duty to take part in efforts for the defense of the state. Therefore, the System of National Defense and Security . . . [requires that] all national forces will be totally and integrally utilized with ABRI as the core in order to defend the independence and sovereignty of the Republic of Indonesia, secure the integrity of the nation and safeguard efforts to attain Indonesia's national goals." Article 30 also asserts that, being born of the people, ABRI has the right and duty to take part in the nondefense and nonsecurity aspects of national life, which would otherwise be the exclusive domain of civilian citizens. In other words, ABRI is not to be excluded from nondefense issues. Rather, "ABRI has a direct interest in contributing to the realization of the society's welfare."

In summary, ABRI is required to act in unity with the civilian social forces not only in time of war or armed conflict but also in time of peace, that is, in the absence of war or armed conflict. The implication of this is that ABRI will continue to play a prominent role in Indonesian society in all fields at all times, in times of peace and in times of war.

EVALUATING *DWIFUNGSI*

Dwifungsi has its critics and supporters. Critics emphasize three points: the temptation for ABRI to become involved in corruption and the abuse of power; the dangers of militarism; and the alleged incompatibility of the dual function with democracy. ABRI personnel, especially middle- and high-ranking officers, seem to be far more privileged than their civilian counterparts in regard to gaining access to strategic positions in government and state institutions. Although in qualitative terms, ABRI's position may be difficult to assess, at least in quantitative terms its dominant role has been reflected in the many ABRI members occupying a majority of the country's key and strategic positions: as ministers in the cabinet, governors in most provinces, district heads, ambassadors in important foreign capitals, and so on.[14] Of no less significance are the powers, authority, and prestige associated with such positions.

The "additional" role of ABRI in the nonmilitary or nondefense fields means that ABRI is not free from excesses of corruption or abuse of power and position for personal interests. When such events become public knowledge, ABRI members, as well as ABRI as an institution, are subject to criticism, suspicion, and accusation. Not infrequently, these are directed against *Dwifungsi,* particularly as part of the process of democratization.

However, even though many of these criticisms are valid, it does not seem fair to direct them to ABRI as a whole, or to *Dwifungsi.* It should be noted, in the first place, that problems with corruption and abuse are not exclusive to ABRI. They are present in the civilian arena, perhaps to an even greater degree given the number of civilians or non-ABRI personnel involved in the nondefense policy arenas. Given evidence of such corruption, is the best solution to abolish the party system altogether? Even further, should the democratization process itself be abandoned, the way "liberal democracy" in the 1950s was abandoned and has continued to be condemned because of the mistakes and failures of past politicians and political parties? In other words, justifying the abolition of *Dwifungsi* with such criticisms seems to assume that without *Dwifungsi,* ABRI members would no longer engage in the behaviors that have been the objects of criticism. This claim sacrifices the merit of the argument for relatively small issues. Instead, the complaint actually is that *Dwifungsi* has widened the scope of military activities and hence has exposed ABRI to more criticism.[15]

Perhaps the most serious critique asserts that *Dwifungsi* is an equivalent or euphemism for military rule. Critics point to the dominant role that ABRI has played under the New Order. Yet it is not accurate to describe the New Order regime as a form of militarism or military dictatorship.

ABRI has never been interested in establishing outright military rule, despite numerous opportunities. The first possibility came with the communist rebellion in 1948, during the struggle for independence against the Dutch. A second opportunity to seize power occurred when the core civilian leadership (including President Sukarno and Vice President Hatta) were taken prisoner by the Dutch in December 1948. Rather than attempting to establish a military dictatorship after the release of the political leaders, the military leadership never attempted to take over the reins of government. One can argue that the military refrained because seizing control would have prevented the independence of Indonesia being recognized by the international community, and therefore would have been counterproductive to the goals of the military. Yet even when independence was no longer an issue, such as after the aborted coup attempt in 1965, the military refrained.

At the beginning of his rule, General Soeharto was aware of the criticisms that would arise from the role played by ABRI in the nondefense arenas. He defended the military's involvement as necessary and argued that ABRI's objective was not to establish a military regime:

ABRI really will not direct state and political life toward militarism or other systems of dictatorship. On the contrary, ABRI desires democratic and constitutional life; that is precisely why ABRI defends *Pancasila* and the 1945 Constitution, opposed the deviations perpetrated by the Old Order and will not repeat the mistakes of the Old Order. . . .

One should not rush to say that there is militarism at present because of the great number of ABRI members . . . in the social and political life. Militarism or no militarism should be judged by existing legal order, whether or not there is freedom and guarantee of human rights and democratic rights based on existing legal provisions on the basis of the constitution; it should not be judged by the number of "ABRI Uniforms.". . .

The presence of ABRI members in government institutions is due to ABRI's role as a functional group and for technical reasons and for reasons of efficiency for the success of the Government's efforts. . . .

By no means does ABRI intend to monopolize a certain position in the Government, nor to seize and occupy as many seats and fields as possible. ABRI is deeply convinced that the problem it faces is not merely one of seats, power, or positions, but the primary national problem is the greatest dedication to the People and the State, one of giving content to independence, to provide welfare for the whole People in the shortest possible time.[16]

Supporters of the concept directly reject the notion that *Dwifungsi* is a guise of militarism. Their view is that Indonesia "adheres to neither militarism, which idolizes the military, nor civilian supremacy, which subjects the military to civilian control." ABRI and the civilian people are equal; both are responsible for the security and development of the country.[17]

Of course, the statement that the military and civilians are equal represents a departure from conventional notions of civil-military relations in liberal democracies. This is the basis for the third critique of *Dwifungsi*. Ultimately, any discussion of the role of ABRI rests on normative rather than social scientific judgments about the process of democratic politics. *Dwifungsi* is not necessarily in conflict with democracy or democratization. All democracies must be based on the liberal principle of a respect for human rights. But civilian dominance of the military is an artifact of the Western experience, rather than a necessary condition.

Supporters of *Dwifungsi*, while not denying that the doctrine has been implemented with problems, base their support of the concept on three factors: its contribution to economic and political development; the support which Indonesians give to the notion of a dual function; and the variety of democratic systems that exist in the world.

Dwifungsi has made significant contributions to Indonesia in the political, economic, and security arenas. It was under the New Order regime that institutional reforms were initiated to create some order in the chaotic and ideologically oriented political party system. It was also the military-led New Order regime that began to pay serious attention to the pursuit of economic development, so long neglected by the Old Order. The result has been increased prosperity for the people. In addition, ABRI saved the nation from disintegration in the face of rebellions by fanatical Muslims in the early 1950s, by regional commanders shortly thereafter, and communists in 1964.[18] Thus, without ABRI, Indonesia could very well have become either a communist or an Islamic theocratic state, or simply might have disintegrated.

From a practical point of view, one needs to recognize that the integration of ABRI into Indonesian politics can hardly be reversed. To put it crudely, ABRI has had a taste of power for more than half of Indonesia's existence as a nation-state. It would seem unrealistic that in the further process of democratization it would simply relinquish its position in the regime. Moreover, ABRI's dual function is firmly established in the legal and institutional basis of Indonesian politics. The democratization process is a pragmatic one, and the challenge for Indonesia is to work within its historical context.

In principle, legislation can always be changed, revoked, or replaced. But transforming the country's political culture is more complicated. Lessons from the past have become deeply embedded in Indonesia's cultural heritage. One of the most prominent lessons Indonesians have learned from their history is that ABRI should never be excluded from participating in a beneficial way in the nation's political life. From this perspective, democratization in Indonesia cannot possibly mean that ABRI should abandon its sociopolitical role and "return to the barracks." Such a turn of events would be contrary to the development of Indonesia's sociopolitical life up to now, in which ABRI's *Dwifungsi* has become an integral part of Indonesians' conceptualization of democracy.

In a 1996 national survey covering fourteen provinces, the majority of respondents accepted *Dwifungsi* as necessary but also believed that its implementation could be improved. Very few of the highly educated and Western-trained respondents favored eliminating *Dwifungsi*. Most respondents also saw the dual function as a constraint on the military budget.[19]

PROSPECTS FOR THE FUTURE

What does the future hold for ABRI's dual function? If the question is whether or not ABRI will continue to perform its dual function, or when that dual function will come to an end, then the question may be irrelevant. ABRI's dual function has become an integral and inseparable part of a growing democratic tradition in Indonesia. And as such it is meant to be a permanent feature of Indonesian democracy.

One of the primary questions that critics of ABRI's dual function may ask is whether the military's sociopolitical role is fundamentally contrary to the principle of democracy. This would be true in definitions of democracy that require civilian supremacy over the armed services. Yet, given ABRI's historical role in domestic politics perhaps a more appropriate question is how will ABRI's dual function manifest itself in the process of democratization? Specifically, what kind of

ABRI-civilian relationship or partnership is likely to take shape in the future? Will ABRI as a sociopolitical force continue to play a dominant role in nonmilitary fields, particularly in the political life of the nation as it has thus far?

Certainly ABRI's dual function is deeply entrenched institutionally and ideologically in Indonesian politics. Its sociopolitical role is understandable given that, in addition to superior administrative and organizational abilities, discipline, and unity, the composition of ABRI membership is much more national in character than that of non-ABRI groups. More importantly, compared to the political parties and other sociopolitical forces, ABRI as a sociopolitical force and as an institution is ideologically much less sectarian and much more nationalist in orientation, and it is unwavering in its loyalty to the state ideology of *Pancasila*.

Indeed, it is no exaggeration to say that ABRI has been the guardian of the state ideology and the unifying force of the nation. This has been proven whenever the country has faced the threat of either division or disintegration in the face of either extreme leftist (i.e., communist) or extreme rightist (theocratic) efforts to substitute their own ideologies for the state ideology of *Pancasila*, whether by violent means or by peaceful means, as in the parliamentary period of the 1950s.

Moreover, it is important to recognize that the dominant role of ABRI has been due to an earlier failure of civilian leadership. When political parties governed Indonesia without ABRI, the welfare of the people at large was neglected and economic development was almost totally ignored. Ultimately, whether or not ABRI will continue to play a dominant role, and what kind of relationship or partnership will develop between ABRI and civilian political parties, depends on the future and further development of the latter.

Yet, ABRI's future role also depends on how the institution itself faces the dual challenges of modernizing its military forces and redefining its role as a sociopolitical force. In the future, ABRI will be faced with pressures to promote the technological advancement of the military institution, particularly with respect to armaments and warfare. Technological modernization will require a higher degree of professionalism and a smaller number of personnel. How such technological advancement in the military field would affect the role of ABRI as the state's apparatus for defense and security is relatively straightforward. How it would affect its role as a sociopolitical force is less clear. One possibility is that ABRI's role as a sociopolitical force will decrease, at least in quantitative terms, because of its preoccupation with the military institution; the pressures of modernization would diminish the time, effort, resources, and personnel available to play its sociopolitical role. This does not mean, however, that the qualitative amount of sociopolitical influence ABRI wields would necessarily decrease. It does mean, however, that the implementation of ABRI's sociopolitical role would be less identified with the physical presence of ABRI personnel in the nondefense arenas.

Another issue ABRI must address is the extent to which it can develop the necessary leadership capacity and political acumen to more fully satisfy its sociopolitical role. Is superiority in terms of administrative and organizational abilities, discipline, structure and composition of membership relevant to the kind of effective leadership needed in the practice of democracy? Leadership in the political field and among civilians cannot rely on automatic support and loyalty as in the case of ABRI leadership, which is sustained by military doctrine and discipline. Political leadership must be earned. This will be a special challenge to ABRI in preparing its members for the performance of its sociopolitical role.

Indeed, for some time to come the kind of leadership style that characterizes the organization of ABRI may still continue to be relevant to the feudal and patrimonial qualities of Indonesian society. But for purposes of political modernization and democratization, serious thought ought to be given to some alternative means of implementing ABRI's sociopolitical role. For example, proposals for changing the system of seat allocation for ABRI members in representative institutions and in the executive and judicial branches of government should be considered. Another issue that needs to be addressed is whether or not ABRI members should take part in general elections, as voters and candidates in lieu of appointment. Mechanisms ought to be developed that subject ABRI members appointed to political positions to a system of checks and balances. Finally, during the period of appointment to nonmilitary positions, especially those of a political nature, ABRI members should temporarily be suspended from their military positions and cut off from the chain of military command. These steps are necessary given that ABRI is in legitimate and rightful possession of the means of violence, which could provide the opportunity for abuse and manipulation of the democratic system.

Those are the future challenges faced by ABRI and the civilian groups, particularly the political parties. The latter's success in developing national and ideological orientations, organizational ability, discipline, and other skills would restore the credibility of the party system after its past failures. Moreover, the success of both ABRI and the political parties in responding to their respective challenges would help promote a dynamic balance and equal partnership between ABRI and the civilian groupings in the future. Considering the geographical structure of Indonesia as the largest archipelago in the world and the demographic composition of its population—the diverse ethnic, cultural, linguistic, traditional, religious, regional, as well as racial backgrounds, and the diversity of their values—such a system may be the most appropriate for the maintenance of national unity and the state's integrity. This system would constitute a workable compromise between one extreme form of government, a military dictatorship, and the other extreme form of government, characterized by civilian supremacy, which in Indonesia has been condemned because of its association with "Western, liberal democracy." Of course, moving toward such a system is the responsibility of both ABRI and civilian groups. Moreover, the regime would have to be responsive to new developments and changing interests over time. Over the long run, the continuation and preservation of such a political system, including the dual function of ABRI, will be determined by the values of future generations of Indonesians. The present generation cannot possibly dictate future outcomes. But one thing is certain: Whatever the system, if it is able to create prosperity and justice for all, then that system will persist. Such a system may finally provide Indonesia with the form of democracy the nation has been searching for through several decades of painful experimentation.

NOTES

1. President Suharto, *State Address as Acting President on the Occasion of Independence Day, 1967,* Jakarta Ministry of Information, 1967.

2. J. Soedjati Djiwandono, "After 50 Years RI Democracy Needs Reform," *Jakarta Post,* August 16, 1995.

3. J. Soedjati Djiwandono, "RI Democracy in 1994: A Tug of War?" *Jakarta Post,* January 2, 1995.

4. Law No. 7/1957 on the National Council and Law No. 80/1958 on the National Planning Council, for example, simply provided ABRI with a legal status as a "functional group." And MPR Decision No. 24 /1958 provided for ABRI representation in the provisional House of Representatives (DPR-GR).

5. The term TNI now is also used to refer to the air force (TNI/AU) and the navy (TNI/AL), whereas the army itself is officially designated as TNI/AD.

6. Cited by David Jenkins, "Soeharto and His Generals: Indonesian Military Politics, 1975–1983," Cornell Modern Indonesia Project Monograph Series (Ithaca: Southeast Asia Program, Cornell University, 1984), 2.

7. For an account of the events surrounding the affair, see for example, T. B. Simatupang, *Membuktikn Ketidakbenaran Suatu Mitos* [To Prove the Falsity of a Myth] (Jakarta: Pustaka Sinar Harapan, 1991), 154–177 and 273–297. The author was Indonesia's first Chief of Staff of the Indonesian Armed Forces, an equivalent of chairman of the Joint Chiefs of Staff in the United States.

8. A good account of political developments in Indonesia during this period is Herbert Faith, *The Decline of Constitutional Democracy in Indonesia* (Ithaca: Cornell University Press, 1962).

9. From a lecture, "ABRI's *Dwifungsi* and the Indonesian National Army: Prospects for the Future," delivered by General Rudini, then Chief of Staff of the Army, to students of the Indonesian Institute for the Promotion of Management, Jakarta, July 31, 1985. Translation in English is my own.

10. The quotations are taken from a special publication (C. 461) by the Department of Information of the Republic of Indonesia, (no date). Translation into English is my own.

11. Ian MacFarling, "The Evolution of the Indonesian Armed Forces: A Case Study in the Fusion of Civil and Military Roles," Ph.D. diss., Politics Department, University College, University of New South Wales, n.d., 196; on the number of Indonesian soldiers of the Dutch colonial army thus integrated, see ibid., 68.

12. An explanation of the legal foundation for *Dwifungsi* is to be found in *Buku Petunjuk Angkatan Bersenjata Republik Indonesia tentang Dwifungsi BRI* [Guidebook for the Armed Forces of the Republic of Indonesia on the *Dwifungsi* of ABRI] (Jakarta: Dept. of National Defense and Security, 1982), hereafter referred to as *Guidebook.*

13. This and the following quotation are taken from *Guidebook,* 13–30. The translation into English is my own.

14. See Harold Crouch, "Indonesia," in Zakaria Haji Ahmad and Harold Crouch, eds., *Military-Civilian Relations in South-East Asia* (Singapore: Oxford University Press, 1985), 60–61.

15. Ali Moertopo, *Srategi Pembangunnan Nasional* [The Strategy of National Development] (Jakarta: CSIS, 1981), 249–251.

16. President Suharto, *State Address,* 1967.

17. Rudini, "ABRI's *Dwifungsi.*"

18. Michael R. J. Vatikiotis, *Indonesian Politics Under Soeharto* (London: Routledge, 1993), 13–14, 16–22; James Mackie and Andrew MacIntyre, "Politics," in Hal Hill, ed., *Indonesia's New Order* (Honolulu: University of Hawaii Press, 1994), 2–3. Editor's note: The nature of the events in 1965 is controversial.

19. Interviews by David R. Mares with Dr. Dewi Fortuna Anwar and Dr. Indria Sanego, Indonesian Institute of Sciences, Center for Political and Regional Studies, November 1, 1996. Jakarta.

CHAPTER FOUR

———————— ■ ————————

Civil-Military Relations in Venezuela

Gisela Gómez Sucre and María Dolores Cornett

Along with Colombia, Venezuela is the oldest continuously democratic country in South America today. The democratic system has been underpinned by a civil-military relationship characterized by civilian domination, to use the framework set out in David Mares's introduction to this volume. Yet the two failed military coup attempts in 1992 demonstrate that Venezuelan democracy, as well as its pattern of civil-military relations, is confronting stress that points to the need for change.

This chapter analyzes the development of civil-military relations in Venezuela, with emphasis on the social, economic, and political factors that have determined the evolution of that relationship since the democratization of the country in 1958. Although the civil-military relationship functioned relatively well to guarantee civilian control over the military, even during the short-lived guerrilla insurgency in the 1960s, it cannot escape the stresses confronting Venezuelan society. The social and economic tensions resulting from Venezuela's underdevelopment and society's growing rejection of oligarchic control of political parties will significantly affect the evolution of the civil-military relationship. Continued civilian domination will depend on successful economic and political reforms and on the continued modernization of the military.

The chapter is divided into four parts. The first part analyzes the structural context influencing civil-military relations, which includes the political culture, the international context, the constitutive rules for the political system, and the civil-military relationship as it currently exists. The second section examines the concerns of the civilian and military sectors. The third section analyses the current crisis of Venezuelan democracy and its effect on the civil-military relationship. In this context, we examine the dilemma of the armed forces in being part of the power structure that produced the crisis, while recognizing that resolution of the crisis will require the military to change and professionalize. The chapter concludes with speculation on the future of the civil-military relationship and democracy in Venezuela.

THE STRUCTURAL CONTEXT

Political Culture

Three factors have fundamentally affected Venezuelan political culture: its history of political authoritarianism, civil-military cooperation in overthrowing dictators, and the wealth generated by oil.

Venezuela experienced long and brutal dictatorships until 1945 and again from 1948 to 1958. The first attempt at democratic government, between 1945 and 1948, failed. The civilian leadership of the Acción Democrática (AD) party assumed it had a mandate to undertake radical reforms. But Venezuelan society was not united in its acceptance of the need for change. Important civilian sectors, including the Christian Socialist Party (COPEI), joined with the military in a coup in 1948. Subsequently, Colonel Marcos Pérez Jiménez consolidated control over the junta and established a dictatorship that lasted from 1952 to 1958. From this experience civilian leaders of most political persuasions, as well as most Venezuelans, became convinced of the need for elite consensus, program limitation, prudent compromise, and controlled but widespread political participation.[1]

Modern Venezuela has experienced important civil-military collaboration in overthrowing authoritarianism.[2] In 1945 and in 1958, military officers participated in the revolts and formed part of the provisional governments whose task was to set up a democratic regime. Civil-military collaboration was accepted by the citizenry as a legitimate way to overthrow an illegitimate government and many Venezuelans developed an image of the military as pro-democratic and the guarantor of democracy. For example, just two weeks after the failed February 1992 coup against a president with declining popularity, 45 percent of the polled respondents believed that had the younger officers succeeded, they would have established economic order, punished corruption, and called new elections (that is, the military would have voluntarily reinstituted democracy).[3]

The majority of Venezuelans feel politically empowered when they vote. Outside of the electoral route, however, they feel politically inefficacious. This may reflect a belief that parties are run by a dominant elite and thus are unresponsive except at election time. The limited ability of citizens to influence parties may also explain Venezuelan rejection of the idea of one-party dominance.[4] It also helps explain why people who do not identify with political parties are willing to allow the military an active role in politics.[5]

The oil wealth of Venezuela significantly affects people's perceptions of the role of government: Government should provide for the people. Petroleum made

Venezuela a rich country for a time but had negative impacts on the country's nonpetroleum sectors. The economy boomed in the 1950s, with the gross domestic product (GDP) growing at the phenomenal average annual rate of 9.4 percent, and again in the 1970s.[6] Even after the price of oil collapsed on world markets in the 1980s and Venezuela became mired in a deep structural economic crisis, almost all Venezuelans believed that the country was rich and could meet everyone's needs if government management were efficient. The issue of the distribution of national wealth became a standard by which to measure the performance of the government. For some analysts, the coincidence of this perception of wealth with the existence of a democratic regime suggests that Venezuelans value democracy in a utilitarian fashion. This would explain the willingness among a large segment of the population, though not among the political elite, to accept extra-constitutional means of replacing a government attempting to implement neoliberal economic reforms.[7]

This political culture results in an ambiguous support of the democratic political system by Venezuelan civil society. The majority of the population is under the age of thirty-five and has never lived under an authoritarian regime; untested by the lessons of 1945–1958, they may value democracy only pragmatically. The government's inability to cope with the socioeconomic problems of the country produces general discontent. The result is that while Venezuelans express the view that the only solution to the crisis is improvement the democratic system, they are inclined toward radical solutions that are characteristic of an authoritarian system.

A recent opinion poll illustrates this ambiguity. Of the 2,000 people surveyed, 86 percent agreed that Venezuela needs radical sociopolitical change. Pro-democracy sentiment can be gauged by the fact that 78 percent considered that democracy was the best political system for Venezuela, 76 percent stated that "democracy had to be defended at any cost," and 69 percent answered that a dictatorship would not be the best solution for the nation's dilemmas. Fully 68 percent believed that democracy can solve these sociopolitical problems. On the other hand, 93 percent demanded a stronger governmental authority and more discipline. Venezuelans polled desired overwhelmingly (86 percent) a strong-fisted administration (un gobierno de mano dura).[8]

In sum, Venezuelan political culture favors democracy, believes in an active state, and places a high value on law and order. Elite and mass public opinion seem to differ on whether "extraordinary" measures (including the extra-constitutional removal of a government deemed "illegitimate") are necessary to save the country and democracy.

International Context

As a developing country, Venezuela acts within certain international constraints. These are not just de facto constraints but have also been accepted as subjective truths. The pragmatism of Venezuelan politics is in evidence here. A foreign minister once explicitly recognized that Venezuela is not a great power, implying that it had to live within this structural context. Civilian and military leaders agree on this point.[9]

The restructuring of the Venezuelan democratic model, which lasted from 1958 until the end of the 1960s, was set within the international framework of the East-West confrontation. Venezuela is a Western, democratic, oil-producing country and an ally of the United States. As such, it opposed Cuba and the socialist bloc, as well as many right-wing dictatorial governments in Latin America. A Cuban-supplied guerrilla movement developed in the 1960s, pushing the government further toward the West.

The Venezuelan-U.S. relationship has been mutually beneficial. The anti-Communist security doctrine of the United States supported Venezuela's national and regional security policy. The United States, in return, gained entry into an important market for investments and reliable access to important raw materials.

The United States continues to influence Venezuela's democracy. In the two coup attempts of 1992, the U.S. government let it be known that any nondemocratic alteration in government would be sanctioned.[10]

CONSTITUTIVE RULES

Political System

The contemporary Venezuelan political model was founded on the unifying spirit that joined together most of the political parties that fought against the dictatorship. The decisive step was taken by the so-called Punto Fijo Pact, signed on October 31, 1958, by the three most significant political parties—AD, COPEI, and the Unión República Democrática (URD). This coalition was joined by the other major Venezuelan social forces (the military, business, unions, and the Catholic church) and established a series of norms underlying the populist system of conciliatory politics. This political system is characterized by the pursuit of consensus and the management of conflicting policy preferences by sociopolitical organizations committed to these norms.[11]

Elite consensus on compromise and coalition supported the development of a strong party system. Venezuelan parties are organized both vertically (linking national, regional, and neighborhood structures) and horizontally (representing functional groups such as students, labor, professionals, etc.), thereby reaching virtually all segments of society.[12] Parties became the basic mechanisms through which political mobilization and action developed and was channeled. In the process, mobilized consent and the electoral process were further institutionalized as the basis of legitimacy for policy.[13]

This political consensus concerning democratic politics, played out in a strong party system, was further strengthened by the increasing share of the oil revenues that flowed into the Venezuelan state's coffers. The politics of plenty meant that parties could colonize the bureaucracy and distribute state resources to party constituents. Furthermore, the Venezuelan state stimulated economic growth and industrialization through an import-substitution development strategy. Virtually all sectors of society benefited, and the combination of political participation and economic distribution provided social peace and political stability.

In summary, the main features of the Venezuelan political regime since the end of the 1960s include the following:

- a model based on consensus and the prevention of conflict through consultation, negotiation, and the mutual responsibility of the elite;
- the abundance of oil revenues;
- a populist-style distribution of state revenues;
- state dependency on public expenses with a subsidy policy and state regulation of economic activities;
- an inward-oriented growth strategy based on import-substitution industrialization and on oil production;
- political parties as mediators par excellence between the state and society.

The Civil-Military Relationship

The basis for a new civil-military relationship, to be characterized by civilian primacy in the political sphere, was established within months of the bloody overthrow of Pérez Jiménez in 1958. Immediately following the fall of the dictator, a five-man military junta seemed to foretell another military government. But in the process of creating a provisional government, the military themselves replaced two members with distinguished civilians and promised elections "at the earliest possible date." Elections were held within a year, and the armed forces accepted the defeat of a military candidate, but along the way there were three major challenges to civilian rule.[14] Each was overcome in a fashion that would strengthen civilian control of the military.

Following the civil disorder that erupted in the wake of U.S. Vice President Richard Nixon's visit in 1958, the military members of the provisional government met with the military high command to discuss the crisis. The civilian members of the junta resigned in protest for having been excluded from what they saw as a task of the government, not the military: investigation of the breakdown of public order. The military accepted this demand and reconstituted a new junta, again combining civilian and military representation. A precedent of civilian involvement in "military affairs" had been set.[15]

Civilian control was further bolstered as a result of attempts by dissident military officers to overthrow the provisional government in July, and again in September, 1958. Although the military situation was quickly dominated by pro-government military forces, massive strikes by students, labor, business, and other civil groups followed to demonstrate their refusal to accept military rule any longer.[16]

Democratic forces within the military not only accepted civilian control, they also facilitated the process. Army domination of the armed forces had previously gone hand in hand with dictatorship. But in 1958 the military junta contained equal representation by the army, navy, and air force. The provisional government, dominated by its military members, issued Decree 288 replacing the unitary general staff (previously controlled by the army) with a joint chiefs of staff. Military influence was now shared among the army, navy, air force, and national guard, and the institutions were formally subordinated to a minister of defense, who reported directly to the president. In addition, when Admiral Wolfgang Larrazabal, junta member and commander of the navy, was runner-up in the December presidential elections and his civilian supporters rioted, the admiral accepted the results and called for calm.[17]

The promulgation of an Organic Law of the National Armed Forces and modifications of the Military Code of Justice explicitly limited the military's overt participation in politics. Article 132 of the 1961 Constitution stipulates that the armed forces must be apolitical and obedient to the constitution and the rule of law above all other considerations.[18] In 1976, the Organic Law of Security and Defense created the National Security and Defense Council and its Permanent Secretariat to provide another mechanism for civilian influence over the military. The efficiency of this linkage, however, is open to question.[19]

Political party oversight of military promotions, which constitute the backbone of the hierarchical pyramid of the armed forces, was another distinguishing feature of the civil-military relationship. According to the 1961 Constitution, the Senate must approve all promotions to colonel and general, as well as all foreign military missions, and parties also influence the lists before they are sent to Congress. Nevertheless, civilians have been careful not to overly politicize the promotion process.[20]

The military did not readily give up its privileges, however negative they had been for the professional development of the armed forces.[21] One of the nine sections in the Minimum Program of Government pact signed by the various groups involved in developing Venezuela's democratic structure directly addressed military concerns. The guarantees given to the military under democracy included amnesty for previous abuses, a commitment to modernization of equipment and training, and an increase in the social-welfare provisions for personnel.[22]

The civil-military relationship is also influenced by informal understandings. The moderation in political conflict that characterizes interelite competition in the civilian realm extends to this sphere as well. Disagreements and controversies are often kept from the public eye, national security issues are easily covered with a cloak of secrecy, and the military is consulted on defense and internal security issues, all of which give the military more influence in politics than a purely formal understanding would reveal.[23]

Civilian control also has more practical aspects. The military serves the civilian-dominated state in a number of ways that might appear strange to analysts in the United States. For example, under a program known as "Plan República," the armed forces are assigned to supervise the election process under the jurisdiction of the Supreme Electoral Council.[24]

Venezuela's civil-military relationship undergoes a constant process of rejuvenation. Military educational institutions serve not only to increase contact between civilians and the military but also to educate and socialize the military in the principles of a democratic state. At the Institute of Advanced Studies in National Defense (IAEDEN), created in 1970, national security issues are understood to include potential threats to the Venezuelan democratic system. Civilians and military officers analyze the concepts of security and national defense in a democratic paradigm that contrasts with the national security conceptions of the military dictatorships operating throughout Latin America in the 1970s.[25] This model of civil-military relations is also reinforced in the military high schools, the Polytechnic Institute of the armed forces (IUPFAN), and the Staff Courses.

In summary, civil-military relations developed under a structure of political rules designed to ensure civilian control over the military while at the same time endowing it with the resources necessary for its modernization. The structure of this relationship is characterized by political clientelism and Venezuelan populist-style procedures. In this way, the concerns of both sectors were addressed. It also enables every new administration to make its impact upon the institution itself.

CIVILIAN AND MILITARY INTERESTS

Within the framework of this analysis, civilian and military concerns form part of the national interest, defined as the system's political stability and the consolidation of democratic rule.[26] The armed forces have become leading actors allied with the civilian sector and identified with and committed to the defense of democracy. But civilians and the military each have specific concerns related to the defense of the national interest.

Civilian Interests

Civilian interests can be summed up in terms of elections, growth, and distribution. Civilians want all three, and party elites want to ensure continued party dominance of the political system that oversees them.

The defense of democracy is clearly an interest of both politicians and the people. For the parties, free elections provide opportunities to implement the policies they favor (if not during the current administration then perhaps after the next election). For the people, democratic politics provides a means of forcing party leaders to distribute resources to their constituencies and generally provide for the public's health and welfare. The February 1992 coup attempt in Venezuela, however, demonstrated that in times of crisis, the interests of politicians and the public may temporarily diverge. Although elected officials and party leaders were virtually unanimous in condemning the attempt, large segments of society seemed willing to accept it as an extraordinary means of deposing a president and his economic policies. They did, however, want Venezuela to continue to be democratic after the termination of President Carlos Andrés Pérez's administration.[27]

Both politicians and the public at large have an interest in the continued economic growth of the country. As noted above in the section on political culture, Venezuelans believe that an efficient government could easily solve the nation's socioeconomic problems. Citizens thus want an efficient and honest government. The dominant elite, however, are wary of disrupting the political parties' continued control over the distribution of resources, and this has led to tension between efficiency and party control.

We cannot forget that since the establishment of democracy in 1958, the Venezuelan political leadership has always been apprehensive of giving the armed forces a major role in decisionmaking. Military participation could threaten the interests of specific parties and undermine the subordination of the military to the civilian sector. There is thus an elite consensus to control interparty competition and keep appeals to the military illegitimate.[28]

Military Interests

The Venezuelan military began to professionalize in the 1930s, but political authoritarianism undermined its efforts. The establishment of democracy allowed the military to focus on professionalizing its personnel, modernizing its equipment and training, and developing strategies appropriate to the threats facing the country.

The professionalization and modernization issue has been addressed through training programs throughout the country in local officers' training schools. In addition, educational scholarships and grants like the "Gran Mariscal de Ayacucho" program finance study programs at various American and European universities, as well as permanent professional and academic educational exchange programs between Venezuelan officers and military personnel from other countries.

In the area of strategy, the Venezuelan armed forces perceive a threat environment composed of four objectives: the defense of petroleum-rich coastal waters; the settlement of territorial conflicts with its neighbors; the need to populate and integrate vast frontier territories with the highly populated and developed north-central region of the country; and the defense of the Caribbean sea lanes.[29]

The political leadership's support of the professionalization of the military was not indicative of a strategy to reorient the future functions of the armed forces but was a response to the demands of officers for the renovation and development of their institution. The military thus became an interest group and inserted itself into the political system on the basis of its role as guardian of the country's sovereignty and democratic order, within the context of a juridical and institutional order that subordinates the military to civilian control.[30]

THE CRISIS OF VENEZUELAN DEMOCRACY

The Political Economy of the Crisis

The major factor affecting Venezuela's current economic context has been the exhaustion of the traditional development model utilized since the end of World War II: import-substitution industrialization financed by petroleum export revenues. In response, Venezuela's economic development strategy shifted toward services and infrastructure. As a petroleum exporter Venezuela financed these new efforts by means of public indebtedness. Following the pattern of other Latin American countries, mismanagement by successive administrations and rising interest rates produced a level of accumulated debt that created significant internal difficulties.

As the economy began to sputter in the late 1980s, the once-populist President Pérez, newly reelected for a second term, decided to undertake massive structural reforms in both the political and economic spheres. The political reforms included the direct election of governors and mayors; the use of a uninominal vote for the election of congressional representatives, legislative assemblies, and municipal councils; and the decentralization of the activities and internal decision-making policies of political parties. There were also discussions for reforming the constitution and the Supreme Court. In addition, between 1989 and 1992, a dramatic decentralization of governmental functions occurred.[31]

The *Paquete Económico* was designed to restructure the economy to permit not only a recovery from its deep crisis, but also to direct it toward a self-sustained economic and social development. These reforms provoked social unrest, including strikes, public demonstrations by labor and public administration unions, students, homemakers, and others, all expressing disapproval of the measures, given the overwhelming level of poverty in the population. The most serious disturbance was the *caracazo* in Caracas and other cities on February 27, 1989, in which hundreds, if not thousands, of anarchic protesters died.[32] The political parties, even the president's, also opposed the reforms.[33]

Oil revenues, however, were still sufficient in 1990 to mitigate social tensions and the political situation appeared to be under control. The socioeconomic crisis, nevertheless, had not been resolved.[34] The administration's inability to stop the growth of poverty and the social injustice affecting Venezuelan society soon developed into a far-reaching legitimacy crisis. The set of agreements between all the country's political players—political parties, private enterprises (FEDE-CAMARAS), Workers Confederation (CTV), the Catholic church, and the armed forces—were starting to crumble, unlocking serious events that could not be controlled by government forces. "The vitality of this phenomenon had not been foreseen by any of the dominant actors, who found themselves not only surprised but also cornered by the force and the character of the popular protest."[35]

The administration's inability to govern further damaged socioeconomic conditions. Important representatives from the political sector and intellectuals, popularly known as *los notables,* proclaimed that the situation had reached its limit and that it was necessary to form an emergency government. FEDECAMARAS, the umbrella organization of industrial and agricultural Chambers of Commerce, as well as the country's financial establishment claimed that President Pérez could not govern. The Venezuelan Workers' Confederation called for a national strike to denounce the effects of the economic measures on the workers' salaries. The Ministry of Defense reported 925 protests between September 1991 and February 4, 1992; of these, 480 were violent enough to require police intervention.[36]

The overwhelming majority of civil society petitioned the government (1) to rectify its economic policies, emphasizing a need for new policies in the areas of education, health, housing, and employment; (2) to fight the impunity of the judicial system in regard to rampant administrative corruption; (3) to devise new security policies; and (4) to fight poverty. In short, the citizens of Venezuela asked for a new definition of democracy in Venezuela.

The subsequent attempt by some junior officers to overthrow the government in February 1992 was rejected by all organized sectors of society, including political parties and business associations. One must note, however, that overtly or indirectly the Venezuelan populace supported the military insurgents. Unlike 1958, the people did not defend the system. Former President Rafael Caldera condemned the coup in a speech before Congress, but he proclaimed that the officers' actions were an inevitable response to the government's economic policies. Not only did this qualification justify the junior officers to some degree, it also propelled Caldera into the presidency in the next election.[37]

There were still challenges ahead. Senior military officers led an even bloodier coup attempt in November 1992. It failed but left everyone with the expectation of more turmoil. President Pérez could not regain support, and he was impeached in June 1993. A caretaker government was installed until the upcoming elections could try to relegitimize the system.

The December 1993 elections became a milestone for the political system. The two traditional parties lost the presidential election to Caldera, running on the platform of a new party, and there were new and more dynamic faces in Congress. Public opinion now weighed more in policy discussions and confrontation became an important element in policymaking. The new politicians searched for an articulate set of criteria with which to challenge the orthodox and very traditional political class in order to restructure Venezuela's sociopolitical system.

The Dilemma of the Armed Forces

Social unrest, increased poverty, public demonstrations by all segments of society, corruption within the government, and the looting following some riots all demanded action, but what type and to what degree? A clash between two realities affected the military's response to the challenge. On the one hand, the military was committed to remaining apolitical and responding to its constitutional role in defending democracy. On the other hand, it also realized that the problems were rooted within the existing structure of political power, of which the armed forces were a major part.

The gravity of the situation made the dilemma all the more acute when the armed forces realized that the threat did not emerge from an external enemy but was generated internally. The threat arose in a society in crisis: its currency devalued, poverty at extreme levels, educational system in crisis, an ever-growing debt, and a decadent political model, incapable of responding to public demands because it defended the interests of historically privileged groups. Finally, the dilemma is underscored by the discovery that within its own ranks, many junior officers perceived that toppling the political system would restore the decency and well-being of Venezuelan society. The threat of a coup d'état had become a reality in one of Latin America's oldest democracies.[38]

Subsequent assessment of the coup attempts indicates that the military's defense of democratic institutions was a fundamental factor in the ability of the system to survive. In this regard, the concerns of the political elite and military coincide.[39] Yet the fissure between high- and low-ranking officers, and between the political elite and ordinary citizens demonstrated the need for a convergence of the civilian and military sectors on different terms.

The armed forces were clearly affected by the situation. Struck by the overwhelming crisis and recognizing their responsibility as leaders, the military leadership worked alongside the political leadership. They confronted the internal discontent and the factionalization of their institution. In these efforts, the institutional regulations that permit the political sector to influence and pressure the military on specific issues and under specific circumstances worked to preserve civilian authority over the armed forces.

The decision was made to reorient the military toward policymaking arenas that would be less threatening to civilian control, while giving the armed forces an important and effective role in Venezuelan life. Foreign affairs, especially the border disagreements with Colombia and Guyana, were to become their new focus. The president appointed the defense minister to replace the outgoing secretary of state and highlighted the importance of the border issues. His message to both public opinion and the armed forces was that the national interests of sovereignty and territorial integrity, as well as the internal institutional order, were safeguarded by these actions.

The Venezuelan armed forces were quite willing to accept these new priorities, as they have always considered border issues to be a fundamental concern. Within the framework set by the civil-military relationship, they have been attentive to what governments have or have not done in this arena.

This shift in security focus does not imply a militarization of the border. Venezuelan military officers have slowly assimilated new forms of conflict resolution, appreciating that relations between neighboring countries are best based on mutual cooperation. Furthermore, the armed forces recognize the importance of

economic issues for regional integration. They also understand that the confidence building between neighbors that is called for in the hemispheric security
agenda is facilitated by mutual commercial exchange. The issues related to public
order and border security have been critical elements in the binational dialogue
between Colombia and Venezuela, and they have defined the nature of the relationship that is developing, particularly since the reactivation of military cooperation, begun in the 1991 presidential summit.[40]

The Venezuelan armed forces, therefore, are undertaking a delicate inner reflection. That self-evaluation is leading to a series of reforms designed to restructure
and renovate the organization and function of the Defense Ministry and its four
components—the army, navy, air force, and national guard.

These reforms are designed to improve management and define the future role
of the armed forces in meeting new and growing threats, within the new security
and defense agenda. This will be carried out within the context of a progressive
reduction of the military expenditure, now less than 2 percent of the GNP, in order to redirect financial resources toward the socioeconomic problems affecting
Venezuela.[41]

THE FUTURE OF VENEZUELAN
CIVIL-MILITARY RELATIONS

The Venezuelan armed forces are entering a new phase in their relationship with
civil society. Today, in 1997, eight years after the first coup attempt, sociopolitical
and economic conflict has continued and increased. The crisis has led the military
to recognize that they confront serious internal problems that require immediate
solutions. As a result, institutional discourse has shifted to a search for a new conceptualization of the Venezuelan armed forces. Venezuela's defense minister, Moisés
Orozco Graterol, articulated this view at the Ministerial Defense Conference of the
Americas in 1995. He argued that the military institution and the democratic
process worked together in a symbiotic manner to give meaning to the notion of
the nation's common good. In light of this relationship, he noted that his country's
armed forces supported an educational process that provided the knowledge to use
technology and professional development to slowly eradicate the economic and social disequilibria that afflict society. He further emphasized that the modernization
of the military must proceed with the reality that the national crisis imposed the
need to decrease the budget and defense expenditures.[42]

Civilians have also been striving to make change. Congress reformed the Organic Law of the Armed Forces (Ley Orgánica de la Fuerza Armada Nacional) to
provide legislative support for all of the proposed changes. The Commission on
Defense created a team of distinguished officials drawn from each branch of the
military who acted as congressional liaisons during the deliberations on reform.

Despite the good will, implementing these changes challenges the civil-military
relationship. In the past, in-depth discussion of problems arising from the institu-

tional values of internal cohesion and principles of authority were considered to be strictly internal military affairs. But now they are open to public debate.

It is important to point out that policies for the modernization of Venezuela's armed forces are viewed as the impetus for transforming the military. For that reason, the Ministry of Defense has reactivated its Office of Education to reinforce the formation of a professional military built on the values of dignity, liberty, and justice, combined with obedience and subordination to civil power. The ultimate objective is the fulfillment of constitutional law and the establishment of the armed forces as guardian and guarantor of democracy through its role in the military defense of Venezuela.

Participating in this discussion and consensus building has not been easy for the armed forces. Knowing where to draw the line between command and subordination, in conformity with discipline, a more liberal education, and freedom of thought, in responding to the new threats facing the contemporary world is not easy. But it is necessary in order to build the type of military organization that a modern democratic society requires. As the minister of defense notes, "The ultimate aim of the military educational system is to form a new individual, shape the future generations in agreement with the type of armed forces that we wish to have. This is the importance and the significance of the military educational problem."[43]

The new civil-military relationship is reflected in the IX National Plan, tellingly called "a project for a country."[44] In this document, the armed forces are seen as an organization that must accomplish new functions regarding security, defense, and development, in line with the new national project. These tasks cannot be accomplished without an effective cooperation with private and public research centers, universities, and the country's productive sector. The active cooperation and joint ventures among these national entities will stimulate more fluid relations between the men in uniform and other sectors of society.

We also need to examine the role played by the political sector. Relations between the civilian world and the armed forces had been calm in the past because the rules imposed by the national leadership functioned. The regulating mechanisms of the public sector wove a tightly knitted system that circumscribed the armed forces to very limited spheres of action.[45] The political elite sought to control and regulate its presence in national affairs, fearing that if they were given other functions in the civilian world, the public institutions would eventually become militarized. Furthermore, the military establishment, although it has maintained an obedient and nonpartisan nature, is still perceived as a threat to the democratic regime.

We consider it vital to support relations between the civilian world and the military in a era of great dynamism and hostility in the international and domestic realms. Nevertheless, despite the political sector's limitations in giving clearer meaning to the security, defense, and development agendas, important steps are being taken toward working together to form those agendas. An example is the symposium on "Goals and Perspectives on the Constitutional Law on Security and Defense in the Framework of the Reform of the Venezuelan State," sponsored by the Permanent Secretariat of the National Security and Defense Council in September 1996. At these meetings, civilians and military personnel spoke and exchanged ideas about security and defense, the viability of democracy in Venezuela, constitutional law and state reform, and the influence on the notion of sovereignty of human rights and environmental concerns.

These issues are also being addressed at the Instituto de Altos Estudios de la Defensa Nacional (IAEDEN), a center for the exchange of knowledge and high-level debate, inaugurated twenty-five years ago. The institute provides a forum for military officers and civilians from the public and private sectors to disseminate their research on security and defense matters, and discuss forms of articulation between civilians and the military. The national and international socioeconomic crises demand an intellectual exchange to develop and implement proposals for developing armed forces that will participate in public life without dominating it, just as do other national sectors. Unfortunately, IAEDEN has not been successful in pulling together the alliances necessary to create a civil-military relationship that can develop an expeditious strategy for national development.

This analysis underscores the dangers that could develop within the military institution as a result of outside pressures emanating from border problems, the demands of the global and economic integration process, the sacrifices demanded by the "neoliberal" political policies, the drug trade, illegal immigration, and the devastation of the country's environment. The "dilemma of the armed forces" still persists and has become graver today. The political fallout from continual illegal immigration into Venezuela from Colombia has weakened an integration process that needs to be consolidated in order to find new strategies for regional economic growth.

Today, throughout the American continent, a deep and serious reflection about the nature of national and regional security and the role of the current armed forces is underway. In the Venezuelan armed forces, the answers are given in the context of a modernization process. The armed forces pursue a professional corporate identity, stressing training, efficiency, and effectiveness. Professionalization will facilitate adaptation to the dynamics of modern society but it also poses a challenge for political and military leadership. However, the demand of social and economic welfare for all Venezuelans is the greatest challenge facing the civil-military relationship.

NOTES

1. Daniel H. Levine, "Venezuela: The Nature, Sources, and Prospects of Democracy," in Larry Diamond, Juan J. Linz, and Seymour Martin Lipset, eds., *Democracy in Developing Countries,* Vol. 4: *Latin America* (Boulder: Lynne Rienner, 1989), pp. 256–257; R. Lynn Kelley, "Venezuelan Constitutional Forms and Realities," and John D. Martz, "The Party System: Toward Institutionalization," both in John D. Martz and David J. Myers, eds.,

Venezuela: The Democratic Experience (New York: Praeger, 1977), pp. 27–46 and 93–112, respectively.

2. For a history of the Venezuelan military in this period, see Winfield J. Burggraaff, *The Venezuelan Armed Forces in Politics, 1935–1959* (Columbia: University of Missouri, 1972); Gene E. Bigler, "The Armed Forces and Patterns of Civil-Military Relations," in Martz and Myers, eds., *Venezuela: The Democratic Experience,* pp. 114–133.

3. Aníbal Romero, *Decadencia y crisis de la democracia* (Caracas: Editorial Panapo, 1994), citing Alfredo Keller, "Venezuela: Escenarios de crisis," unpublished manuscript, Caracas, 1992, p. 8; also, Felipe Agüero, "Las fuerzas armadas y el debilamiento de la democracia en Venezuela" in Andrés Serbin et al., *Venezuela: La democracia bajo presión* (Caracas: INVESP and Editorial Nueva Sociedad, 1993), p. 187.

4. Enrique Baloyra, "Public Attitudes Toward the Democratic Regime," in Martz and Myers, *Venezuela: The Democratic Experience,* pp. 50–51, 62.

5. David J. Myers and Robert E. O'Connor, "Venezuelan Political Attitudes 1973 and 1993: Parties, Performance, and the Military," paper delivered at the 1994 Annual Meeting of the American Political Science Association, New York, September 1994, pp. 17–18.

6. James A. Hanson, "Cycles of Economic Growth and Structural Change Since 1950," in Martz and Myers, eds., *Venezuela: The Democratic Experience,* p. 64; for the 1970s and 1980s, see Moisés Naim, *Paper Tigers and Minotaurs: The Politics of Venezuela's Economic Reforms* (New York: Carnegie Endowment, 1993).

7. Romero, *Decadencia y crisis de la democracia,* pp.17–28; Levine, in "Venezuela: The Nature, Sources, and Prospects of Democracy," argues that Venezuelans have a "shared commitment to democracy as a central value," p. 248.

8. "The Venezuelan Value System," *El Globo,* November 2, 1995.

9. Elsa Cardozo da Silva, "Militares y política: Propuestas para el estudio del caso venezolano," in Carlos Juan Moneta, ed., *Civiles y militares* (Caracas: Editorial Nueva Sociedad, 1990), pp. 81–85.

10. Heinz R. Sonntag and Thais Maingon, *Venezuela: 4-F 1992* (Caracas: Editorial Nueva Sociedad, 1992), p. 46.

11. Aníbal Romero, "El sistema político venezolano," *Temas del IAEDEN,* no. 6 (1990). "The Venezuelan political system is a unique and noteworthy example of the establishment of a series of rules that have created an elite pact of heightened solidness. There is not just one exclusive group that monopolizes power, but rather a complex game of negotiation and commitments of this powerful group." [Authors' translation.]

12. Levine, "Venezuela: The Nature, Sources, and Prospects of Democracy," p. 252.

13. Miriam Kornblith and Daniel H. Levine, "Venezuela: The Life and Times of the Party System," in Scott Mainwaring and Timothy R. Scully, eds., *Building Democratic Institutions: Party Systems in Latin America* (Stanford: Stanford University Press, 1995), pp. 37–38.

14. Burggraaff, *The Venezuelan Armed Forces,* pp. 138–189.

15. Burggraaff, *The Venezuelan Armed Forces,* pp. 177–178; Bigler, "Armed Forces and Patterns of Civil-Military Relations," p. 120.

16. Burggraaff, *The Venezuelan Armed Forces,* pp. 178–187. A third conspiracy was discovered in November but put under control. See also Bigler, "Patterns of Civil-Military Relations," p. 119.

17. Burggraaff, *Venezuelan Armed Forces,* p. 187.

18. Article 132 is cited in Andrés Serbin, "Percepciones de amenazas y equipamiento militar en Venezuela," in V. A. Rigoberto Cruz Johnson and Augusto Varas Fernandez, eds.,

Percepciones de amenaza y políticas de defensa en América Latina (Santiago: FLACSO, 1993), p. 274; Cardozo da Silva, "Militares y política," pp. 88–89.

19. Antonio Gil Yepez, "El encaje político en el sector Militar: Caso Venezuela," in Augusto Varas, ed., *Autonomía militar en América Latina* (Caracas: Nueva Sociedad, 1988), p. 135. "There is not a practical instrument that could fulfill the link, even with the existence of the Permanent Secretariat of the National Security and Defense Council; the policies and military programs are not connected with the development policies of the Office of the Presidency of the Republic (CORDIPLAN), in charge of the national management and coordination."

20. Bigler, "Pattern of Civil-Military Relations," pp. 122–125.

21. See the discussion in Burggraaff, *The Venezuelan Armed Forces*, pp. 195–205.

22. Cardozo da Silva, "Militares y política," pp. 89–90; Levine, "Venezuela: The Nature, Sources, and Prospects of Democracy," pp. 237–238; Elias Daniels, *Militares y democracia* (Caracas: Editorial Centauro, 1992), pp. 42–44.

23. Serbin, "Percepciones de amenazas y equipamiento militar en Venezuela," pp. 272–281; Cardozo da Silva, "Militares y política," p. 90.

24. José Machillanda P., "Poder político y poder militar en Venezuela, 1958–1986," bachelor's thesis, Simón Bolívar University, Caracas, 1988, p. 98.

25. Serbin, "Percepciones de amenazas y equipamiento militar en Venezuela," p. 284.

26. Cardozo da Silva, "Civiles y Militares"; Felipe Agüero, *Las fuerzas armadas y el debilitamiento de la democracia en Venezuela* (Caracas: Editorial Nueva Sociedad), no. 2 (April-June, 1993); Burggraaff, *Venezuelan Armed Forces*, pp. 190–207; Bigler, "Pattern of Civil-Military Relations."

27. Compare the reactions in Sonntag and Maingon, *Venezuela: 4-F 1992* and Romero, *Decadencia y crisis*. Naim, in *Paper Tigers and Minotaurs* analyzes popular discontent with economic policies.

28. Bigler, "Patterns of Civil-Military Relations," pp. 119–120.

29. Serbin, Percepciones de amenazas y equipamiento militar en Venezuela, pp. 282–283.

30. Gil Yepez, "El encaje político en el sector militar," p. 132; Carlos Celis Noguera, *Introducción a la seguridad y defensa* (Caracas: Librería Militar, S.A., 1989), p. 104.

31. The political reforms began a few years before. For a discussion, see Andrés Stamboli, "Déficit Democrático y gobernabilidad del sistema político venezolano," in Carlos Blanco, ed., *Venezuela del siglo XX al siglo XXI* (Caracas: COPRE/PNUD/Editorial Nueva Sociedad, 1993), pp. 29–44.

32. For a discussion of these figures, see Sonntag and Maingon, *Venezuela: 4-F 1992*, .p. 66; see also the special issue of *Cuadernos del CENDES*, no. 10 (January-April 1989).

33. For a discussion of the political economy of the reform process, see José Toro Hardy, *Fundamentos de teoría económica* (Caracas: Editorial Panapo, 1993); Rafael De la Cruz, ed., *La estratégia de la descentralización en Venezuela: Descentralización, Gobernabilidad, Democracia* (Caracas: COPRE/PNDU/Editorial Nueva Sociedad, 1992), pp. 15–73; Naim, *Paper Tigers*.

34. The economic and social indicators can be found in Naim, *Paper Tigers*, pp. 34–44.

35. Carvallo Gaston y Margarita López Maya, *Crisis en el sistema político venezolano* (Caracas: Editorial Vadell Hermanos, 1989); special issue of *Cuadernos del CENDES*, no. 10 (January-April, 1989).

36. *El Globo*, May 26, 1992, p. 9.

37. Romero, *Decadencia y crisis,* pp. 36–39.

38. Sonntag and Maingon, in *Venezuela: 4-F 1992* note: "It was a movement that had been planned a dozen years ago, whose members were capable and ambitious officers, the majority with a college degree (other than their military academic degree) and a considerable ability in troop command; it was created through joint motivations, in small groups that discussed the sociopolitical and economic situation of the country, who shared a common dissatisfaction with the economic model implanted by Pérez, with the decline of the social situation of a great part of the population, and the ambiguous attitude of the government with respect to the border problems with Colombia over the Gulf of Venezuela." [Authors' translation.]

39. Agüero, "Las fuerzas armadas y el debilamiento de la democracia en Venezuela," p. 8.

40. Elizabeth Azuaje, Francisco Mijares, and Francisco Rangel Gomez, "Venezuela-Colombia: Relaciones político-militares," bachelor's thesis, Instituto de Altos Estudios de la Defensa Nacional (IAEDEN), Caracas, Venezuela, 1996, p. 31.

41. See the declaration by General Alvaro Barboza R., former director of IAEDEN, in *Revista Española de Defensa* 97 (March 1996). See also Alaña Leopoldo, Jesús A. Cárdenas, and Eugenio Gutierrez, "Migraciones rural-urbana en Venezuela y su incidencia en la seguridad y defensa nacional," master's thesis, IAEDEN, Caracas, 1996, pp. 97–103.

42. Moisés Orozco Graterol, "Discurso las fuerzas armadas en las democracias del siglo XXI" Perspectiva Venezolana, conferencia ministerial de Defensa de las Américas, Williamsburg, Virginia, September 1995.

43. Moisés Orozco Graterol, "Políticas para la modernización educativa de las fuerzas armadas nacionales," speech made in Caracas, Venezuela, 1995.

44. CORDIPLAN, *Un proyecto de país, IX plan de la nación* (Caracas, Venezuela, February 1995).

45. Those spheres were not always strictly military. At times, the military participated in the government's social programs, and it is also available for special events, such as the visit of the Pope John Paul II, when 26,000 soldiers were mobilized for logistical and security activities.

- ∎ -

PART TWO

Civilian-Dominated Relationships

In this section of the volume we analyze the civil-military relationships that can be classified as civilian-dominant. Four countries in this project enjoy such a relationship: Argentina, the Czech and Slovak Republics, and Poland. The in-depth analyses of these authors illuminate how *a particular form of the civil-military relationship* affects both the consolidation of democracy and the tenor of regional relations.

Among Latin American countries, Argentina has experienced the most dramatic changes in its civil-military relationship. David Pion-Berlin's chapter contrasts Argentina's current foreign policy, emphasizing regional cooperation, with that under previous military dictatorships, in which competition was the norm. He analyzes the changes in the civil-military relationships that developed a civilian-dominated relationship on the ashes of the previous military-dominated and pacted relationships.

Under communist rule, civil-military relationships in Central Europe were civilian dominated. The collapse of communism affected countries differently, but they all had one thing in common: the continuation of a civil-military relationship characterized by civilian dominance. Thomas S. Szayna explores the different paths to civilian leadership taken by the Czech and Slovak Republics after the breakup of Czechoslovakia. In the Czech Republic the military is largely discredited and plays no role in domestic or external policy. But in the Slovak Republic civilian politicians are stimulating the creation of nationalist myths as a way of maintaining their hold over democratic politics. In the process the military is being developed and legitimized as a national institution that can help bind the country together. The implications for the future preservation of civilian control and regional cooperation are problematic.

The Polish transition to democracy after the fall of communism is a particularly interesting one for this volume. The Polish military, unlike that in the Czech

Republic, enjoys a high level of popularity. The challenge for Poland's democracy, according to Mark Kramer, is to maintain civilian control over such a popular institution at the same time that competition among civilian politicians produces a political process that appears virtually chaotic to Poles. Kramer undertakes a detailed analysis of the process by which civilian control has not only been maintained, but strengthened.

CHAPTER FIVE

From Confrontation to Cooperation: Democratic Governance and Argentine Foreign Relations

David Pion-Berlin

Argentine civil-military relations have fundamentally changed in a way that affects the nation's foreign policy decisions. Whereas politicians were thoroughly subordinate to the tyranny of a military state from 1976–1983, it is now the armed forces' turn to submit to the will of politicians. With elected, civilian authorities in charge, the formation of foreign policy in the realm of security and economic affairs reflects their interests and perceptions, and not those of the military. Civilians have opted to replace policies of regional and international confrontation with ones of cooperation. But the sheer force of their diplomatic efforts has also pulled the armed forces along with it, causing positive changes in military behavior and attitudes.

In 1983, the rapid transition from authoritarian to democratic rule was completed. The political and economic failures of the 1976–1983 dictatorship—known as the Proceso de Reorganización Nacional or simply "Proceso"—combined with the cataclysmic effects of the Malvinas War to undermine the military's historic role as Argentina's political power broker.[1] Failures caused it to collapse, sending the military into a hasty retreat from political office. The balance of forces shifted decisively in favor of the incoming Alfonsín administration, which assumed office in December 1983 with an impressive electoral mandate and irreproachable moral authority. In an interregnum such as this one, characterized by an authoritarian collapse and civilian renewal, incumbents can find they have a freer hand in shaping national and foreign policy and are less burdened by the old order, whose interests can no longer be adequately safeguarded.[2]

The armed forces have complied, with a few exceptional moments, with governmental policies and the civilians who make them. Perhaps the greatest test of compliance has been the military's extraordinary restraint in the face of declining prerogatives and a diminished sphere of influence. Unprecedented and unrelenting have been the reductions in the budget going toward military salaries, operations, and procurement; the privatization of military holdings; the termination of important missile projects; and the legislative prohibition on all internal security missions. In the past, these moves would have represented an unacceptable and reversible erosion of military power but now go unchallenged by the armed forces.

This is not to say that the military is pleased with these developments and does nothing about them. The armed forces remain an important institution with interests to defend and are a force to be reckoned with still. But the reckoning occurs inside governing institutions, not outside of them. There is a great difference between the extra-legal forms of pressure used in bygone days and the institutionalized forms of pressure exhibited today. Now, officials privately and diplomatically register their concerns with the defense minister while military *enlaces* (liaison officers) take their cause directly to the congress or to the foreign affairs ministry. With a few exceptions, military objections to policy are expressed through proper channels. And although those channels represent pathways of influence, power is expressed more forcefully from the top down than it is from the bottom up: Officers may complain, but civilians decide. This then is the new civil-military relationship, one where politicians clearly have the upper hand. As a result, there has been a dramatic shift from military-dominated to civilian-dominated thinking about foreign affairs. To understand that shift, it is important to first briefly recount the military view that guided preferences during the years of dictatorship, before turning to an account of democratic foreign policy makers and their preferences.

MILITARY DOMINATION, THREAT PERCEPTION, AND FOREIGN POLICY

The Proceso dictatorship was preoccupied with security threats from without and from within. Conforming to a realist's view of the world with heavy geopolitical overtones, the military junta believed that states are situated in an anarchic, unceasingly competitive, and oftentimes hostile environment.[3] To survive in this brutal world, Argentina has no choice but to keep its guard up. If it does not, rivals will spare no expense to expand their power to Argentina's detriment. International organizations and treaties provide scant protection against countries determined to dominate others.

Neighbors are particularly worrisome, because they are in a position to widen their sphere of influence by seizing territory. As geopolitical theory suggests, political borders are not irrevocably fixed. They are "living frontiers" which are permeable, malleable, and movable.[4] They are subject to pressures from either side, as each nation attempts to push its border outward. Obviously then, the stronger and more persistent state will succeed at expanding its frontiers through military action unless its neighbor remains vigilant and prepared to defend its sovereignty at any costs.

To the west, Chile is Argentina's perennial nemesis. The two countries share an extremely long, unguarded, and at places, disputed mountainous border. The length of the territorial divide only adds to the military's sense of uncertainty, since there are many locations where a cagey enemy could strike. Were Chilean soldiers to cross over the Andes to the south, they would find waiting for them the vast, wind swept plains of Patagonia. This is Argentina's weak southern flank because its armed forces haven't the strength to adequately defend such an expanse. In addition, the area is largely underpopulated, underdeveloped, and poorly integrated with the rest of the nation. Without a network of economically healthy population centers scattered throughout Patagonia and particularly along the border, Argentina is granting Chile an open invitation to invade, or so the military thought.

With the region's best-trained army, Chile certainly had the capacity to harm Argentina. Did they have the motive? Perhaps. Chile's narrowness and its inhospitable climates to the north and south have always constrained national agriculture, development, and transportation with, according to the military, important consequences for the country's security.[5] Argentina, on the other hand, has vast amounts of cultivable land and a suitable climate to match, not to mention an abundance of minerals and offshore gas and oil deposits that Chile covets. To Argentina's south lies the much-contested Beagle Channel. Were Chile to win possession of the islands within the channel, it would have nautical control of a key passageway to the Atlantic. In any event, Argentine officers certainly thought there was sufficient reason to treat Chile with great caution. When preparing their own forces to wage war, they had Chile uppermost in their minds. That the two countries nearly went to war in 1978 over the Beagle Channel speaks volumes about the impact of military views on the nation's foreign affairs at the time.

The Argentine military was also suspicious of its giant neighbor to the north, Brazil. As the most populous and geographically and economically largest nation in South America, Brazil has sizable comparative advantages over other nations in the region. It could use those advantages to extend its influence (or its borders) deep into the heartland of the continent. Whether in line with reality or not, Argentine officers tended to assume Brazil had imperialist aspirations. Moreover, they believed that as the second-largest country in the region, Argentina was the principal agent charged with stopping Brazil's threatening advance. This then shaped the perennial, Argentine-Brazilian rivalry for subregional domination.

That rivalry has had an impact on Argentine military thought as well. The military studies Brazilian geopolitics with great passion. They understand that many of Brazil's most noted military theorists, some of whom have held positions of

authority and have thus had a significant impact on decisionmaking in the realm
of security, have vigorously championed the cause of Brazilian expansion.[6] Year in
and year out, military journals such as *Geopolítica* devote extensive coverage to
Brazil's strategic doctrines. Argentine officers fashion their own views not as in-
ventions so much as reactions, mainly to Brazilian thinking. What are the Brazil-
ians up to? How will their ideas, if implemented, pose potential threats to us?
How should we respond? And can we ever gain an advantage?

The Argentine obsession became more than just an intellectual rumination
found in the pages of journals. When Brazil tried to overcome its lack of energy
self-sufficiency by signing an agreement with Paraguay in 1966 to finance (in exchange for Brazilian use) the construction of Itaipú, the largest hydroelectric facility in the world, it posed a threat to Argentina. Barely twenty-three kilometers
from the Argentine border, the project, once completed, would impinge on Argentina's own supply of water downstream, challenge Argentina to make similar
arrangements with its landlocked neighbor to the north, which it had so far failed
to do, and serve as a flash point in the uneasy relations between these two South
American giants.[7] Although the military governments of the three countries managed to sign an accord in 1979 intended to resolve this dilemma, tensions still persisted, and the Proceso government could not, in Roberto Russell's words, "take
significant steps on stable foundations in the relationship with Brazil."[8]

Rather than search for common ground with foes, the Argentine armed forces
tended to accentuate the divisions. Rather than suppose a probable peace with
their rivals, they planned for an inevitable war. They tended to invoke worst-case
scenarios designed to elevate their own levels of anxiety, which in turn would
cause them to elevate their state of alertness. Of course this kind of threat perception is, in one sense, standard operating procedure for a military institution
charged with providing for the common defense. The military tends to view the
world suspiciously so that it is prepared should the day of reckoning arrive. The
problem is that under dictatorship, military perceptions alone determine national
priorities; the organizational imperatives of the armed forces become the unim-
peded driving force behind state policy. Countervailing views cannot easily find
their way into the closed decisionmaking circles of a de facto regime. However exaggerated or erroneous military perceptions of its competitors may be, they
nonetheless prevail and singularly define how the nation will relate to others.

But those perceptions also define how the state will relate to its own society.
Under authoritarian rule, military threat perception not only guided foreign policy, it steered domestic policy as well. The armed forces were preoccupied with internal enemies of state which they believed were poised to subvert the political
and economic order. True, Argentina had its share of radical insurgents. In the
early to mid–1970s some of these groups staged daring raids on military installations or escaped to the hills to engage in guerrilla-style warfare. But although they
may have posed a limited security risk, these organizations were soon mercilessly
rebuked, reduced first to the commission of random acts of futile terror and then

liquidated entirely. Yet even *after* their opponents had been soundly defeated, the armed forces continued a relentless campaign of intimidation and coercion against an unarmed and harmless civilian population.[9]

At a time when it would have been logical to de-escalate, the military expanded its operations, intervening in industrial, educational, cultural, professional, and religious organizations with a full show of force in what became known as Argentina's Dirty War. In hindsight, much if not most of this repression seems to have been excessive and unnecessary. Yet from the military angle of vision at the time, the enemy was formidable, omnipresent, and unceasing in its efforts to destroy the economic, social, and political order. Soldiers believed that ultimately the very survival of the armed forces was at stake as well. The military's insecurities seemed to grow over time. It felt itself under siege from enemies all around it. Hence while the military acted to restore some measure of certainty and stability to its environment, as all militaries do, it did so on the basis of perceptions and beliefs that inflated the security risks clear out of proportion.[10]

The centerpiece of the military *weltanschauung* was their doctrine of national security (NSD).[11] The NSD was an amalgam of ideas about enhancing the state's security that borrowed from U.S., French, and Argentine sources. Chief among these ideas was the principle that a state of permanent or total war existed within and outside of society. Subscribing to a fundamentally conspiratorial view of the world, the generals of the Proceso were convinced they were in the midst of a Third World War, one which pitted capitalist, Western, Christian civilization against the socialist, atheistic, Marxist-inspired East. Argentina, they believed, was a major theater of operations in this ongoing global confrontation. Although it sided with the United States in its East-West struggle, Argentina had its own peculiar problems, its own vital interests, and thus had to fight its own battles right at home. The logic of war dictated that politics and policy be subordinated to the demands of combat. This produced a simplistic and dichotomous view of the Argentine polity, where all those who refused to demonstrate total loyalty to the military regime were thrown into the enemy camp. And since their foes could not be trusted to abide by negotiated settlements, only their complete extermination would create the more secure environment the military was striving for.[12]

In sum, during the years of dictatorship, military threat perception led to interstate tension and intrastate persecution on an unprecedented scale. The armed forces could not get beyond their historic mistrust of neighboring countries or their infatuation with internal subversion. Ironically, its internal war against subversion and its external conflicts with neighbors did nothing to enhance the regime's sense of security. In fact, the regime grew increasingly insecure about its political bases of support, which prompted it to plunge the nation into war with Great Britain in 1982 in order to galvanize the popular wrath against the enemy. Meanwhile, the military engorged itself unabashedly, using national security as the excuse to bloat its defense budgets. Yet it never spent its money wisely to build the kind of fighting machine that would have given Argentina some comparative edge over its Brazilian or Chilean rivals. The reason was that the military had been lulled into self-assuredness as a result of its easy victories over leftist insurgents during the 1970s. Those victories helped to mask underlying differences in its capabilities to fight and win a conventional war against an external foe.

CIVILIAN DOMINATION, THREAT PERCEPTION, AND FOREIGN POLICY

Only a change in regime could shift the emphasis. Only the replacement of a junta by a democratically elected government could prompt the kind of reappraisal of foreign and domestic policy that occurred in Argentina beginning in 1983. And yet a changing of the guard would not suffice; there had to be a decisive alteration in the balance of power. In the past, weak civilian governments had felt beholden to military interests and views when it came to making foreign policy. They feared retaliation should they not conform to certain precepts espoused by the armed forces. And so conform they did. Even under democratic rule, Argentina remained deeply suspicious of its neighbors, pursued policies of isolation, and engaged in geopolitical rivalry with neighbors and occasional confrontation with Western powers.

With the collapse of the Proceso and the ascension of a new democratic regime, all that would begin to change. Now, the civilian government enjoyed sufficient autonomy from the armed forces to conduct its own foreign policy based on its own views.

Democratic leaders no longer had to operate within the long shadow of the armed forces because military might and prestige had been so decimated by the events of the recent past. The Proceso government's economic blunders, its systematic abuse of human rights during the infamous Dirty War, and its humiliating defeat at the hands of the British in the Malvinas conflict precipitated not only a loss of military power but a loss in public confidence about military-imposed solutions to political problems, both domestic and foreign.

Argentine political culture had traditionally tolerated and even condoned military intervention in politics. Frustrated with their inability to advance their interests through democratic channels, many Argentines eagerly turned to the armed forces for quick, authoritarian solutions. The military coup was a societal coup, one launched only after a sufficiently large proportion of the public had turned its back on its own democratic system.[13] But the Proceso's terrible blunders and unspeakable atrocities significantly raised the costs of authoritarian solutions for the nation as a whole. The Proceso was one of those defining moments in a nation's history when virtually all sectors of society are so adversely affected that each is compelled to question its own assumptions and practices. That self-scrutiny has resulted in a change in Argentine political culture. Citizens, frightened by the prospects of a return to the past, have eschewed extremist solutions, moved to the political center, toned down the rhetoric, and learned to play by the institutional rules of the game. Neither civil nor political society trusts military rule or military perspectives. All of this benefits the politicians who may now conduct military policy without fear of public betrayal.

With the return to democratic governance in 1983, the military's view of the world became suddenly less salient, while the civilian view rose quickly to prominence. This is important because the Argentine armed forces continued to cling to their antiquated doctrines of national security, even as a new political environment was rapidly unfurling around them. Interviews by this author with army officers in 1986 and again in 1989 revealed a preoccupation with internal threats to security, specifically with a resurrection of left-wing subversion which they believed had risen from the ashes of defeat in the counterinsurgency wars of the 1970s to resume its offensive in disguised forms.[14] Subversives, they believed had not only penetrated the media but had occupied important posts within the Alfonsín government. The sudden left-wing attack on the military base known as La Tablada in January 1989 validated the military's preoccupation with domestic subversion. But although such views still had a grip on the military mind (at least for a while), they had already lost credence with civilians inside and outside of government and across party lines. Radical and Peronist legislators joined together in April 1988 to pass a new national defense law, which served a legal death warrant on the national security doctrine by outlawing military involvement in domestic political affairs.[15]

Hence, it is fortunate that the shift in the balance of power that occurred as a result of the collapse of the Proceso government and the transition to democracy were so decisive. Military threat perceptions had failed to keep up with a changing world but could not and did not hinder the advance of Argentine foreign policy. The military has not been able to challenge, veto, or reverse the diplomatic initiatives to which it takes exception. The tail no longer wags the dog.

Although politicians clearly have the upper hand, this is not to suggest that they have gained total supremacy over the armed forces. Civilian control is a difficult objective to achieve. It connotes much more than a legal adherence, however habitual that adherence may be. It goes beyond restrictions on military means, ends, and prerogatives to the issue of values. In the final analysis, compliance must be not only ritualized but internalized.[16] The notion that a professional soldier submits to a higher, political authority or that he executes but does not question policy and those who make it must represent a principle, an article of faith. The full realization of civilian control—if it is to be realized at all—must await a profound reorientation of values among soldiers. Currently, military compliance in Argentina is simply a rational adaptation to a new political environment.

And yet for now, military adaptation to democratic, civilian-led government seems sufficient, at least in the realm of foreign policy. The president is served by a well-trained diplomatic corps that enjoys a considerable degree of autonomy from military pressure. Accordingly, foreign policy making can and does more easily reflect the priorities of the chief executive and the advice of his foreign affairs ministry. Contrast this with the Proceso years, and one can immediately see the progress made. During the Proceso, the chancellery often competed with the armed forces for policy influence. For example, during the brief tenure of General Roberto Viola as president (March-December 1981), General Galtieri, then head of the army, developed his own diplomatic initiatives in Washington, often undermining the work of the president's foreign affairs minister, Oscar Camilión.[17]

With the return of democratic rule, the foreign affairs ministry has fully recovered and in fact enhanced its powers. The ministry has no rivals when it comes to making foreign policy. Neither the armed forces, nor any other ministry, nor the congress can compete with it for influence over external affairs. Staffed by a highly trained, politically savvy team of specialists, the ministry has won unprecedented influence in the realm of security and defense affairs.[18] Interministerial work groups have been set up between defense and foreign affairs to coordinate the use of military power abroad. Liaison offices have been established to provide the military with direct links to the foreign affairs ministry. And the ministry has sent a number of directives to the armed forces reminding them of their obligation to collaborate in the execution of foreign policy.[19]

For the first time in recent memory, foreign affairs policy now defines how the nation's external defense and security objectives will be fulfilled, and how the armed forces will fit in. Argentina's entrance into the 1991 Gulf War, its participation in United Nations peacekeeping missions, its historic nuclear treaty with Brazil and treaty of peace and friendship with Chile, its mending of relations with Great Britain, and its efforts to spearhead a drive toward regional security cooperation are just some of the steps taken at the prodding of the president's foreign affairs ministry.

What is the nature of Argentina's new foreign policy agenda? And what are the civilian perceptions behind the policy? First and foremost, it is a policy that has acknowledged and learned from the errors of the past. Reliance on military force to resolve long-standing political problems is untenable. The Argentine defeat in the Malvinas War at the hands of the British conveyed this lesson in the strongest terms. Unfortunately, it took such a defeat to instill in Argentine leaders the knowledge that diplomacy would have to supplant warfare if the nation was to ever achieve its foreign policy objectives.

Although the Argentines did not expect to easily defeat the British in the 1982 Malvinas War, its decisive loss came as a surprise for two reasons. The first was the armed forces' contention that they had achieved an adequate if not superior level of force modernization. The second was the military's belief that their victory over leftist insurgents had confirmed their status as able warriors. Neither view was well founded. Having had its attention diverted for so long toward counterinsurgency and away from conventional warfare, the military had left itself vulnerable to defeat from foreign military powers: Weapons were not carefully procured for use in modern warfare; technical training lagged behind; and separate service branches were strategically and tactically uncoordinated. However, with its impressive victory over guerrilla forces during the mid-1970s, the military was not exceedingly preoccupied about such deficiencies. In all likelihood, the illusion of military preparedness would have persisted for years had the Malvinas War not intervened so dramatically. The War of the South Atlantic exposed the wide gulf that existed between the image of Argentina's professional skills and its reality.[20]

The war also exposed the danger of placing foreign policy decisions in the hands of misguided, uninformed generals. When it made the fateful decision to invade the Malvinas, the Argentine junta seemed oblivious to the strength and seriousness of Washington's security commitments to NATO. The United States would not and could not stand idly by as their British allies went to war. The military government failed to recognize that essential fact because for too long it suffered from delusions of grandeur. The junta believed Argentina's international importance to be far greater than it really was. Thus, when the Argentine military launched its messianic campaign to liquidate the nation's "subversive" left, helped foment a right-wing coup in Bolivia, and sent military advisors to Central America to help train the *contras* in their war against the Sandinistas (at a time when Reagan had been prohibited by law from doing the same), it envisioned itself as an indispensable ally of the United States in its global struggle against the Soviets and their proxies. As a quid pro quo for its assistance, the junta surmised that the United States would not interfere in the Malvinas conflict. Wearing ideological blinders, the Argentine armed forces could not see that although the Reagan administration may have been grateful for Argentinean collusion, it was not dependent upon it.[21]

Argentina was not then and is not now in a strong bargaining situation. It is a nation on the periphery that needs the core countries more than they need it. It is a relatively poor, geopolitically insignificant nation-state, whose influence seldom extends much beyond its own borders; it should not pretend otherwise, by engaging in reckless military adventures beyond its shores aimed at fueling nationalistic pride at home. It can no longer assume that it is an important enough actor such that it can automatically purchase U.S. support by following certain policies that are pleasing to Washington, while evading the political costs that come with pursuing actions that provoke Washington's enmity.[22]

It was not just the Malvinas incursion that revealed Argentina's weak hand. So too did the policy of systematic repression. The Proceso generals discounted the international repercussions of violating the human rights of their own citizens. They believed they could thumb their noses at the Carter administration, which had made the protection of human rights a cornerstone of its foreign policy. But as a result of its defiance, Argentina quickly became a pariah state, ostracized by the world community and cut off from important sources of U.S. military and economic assistance.

Civilian leaders now understand that Argentina's policies must realistically conform to its more modest position in the world. The country cannot occupy a more critical role in the world than its political, economic, and military influence will allow. It cannot push weight around that it doesn't have, or in the words of one of Argentina's foremost authorities on foreign affairs, Carlos Escudé, design "policies of power without power."[23] In overplaying its hand, Argentina only brought harm to itself by triggering reprisals from states far more powerful than it. But the antidote to overextension is not withdrawal, claims Escudé. Argentina cannot afford to retreat into a political shell, oblivious to events outside itself. Political isolationism fosters ignorance and misperception, which in turn leads to foreign policy blunders, he adds. Also, Argentina hasn't the luxury to remain detached precisely because it depends on the cooperation of other nation states for trade, investment, financing, and technology. To firm up that support, Argentina must prove to its neighbors, to the world, and to the powers that be that it can act prudently.[24] In this respect, it may have more to prove than any other Latin American state, since it had long been the region's unpredictable, unreliable outsider. Its current president, Carlos Menem, recognized the need for greater prudence, when he said: "My government is guided by realism and pragmatism; we only want to occupy the international space that corresponds to us, without ideological commitments, that are today void of meaning."[25]

If civilians perceive threats, they are ones associated not with other nation-states, but with erroneous practices of the past: military provocation and overextension, and political isolation and defiance. The threat to Argentina is to act threatening toward its neighbors, toward Great Britain, and toward the United States. The remedy is to take measures designed to dissipate tensions with each of these partners.

Let us take regional neighbors for example. Not surprisingly both the Alfonsín and Menem administrations largely abandoned hypotheses of interstate conflict in favor of hypotheses of confluence and cooperation. This has been a point of contention with the armed forces, which wishes to clarify what Argentine leaders believe will be the nation's likely future conflicts. Traditionally it is the task of the governing authorities to identify probable flash points so that difficulties can be anticipated. Equipped with these forecasts, the military could then devise contingency plans should political disputes spill over into violent confrontations. Without knowledge about who the enemy is, the armed forces have difficulty understanding how to train, equip, and organize their troops.

Yet democratic administrations have resisted handing the military what it wants because by doing so, they pit Argentina against the very states they want to draw closer to. Hence Alfonsín's foreign affairs minister, Dante Caputo, publicly asserted that Argentina would never contemplate offensive engagements against its neighbors.[26] In November 1984, the Alfonsín administration signed a treaty of peace and friendship with Chile, which obliged both countries to abstain from the threat or use of force and to resort always to peaceful means of conflict resolution.[27] Civilian foreign policy makers started searching for common ground with their counterparts next door because they perceived it was in Argentina's national interest to do so.

There is nothing to be gained, and everything to be lost, by Argentina signaling its apprehensions about Chilean and Brazilian intentions, as it did in the past. Distrust only bred uncertainty, which fostered greater distrust. As mutual suspicion escalated, so too did the arms buildup. Any move by Chile to fortify its defenses was, in the absence of incontrovertible evidence to the contrary, interpreted as offensive in nature and therefore of potential danger to others. This compelled fearful neighbors to attempt to respond in kind. But lacking Chile's resources, Argentina could never keep up with its rival, thus generating not only greater animosity, but a deeper sense of insecurity. Consequently, the acknowledgment of a threat to national security would signal a return to this uncertain past and a refusal to take advantage of a historic window of opportunity to improve Argentina's situation through a rapprochement with its erstwhile adversaries. Security is being visualized in terms of a regional peace, not a military edge.

Argentine-Chilean Relations

Democratic Argentina has promoted a policy of regional engagement. Increased contact has taken the form of a series of confidence-building measures designed to ameliorate sources of historic friction between Argentina and its former adversaries. With Chile, it has moved a long way since 1978, when the two nations stood at the brink of war over control of the Beagle Channel and its islands. The Treaty of Peace and Friendship signed in November 1984 put an end to that century-old conflict. The accord established a boundary line through the channel, permitting Argentina and Chile to enjoy political sovereignty and zones of economic control to their east and west respectively. At the same time, each nation was assured navigational safe passage through the other's waterways.[28] The treaty did more than end an old dispute about land and water at the South American tip; it established a permanent mechanism for submitting all future conflicts between the two nations to peaceful resolution. The parties must hold regular meetings to "prevent discrepancies in their viewpoints from becoming controversies."[29] Should controversies arise nonetheless, the parties are then obligated to find a settlement through direct bilateral talks, or failing that, conciliation and if needed, arbitration.[30]

Foreign Minister Caputo left no doubt about the historic significance of having achieved peace through diplomacy, when he said: "We were clearly aware that the long-term effects not only of a war but of the maintenance of a state of high tension between Chile and Argentina would seriously curtail our limited possibilities."[31]

The possibilities he had in mind were largely economic. Under civilian leadership, the two countries now wanted to find a way to harness their comparative economic advantages to achieve mutual gains. This would necessitate forging closer commercial ties, building gas pipelines, and improving transportation routes across the Andes, among other things. But to hasten these projects, these Southern Cone neighbors would first have to put an end to some two dozen outstanding border disputes that stood in the way of progress. The Beagle accord set both nations on a fast track toward resolution. By August 1991, Presidents Menem and Aylwin had signed an agreement ending twenty-two out of twenty-four border conflicts, leaving to be settled only the conflict over Laguna del De-sierto,[32] a 500-square-kilometer zone comprised of a lake and mountains, and an-other dispute over continental glaciers. By October 1994, the first was resolved (in Argentina's favor), this time through an arbitration tribunal as provided for in the Beagle treaty.[33] The second dispute was conditionally settled pending congres-sional ratification, which has yet to occur.[34]

These diplomatic moves have also had military repercussions. The armed forces of Argentina and Chile continue to harbor a profound distrust of each other. They view bilateral compromises with some suspicion, either because they believe there is nothing to concede or that once having made concessions, the other side could not be trusted to honor its own commitments. Indeed, the Ar-gentine military did not look upon the government's diplomatic peace offensives with great enthusiasm. They could not understand the reason for submitting the Laguna del Desierto dispute to arbitration (since it was unquestionably Argentine territory, in their view) and complained directly to Foreign Minister Guido di Tella for not having been consulted in advance about the matter.[35]

Yet despite it all, the diplomatic achievements have slowly but surely earned some grudging acceptance from the armed forces. Diplomacy has pulled the armed forces along with it. Commissioned and noncommissioned officers now participate in ski competitions across their border. The naval commands of both nations meet annually to exchange information about the location and move-ment of their respective forces. Officers from the two armies have begun to visit each others' units. And the Argentine and Chilean border patrols have agreed to improve communications and coordinate their frontier activities in order to avoid misunderstandings and harmful clashes.[36]

The Argentine armed forces really have no other choice but to go along with the peace offensive. Civilians are in charge, and they have cut the military budget to the bone. This has added to the deterioration in defense readiness that began with the Malvinas defeat. The military is neither in a position to credibly threaten Chile nor to credibly dissuade a Chilean attack. Although the country may not be defenseless, it is vulnerable. And yet, that vulnerability is less worrisome than it might have been two decades ago, precisely because diplomacy has dramatically reduced the risk of attack from across the Andes.

Argentine-Brazilian Relations

Prior to the democratic change, a general climate of mutual suspicion continued to persist between Argentina and its longtime rival, Brazil. That suspicion was specifically pronounced when it came to matters of nuclear power. As the only countries in Latin America with atomic capacities, distrust between the two ran rampant regarding nuclear ambitions. Clearly, if one nation were to move from the production of energy to the production of nuclear arms, the other would find itself at a decisive military disadvantage. Mutual distrust was aggravated by a lack of transparency in the relations between the two states, characterized by a complete absence of informational exchanges, reciprocal visitation, or controls.

With the return to democracy, a vigorous diplomatic effort was launched from the nuclear platform as a way of building political bridges between the two nations. With the signing of the Foz de Iguazú Declaration of November 1985, that process officially commenced.[37] The agreement committed both sides to develop nuclear power for peaceful uses only and to collaborate in making their nuclear energy policies compatible with one another. To accomplish this, the foreign affairs ministries would establish a working group to create mechanisms of compliance and enforcement. The Foz de Iguazú agreement thus generated future protocols that (1) intensified the exchange of information, (2) increased visitation of nuclear sites,[38] (3) expanded the number of facilities that would be open to inspection by the other side, (4) established systems of reciprocal control and comprehensive safeguards, (5) strengthened the consultative and coordinating mechanisms designed to produce a convergence of nuclear strategies, (6) amended the Treaty of Tlatelolco (which called for a nuclear-free zone) in a manner that cleared the way for Argentine congressional ratification on November 10, 1992, as well as Chilean compliance, and finally, (7) established a supranational agency of accountability and control of nuclear materials that obliges both countries to submit to verification and offers the international community guarantees regarding the peaceful aims of the two countries' programs.[39]

The agreement and protocols had significance that reached well beyond the nuclear issue itself. Through the process of diplomatic negotiation, the two nations began to break down the political and psychological barriers that had separated them for so long. This paved the way for other kinds of bilateral and multilateral understandings. Economically, it set the stage for talks between Argentina and Brazil that widened to include Uruguay and Paraguay and that culminated in the March 1991 Treaty of Asunción, creating the Southern Cone common market, known as MERCOSUR (Mercado Común del Sur).[40]

MERCOSUR pushed Argentina and Brazil even closer toward economic coordination and integration. It was not enough that each member of the trading bloc had endorsed the pact. In doing so, each had also made a commitment to "a shared view about fundamentals of economic policy . . . as well as macroeconomic visions and goals."[41] Consensus implies coordination. Since these Southern Cone nations started out with incompatible economic policies and structures, it compelled them to undertake some significant internal adjustments in order to bring their systems into greater harmony with one another. But that could only be accomplished cooperatively; they would have to first agree on what the problems were, and then find solutions to alleviate harmful economic asymmetries. Obviously, a schedule of tariff liberalization would have to be agreed to, as is custom-ary whenever a common market is being designed. But this was only the beginning, as MERCOSUR required member states to coordinate macroeconomic and sectoral policies on foreign trade, agriculture, industry, fiscal, monetary, and exchange-rate matters, as well as policies on services, customs, transportation, communication, and other areas that might be necessary to ensure economic integration and competition.[42]

Although national interest has motivated this process, members realize that the strength of the collective may be more important than the strength of any one nation. The growth and employment gains to be had for one country come only from the expansion to a regional level of trade and investment opportunities, made possible by the enlargement of cross-national consumer markets and labor and capital flows. The members must hang together if each is to gain. Should any one country feel slighted by these arrangements, it will withhold cooperation or withdraw entirely, thereby breaking the pact. But when no one defects and the trade bloc works, it epitomizes the concept of a non-zero-sum game.

The notion of mutual gain must seem peculiar to the armed forces of Brazil and Argentina, which have traditionally seen themselves as zero-sum competitors. But as a result of the nuclear and economic accords, those perceptions are shifting to a recognition of the advantages of cooperative security arrangements with Brazil and other MERCOSUR members. Still, none of the armed forces is prepared to abandon its primary mission, which is to defend its nation's territorial sovereignty. Although state boundaries may be slowly dissolving in the waters of economic unification, they remain very much a solid fixture in the minds of soldiers. Hence, neither is the military ready to follow MERCOSUR's lead by moving into the unknown realm of military *integration;* each force still very much wants to maintain its own institutional integrity. However, improved military *cooperation* has been a highly visible outgrowth of the political rapprochement and economic convergence achieved between these two South American giants.[43]

As in the case of Chile, the Argentine military seems to be following the lead of the nation's diplomats. The Argentines have commenced joint naval exercises with Brazil (and Uruguay and Paraguay as well) that include the exchange of cadets between ships and submarines. The navies have also set up liaison offices at each other's headquarters so that visiting sailors can view the operations of their counterparts. All the Argentine armed services have opened various command centers and combat units to periodic visitation by officers from MERCOSUR countries. Argentina and Brazil have welcomed military observers from the other side whenever the two forces are conducting border exercises. And the air force war colleges from Argentina, Brazil, Peru, and Venezuela have joined in a student exchange program.[44]

Evidence suggests that military attitudes, as well as behavior, are changing in step with diplomatic advances. Lt. Gen. Martín Balza, army chief of staff, recently stated, "No hypothesis of conflict exists or ought to exist among members of MERCOSUR, since all actions geared toward maintaining the military capacity ought to orient themselves toward multilateral cooperation that safeguards the autonomy of each of the states and at the same time supplies efforts to the common defense of the region."[45] Balza and other generals recognize that the democratic wave that has swept the region and the diplomatic energies that it has unleashed have made the use of force an increasingly remote possibility, while making possible steps toward military cooperation that were unimaginable just a short while ago. "Democratization, to which the nations [of MERCOSUR] are committed, turns out to be of fundamental importance because it gives the continent a pronounced homogeneity of shared principles and values . . . which together with the development of economic interaction produce the necessary reasonableness and foresight to make the possibility of resorting to force in the solution of conflicts remote."[46]

Democratization induces a greater transparency in relations that used to be distinguished by their secrecy. This new openness is marked by the willingness to exchange information, to open nuclear facilities to inspection and verification, and to allow foreign armies to visit one's own military installations. Familiarity tends to breed respect. As the armies of the region come to know more about each other, their mutual anxieties and uncertainties are diminished. The lowering of uncertainty is particularly important when it comes to security affairs. Any military action, in the absence of concrete information, is open to wide interpretation. Is, for example, the Argentine procurement of a fleet of planes for offensive or defensive purposes? What is the significance of troop movements near a border? Absolute certainty about such actions can seldom be achieved. But unless there is a sense of mutual confidence, each side is likely to assume the worst about actions undertaken by the other.

Argentine-U.S. Relations

Democratization brought with it a shift in Argentine foreign policy toward the United States, but so too did changes in administration. The Radical Party government of Raúl Alfonsín began healing some of the wounds that had been inflicted on Argentine-U.S. relations as a result of the Malvinas War. But Alfonsín also kept his distance, taking strong exception to Reagan's ideologically inspired entanglements in Central America. Since assuming office in 1989, Carlos Menem's Peronist government has sought increasingly close ties with Washington. In fact, relations have gotten so close that they were described by Foreign Affairs Minister di Tella as "relaciones carnales" (carnal relations).[47] The objective has been to remove practically all points of contention between the two countries. Although Argentina still reserves the right to occasionally take issue with the United States on economic matters that directly affect its material well-being, it has completely abandoned all political confrontations with the great power to the north.[48] No other country in Latin America has joined so tightly with U.S. foreign policy objectives as has Argentina in recent years. No other country has so willingly followed the U.S. lead on so many issues.

For some states in the region, the strategy smacks of weakness or dependency. Why should a Latin American state intentionally subordinate itself to an expansionist power? Aren't national strength and independence linked? On a philosophical level, the nations of the region can easily join with the United States to express their unity on shared principles of democracy, freedom, and human rights. On a more pragmatic level, they keep some distance, remembering that in the not too distant past, Washington unilaterally engaged in military and covert actions against Latin American states, allegedly on behalf of those same principles. When push comes to shove, the United States has followed and will always follow its own national interests, not those of its southern neighbors. For this reason, Argentine rapprochement with the United States is viewed with some circumspection by other states in the region.

But from *Menem's* vantage point, there is a persuasive logic to this foreign policy.[49] Regional and hemispheric strategies represent two sides of the same coin. On one side is the effort to eliminate tensions with neighbors in order to pave the way for economic integration. Free trade agreements, along with drastic transformations of the domestic economy, should, in theory, make Argentina a more attractive host to North American investors and traders. But none of this can be taken for granted. The United States has many other new markets it can explore (China, Eastern Europe). Why should it invest in Argentina's, given that country's troublesome history of political defiance? Autonomy, Argentine style, has often amounted to a purposeful confrontation with other nation-states, including the United States.[50] The country has paid a price (in the form of sanctions, embargoes, aid cutoffs) for that confrontation—a price it should prudently avoid paying in the future. But to fully exculpate itself, Argentina must go beyond avoidance; it must demonstrate acceptance of world leadership of the United States if it is to earn Washington's confidence. Hence, on the other side of the coin is Menem's devotion to the United States, which he hopes will give his country a comparative edge over others seeking the same kind of economic attention.

As part of that new devotion, the Argentine government made the decision in 1990 to send two naval vessels and several hundred cadets to the Middle East to join Western powers in the U.N.-endorsed war against Iraq.[51] This was a politically bold move. It was made over and above objections from the president's own cabinet and political party.[52] It dramatically broke with Argentina's long-standing policy of neutrality in internationalized conflicts. And no immediate national interests were served in the Gulf. Thus, were fatalities to be suffered, Menem would have to answer to an angry public that had not forgotten the victims of the Malvinas War.

And what about the armed forces? How would they react to this unusual request? They had not been consulted prior to the decision to send troops abroad, only after. The Gulf War involvement was never designed with the armed forces in mind. Aside from the president himself, it was the foreign affairs minister, Domingo Cavallo, who was the driving force behind the decision, not the minister of defense, nor the military high command. Menem and Cavallo had as their primary objective the improvement in Argentina's international image and especially its standing with the United States. Whether the mission would have delivered a military payoff or not was beside the point; it was assumed the armed forces would be ready and willing to fulfill whatever policy objective was stipulated by their political superiors. They were. Not only did they comply, but upon return from their mission, expressed gratitude for the experience. Argentine servicemen got to rub shoulders with the finest-trained soldiers in the world and found that to be a valuable learning experience. Hence a foreign policy mission that was taken for purely political reasons had in the end fortuitous consequences for the military profession.

Moreover, the Gulf War set the stage for Argentina's participation in U.N.-sanctioned peace missions. Here, too, the foreign affairs ministry quickly realized the political mileage (and visibility) to be gained by Argentina's involvement. By participating in internationally sanctioned peacekeeping operations, Argentina could demonstrate support for the new world order, further endear itself to Washington, and yet accrue benefits for its armed forces as well. Since all operations were paid for by the United Nations, soldiers would gain professional experience while sparing the government the expense. Having won praise for their exploits in the Gulf, and having bolstered their own image back home, the armed forces (and the navy in particular) now eagerly awaited the opportunity to again follow the diplomatic lead.

Under U.N. auspices, Argentina has been sending about 2,600 new troops annually to various trouble spots around the globe. Nine hundred men were stationed in Croatia alone during the height of the Bosnian conflict.[53] The Argentine military now commonly defines its U.N. work as one of its ongoing (although secondary) missions of defense. This represents the first time in Argentine history that the nation's military has been asked to serve the goal of international rather than national security.

CONCLUSION

With the transition from military to civilian rule has come not only a decisive shift in the balance of power but a fundamental change in foreign policy outlook. This change commenced under Alfonsín and was then deepened and to some extent altered under Menem. Undoubtedly there are some differences in style and emphasis that can easily be attributed to the different approaches adopted by the two democratic administrations. But of greater significance is the radical departure from military-dominated policy that the advent of democratic governance itself has brought. Although full civilian control has not as yet been achieved, democratic leaders enjoy enough of an advantage over the armed forces to be able to construct, without hindrance, a new foreign policy agenda. In doing so, they are guided by their own set of perceptions governing the making of Argentine foreign policy.

Central to the new perception is the notion that Argentine national interests and security can be protected without confrontation—whether that confrontation be with citizens, neighbors, or great powers. For all its past obsession with internal and external threats, for all its devotion of political, financial, and coercive resources to the systematic elimination of those threats, Argentina had little to show for the effort. In fact, it could be safely said that the nation's *insecurity*, in political, economic, and military terms, seemed to grow in proportion to the dictatorship's determination to combat and even exterminate those it perceived to be enemies of state and nation.

While keeping a keen eye on Argentine interests, civilians have traded in past notions of geopolitical rivalry, ideological confrontation, and national arrogance for new notions of regional cooperation, political pragmatism, and national modesty. Since Argentina is unlikely to ever achieve a decisive military edge over, let alone parity with, its neighbors, it is pointless to pursue a strategy that hangs national security on the hook of military superiority. Certainly the nation's defense force ought to be maintained and strengthened so that it can act as a deterrent if need be. But civilian leaders understand that since defensive needs are measured in proportion to risk, why not use diplomacy to lower that risk? With that concept in mind, and with the foreign affairs ministry at the hub of operations, Argentine democratic governments have spearheaded an unprecedented and so far successful effort to jettison historic hypotheses of conflict in favor of hypotheses of confluence and cooperation, which they hope will turn the regional neighborhood into a safer, less hostile community.

The diplomatic offensive has locked erstwhile regional adversaries into a series of agreements that arrest bilateral tensions, resolve border disputes, submit all future disputes to peaceful means of conflict resolution, and commit those same parties to strategies of economic integration. Internationally, it has reinstated Argentina into the world community in a way that acknowledges the nation's status as a poor, third world state and draws it closer to the United States and other Western powers. This, too, is a strategy of risk reduction because it is designed to avoid the punitive costs of political and economic sanctions that had been heaped upon Argentina as retribution for its past insolence.

Finally, the advancing tide of these diplomatic innovations has swept the armed forces along with it. Because of their relative organizational weakness in the wake of the Proceso and Malvinas disasters, and as a result of their reduced budget, the Argentine armed forces have had to comply with and adjust to the new political orientation. Foreign policy decisions are no longer theirs to make or to dispute. Even if they have some lingering suspicions and fears about their neighbors—and in all likelihood they do—those views no longer penetrate the inner circles of power as they once did. Nationalistic soldiers may have qualms about the new, cozy relationship with the United States. But they keep those views to themselves.

Moreover, military attitudes *have* incrementally changed as well. Officers seem more receptive to civilian thinking in the realm of security relations. The armed forces have begun to see the benefits that accrue to themselves from regional and international engagement. And with this change in behavior and mind-set, with soldiers ready to place themselves at the service of a constitutional regime's foreign policy, Argentina seems poised to enter the twenty-first century as a more stable and self-confident democracy.

NOTES

1. Accounts of the Proceso's failures can be found in P. Waldmann and E. G. Valdez, eds., *El poder militar en la Argentina: 1976–1981* (Buenos Aires, 1983); J. Schvarzer, "Martínez de Hoz: La lógica política de la política económica," Centro de Investigaciones Sociales Sobre el Estado y la Administración, *Ensayos y Tésis* 4 (Buenos Aires, 1983); William C. Smith, *Authoritarianism and the Crisis of the Argentine Political Economy* (Stanford: Stanford University Press, 1989), pp. 224–266.

2. On transition through collapse, see Constantine Danopoulos, "From Military to Civilian Rule in Contemporary Greece," *Armed Forces and Society* 10 (1984):229–250; David Pion-Berlin, "The Fall of Military Rule in Argentina: 1976–1983," *Journal of Latin American Studies and World Affairs* 27 (1985):55–76. The effects of the Argentine transition on the balance of power between the armed forces and the new democratic leadership has been well documented. See Andrés Fontana, "Fuerzas armadas, partidos políticos y transición a la democracia en Argentina, 1981–1982," *Kellogg Institute Working Paper* 28 (July 1984), pp. 29–32, and "La política militar del Gobierno Constitucional Argentino," *CEDES Working Paper* 28 (July 1987), p. 6.

3. On realism, see Kenneth Waltz, *Theory of International Politics* (Reading, Mass.: Addison-Wesley, 1979). On geopolitics, see Philip Kelly and Jack Child, eds., *Geopolitics of the Southern Cone and Antarctica* (Boulder: Lynne Rienner, 1988); General Golberry Do Cuoto e Silva, *Geopolítica del Brasil* (Mexico: El Cid Editor, 1978); David Pion-Berlin, "The National Security Doctrine, Military Threat Perception, and the 'Dirty War' in Argentina," *Comparative Political Studies* 21 (October 1988):382–407.

4. Jack Child, "Geopolitical Thinking in Latin America," *Latin American Research Review* 14 (1979):89–111; Augusto Pinochet, *Geopolítica* (Santiago, Chile: Editorial Gabriela Mistral, 1968).

5. Howard T. Pittman, "From O'Higgins to Pinochet: Applied Geopolitics in Chile," in Kelly and Child, eds. *Geopolitics of the Southern Cone,* pp. 173–174.

6. Bernardo Quagliotii de Bellis, "The La Plata Basin in the Geopolitics of the Southern Cone," in Kelly and Child, eds., *Geopolitics of the Southern Cone,* p. 119.

7. Quagliotti de Bellis, "The La Plata Basin in the Geopolitics of the Southern Cone," pp. 133–134; Joseph S. Tulchin, *Argentina and the United States: A Conflicted Relationship* (Boston: Twayne, 1990), p. 135.

8. Roberto Russell, "Argentina: Ten Years of Foreign Policy Toward the Southern Cone," in Kelly and Child, eds., *Geopolitics of the Southern Cone,* p. 74.

9. David Pion-Berlin, *The Ideology of State Terror: Economic Doctrine and Political Repression in Argentina and Peru* (Boulder: Lynne Rienner, 1989), pp. 3–5.

10. Pion-Berlin, "The National Security Doctrine, Military Threat Perception, and the 'Dirty War' in Argentina."

11. The Argentines subscribed to a hard-line version of the national security doctrine. For more on this see David Pion-Berlin, "Latin American National Security Doctrines: Hard and Softline Themes," *Armed Forces and Society* 15 (Spring 1989):411–429.

12. David Pion-Berlin and George A. Lopez, "Of Victims and Executioners: Argentine State Terror, 1975–1979," *International Studies Quarterly* 35 (1991):63–86.

13. Alaine Rouquié, *Poder militar y sociedad política en la Argentina*, Vol. II (Buenos Aires: Emece Editores, 1982).

14. The author's interviews with the following officers confirmed this point: General Heriberto Auel, Buenos Aires, July 31, 1989; General José Teófilo Goyret, Buenos Aires, September 18, 1986; General Julio A. Fernandez, August 11, 1989; General Jorge Arguindeguy, August 22, 1989.

15. David Pion-Berlin, "Between Confrontation and Accommodation: Military and Government Policy in Democratic Argentina," *Journal of Latin American Studies* 23 (1991):543–571.

16. S. E. Finer, *The Man on Horseback: The Role of the Military in Politics*, second enlarged edition, revised and updated (Boulder: Westview Press, 1988), pp. 24–26.

17. Roberto Russell, *Cambio de régimen y política exterior: El caso de Argentina, 1976–1989* (Buenos Aires: Facultad Latinoamericana de Ciencias Sociales, December 1989), pp. 20–21.

18. Ibid., p. 22.

19. Rut Diamint, "Cambios en la política de seguridad: Argentina en busca de un perfil no conflictivo," *Fuerzas Armadas y Sociedad* 7, no. 1. (January-March 1992):3, 9.

20. Defense specialists agree that although the nation has accumulated a large stockpile of weapons, these have not always been carefully selected for deployment in a modern war. Problems in procurement were evidenced during the Malvinas engagement by the navy, which remained reliant on surface attack ships whereas the British (and virtually all other advanced Western powers) had moved to nuclear-powered submarines and aircraft carrier warfare long before. The sinking of the Argentine destroyer *General Belgrano* by undetected British nuclear submarines, with the resultant loss of nearly four hundred lives underscored just how far behind Argentina had lagged in naval readiness. But the procurement problem was just symptomatic of a more profound, underlying malady: the lack of proper planning, training, and coordination.

21. See David Pion-Berlin and Ernesto López, "A House Divided: Crisis, Cleavage, and Conflict in the Argentine Army," in Edward C. Epstein, ed., *The New Argentine Democracy: The Search for a Successful Formula* (Westport, Conn.: Praeger, 1992), p. 71.

22. This idea can be found in Carlos Escudé, *Realismo periférico: Fundamentos para la nueva política exterior Argentina* (Buenos Aires: Planeta, 1992).

23. Carlos Escudé, "La política exterior de Menem y su sustento teórico implícito," *Perspectiva Internacional Paraguaya* 3, no. 5 (January-June 1991):115.

24. See Escudé, *Realismo periférico;* also Escudé, "La política exterior de Menem."

25. Carlos Saul Menem, *Estados Unidos, Argentina, y Carlos Menem* (San Isidro, Argentina: Editorial Ceyne, 1990), p. 32.

26. For example, in the fall of 1984, the government ceded responsibility to devise a new strategic plan to the Policy and Strategy Department within the Estado Mayor Conjunto. The director of that department, General Heriberto Auel, drew up such a plan only to have it summarily rejected by Alfonsín. Auel stated that in turning it down, the president had argued that there were no "hypotheses of conflict" worth contemplating since Argentina was

at peace with her neighbors and with other countries in the region. General Heriberto Auel, interview with the author, Buenos Aires, July 31, 1989.

27. Article 2 of the treaty, reprinted in the *Foreign Broadcast Information Service-Latin America* (FBIS-LAT), October 23, 1984, p. B3.

28. *Foreign Broadcast Information Service-Latin America* (FBIS-LAT), October 23, 1984, p. B4–5.

29. Ibid., art. 1, p. B3.

30. Ibid., arts. 4, 5, 6, p. B4.

31. *FBIS-LAT,* November 30, 1984, p. A2.

32. *FBIS-LAT,* August 5, 1991, pp. 36–37.

33. *FBIS-LAT,* October 18, 1995, p. 35.

34. Marcela Donadio, "Integración y defensa nacional en el Cono Sur," *Seguridad Estratégica Regional* 8 (October 1995):62.

35. *FBIS-LAT,* August 2, 1991, pp. 20–21.

36. Organización de los Estados Americanos, "Exposición del Gobierno de la República Argentina sobre puntos del temario de la Reunión de Expertos Sobre Medidas de Fomento de la Confianza y Mecanismos de Seguridad en la Región," (Washington, D.C.: OEA, doc. 29, March 15, 1994), pp. 3, 6.

37. Organización de los Estados Americanos, "Argentina-Brasil: Medidas Bilaterales de Fortalecimiento de la Confianza Mutua," (Washington, D.C.: OEA, doc. 7, March 15, 1994), p. 4.

38. Brazilian President José Sarney visited a uranium enrichment plant in Argentina in July 1987, and that was followed by Raúl Alfonsín's visit to the same kind of facility in Brazil in April 1988.

39. Organización de los Estados Americanos, doc. 7, March 15, 1994, pp. 6–13.

40. Luigi Manzetti, "The Political Economy of Mercosur," *Journal of Interamerican Studies and World Affairs* 35 (Winter 1993–1994):101–141.

41. Felix Peña, "Strategies for Macroeconomic Coordination: Reflections on the Case of Mercosur," in Peter H. Smith, ed., *The Challenge of Integration: Europe and the Americas* (Miami: North-South Center, 1993), pp. 184, 185.

42. Ibid., p. 192.

43. Relaciones Internacionales de America Latina (RIAL), "Actitud de las Fuerzas Armadas del Mercosur," *Seguridad Estratégica Regional* 7 (March 1995):15–16.

44. Organización de los Estados Americanos, "Exposición del Gobierno," doc. 29, March 15, 1994, pp. 9–10.

45. Lt. Gen. Martín Balza, "La Seguridad Entre los Paises del Mercosur," *Seguridad Estratégica Regional* 8 (October 1995):26.

46. Ibid., p. 27.

47. This famous remark prompted two Argentine journalists, Eduardo Barcelona and Julio Villalonga, to name their book about the suspension of the Condor II missile project, *Relaciones Carnales: La Verdadera Historia de la Construcción y Destrucción del Misíl Condor II* (Buenos Aires: Planeta, 1992).

48. Escudé, *Realismo periférico,* pp. 46–47.

49. Menem, *Estados Unidos, Argentina, y Carlos Menem,* pp. 32–33.

50. Ibid.

51. Diamint, "Cambios," p. 13.

52. A point made to me by Hernan Patiño Mayer, former Argentine ambassador to the Organization of American States, interview with author, Washington, D.C., July 5, 1994.

53. Data on the dispatching of peacekeeping troops provided to author by Gen. Carlos M. Zabala, former Argentine military attaché to the United States, in an interview held in Washington, D.C., June 29, 1994.

CHAPTER SIX

■

Civil-Military Relations in the Czech and Slovak Republics

Thomas S. Szayna

The evolution of Czechoslovakia and its two successor states between 1989 and 1996 provides some unique lessons about the relationship between domestic politics, civil-military relations, and regional relations, both in comparison with the country's European neighbors and with democratizing states around the globe. The Czechoslovak case differs from that of its central European neighbors (such as Hungary or Poland) in that the country experienced two fundamental shocks: the end of the Communist regime in 1989 and the country's peaceful division into two sovereign states, the Czech Republic and the Slovak Republic (Slovakia) in 1992–1993. Nevertheless, the Czechoslovak case can be usefully compared with other developing states undergoing transition in a context of deeply entrenched ethnic cleavages and secessionist tendencies. The comparison provides an opportunity to evaluate the claim that modernization can accentuate ethnic cleavages, and hence may offer important lessons for some of the countries in southeast Asia (for example, Indonesia) or parts of Latin America.

This chapter begins with an outline of the civil-military and ethnic dimensions of the situation in Czechoslovakia prior to 1989, as background for discussion of the post-transition period. A review of these historical patterns and myths is essential to understanding the problems evident in Czech and Slovak civil-military relations since 1989, the political evolution of both countries, and their relations with neighboring states. The chapter then examines the domestic and international context, civil-military relations and regional relations in post-Communist Czechoslovakia, in the Czech Republic, and finally in Slovakia. The conclusion summarizes the patterns observed and offers some explanations for the countries' differences.

PRE-1989 CZECHOSLOVAKIA: BACKGROUND TO THE TRANSITION

The following section examines both the evolution of interethnic relations in Czechoslovakia and the changing stature of the military in society. Both the country's history of ethnic tensions and the low esteem of the armed forces observed in post-Communist Czechoslovak civil-military relations are essential to understanding the recent political development of the country and its successor states' relations with neighboring countries.

The Ethnic Issue

Teleological interpretations of the evolution of the Czechoslovak state from its multiethnic beginnings in 1918 through its division in 1992–1993 into two homogenous nation-states are tempting but misguided because there was nothing inevitable about the process. With that said, it is also impossible to understand the breakup of Czechoslovakia without taking into account the vitality and appeal of nationalist ideologies and the processes of state-sponsored assimilation, expulsion, and ethnic discrimination that contributed to the establishment of the Czech and Slovak republics. From this perspective, the formation of Czech and Slovak states represents another step on the lengthy road of ethnic "unmixing"— a process that has proceeded with fits and starts since the end of the Austro-Hungarian empire in 1918 and still has not ended in Slovakia.

The Czechoslovak state, named after two West Slavic ethnic/national groups (the Czechs and the Slovaks) that inhabited it, was carved out of the Austro-Hungarian empire in 1918, in the aftermath of World War I. The political union of Czechs and Slovaks had no historical precedent, and in fact, the outward linguistic similarities between the two peoples hid substantial differences between them. The lands inhabited primarily by the Czechs (the historical provinces of Bohemia and Moravia), were the most industrialized portion of the Austro-Hungarian empire and among the most industrialized parts of Europe in general. On the other hand, the lands inhabited primarily by the Slovaks (the various mountain ranges of the western Carpathians and the Vah-Danube lowlands), were primarily an agricultural backwater of the Austro-Hungarian empire. Most Czechs were Protestant and secularized whereas most Slovaks were Catholic and devout. The Czech-inhabited areas had been under Germanic rule for several centuries whereas the Slovak-speaking peoples had been under Hungarian rule dating back to the Middle Ages.

Czechs constituted a much larger portion of the population of the new state (50 percent of the population, as opposed to 15 percent Slovaks), and they dominated the politics of the country. Some Czech-Slovak friction emerged between the two world wars primarily because of the perception among many Slovaks that they were "second-class" citizens in Czechoslovakia and that the Czechs ran the country from Prague. However, the Czech-Slovak friction was dwarfed by the problems with other ethnic minorities. Befitting a state that had emerged from a portion of an empire, Czechoslovakia contained substantial ethnic minorities (Germans, Hungarians, Ruthenians/Ukrainians, Poles), so many that the Czechs and Slovaks constituted only two-thirds of the population of the new state and ethnic Germans outnumbered Slovaks.[1]

Problems with the ethnic minorities—primarily the ethnic Germans and Poles in the Czech lands and ethnic Hungarians in Slovakia—plagued the state and caused friction and disputes with the neighboring countries (including a brief border war with Poland soon after the end of World War I). The minority problems finally led to the destruction of the Czechoslovak state in 1938–1939, when the Czechoslovak government capitulated to German territorial demands and allowed Germany to annex the primarily ethnic German-inhabited areas of the country. By March 1939, Czechoslovakia ceased to exist. Germany annexed most of the Czech lands, Poland took a small chunk of Czech and Slovak territories, and Hungary annexed southern portions of Slovakia and all of Ruthenia (the easternmost portion of Czechoslovakia). An authoritarian Slovak state, closely allied with Germany and openly espousing a fascist ideology, also emerged.

To Slovak nationalists, the carving up of Czechoslovakia led to the disappearance of what they had interpreted as an "internal colonial" situation of the Slovaks in a Czech-dominated state and the formation of the first independent Slovak state. Although the notorious anti-Semitism and fascist ideology of the Slovak wartime state has caused most Slovak nationalists to look with ambivalence on the first experiment with Slovak statehood, they also see emergence of that state as an important first step on the road to current Slovak statehood.

The democratic government of the reborn Czechoslovak state after World War II decided to eliminate the minority problem that had led to the destruction of Czechoslovakia in 1938–1939. The passage of the Benes decrees, a set of laws that assigned collective blame for collaboration, provided the legal framework for the forced migrations of ethnic minorities. Several million ethnic Germans who had inhabited primarily the outer mountainous areas of the Czech lands were forcibly expelled. On a smaller scale, some ethnic Hungarians were also expelled from Slovakia. As a result of the expulsions (and the annexation of most of the Ruthenian/Ukrainian-inhabited areas by the USSR), the post–World War II Czechoslovak state emerged as primarily a state of Czechs and Slovaks. Only ethnic Hungarians remained a substantial minority, inhabiting mainly a geographically compact area of southern Slovakia.

The Communist seizure of power in a coup in 1948 began the process of integrating Czechoslovakia into a Soviet-dominated bloc and its formal security and economic institutions that were established with time—the Warsaw Pact and CMEA (Council for Mutual Economic Assistance). Ethnic friction did not disappear with Communist rule in Czechoslovakia, though its discussion became tightly curtailed through strict censorship. In terms of the Czech-Slovak relationship, the administrative division of the country into three provinces—Bohemia, Moravia and Silesia, and Slovakia—was abolished in 1948 in line with Communist centralization and the official disfavor toward "bourgeois" ethnic allegiances in favor of "workers' solidarity." In contrast with the "independent" Slovak state during World War II, the administrative change represented a complete rollback of Slovak nationalist thinking because not even an autonomous administrative-territorial unit existed over all of Slovakia. During the lengthy and harsh Stalinist period in Czechoslovakia, all public references to any Czech-Slovak problems disappeared so as to present an image of a unified society. Similarly, all references to any problems with ethnic Hungarians and Poles ceased in public discourse because of the need to present an image of a unified socialist bloc.

Reform Communists came to power in Czechoslovakia in the 1960s. The Czech-Slovak friction emerged clearly in the orientations of the reformers. In the Czech lands, the thrust of the reforms was an attempt to bring about "socialism with a human face." However, in Slovakia, there was a clear ethnic component, and the demands focused on the setting up of a federal state to give Slovaks a measure of self-rule and some freedom from what many saw as overbearing Czech domination.

Ultimately, the entire reform movement was crushed because it led to the Soviet proclamation of the "Brezhnev doctrine" of limited sovereignty for the Soviet satellite states and a Soviet-led military intervention (in which Warsaw Pact contingents from Poland, Hungary, East Germany, and Bulgaria also participated) and the installation of hard-line Czechoslovak Communists in power. In terms of Czech-Slovak tensions, in an attempt to win some popular legitimacy the Soviet-installed government transformed the centralized administrative structure of the country by setting up a federation of two ostensibly equal entities: the Czech Socialist Republic and the Slovak Socialist Republic. The official name of the country was changed to the Czechoslovak Socialist Federal Republic (CSFR)—from the post-1948 name of Czechoslovak Socialist Republic (CSR)—to underline the new federal status of the country. Although some power devolved from the center, the CSFR was not a federal state in the Western understanding of the term, and a substantial degree of centralization remained. Just as in the pre-1968 period, the reinstatement of strict censorship put a stop to all public discussion of any ethnically based tensions. These conditions existed up until the very end of the Communist regime and set the stage for the political developments that followed the ouster of the Communists from power at the end of 1989.

The Image of the Military

The low esteem of the armed forces in Czechoslovakia has been especially pronounced in the Czech lands, and it has affected greatly the political role that the Czechoslovak armed forces have played in the country. The strong antimilitary and even pacifist outlook in the Czech lands can be traced back to the fact that in modern Czech history the military always has been associated with foreign domination (prior to 1918, it was seen as a tool of Austrian interests). The popular image of a soldier as a bumbling fool also comes across in classic nineteenth-century Czech literature. Despite the setting up of a Czechoslovak state, there is no history of the Czechoslovak military ever defending the state; thus, the military could not point to any one experience to form the core myth of its role as the protector of Czechoslovak state sovereignty. Indeed, the harnessing of the Czechoslovak military for Soviet ends and its participation in domestic crackdowns under the Communist regime only strengthened the old negative images. The exploits of the Czechoslovak Legion during the Russian Civil War or a few Czech combat units' participation on both Eastern and Western fronts during World War II could not serve as substitutes for a battle in defense of the state. Indeed, in popular perceptions, the military proved useless during the several occasions in the twentieth century that the Czechoslovak state was threatened.

The first instance was in 1938–1939, when Czechoslovakia was threatened by Germany. In a pragmatic move, the Czechoslovak government surrendered to the German demands even though the Czechoslovak armed forces were as modern (if not more so) than the German armed forces, and the territory bordering Germany and Austria was forested, mountainous, fortified, and favored defense. The second instance was in 1948 during the Communist coup. The Czechoslovak armed forces stayed in the barracks. The inaction is explained by the genuine popularity of the Communist Party, the absence of an anti-Russian outlook among the Czechs and Slovaks (unlike in neighboring Poland, pan-Slavic and Russophile views had been strong, especially in the Czech lands prior to World War I), and the image of the USSR as the main force responsible for the defeat of Nazi Germany. Another instance was in 1968, during the Warsaw Pact intervention, when the Czechoslovak military again stayed in the barracks. The inactivity is easily explained since, by the late 1960s, the Czechoslovak military was thoroughly Soviet-penetrated and the officer corps itself was paralyzed because of the split among its ranks between those who supported the reformers and those whose allegiance was to the hard-liners and the Warsaw Pact.[2]

But in popular perceptions, on all three occasions (1938–1939, 1948, 1968), the military proved useless. Driving the point home, following the 1968 intervention the Soviets retained a permanently stationed force in Czechoslovakia, deployed primarily in Moravia and Slovakia (prior to 1968, the Soviets had not stationed troops in the country, unlike in Poland, East Germany, and Hungary). To many Czechs and Slovaks, the period after 1968 felt like a foreign occupation. Moreover, the use of the Czechoslovak military to assist internal security forces in repressing strikes in 1953 and, in 1969, again to assist in controlling demonstrations on the first anniversary of the Warsaw Pact intervention only strengthened the popular perceptions (especially in the Czech lands) of the armed forces as a tool of foreign powers.

This image is especially pertinent to the Czech lands. In Slovakia, the antimilitary outlook has not been so prevalent. The wartime Slovak state created its own

armed forces, and in accordance with the fascist inclination of that state, the Slovak military was officially glorified. Slovak units took part in the German invasion
of Poland and in the fighting against the USSR. In 1944, as Soviet forces approached Slovakia, a popular uprising against the authoritarian government took
place. The uprising was crushed by Hungarian and German forces, but it provided an important material for a nationalistic myth regarding the determination
of Slovaks in fighting foreign occupation and provided an example of a "glorious
fight" by the Slovak military on home territory. No experience that could give rise
to a similar myth existed in the Czech lands.

The net effect of the more than forty years of subservience of the country toward the USSR and the subordination of the Czechoslovak armed forces to Soviet
goals had a far-reaching impact on the stature of the armed forces in the society
by deepening the antimilitary outlook and pacifistic proclivities in Czechoslovakia at the popular level (particularly in the Czech lands). Especially after the 1968
intervention and the purges in the military that followed, the Czechoslovak officer corps became associated at the popular level with little more than a group of
traitors serving a foreign power. Despite the incentives offered by the regime, few
young people wanted to choose the military as a career. The popular perception
of the officer corps was that of a place for rejects who were not smart enough to
do anything else. This image has constrained the military in post-1989 Czechoslovakia, leaving it a weak actor in domestic politics. Not surprisingly, after 1989
many in Czechoslovakia called for the complete abolishment of the armed forces.

Decline in prestige of the armed forces took place in the other Soviet satellite
states. But the extent of the antimilitary outlook and the low esteem of the military clearly went the furthest in Czechoslovakia because it built on earlier proclivities. Only Hungary comes even close to the Czechoslovak case in this sense.

Civil-Military Relations

The stages in the political evolution of Czechoslovakia yielded quite different
forms of civil-military relations. Between the two world wars, Czechoslovakia was
a genuine functioning democracy, and its pattern of civil-military relations did
not differ significantly from other democracies in Western Europe. Civilian defense ministers were in charge, and the professional military respected the constitutional system and did not question the authority of the civilians to determine
the threat perceptions to the country. The main orientation of the Czechoslovak
armed forces was against an external attack. Although the popular esteem of the
military was lower than in many other European countries, the existence of the
institution as a whole was not questioned. In terms of regional relations, the
dominant dividing lines in central Europe in the period between the two world
wars were those between the status quo-oriented countries that gained from the
post–World War I peace arrangements (such as Czechoslovakia) and the revisionist states that lost as a result of the peace arrangements (Germany, Hungary). The

domestic ethnic makeup of Czechoslovakia amounted to a weakness that could be (and was) exploited for irredentist ends by revisionist states such as Hungary and Germany.

During the Communist period, the full Soviet pattern of civil-military relations was imposed in Czechoslovakia. This entailed the elimination of the defense ministry as a civilian-controlled part of the government and its transfer to a role akin to that of an operational military headquarters. The Communist Party fully penetrated the military. Communist Party membership was expected of the officer corps and it was required at mid- and upper-level ranks. Education in Soviet military schools was a requirement for promotion to a high rank. Political officers, belonging to the Main Political Administration of the armed forces—actually a department of the Communist Party's central committee—were posted down to the small unit level to ensure compliance to the regime. A secret net of informers throughout the armed forces kept an additional check on the officers' reliability. Under the Communist regime, the military's assigned role was to deal with both foreign and domestic threats to the regime, as defined by the regime. Two large-scale purges of the officer corps took place during the Communist period. The first, during the Stalinist period, centered on elimination of Western-trained officers from the ranks. Then, following the 1968 Warsaw Pact intervention and the reinstatement of Communist orthodoxy, the military went through massive purges, as officers who had sided with the reformers were forced out or imprisoned. For a few years, the Czechoslovak armed forces lost their operational effectiveness as the officer corps was being rebuilt.

Because of the satellite status of Czechoslovakia vis-à-vis the USSR, determination of threat perception was a moot point. The Czechoslovak armed forces became de facto detached from the Czechoslovak state and were responsible directly to the Soviet General Staff in Moscow as part of the integrated Warsaw Pact structure. Soviet generals gave orders directly to the Czechoslovak military and assigned planning objectives to them. Because of the Western-exposed geographic location of Czechoslovakia, its units were to be in the first echelon of a Warsaw Pact offensive against the North Atlantic Treaty Organization (NATO). They were to engage U.S. and West German forces in Bavaria as part of an overall operational westward thrust.

CZECHOSLOVAKIA, 1989–1992

Domestic Political Context

The transition began in Czechoslovakia in the form of a sudden rupture in November 1989. In the space of six weeks, the hard-line Communists associated with the Soviet intervention in 1968 (who still occupied the top political posts) were ousted and replaced by former dissidents. The initial transition period came to a close with the "founding elections" in June 1990. The fully contested elections brought into the parliament people associated with the two opposition umbrella groups—the Civic Forum in the Czech lands and the Public Against Violence in Slovakia. Since the most famous dissident, the playwright Vaclav Havel, already had become president in January 1990, the elections and the formation of a new government completed the early stage of the transition. The new Czechoslovak leadership rejected the Communist model and launched steps to put into place a market economy and a democratic political system.

The newly elected parliament was also a constituent assembly, and it stipulated that it would complete a new constitution for the country within two years. From the very outset of the transition process, Czech-Slovak friction appeared in the political realm. In April 1990, under pressure from some of the Slovaks and after a debate on whether the name Czechoslovakia should be hyphenated (and written as Czecho-Slovakia), the name was changed to the Czech and Slovak Federal Republic (CSFR).[3] Inconclusive and increasingly bitter negotiations between Czech and Slovak representatives regarding the new constitution went on in 1990–1991 so that, by early 1992, the future of the federation was in question. The elections in June 1992 revealed the divide between the Czech lands and Slovakia at the legislative level.[4] Recognizing the impasse and the futility of further debate, the two sides agreed to dissolve the federation and set up two independent successor states. During the latter half of 1992, Czech and Slovak representatives negotiated the breakup and the two new states officially came into being on January 1, 1993.

The political-party systems that formed in the two parts of Czechoslovakia in 1990–1992 showed different dominant orientations. In the Czech lands, strong civic-democratic liberal parties emerged out of the Civic Forum. Their primary policy goal was rapid transition to a free market economy and a quick integration into Western international institutions. However, illustrating the persistent and unsolved national issue in Slovakia, nationalist aspirations and the striving for greater autonomy or outright independence became the dominant concern of the parties and movements that emerged out of the Public Against Violence. Most of the Slovak parties and movements also evidenced a greater appreciation for state intervention in the economy than did Czech parties. These trends emerged early on and they gained in strength commensurately with the impasse over the constitutional setup at the federal level. The June 1992 elections led to a hopelessly deadlocked parliament—a center-right coalition in favor of rapid reforms emerged as the dominant political grouping in the Czech lands, whereas a populist-statist movement appealing to Slovak nationalism emerged as the dominant political grouping in Slovakia. Because of the rules concerning the passage of laws in the bicameral Czechoslovak parliament, the dominant Slovak and Czech groupings could block any measure proposed by the other side.

The difference in the ideological spectrums of Czech and Slovak politics is illustrated well with the help of Herbert Kitschelt's portrayal of axes of political-party competition in post-Communist countries.[5] Kitschelt has proposed an ideological spectrum (or party competition political space) with two axes: libertarian and authoritarian politics (closely related to civic and nationalist orientations, respectively) and market and statist economic distribution (or capitalist and socialist orientations, respectively). In such a construct, the main axis of party cleavages and competition in 1990–1992 Czechoslovakia ran along a diagonal from civic and market orientations to authoritarian and statist orientations. Showing the depth of differences between the Czech lands and Slovakia, the parties that dominated in the Czech lands were predominantly on the market and civic side, whereas the main parties in Slovakia were largely on the authoritarian and statist side.

The differences reflected the distinct dominant norms and values in the two parts of Czechoslovakia (with more liberal tenets dominant in Czech nationalist thought and the more corporatist outlook present in the paternalistic and clericalistic Slovak nationalist thought), but they were strengthened by the different impacts that economic reform had on the two parts of Czechoslovakia. Because of the structure of the Slovak economy, including a greater reliance on the defense industry,[6] unemployment in Slovakia quickly rose to rates double those of the Czech lands. There were good economic reasons for such a turn of events, but because economic reform policy was formulated by the government in Prague, the issue was seized upon by Slovak nationalist politicians and portrayed as another example of Czech "overbearing domination."

But in an overall sense, the period 1990–1992 demonstrated a fundamental conflict between the Czechs and Slovaks over which set of constitutive rules would be established for the country. The cleavage was related to the different dominant sets of norms and rules in each part of the country. In the Czech lands, a primarily liberal model of state-society relations was dominant, whereas in Slovakia frustrated nationalist aspirations existed alongside a mixture of liberal and corporatist orientations. The inability to agree on the administrative setup of the country and on a constitution was a symbol of the deeper disagreements.

International Opportunities

The gaining of full sovereignty, ensured by the dissolution of the Warsaw Pact and then the breakup of the USSR, opened up the potential for the integration of Czechoslovakia into West European international institutions. Such integration formed the international component of the domestic transition away from the Communist autarkic and authoritarian model and toward a market economy and a democratic political system. The systemic change had overwhelming support, demonstrated by the elections in 1990. Recognizing the opportunity, the new Czechoslovak government's central goal was the integration of the country into Western economic and security structures, including economic integration with the European Community (now the European Union [EU]). In security terms, Czech efforts were initially concentrated on the transformation of the Conference on Security and Cooperation in Europe (CSCE) (now the Organization on Security and Cooperation in Europe) into a pan-European security organization that would transcend the Cold War divisions and alliances. However, Czechoslovak appreciation for NATO and its continued role grew steadily, advanced by such events as the attempted coup in Moscow in August 1991.

Because of the need for Western diplomatic, economic, and financial support to ensure the success of the Czechoslovak domestic transition, relations with the United States and West European countries went almost overnight from adversarial to close and friendly. Conversely, the new leadership implicitly identified the USSR as the main potential threat because of an attempt to reimpose a satellite status on Czechoslovakia and constrain its reformist path. As long as Soviet troops were stationed in the country and the Warsaw Pact continued to exist, the Soviet threat to roll back the regime change was real. In the view of the new Czechoslovak authorities, the Czechoslovak military, with its direct and deep ties to Moscow, could have been the agent of such a Soviet policy. Thus, the Czechoslovak armed forces had to be brought under full national control as part of securing the newly gained sovereignty.

Besides the nearly 180-degree shift in international orientation, there also existed an opportunity for a change in relations with immediate neighbors. Driven by similar goals vis-à-vis the USSR, Czechoslovak policies included genuine cooperation and coordination with Poland and Hungary. Cooperation built on connections among the dissidents in the three countries, all of whom had assumed power. By 1991, the cooperation (spurred by Western encouragement) took on a formal nature and the three countries became known as the Visegrad group (for the name of the city where the leaders of the three countries met and agreed to coordinate some of their policies).

Finally, the breakup of the Communist federal states (the USSR and Yugoslavia) were a vivid demonstration that, in the aftermath of the downfall of communism in Europe, fundamental rules regarding the future setup of Czechoslovakia were up for grabs.

Civil-Military Relations

Conditioned by their own experience as well as the behavior of the armed forces in November 1989, the new leadership's view of the military was overwhelmingly negative. The new officials came to power having little experience in foreign and defense matters (understandable in view of the veil of secrecy that surrounded national security under the Communist rule). As former dissidents, they viewed the armed forces as a tool of repression and an armed wing of the Communist Party. In addition, the intellectual roots of the new leadership were in the Helsinki process and pan-Europeanism, and their contacts with the West were often through the West European left or peace movements with their concomitant strong pacifist outlook. These views built on the preexisting and widespread negative perceptions of the military in Czechoslovakia. In this sense, the magnitude of the intellectual gulf between the military and the new political leadership was so wide that it has few parallels.

The Czechoslovak armed forces came close to intervening internally in November 1989. As the regime teetered on the brink of collapse, the defense minister, General Milan Vaclavik, gave orders to the armed forces to prepare for possible armed domestic intervention to defend the regime. Although plans were in place, the orders were never implemented and the regime capitulated. In this sense, the role of the military during the crisis stage was close to that in East Germany (and unlike the passive role of the military in Hungary and Poland, though also unlike the direct intervention of the military in Romania).[7] Once the regime capitulated, the military's political interference in the transition process was negligible. A new defense minister, General Milan Vacek, struck a deal with Havel in early December 1989: In return for respecting Czechoslovakia's Warsaw Pact obligations, the armed forces would stay on the sidelines in the political struggle. The deal worked for much of 1990. Put differently, the top leadership of the armed forces was ready to intervene, but it had no allies because the top Communist political leadership had capitulated to the opposition, neighboring Communist regimes had fallen, and the crucial Soviet backers were in the forefront of sponsoring the regime changes (through the abandonment of the Brezhnev doctrine and the initiation of reform of the USSR at the systemic level).

The government negotiated the withdrawal of the Soviet troops from Czechoslovakia (agreed on in February 1990 and completed by mid-1991) and took steps to bring about the dissolution of the Warsaw Pact, but domestically it focused on the internal security apparatus built up to huge proportions under the Communist regime (so much so that the various militias and internal security forces rivaled the military in terms of size). With the Havel-Vacek deal in place, the military was left largely to reform itself, with guidelines from the new leadership but without its direct supervision.

The military was instructed to change its planning, overall size, and force structure and to weed out the personnel whose loyalty to a sovereign and non-Communist Czechoslovakia was suspect. More specifically, by mid-1990, the new political leadership directed the military to abandon planning against any one specific enemy and to prepare a new military doctrine that would rely on territorial defense against a threat from—theoretically—any direction. In practice, this meant the abandonment of planning against NATO and a military stance akin to that of the European neutrals. As a part of such a move, the military was also directed to move to a more defensively oriented and lighter force structure that was substantially smaller in number. This implicitly represented the curtailment of Czechoslovak membership in the Warsaw Pact. In March 1991, the parliament adopted a new draft military doctrine based on these precepts. Czechoslovak representatives also played a leading role in pressing for a fundamental reform of the Warsaw Pact and, when that proved unfeasible, for its disbandment (by mid-1991). In terms of verifying loyalty of the officer corps, the military quickly disbanded the institutions of Communist control and launched a process of verification of the entire officer corps. By September 1990, some 15 percent of the professional soldiers had left the armed forces, with over half of the generals leaving the military. All officers went through an interview process to weed out the most undesirable elements.

Despite these changes, the military came under attack for being too slow to rid itself of the Communist influence. Revelations about Vacek's role in preparing for a military intervention in November 1989, the obsolescence of the Vacek-Havel deal because of the disintegration of the Warsaw Pact, and pressure by reform-minded intramilitary groups, such as the Free Legion, led to the ouster of Vacek from the post of defense minister and his replacement by a civilian and former dissident, Lubos Dobrovsky, in October 1990. In addition, in a step designed to extend direct civilian oversight of the military, the parliament established the office of an Inspector General (appointed by the parliament) in December 1990.[8] These steps represented the beginning of the implementation of the full democratic liberal model of civil-military relations, with civilians in direct control of the defense ministry. Because of the vivid demonstration of the Communist Party's lack of popular support in the 1990 elections, the disruptions and personnel ousters within the military that had already taken place, and the apparent signs that the Warsaw Pact would soon be disbanded, the military was in no position to reject the extension of direct civilian supervision over its apparatus. Whereas in December 1989 the military agreed to a relationship with the new government akin to that of two separate spheres of responsibility (keeping its previous autonomous position within the state), it seems to have envisioned a gradual easing of East-West tensions and did not expect such a complete and rapid breakdown of the entire domestic and international components of the Soviet Communist system. When the magnitude of the change was clear by the second half of 1990, it was in too weak a position to act against the further usurpation of its autonomy by the civilians.

Dobrovsky speeded up some of the reforms initiated by Vacek, most of all by reexamining the retention of armed forces personnel who served in the Communist Party's institutions of control over the military and by reinvestigating Vacek's overall personnel verification process. The reinvestigation basically confirmed the earlier results. Dobrovsky's reforms of the defense ministry—aimed at separating the ministry from actual troop command—were put in place in 1991.[9] However, by mid–1991, the entire process of reforming the Czechoslovak defense establishment in line with the model of civil-relations in the democratic states of Western Europe was overtaken by the ethnic tensions that had affected the functioning of the entire state administration, including the military.

The impasse in the Czech-Slovak deliberations on a new constitution and the Slovak nationalists' increasingly stronger demands regarding the future setup of the country affected the military by the end of 1990. In this sense, the Czechoslovak armed forces became another battleground for the Czech-Slovak tensions. The most important of the secessionist Slovak nationalist political parties, the Slovak National Party (SNS), called on its sympathizers in the armed forces to form the Association of Slovak Soldiers (ASV). Personnel belonging to ASV soon began to criticize the supposed discrimination against Slovaks in the military and the alleged inattention to Slovak defense needs by the Czech-dominated leadership of the federation and they called for the formation of two separate Czech and Slovak militaries. Put in different terms, the Slovak nationalists mobilized their sympathizers in the armed forces and tried to split the military along ethnic lines.[10]

The Slovak nationalists exploited the Warsaw Pact legacy and the attempt of the Czechoslovak authorities to deal with it. More specifically, as part of the shift to an "all-around defense," the military made plans to redeploy forces more evenly throughout the territory of the country. Until then, the Czechoslovak armed forces were deployed almost exclusively in Bohemia, a legacy of the armed forces' offensive mission as part of the Warsaw Pact. The plans envisioned that, as Soviet forces pulled out of their bases (mainly in Moravia and Slovakia), Czechoslovak troops would be redeployed to those bases. However, Slovak nationalists claimed Hungarian irredentist designs on the largely ethnic-Hungarian-inhabited southern Slovakia, and they urged quicker redeployment so as to "protect Slovakia." In the same vein, Slovak nationalists called for the formation of a Slovak Home Guard, which would be, in effect, a nascent Slovak military. The strong anti-Hungarian tenets of Slovak nationalism were an important reason for the Slovak use of the "Hungarian threat," but the conservative-nationalist Hungarian government's policy of support for ethnic Hungarian minorities and the political mobilization of ethnic Hungarians in Slovakia provided additional fodder for a genuine increase in Slovak fears about Hungary.

In an overall sense, the Slovak nationalists heightened Czech-Slovak friction by exploiting popular anti-Hungarian prejudices in Slovakia. Coming in the context of an increasingly bitter impasse in negotiations between Czech and Slovak representatives on the future division of authority between the federal units and amidst an economic transition that affected Slovakia to a much greater extent than the Czech lands, the engagement of the military in the ethnic tension further fueled the dispute. Although the military establishment tried to stay out of the political-ethnic tensions, distrust between officers and a sense of uncertainty over the future spread.

After the June 1992 elections and the agreement to divide the country, the Czech and Slovak representatives agreed to split the military in a 2:1 ratio in favor of the Czechs (roughly approximating the territorial and population ratio of Czechs and Slovaks). A Slovak general, Imrich Andrejcak, was appointed defense minister (in a compromise choice) to preside over the division of the armed forces. Interestingly enough, the actual split was largely free of problems and bickering over specific weapons systems, as Slovak and Czech officers worked out the technical issues of the division of military assets. The absence of problems showed that the Czech and Slovak officers did not view each other as potential adversaries; they followed orders but most of them did not support the breakup.

To sum up, for reasons tied to the role the military played under the Communist regime and its low social standing, the military as an institution suffered greatly following the regime change in 1989. Its budget was slashed by approximately 50 percent between 1989 and 1991; its personnel were subjected to a humiliating verification process designed to ensure loyalty to the country; the basic tenets of its military planning were altered; its very existence became publicly and vocally questioned in the media and in the parliament (for example, poll results in 1991 showed that some 25 percent of the Czechoslovak population felt that the armed forces were unnecessary); and it became a battleground for the open political friction between Czechs and Slovaks. And yet, throughout this period, there were no signs that the military contemplated any challenge to the new political authorities (except for the crisis period in November 1989). The situation was one of clear dominance of civilians over the military. One may question the extent of direct control the new civilian leadership actually had over the military and the central problem in civil-military relations was about the extension of such control, but the problems in extending the control were related partly to civilian lack of interest in and especially lack of expertise about the military. The military clearly feared the extension of such control, but it proved unable to stem it or even to challenge it seriously. As an institution that was closely identified with the old regime, it was discredited and weakened when the regime was delegitimized and deposed. The liberal model of state-society relations clearly guided the development of post-Communist Czechoslovakia, even if the model was just being implemented.

Regional Relations

The unity of Czech and Slovak umbrella political groupings broke up soon after they achieved their main goal of deposing the Communist regime. Then, regional differences between the Czech lands and Slovakia came out into the open. In the Czech lands, the broad-based political coalition that was in favor of integration into larger international structures held together. It identified transnational forces as an ally. The coalition clearly aimed for Czechoslovakia to become a trading state, exploiting its economic comparative advantages. Its most important neighbors—Germany, Austria, and Poland—followed the same inclinations. Hungary was in a slightly different category, since its economic reform was not as rapid and its foreign policy had a strong nationalist line. But it was the USSR that emerged as a threat because of its potential to roll back the reforms in Czechoslovakia. After the breakup of the USSR in late 1991, Russia and Ukraine were identified as sources of instability that could threaten Czechoslovakia's transformation.

In Slovakia, the broad-based political coalition that had formed in order to overthrow the Communist regime did not survive for long. Because of the negative effect that economic reform had in Slovakia, an industrial-labor coalition that appealed to populism and nationalism came to power. The coalition aimed to protect Slovak industry through greater subsidies from the federal government. When that policy had limited success, the coalition openly opted for secession. Because of the inherent anti-Hungarian outlook in Slovak nationalism and the raising of tensions by Hungary through its more active policy in support of ethnic Hungarian minorities, Slovaks began to identify Hungary as an adversary.

How much did civil-military relations have to do with the divergent threat perceptions and growing differentiation between the Czech lands and Slovakia? Slovak nationalists interpreted the compliance of the Czechoslovak armed forces to the directives of the federal government as evidence that it was a mere tool of the Czech-dominated power structure. In this view, the military clearly did not represent Slovak interests. The nationalists' attempt to redeploy it faster to Slovakia and to increase the proportion of Slovaks in top positions in the military could be interpreted as a logical solution that Slovak nationalists had to seek in view of their concerns about Hungary.

But the situation that existed in Czechoslovakia in 1990–1992 was unique in so many ways that it makes it difficult to think about civil-military relations as a determinant of regional relations. Indeed, the military's stature and political clout were so low that the military ceased to be much of an actor or to have much of an influence in shaping foreign policy. If anything, the military was absent from the larger debates and treated as irrelevant by most actors. The regular jeering of the military and open debates in the Czechoslovak parliament on whether to keep a military at all reduced the institution's significance. The weak position of the military in Czechoslovakia stands in contrast to the other former Communist states. For example, only in Czechoslovakia was there a verification of loyalty launched in the military. But the situation of the military is not unique. Because of the post-1968 purges and the image of those occupying high positions as traitors serving a quisling government, the new Czechoslovak parliament passed a law that prevented personnel associated with the apparatus of the Communist regime from taking positions of political influence. No other former Communist state in central Europe passed such a law (and its passage had much to do with the Warsaw Pact crushing of the Prague Spring in 1968 and its aftermath). Similar measures were considered in other countries (such as Poland) but were not implemented.

THE CZECH REPUBLIC, 1993–1996

Domestic Political Context

The Czech assembly, elected in the June 1992 elections, became a national parliament of the Czech Republic when the country came into being in 1993. Czech political institutions largely retained continuity with the former Czechoslovak structures. Havel became the president of the new country and the dominant pro-Western integrationist policy became even stronger. Even in terms of symbols, the Czech Republic clearly represented the "true" successor state; for example, the Czechoslovak flag became the flag of the Czech Republic. Shortly before the official independence of the Czech Republic, the assembly adopted a constitution. The document was heavily influenced by the constitutions of Western Europe and the United States, and it stressed the civil basis of Czech citizenship. The constitution codified the predominant liberal orientation of the country.

A coalition of liberal and predominantly civic-democratic parties (with the Christian Democrats also participating) formed a government led by Vaclav Klaus. The government stayed in power for four years, aided by a weak opposition. In Kitschelt's terms, the Czech political-party system in 1993–1996 was heavily concentrated on the libertarian-market side. Unreconstructed Communists (on the far-statist side with a dose of authoritarianism), socialists (statist-centrist), and social democrats (libertarian-centrist) comprised the main opposition. It is too soon to look at the consequences of the June 1996 elections. However, the elections produced less one-sided results, and they seem to have ushered in a period of more splintered Czech politics and greater political volatility.

International Opportunities

Upon independence, the Czech Republic became geographically the westernmost of the former Communist states in central Europe, with over half of its territory bordering on the EU and NATO member Germany, and soon-to-be EU member Austria. Combined with the high level of development of the country and the successful reform measures up until 1993, the factors were in place to push for a rapid Czech integration into Western international structures.[11]

The Czech foreign policy line became a more radical variation of the earlier Czechoslovak policy. Klaus and his leadership previously had been uneasy with Slovak political trends and looked at Slovakia as unnecessary baggage that acted as a brake on the Czech aspirations to "rejoin the West." With the Slovak "baggage" discarded, Klaus felt free to implement the full range of policies in order to integrate into Western institutions as soon as possible. Thus, the Czech Republic downgraded regional cooperation in the Visegrad group (Czech Republic, Slovakia, Poland, Hungary) in favor of a unilateral attempt to join the EU and NATO. The rationale for such a policy stemmed from the perception that the Czech Republic was best suited as the front-runner in the race with neighbors to join the Western institutions. Similarly, in terms of ties with Slovakia, the Klaus government quickly proved that it treated Slovakia as any other neighboring country, as evidenced when it allowed its monetary union with Slovakia to dissolve soon after the breakup.

The Czech "defection" from regional cooperation was greeted with resentment by the other Visegrad members and, for their own reasons, by the EU and NATO. In turn, the Western institutions acted to curtail the Czech unilateral approaches. As a result, Klaus modified the policy line, though without fully abandoning the goal of being the first of the former Communist countries to join the EU. The acceptance of the Czech Republic into the Organization for Economic Cooperation and Development (OECD) in 1995 as the first of the former Communist states and the continuous Czech policy of rapidly changing its economic-legal system to EU standards bears out the determined Czech push for integration. Showing confidence in free-market approaches, the Czech leadership also pursued a policy of regional trade liberalization, both through acting as a catalyst in the formation of the Central European Free Trade Area (or CEFTA, at first consisting of the Czech Republic, Slovakia, Poland, and Hungary, and later joined by Slovenia) as well as through a series of bilateral free trade agreements.

In the security sphere, the Czech Republic was physically more secure because of the greater distance between the country and the former USSR. Whereas previously Czechoslovakia had bordered the former USSR (Ukraine), the Czech Republic was now separated from Ukraine by Slovakia, and two countries were in between it and Russia. Also because geographically the country is "wedged in" against the unified Germany, Czech planners could assume that in case of a Russian threat to the Czech Republic, they would receive substantial German assistance. Indeed, in view of the friendly relations with all of the Czech Republic's neighboring countries, it became exceedingly difficult even to come up with hypothetical military threats to the country.

In terms of specific security orientations, the central goal of Czech policy was membership in NATO, the earlier idealistic views of OSCE having been discarded. For the Czech Republic, integration into NATO would serve as a way of ensuring its security against any residual Russian attempt to reimpose control over central Europe while at the same time the continued survival of the alliance prevented the renationalization of German security policy. In addition, Czech and German membership in the same alliance held out the prospect of finally putting Czech-German relations on the same "normal" level as, for example, Dutch-German relations. As part of the NATO orientation, Czech ties with the United States and Germany became especially close. The Czech Republic joined the Partnership for Peace (PfP) program that NATO offered in 1994 so as to postpone the decision on accepting new members into the alliance and it has participated extensively in PfP activities, especially with German and U.S. armed forces. The participation has a clear motive of preparation for entry into NATO. In order to assuage fears in NATO about the Czech Republic becoming a "free rider" in the alliance, the Czech leadership has taken pains to show that it will take its obligations as part of NATO seriously: The Czechs have participated extensively in UN peacekeeping operations (stepping up the earlier, Czechoslovak 1991–1992 involvement). In the same vein, a Czech battalion has taken part in the IFOR operation in Bosnia-Herzegovina.

Ties with Poland in the security realm also tightened following the realization that, for geostrategic reasons, Poland is the most important country to NATO of the aspiring new members and that close security ties with Poland made most sense for the Czech Republic for they opened up the prospect of simultaneous Czech-Polish integration into NATO. In addition, the step-up in Czech relations with Poland was motivated by similar Polish and Czech concerns about Germany. While Czech-German relations were good, problems arose in Bavarian ties with the Czech Republic which, in turn, were related to the issue of compensation to the ethnic Germans expelled from Czechoslovakia (mostly the Czech lands) shortly after World War II. Many of the expellees settled in Bavaria and they have had substantial influence on Bavarian politics. Since the Bavarian-based Christian-Social Union is a partner in the ruling coalition in Germany, the influence has translated into an irritant in Czech-German relations. The issue is more of a domestic problem in Germany, but combined with the fact that most of the foreign direct investment into the Czech Republic since 1990 has come from Germany, there are some residual fears among Czechs about the eventual nature of German influence over the Czech Republic. Both the Communist as well as extreme nationalist political forces in the Czech Republic have used fear of Germany to discredit the Klaus line of integration.

Civil-Military Relations in the Czech Republic

Just as there was continuity between the overall Czechoslovak and Czech outlooks, the dominant negative views of the military persisted in the Czech Republic (since the antimilitary outlook was primarily in the Czech lands rather than in Slovakia). Anton Baudys, a civilian from the Christian Democratic Party, became the Czech Republic's first defense minister. Baudys's first comments were to the effect that no major changes had taken place in the armed forces since 1989. Consequently, another round of verification, or screening, was launched by mid-1993. Every Czech professional soldier was interviewed and assessed in regard to loyalty and qualifications one more time. The screening was completed by the end of 1993, and it led to more personnel departures. Although the results confirmed the loyalty of the officer corps, some voices in the parliament continued to question the extent of the changes. When, after some coalition squabbling, a new civilian defense minister, Vilem Holan, replaced Baudys in September 1994, he too began his tenure by criticizing the earlier verifications as not sufficiently far-reaching.[12]

   The criticism of the officer corps and the questioning of its loyalty have become almost a standard feature of Czech politics. Undoubtedly, the repeated personnel verifications and criticisms have had a negative impact upon the morale of the military. Most of all, the treatment of the military by the political leadership shows the unquestioned dominance of civilians in the security sphere—an outlook that is extreme even in terms of a liberal political model. But more than that, the civilians' treatment of the military also shows the deep distrust of the military among the ruling circles in the Czech Republic and the Czech politicians' determination to start anew by breaking down the military institution as it had existed. They could do so because, by 1993–1994, officers who had gone through training in Western military educational facilities could take over some of the top posts and steer the Czech military toward integration into NATO. In addition, the verification process was also a convenient tool to implement radical cuts in the size of the armed forces. Finally, the secure situation of the Czech Republic offered time and allowed the Czechs the luxury of letting their military become a force of questionable operational effectiveness.

The eventual goal of entering NATO has driven the whole gamut of Czech thinking about reform of the defense establishment. A long-range concept for the transformation of the Czech armed forces was put together in 1993–1994. The concept calls for a transition to a NATO-like force consisting of corps and brigades deployed fairly evenly in Bohemia and Moravia. The entire force will be less than 65,000 and this goal was already reached in 1995. Within a few years, the force will be made up almost exclusively of professional soldiers, and the conscription system will be in place only to train the manpower for the territorial forces.[13] Procurement decisions on weapons systems (primarily modification of existing systems due to low budgets) have been driven by the need for compatibility with NATO. Even the drive to restructure the defense ministry and the influx of civilians into positions of authority in the ministry is part of the overall transition to a NATO-like defense establishment, and it is driven by the fact that NATO has made civilian control over the defense ministry one of the criteria for accepting new members. The potential for success of the Czech armed forces in becoming a NATO-compatible organization remains cloudy because the military's low standing in the public eye makes defense expenditures unpopular. Although the Czech defense budget has remained fairly steady, it is low in relation to the Czech GDP (approximately 2.0 to 2.5 percent), lower than that recommended by NATO (3.0 percent), and extremely low in relation to the outlays for the military during the Communist era.

To sum up, the Czech military is engaged in a long process of rebuilding and restructuring. It faces a lack of interest and even hostility from many Czech politicians, the officer corps has been subjected to repeated humiliation, social approval of the military has not risen (indeed, polls indicate that, since 1993, distrust of the military has grown), and it still has a long way to go to achieve compatibility with NATO. However, since NATO membership is ultimately a political decision, the success of the overall Czech political and economic transformation is more important than any military measures per se. There is little question that the civilian leadership clearly dominates civil-military relations and that, so far, a liberal model of state-society relations has guided the development of the Czech Republic. Despite its difficult situation, the military has not shown any signs of questioning the principle or extent of civilian control. Indeed, the military appears to support the overall goal of professionalization and eventual NATO entry probably because such an evolution ensures the survival and competence of an admittedly small but effective Czech armed forces. Such an evolution also offers the prospect of greater social approval for the armed forces, for it puts the military in the forefront of integration with pan-European institutions—a goal that has overwhelming public approval.

Regional Relations

The Czech political coalition that has governed since the creation of the Czech Republic has advocated strongly the integration of the country into international structures. The Czech leadership clearly aims for the country to become a trading state, and it sees transnational forces as an ally. In this sense, the Czechs have looked upon the EU-integrated trading states of Germany and Austria as allies. Despite the coming to power of socialists in Poland in 1993, the Polish market orientation has not changed, and the many similar concerns and interests between Poland and the Czech Republic have led to close ties between the two countries. The two countries even agreed to a mutually profitable exchange of weapons in 1995–1996.

Relations with Slovakia have been difficult at times, and Czech officials seem resigned to accepting Slovakia as a politically unstable and potentially threatening (in the sense of causing refugee flows) country. The uncertain political and economic reform process in Slovakia has given rise to a number of concerns. One stems from the potential closer Slovak ties with Russia that could lead to Russia using Slovakia as a tool to promote instability in central Europe. Another concern stems from the nationalistic policies in Slovakia and Slovak-Hungarian friction. Czechs fear that an escalation of tensions might spill over to the Republic. However, the extensive personal ties between individual Czech and Slovak politicians, administrators, and military officers have mitigated the perception of Slovakia as a military adversary.

Czech leadership implicitly perceives Russia as an adversary because, above all, Russian opposition to Czech membership in NATO has delayed the implementation of a fundamental Czech foreign policy goal that underlies a whole range of Czech policies. In addition, increasing signs of restoration of expansionist political forces in Russia raise the specter of renewed Russian attempts to expand influence over central Europe. Finally, the uncertain political and economic situation in Russia and Ukraine has led to the proliferation of organized crime and drug smuggling rings, which have established a strong presence in the Czech Republic. Dealing with such threats has become a specific security problem for the Republic.[14]

The weak political standing of the Czech armed forces has meant that the policies of integration into Western structures have met with little if any modification from the military. Indeed, the military has jumped on the pro-NATO bandwagon, seeing it as one of the few ways of obtaining higher allocations of funds and new weapons and ensuring the viability and long-term survival of the Czech military establishment. The military's embarking on new missions (for example, peacekeeping) shows its search for a role in the post–Cold War period and an attempt to create a role for itself in a democratic Czech Republic. Seen from a different standpoint, since the Czech military is but an echo of the Czechoslovak military in terms of size, the Czech officer corps has had to adjust to being a small and comparatively weak force. Integration into a multinational alliance and shrinking to a small but high-quality core may allow it to persist and prosper as an institution. Although other Communist states in central Europe have jumped on the NATO bandwagon, the Czech Republic is an outlier in terms of its motivations.

THE SLOVAK REPUBLIC, 1993–1996

Domestic Political Context

The Slovak assembly, elected in the June 1992 elections, became the Slovak parliament when the country gained sovereignty in 1993. Significant differences emerged between Slovak policies and those of Czechoslovakia. Some economic reforms slowed and were even reversed (especially in the realm of privatization). The integrationist line remained the official policy but Slovak determination in pursuing it in practice became questionable. The Slovak constitution stressed the national—Slovak—basis of citizenship. Overall, the document reveals a corporatist outlook (with some liberal components) regarding the preferred model of state-society relations.

The political evolution of Slovakia has reflected mixed liberal and corporatist orientations. Initially, the Movement for a Democratic Slovakia (or HZDS), an umbrella political organization favoring Slovak autonomy or outright independence, led by Vladimir Meciar (an alleged former Communist secret police agent), achieved close to a majority of representatives in the parliament. The former Communists, reformed into a socialist party and running under the label of the Party of the Democratic Left (SDL), came in a distant second. Christian Democrats came in under 10 percent, as did the SNS, an outright secessionist and nationalistic party. Finally, a coalition of ethnic Hungarian parties also entered the parliament. All parties that entered the parliament, with the exception of ethnic Hungarians, had appealed to Slovak nationalism, varying from mild (by SDL) to militant (SNS). Fearing that Slovak nationalism would no longer be filtered through federal institutions, only the ethnic Hungarians strongly opposed the Slovak drive for greater autonomy or independence. The HZDS and SNS cooperated in forcing the dissolution of Czechoslovakia.

Being an umbrella group, the HZDS soon splintered after achieving Slovak independence, the goal for which it was formed. Although the HZDS twice formed a coalition with SNS, in 1993 and early 1994, the period is most notable for the inability to form a viable government. As the political struggle went on, the president's office became engaged in it, leading to institutional rivalry between the prime minister and the president over their respective areas of responsibility.[15] In March 1994, several parties and groupings opposed to Meciar formed a government led by Jozef Moravcik. The government tried to push forward a number of market-oriented economic reforms. But early elections (in September–October 1994) led to another victory of Meciar and his peculiar brand of populism, statism, and nationalism.[16] A socialist–social democratic coalition came in a distant second. The ethnic Hungarian coalition, the Christian Democrats, the splinter group from HZDS, the SNS, and a populist reactionary Communist group (the Association of Workers of Slovakia [ZRS]) also entered the parliament. The elections led to an odd coalition of a Meciar-led government of HZDS, SNS, and ZRS. The coalition has remained in place since that time even though it is shaky and volatile.

In Kitschelt's terms, the Slovak political-party system in 1993–1996 was weighted in favor of the authoritarian-statist side, with the HZDS (and Meciar himself) representing a strong authoritarian current. The SNS (which, by 1994, had rid itself of its moderate wing) became even more authoritarian, since its leadership seems to have misgivings about a democratic political system (as evidenced by its nostalgic view of the World War II fascist Slovak state). Centrist-authoritarian Christian Democrats, statist-centrist social-democrats and socialists, a centrist group that split apart from HZDS, and the far statist-authoritarian ZRS completed the Slovak political scene. The centrist ethnic Hungarian coalition does not come into play in the Slovak political scene since other parties are reluctant to form an official coalition with it for fear of alienating the nationalist proclivities of the electorate. The Slovak political-party system remains at an early stage of democratic development, since the main party, the HZDS, retains many elements of being a vehicle of a populist figure rather than an organization with a coherent set of views.

International Opportunities

Just as the emergence of a sovereign Czech Republic moved the country westward, the setting up of a sovereign Slovakia moved the country eastward in the sense of eliminating the border with Germany and, save for a short border with Austria, surrounding it by former Communist states. Correctly or not, other central Europeans as well as Western Europeans identified Slovakia as the culprit in the breakup of Czechoslovakia. Already suspect in terms of its commitment to a free market, democratic state, facing severe structural adjustment problems, perceived as breaking international norms on the treatment of the ethnic Hungarian minority, and led by populist and unsavory figures, Slovakia faced greater problems than the Czech Republic in gaining acceptance as a serious candidate for rapid integration into Western structures.

Slovak foreign policy has attempted to square the circle. It has paid lip service to integration into Western structures, but it also has looked to Russia for economic cooperation. Because of its linchpin geographic location and crucial role in the proposed enlargement of NATO (as the only country bordering the other three Visegrad states), Slovakia has received special support and assistance from the Western countries. It also has continued to engage in cooperation with other central European states, for example, by joining CEFTA to gain the benefits of regional trade liberalization. But for the same reasons of crucial location, Slovakia also has played its "Russian card" to secure special economic support from Russia. Russia has been willing to play along because the special relationship with Slovakia allows it to drive a wedge in the central European grouping and cause problems for NATO enlargement. The Slovak policy has met with only partial success because it elicited distrust among other central European states and frustration among the EU and NATO countries. Because of Russia's economic weakness, its assistance has not made much difference to Slovakia.

Slovak policy initially (in 1993) wavered on NATO membership, then came out in favor of joining the organization (especially during the short-lived tenure of Moravcik as prime minister in 1994), and it has remained in place, though there is little enthusiasm in the policy and one of the current coalition partners, the ZRS, is opposed to the idea. Slovakia joined the PfP program and it has taken part in PfP activities, though its participation has been hampered by lack of funds. Slovak participation in UN peacekeeping operations has persisted, though it has not been at as high a level as the Czech Republic. A Slovak unit has not been assigned to the IFOR operation, although a support unit has been stationed in eastern Croatia as part of the United Nations Administration in Eastern Slavonia (UNTAES).

In the security sphere, unlike the Czech Republic, Slovakia became physically less secure because it faced potential threats as a much smaller and weaker entity than when it was a part of Czechoslovakia. The most problematic bilateral Slovak ties have been with Hungary. Tensions over the treatment of the ethnic Hungarian minority and a dispute over a massive hydroelectric project on the Danube (on the Hungarian-Slovak border) on top of historical animosities heightened by politicians in both countries have led to implicit Slovak perceptions of Hungary as an adversary. In this context, whereas Czechoslovakia had a larger population (3:2 ratio) than Hungary and a substantially better and larger military than Hungary, a sovereign Slovakia shrank to one-half the size of Hungary in terms of territory and population. Moreover, the Slovak military was just being built from scratch and its effectiveness was in question. The Hungarian government's active policy in support of ethnic Hungarian minorities in the neighboring countries, combined with the ethnic Hungarian minority in Slovakia (concentrated in southern Slovakia and bordering Hungary—an area annexed by Hungary in 1938–1939) raising demands for group rights and territorial autonomy, provided fuel for Slovak fears. In addition, the international context led to further Slovak suspicions, in view of the perceptions of Western (especially German) complicity in the breakup of the former Yugoslavia, the assistance provided to Hungary by Germany (including in the military realm), and the Hungarian arming of Croat militia just before the breakup of Yugoslavia.

Civil-Military Relations in the Slovak Republic

The different views of the military and the state-society relationship in Slovakia than in the Czech Republic are summed up in Article 25 of the Slovak constitution: "The defense of the Slovak Republic is a matter of honor for each citizen." The extreme nationalist party, the SNS, has had a special interest in military issues, and because of its participation in the government, it has had a prominent role in shaping the building of the Slovak military. Rather than attempting to humble the military, the new Slovak civilian leadership has approached the military as an important national institution and a symbol of the Slovak state.

In creating a new military institution, Slovakia has faced much greater challenges than has the Czech Republic. As part of the Warsaw Pact and its anti-NATO orientation, almost all Czechoslovak armed forces were stationed in the Czech lands (and mostly in Bohemia). Only some reserve and training units were stationed in Slovakia, and other than a few Soviet bases, there was little infrastructure to support military units there. When the Czech Republic became a sovereign state, the existing Czechoslovak units simply became Czech units. The Czechoslovak ministry of defense became the Czech ministry of defense. But in Slovakia everything had to be put together from scratch. A further complication resulted from the country's financial situation. Because of Slovakia's weaker economy, the defense budget was more constrained than in the Czech Republic. Consequently, the Slovaks have had to accomplish more with fewer resources.

Because of the need to build the military and the different orientation of the political coalition in Slovakia than in the Czech Republic, the Slovak personnel policy in the military also differed from that in the Czech Republic. One, the Slovaks needed personnel to build the military, and because of the limited military presence in Slovakia, they were willing to take in officers who could not serve in the Czech armed forces because of the verification campaigns. Two, the Slovak coalition contained many people who had a Communist past (as exemplified by Meciar himself), and it was more forgiving of such people. The Czechoslovak policy of legally barring people with a Communist past from public office was abandoned in Slovakia (unlike in the Czech Republic), and if an ethnic Slovak former political officer wanted to transfer to the Slovak military from the Czech lands, few questions were asked. No verification campaigns took place in the Slovak armed forces.

Personnel policy took a different form in Slovakia. Led by SNS (and the ASV), the Slovak nationalists attempted initially to play a crucial role in forming the Slovak armed forces and in preventing the evolution of the Slovak military along the same lines as the Czech military. Thus, in late 1992 and early 1993, the Slovak nationalists tried to limit the outflow of ethnic Slovak officers from the Czech lands to Slovakia by threatening them and forcing them to make a quick decision on whether to move to Slovakia or not. When Meciar appointed the retired general Andrejcak (and the last Czechoslovak defense minister) as the first Slovak defense minister, the SNS quit the coalition in protest, for the SNS saw Andrejcak as an example of a Slovak polluted by "Czechoslovakism."

In 1993 and early 1994, because HZDS still contained centrist elements, the Slovak leadership approved a defense doctrine that did not point to a specific adversary and expressed interest in joining Western security structures. These policies became more pronounced during the tenure of Moravcik government. Under the first true Slovak civilian (not a recently retired officer) defense minister, Pavol Kanis from the socialist coalition, the Slovak defense doctrine was revised to stress more strongly NATO membership as a fundamental security goal. But that goal was watered down with the return of Meciar to power at the end of 1994. The new civilian defense minister, Jan Sitek, from the SNS, has placed less emphasis on NATO than his predecessor.

The SNS exemplifies a corporatist outlook, seeing the nation as an organic group, linked by linguistic-cultural traits, and viewing ethnicity as something that is predetermined. It sees the group as more important than the individual. In a throwback to another era, the SNS also glorifies the military as an embodiment of the martial traits of the nation. In view of the anti-Hungarian views embodied in Slovak nationalism, the presence of an SNS defense minister seems to have led to some anti-Hungarian aspects in personnel training in the Slovak military. In this sense, the Slovak military has taken on an implicit outlook of Hungary as the adversary.

Such views would have been even stronger had it not been for the tension that has emerged between the top two civilian officials in the defense ministry, Sitek and Jozef Gajdos, the State Secretary at the Ministry of Defense and an HZDS appointee. The rivalry between the two has led to indecision on a number of major military issues. The rivalry has combined with the power struggle between the General Staff and the Defense Ministry over the scope of responsibilities. The General Staff, physically separate from the Defense Ministry (in Trencin, 100 miles north of Bratislava), was established first, in place of the old Czechoslovak Army Command East. Initially, the General Staff played a critical role in setting up the Slovak military, and it has not been willing to cede some of its responsibilities to the civilian-controlled ministry of defense even once the ministry was established.[17] The political instability in Slovakia has not made the military any more eager to be under civilian control. Sitek, as befitting his SNS corporatist orientations and the perception that the military should be in full control of the defense sphere, has given the military leadership a good deal of leeway, with his role limited to making sure that funds are available and that a proper "martial-patriotic" spirit exists in the armed forces. But Gajdos, as befitting the more centrist if populist outlook of HZDS, has been more interested in subordinating the military to the political authorities. In effect, the intracoalition tensions have drawn the military into the political rivalries in Slovakia. The end result has been a mixed system of corporatist and liberal models as far as the role of the armed forces in the society is concerned.

Despite the higher popular esteem for the military in Slovakia than in the Czech Republic, the budget squeeze has been a tremendous constraint on the development of the Slovak armed forces. Since Slovakia did not emerge out of its post-transition recession until 1994–1995, the funds to build a Slovak military have not been available. In view of the basic problems still faced by the Slovak armed forces, their operational effectiveness remains questionable. The lack of funds has delayed the planned Slovak transition to achieve compatibility with the NATO forces. Although the Slovak military had prepared reform and restructuring plans much like those prepared by the Czechs, it has not been able to implement them. The planned force levels of the Slovak military are to be approximately 35,000 troops, organized in brigades and with NATO-compatible weapons, and backed up by a territorial militia. But the military remains organized into divisions and regiments and there is not even a prospect of any procurement or modification of weapons toward NATO compatibility. The lack of funds also has driven Slovakia to obtain some weapons from Russia in a noncash transaction, a move that both Poland and the Czech Republic have avoided because of the complications it poses for NATO membership. In exchange for some Soviet-era debts, Slovakia obtained a dozen MiG-29s (an earlier similar deal by Hungary probably played a part in the Slovak decision). In addition, Slovakia has secured further cooperation with Russia in the defense industry. The fact that Meciar exploited the problems of the Slovak defense industry for his own political ends also seems to have played a part in the continuing ties with Russia. The choices put into question NATO membership and eventual integration into Western structures.

The Slovak military faces problems of a fundamental nature. It has become the subject of political infighting over the nature of the military's role in the society while still at a formative stage.[18] The tensions also extend to intramilitary institutional rivalries. Consequently, the civilian leadership shares responsibility with the military in the realm of defense—a mixture of corporatist and liberal models of state-society relations. This confusion in the civilian sphere is complicated by the military's own effort to define itself in relation to different models of civil-military relations. Although the military leadership shares the legacy of the Communist model (unlike the Czech military, some in the Slovak military have a strong Communist background), with its separation of the military and political spheres and clear civilian dominance over the military, they have also been exposed to the liberal model in the initial transition in Czechoslovakia. Thus the leadership also recognizes the benefits of the liberal model (protection of the military's corporate interests in a situation of parliamentary support and popular approval through democratic processes). Moreover, the military's effort to define its relation to the state is complicated by the degree of alienation and even disgust exhibited by the professional military at the bickering among the politicians and its adverse effect on the military (wasting of resources, the failure to address key decisions, favoritism in the promotion process). This is compounded by the negative feedback regarding the country's internal instability that Slovak military leaders are sometimes exposed to when they attend NATO-sponsored meetings as part of the PfP process.

In short, the military is dissatisfied with the political instability, seeing it as a threat to the security of the country. Yet, although the military is not happy with the situation, it is very weak in terms of resources and funding. Moreover, it still exhibits the Communist era attitudes of shunning involvement in politics. Does all this mean that the relationship is civilian dominated? Yes, with some qualifications, in that the country's political instability has confused the direction of security policy. Politicians can't agree on where to go both in terms of the country's security orientation and in establishing an appropriate model of civil-military relations. Ultimately the problem resides in the fact that the parliamentary system itself is still only in its formative stages and much is still undecided in the civilian arena.

Regional Relations

The Slovak political coalitions that have governed since setting up the country have had predominantly an industrial-labor base, interested in protecting certain sectors of industry (and keeping it under state control) and catering to the interests of workers. Other than the short-lived non-Meciar period in 1994 (which tried to represent a broader range of interests), the coalition has had mixed views toward transnational forces and toward the integration of the country into international structures. It has gone along with CEFTA, but it does not envision Slovakia becoming a trading state. The coalition wants the impossible: benefits of EU membership without giving up the industries that cannot function in the EU. This has led to guarded views of Poland and the Czech Republic. Based on perceptions of disputed territory and on the exclusivist nature of the Slovak state, Hungary has been perceived as a potential adversary.

Slovak bilateral relations with the Czech Republic have the form of "special relations" because of the contacts between officials in the two countries, though the ties have been plagued by irritants. Although bilateral relations with Ukraine are free of major problems, some fears about the evolution of Ukraine remain, mostly in the context of political and economic uncertainties in Ukraine and the spillover problems they might cause for Slovakia. There is also an ethnic aspect to Slovak-Ukrainian relations, since Slovak policy has been supportive of the mobilization of Ruthenians inhabiting eastern Slovakia as a separate ethnic group. The Ukrainian government has pursued an opposite policy regarding the much larger Ruthenian population in the area of Ukraine bordering Slovakia. While not a major bilateral problem, the issue has become an irritant in Slovak-Ukrainian relations.

The Slovak leadership perceives Russia as a potential ally, though it recognizes the negative aspects in regional relations and relations with the EU and NATO countries if that were to be adopted as a formal policy. Russian opposition to NATO enlargement is of little concern to the Slovak leadership, since Slovak chances to enter the alliance are limited and the Russian role in preventing a potential Hungarian challenge to southern Slovakia remains an ace in the hole for the Slovaks. Russian political evolution presents only limited concern to the Slovak leadership in view of the shared outlooks in the ruling coalitions (protectionist and populist) in both countries.

The instability in the Slovak political sphere has meant that the Slovak military has been able to play off the various political actors and establish a significant autonomous zone for itself. As the option of NATO membership seems ever more distant (even though it remains desirable to the Slovak military), the identification of the neighboring state—Hungary—as an adversary brings up some ways in which the military can gain access to more resources (which it desperately needs). Yet, the military faces fundamental conflicts of interest in identifying threats. On the one hand, it has favorable relations with Hungary at the bilateral military level (the legacy of Warsaw Pact era ties and the more recent NATO-sponsored meetings and the Visegrad cooperation), and it does not greatly believe that Hungary constitutes a real threat to Slovak security. The military is also wary of the long-term negative consequences of characterizing Hungary as a threat—difficulties in joining NATO, being an outcast in the region, and eventually creating a real threat to the country. On the other hand, identifying Hungary as an adversary would lead to an increase in resources for the Slovak military. Such a funding increase is essential to gaining entry into NATO that is currently difficult to obtain because of the country's political instability. And, in any event, a funding increase on the basis of a Hungarian threat would be counterproductive to the goal of NATO accession. Nonetheless, the mistrust of Hungary remains at the popular level and is exploited by the ruling coalition. Moreover, the probability of an earlier Hungarian entry into NATO and the consequent greater modernization of the Hungarian armed forces magnifies the Slovak threat perceptions. Yet, for a number of reasons, such as the necessity not to alienate NATO or Slovakia's other central European neighbors, the identification of Hungary as a threat has to remain implicit.

Because of its financial situation, the Slovak military has shown more reluctance than the Czech or Polish militaries to embark on post–Cold War missions, preferring to limit its involvement in peacekeeping operations and not being eager to spend the resources required to participate at a higher level in PfP activities. The actions make sense from the standpoint of the formative stage of the Slovak military as well as a focus on more traditional (state defense) missions. In view of the corporatist outlook in Slovakia, the role of a nation-protector (with the nation interpreted in an exclusivist fashion) allows long-term viability for the military as an institution in Slovakia. Because of the mixture of liberal and corporatist inclinations in Slovakia, paying lip service to NATO membership probably will continue, but it will lack the determination of the Czech efforts to join the alliance. Moreover, the military does not want to alienate Russia; it does not have the condescending attitude toward Russia held, for example, by the Polish military. Hence, greater reliance on Russia and on its own resources increasingly looms as the likely, though not all that preferable, option.

CONCLUSION

The cases of Czechoslovakia, the Czech Republic, and Slovakia in the post-1989 period illustrate the divergent paths of post-Communist politics and the development of different forms of civil-military relations. The Czech case represents a situation in which the military retains only a minor role in domestic politics. The establishment of civilian control has allowed the Czech leadership to implement its policy of rapid integration into the international economy. Only states that could conceivably put obstacles in the path of Czech integration are considered potential adversaries. Moreover, the Czech military has put in place a reform plan that clearly bases the future security of the country on Western security institutions, such as NATO.

In contrast, in Slovakia, civil-military relations have been by influenced by the country's political instability and the absence of a consensus on the proper role of the military in the society. Slovakia appears to be still trying to come to grips with its independence and to establish its regional identity. This process has been complicated by the integrative trends in the West and the general discrediting of thinking about security in strictly national terms in Europe. There is discord in the process as pro-integrative forces exist uneasily alongside corporatist and nationalist elements. The military has been torn between the poles. It has tried to protect its autonomous status to prevent itself from being drawn in on the side of one of the domestic political actors. As a result, pro-Western integrationist elements, narrow national and nationalist-based perceptions, as well as reluctance to abandon ties to Russia all seem to exist in Slovak foreign and security policy.

In general, the cases bear out the main elements of David Mares's outline regarding the role of civil-military relations in shaping threat perceptions and regional relations (see Chapter 1). Yet the analysis also yields two insights regarding these relationships. First, the Czech case illustrates that an important variable is the level of esteem the military enjoys in society. In democratic countries where the military is viewed as an unnecessary and irrelevant institution, the military may have little influence in identifying threats to the country; the dominant civilian coalition is largely in charge of such processes. Second, the Slovak case suggests that political instability may motivate the military to seek autonomy from civilians and may complicate its effort to identify potential international threats and opportunities.

In conclusion, the applicability of the Czech and Slovak cases to democratizing countries in Latin America and southeast Asia seems limited. But the parallels that do exist, such as democratization and the extent of the military's autonomy, may offer some useful insights. Moreover, the Czechoslovak example helps to illustrate how states, even when formerly unified, can establish very different models of civil-military relations and can have widely different perceptions of the regional environment.

NOTES

1. For background on pre–World War II Czechoslovak history, see Joseph Rothschild, *East Central Europe Between the Two World Wars* (Seattle: University of Washington Press, 1974).

2. Condoleezza Rice, *The Soviet Union and the Czechoslovak Army, 1948–1983: Uncertain Allegiance* (Princeton: Princeton University Press, 1984).

3. This was a second change in the country's official name in 1990, since in March, in recognition of the deposing of the Communist regime, the name had been changed to the Czechoslovak Federal Republic (dropping "Socialist").

4. Gordon Wightman, "The Czechoslovak Parliamentary Elections of 1992," *Electoral Studies* 12, no. 1 (March 1993):83–86; Sharon Wolchik, "The Repluralization of Politics in Czechoslovakia," *Communist and Post-Communist Studies* 26, no. 4 (December 1993): 412–431.

5. Herbert Kitschelt, "The Formation of Party Systems in East Central Europe," *Politics and Society* 20, no. 1 (March 1992):7–50.

6. The problems of the Slovak defense industry became a symbol of the supposed Czech domination because of the initial policies pursued by the Czechoslovak government. The former dissidents who came to power in 1990 were led by intellectuals with strong pacifist outlooks (exemplified by Havel). Few of them had any experience or background in foreign and defense security issues and their initial policies were idealistic to the point of being naive. In recognition of the previous role that Communist Czechoslovakia had played as a supplier of arms to many of the world's terrorists and rogue states, the new government arbitrarily stopped all arms sales. However, because the defense industry was concentrated to a greater extent in Slovakia than in the Czech lands (and the Slovak defense industry also faced greater problems of adaptability to market conditions), the impact was much greater in Slovakia. For more information, see Thomas S. Szayna, "Defense Conversion in East Europe," *East-Central Economies in Transition, Study Papers* of the Joint Economic Committee, United States Congress (Washington, DC: U.S. Government Printing Office, 1994), pp. 133–146.

7. On this point in a comparative perspective, see Zoltan D. Barany, *Soldiers and Politics in Eastern Europe, 1945–1990: The Case of Hungary* (New York: St. Martin's Press, 1993), pp. 155–159.

8. For more information, see Thomas S. Szayna, *The Military in Post-Communist Czechoslovakia* (Santa Monica, CA: RAND,1992); Thomas S. Szayna and James B. Steinberg, *Civil-Military Relations and National Security Thinking in Czechoslovakia: A Conference Report* (Santa Monica, CA: RAND,1992).

9. For more detailed information, see the chapter on Czechoslovakia in Jeffrey Simon, *Central European Civil-Military Relations and NATO Expansion,* McNair Paper 39, Institute for National Strategic Studies (Washington, DC: National Defense University, April 1995), pp. 111–128.

10. Szayna, *The Military in Post-Communist Czechoslovakia,* pp. 72–79.

11. For a full elaboration of Czech national interests, as envisioned by an advisory group to the Czech leadership on foreign policy, see *Czech National Interests* (Prague: Institute for International Relations, 1993).

12. For more detailed information, see Simon, *Central European Civil-Military Relations and NATO Expansion,* pp. 129–139.

13. For more information on the extent of reform of the Czech armed forces, see Stephane Lefebvre, "The Army of the Czech Republic: A Status Report," *The Journal of Slavic Military Studies* 8, no. 4 (December 1995):718–751.

14. For a full exploration of threats to the Czech Republic, see "The Security Policy of the Czech Republic," *Study Papers,* no. 3 (Prague: Institute for International Relations,

1994); Emil Antusak, "European Security and Its Influence upon the Development of Military Art," *European Security* 4, no. 2 (Summer 1995):306–317.

15. The situation is not unusual, in that all of the former Communist states in central Europe with the exception of the Czech Republic have had problems with rivalry between the president and the prime minister. Thomas A. Baylis, "Presidents Versus Prime Ministers: Shaping Executive Authority in Eastern Europe," *World Politics* 48, no. 3 (April 1996):297–323.

16. John Fitzmaurice, "The Slovak Election of September 1994," *Electoral Studies* 14, no. 2 (June 1995):203–206; Samuel Abraham, "Early Elections in Slovakia: A State of Deadlock," *Government and Opposition* 30, no. 1 (Winter 1995):86–100.

17. For more detailed information, see the chapter on Slovakia in Simon, *Central European Civil-Military Relations and NATO Expansion*, pp. 141–151.

18. Of course, such a development has been common to most of the former Communist countries in central Europe though its intensity has varied from country to country; Thomas S. Szayna and F. Stephen Larrabee, *East European Military Reform After the Cold War: Implications for the United States* (Santa Monica, CA: RAND, 1995).

CHAPTER SEVEN

■

The Restructuring of Civil-Military Relations in Poland Since 1989

Mark Kramer

Over the past forty years, Western scholars have acquired a much better understanding of civil-military relations. Elaborate theories have been derived from the experiences of Western industrialized democracies (including Israel), Third World military regimes, and "indigenous" Communist states such as the Soviet Union and China. For Eastern European countries, however, most of this theoretical work has been of little relevance. Theories that applied reasonably well to the Soviet Union could not readily be adapted to explain civil-military relations in countries where Communism was imposed from outside and maintained by the threat of Soviet military intervention.[1]

Similar analytical problems have arisen in the post-Communist era. Western analysts have tried to discern patterns of civil-military relations in newly democratizing Third World and south European countries, but this work has dealt almost entirely with former military regimes and thus has little bearing on the East European states. In 1989, East European members of the Warsaw Pact were not military regimes but externally dominated Communist systems. This chapter's analysis of civil-military relations in post-Communist Poland draws on existing concepts where possible, but also highlights unique aspects that appeared after the demise of Communism.

The chapter has three parts. The first develops an analytical framework presenting concepts useful for the analysis of the internal and external dynamics of the civil-military relationship. Three sets of hypotheses about changes in civil-military relations in Eastern Europe after 1989 are derived from recent literature about political and economic institutions and principal-agent theory, as well as the points raised by David Mares in his introductory essay.

The second part examines the period between 1989 and 1995 to show how a series of post-Communist governments in Poland sought to expunge the military
legacy of the Communist era while attempting to benefit from the popularity that
the Polish armed forces have traditionally enjoyed. This section explains why, despite turbulence and uncertainty in civil-military relations, the "prerogatives" of
the army in post-Communist Poland are highly circumscribed. The section also
considers the effects of external actors, especially the North Atlantic Treaty Organization (NATO), on civil-military dynamics within Poland. Recent changes in
Poland's civil-military relations and the implications for regional security are discussed in the conclusion along with findings about political institutions in post-
Communist societies.

ANALYTICAL FRAMEWORK AND HYPOTHESES

The institutional roles and interests, or "prerogatives," of the military are the areas
in which "the military as an institution assumes that [it has] an acquired right or
privilege, formal or informal, to exercise effective control over [the army's] internal governance, to play a role within extramilitary areas within the state apparatus, or even to structure relationships between the state and political or civil society."[2] The scale of military "prerogatives" is a continuum: At the higher end, the
military is involved in a wide range of activities normally reserved for civilian authorities, such as public administration, law and order, primary education, and
economic decisionmaking. In some instances, this simply amounts to "military
role expansion," but in more extreme cases, the army displaces the civilian government and rules the country.[3] By contrast, at the low end, the military remains
under full civilian control and does not intrude into civilian functions. Most
armies in Latin America, Africa, and South Asia fall in the moderate to high
ranges of the continuum, whereas most armies in North America and Western
Europe are at the low end.

The Polish army enjoyed a high level of prerogatives during much of the inter-
war period, especially after Marshal Jozef Pilsudski launched a coup d'état in May
1926. A full-fledged military regime was entrenched in Poland between 1935 and
1939. Under Communist rule the prerogatives of the Polish military shrank, with a
few notable exceptions: In 1956 the Polish army violently suppressed worker
protests in Poznan; in 1968 the Polish leader Wladyslaw Gomulka tried to gain
support from the military against his political rivals; and in 1970 the army fired on
striking workers along the Baltic coast. In the early 1980s, martial law was declared
in Poland and military officers were given national and local administrative posts,
marking the high point in the Polish army's prerogatives during the Communist
era. Nevertheless, in no instance was there a return to the situation of the mid- to
late 1930s. Moreover, the expansion of the Polish military's roles under Communism was only temporary (though to a lesser extent in 1983–1989) and was carried
out with the full approval of the Communist authorities. Throughout, the Polish

army remained under tight civilian control, albeit the control of a single political party that in turn was accountable to a preponderant external actor.

The emergence of a new pattern of civil-military relations under Communism imposed from without suggests that changes of similar magnitude would occur during the transition from that form of Communism to a sovereign multiparty democracy. Hypotheses derived from theories of political and economic institutions,[4] including principal-agent theory, about civil-military relations in post-Communist Eastern Europe can be grouped around three broad themes: expected changes in principal-agent relationships; potential obstacles to the principal's objectives; and the likely impact of external circumstances. The terms "principal" and "agent"—referring to the civilian government and the professional military, respectively—are used here to examine a civilian-led dominant-subordinate relationship discussed by Mares in this volume's introduction.

All principal-agent relationships are based on a formal or informal contract obligating the agent to act on behalf of, and in response to, the principal. The principal's authority to issue orders to the agent is usually derived from legal, political, administrative, or historical/cultural sources. Because the agent is expected to comply with the principal's orders on all matters covered by the agency contract, these issues are usually described as being within the agent's "zone of acceptance."[5] In the case of civil-military relations, the zone of acceptance encompasses the norm of civilian control over the military, the basic guidelines for military policy, and specific aspects of military affairs. For example, civilian leaders (i.e., the principals) determine whether the country goes to war, and they exercise at least some guidance over how the war is fought. Military officers (i.e., the agents) are responsible for the prosecution of war. This same general type of principal-agent relationship applies to the full range of civil-military issues.

If the principals knew exactly what the agents were doing at all times and the agents knew exactly what the principals wanted, the agency relationship could be enforced relatively easily. Yet agents might try to gain undue latitude by exploiting divisions among the principals or by appealing to third parties outside the contractual relationship. Problems also are likely to arise from information asymmetries. Agents normally have detailed knowledge of their assigned tasks and of what they are actually doing (or have done), whereas the principals often know comparatively little about either matter.[6] For example, military officers have a better grasp of military strategy, logistics, weapons technology, and the status of the army than do most civilian leaders. These information asymmetries tend to give agents considerable leeway in fulfilling—or, possibly, circumventing—the principals' wishes. Some agents may be tempted to engage in opportunistic behavior, exploiting the information asymmetries for their own ends.[7] In exceptional cases, agents may openly defy the principals, reneging on key contractual obligations. To forestall opportunistic behavior by agents, the principals monitor agents. The more elaborate the monitoring, however, the more expensive and time-consuming it becomes. Moreover, intrusive monitoring may deprive agents of flexibility needed to complete their tasks. Hence, although information asymmetries can be mitigated, they are likely to persist in most agency relationships, leaving the way open for unauthorized actions.

Litigation is not always a feasible response to illicit behavior or an open challenge by the agent. In some cases, punitive measures (e.g., the dismissal of insubordinate officers) are likely to be politically costly, unpleasant, and even dangerous.[8] Yet, failure to punish infractions or overt challenges also creates serious problems, especially if it tempts other agents into illicit acts. If further transgressions occur and the principals do not forcefully reassert their authority, they risk undermining the agency relationship. Over the long term, then, the only way principals can ensure compliance with the agency contract is by demonstrating "a credible commitment to punish" noncompliance.[9]

This general framework, supplemented by other key tenets of the institutionalist literature and by considerations about the external environment, suggests some hypotheses about civil-military relations in post-Communist Eastern Europe.

Expected Changes in Principal-Agent Relationships

At an early stage of the transition, the political "winners" (i.e., the new civilian elites) will adopt legal and constitutional reforms and personnel changes to ensure that the military will serve (or at least not act against) the interests of the new system.

To forestall opportunistic behavior by military officers, the civilian authorities are likely to seek tighter control of the defense ministry by appointing a civilian minister, by increasing civilian representation within the ministry, and by establishing independent oversight mechanisms.[10]

If military forces during the Communist era were involved in the suppression of internal unrest, a broad consensus is likely to emerge during the post-Communist transition that the army should be used only against external threats.[11] This consensus should provide an additional check against increased military prerogatives.

Once changes in civil-military relations are codified, they will be difficult (though not impossible) to reverse because (1) key actors acquire a vested interest in maintaining those arrangements; (2) the transaction costs of undoing the changes are excessively high; (3) elites are uncertain whether new arrangements will be more desirable than extant institutions; (4) patterns of civil-military relations become bound up with culture, tradition, and custom; or (5) bureaucratic inertia sets in.

If interservice rivalries emerge (or intensify) during the post-Communist transition (perhaps because of disagreements about how to apportion cuts in troop strength and budgets), civilian authorities can use these splits to tighten their grip over the military establishment as a whole.

As a deterrent to unauthorized behavior, civilian leaders will punish transgressions, thus demonstrating a credible commitment to enforcement.

Potential Obstacles to Achieving Principal's Objectives

If the lines of authority for civil-military relations are left ambiguous during the early transition period (whether deliberately or otherwise), contending civilian leaders (or organs of government) will vie for support from the army leadership.

The jockeying among civilian authorities (including executive-legislative disputes) will enable military officials to seek greater budgetary outlays and engage in other forms of opportunistic behavior.

If no authoritative mechanism exists to adjudicate intragovernmental disputes, opportunistic behavior by military officers is likely to go unpunished and to recur, with the result that military prerogatives will increase.

If popular esteem for the army is high, senior officers will have greater leeway to expand military prerogatives.

Hypotheses Concerning the External Environment

The absence of perceived imminent external threats should facilitate reductions in military force levels and defense spending.

When serious external threats are perceived to exist, however, military prerogatives are more likely to increase.

If civilian elites are seeking country membership in NATO, they will be more inclined to keep a check on military prerogatives, in accordance with alliance norms and expectations.

POST-COMMUNIST TRANSFORMATION

Poland's subordination to Soviet hegemony for nearly forty-five years after World War II denied the Polish Communist regime any hint of legitimacy (aside from a very brief period in the autumn 1956), creating an artificial—and ultimately unsustainable—structure of civil-military relations.[12] Six years after the lifting of martial law, Communism collapsed in Poland. Unrest in the mid- to late 1980s culminated in a wave of strikes in the spring and summer of 1988, forcing major concessions by the authorities. In early 1989, the Polish government sought to allay public discontent by entering into "roundtable" negotiations with leaders of the still-banned Solidarity movement. Talks produced a historic agreement in April 1989 that provided for partly free parliamentary elections in June. Not surprisingly, Solidarity gained a crushing victory in the elections. This humiliating defeat of the Polish United Workers' Party (PZPR) spurred calls for the formation of a Solidarity-led government. In August 1989, Polish Communist officials agreed to relinquish power. The advent of a Solidarity-led government in September 1989, under prime minister Tadeusz Mazowiecki, began Poland's post-Communist transformation.

Soon after Mazowiecki took office, the new civilian elites began making sweeping military reforms, which continued for throughout the 1990s under a succession of governments. Force restructuring and personnel changes were not as drastic or rapid in Poland as in the Czech Republic, but the composition, management, and force posture of the Polish army were greatly altered. Moreover, Poland's realignment from the Warsaw Pact toward NATO was as far reaching as that of Hungary and the Czech Republic. In all these respects, expectations of fundamental institutional change were amply borne out. Even so, Poland did not always enjoy a harmonious civil-military relationship in the first half of the 1990s. The army was no longer beholden to a single party and external actor, but political scandals and military interference in politics still occurred surprisingly often. Although civilian control of the military was never in doubt—despite exaggerated claims to the contrary both inside and outside Poland—institutional change often did not go as far as expected.

Constraints on Institutional Change

The setting in which institutional change and formation takes place can often be decisive.[13] Military reform in Poland was impeded by four circumstances that either inhibited major changes in existing institutions or slowed the formation of new ones.

Personnel Holdovers.   The deal permitting Solidarity to form a non-Communist government in August–September 1989 stipulated that key national security organs—the presidency, the national defense ministry, and the internal affairs ministry—were to be left under the control of the PZPR. Wojciech Jaruzelski continued to serve as head of state (in his newly created role as "president"), General Florian Siwicki retained his post as national defense minister, and General Czeslaw Kiszczak stayed on as internal affairs minister. These three positions were wrested from the PZPR's jurisdiction sooner than expected—Siwicki and Kiszczak were both removed in July 1990, and Jaruzelski stepped down in December 1990—but during the transition's crucial first year, Communist officials still . dominated the top layer of the national security apparatus.

Delay in Adopting a Constitution.   During the first seven years of the post-Communist transition, Poland failed to approve a full-fledged democratic constitution. A stopgap document, the "Small Constitution," was adopted in October 1992 as a temporary replacement for the country's Stalinist constitution of 1952.[14] Western scholars have disagreed about the desirability of a full-fledged constitution for economic reform.[15] There is little doubt, however, that a full-fledged constitution would have been beneficial for civil-military relations. Often a permanent constitutional framework is the only means of reducing ambiguity about lines of command. By specifying the duties and responsibilities of the president, prime minister, defense minister, and chief of the General Staff in war making, appointments, and other aspects of military policy, and by clarifying the division of functions between the executive and legislature, a well-designed constitution can minimize the likelihood of serious splits among civilian principals. By contrast, the lack of a constitution will increase the likelihood of disputes among principals and make it far more difficult to resolve those disputes. It also may tempt military agents to align with certain principals or to play the principals off against one another. This is precisely what happened in Poland in the first half of the 1990s.

In the absence of a new constitution, civil-military relations in Poland from 1989 through May 1997 were governed primarily by the 1967 Law on Universal Military Duty and by the Small Constitution. The 1967 law, amended some twenty times over the years, was of little importance so long as the PZPR held supreme power.[16] The law imposed vague—though potentially far-reaching— limits on the military-related duties of the head of state (known until April 1989 as the "head of the Council of State," largely a figurehead post during the Communist era). The law obligated the head of state to uphold national sovereignty and security by directing the armed forces both in peacetime and in war, but it required him to consult with the minister of national defense. Similarly, the head of state had responsibility for appointing the chief of the Polish General Staff, but the appointment was at the recommendation of the national defense minister. Under a 1983 amendment, the head of state chaired the State Defense Committee (KOK). The other members of the committee, including the national defense minister, could in principle outvote him.[17]

The potential significance of these provisions became evident in the summer of 1989 when the PZPR finally agreed to relinquish its "leading role" in Polish society. This development ensured that the newly created "presidency" (a post established through a constitutional amendment in April 1989) would be vested with genuine power, rather than simply being a tool of the Communist party. After Mazowiecki's government took office, the Polish parliament set out to remedy the vagueness of the 1967 law and to establish a clearer demarcation of the president's and government's responsibilities vis-à-vis the army. However, because Jaruzelski was president, many legislators wanted to avoid doing anything that would strengthen presidential power. As a result, the contours of civil-military relations were left even murkier than before.

The Small Constitution, though a vast improvement over Poland's previous constitution, was surprisingly ambiguous and convoluted in its treatment of national defense and did not alleviate the problem. On a few issues the document was relatively straightforward. Article 35 gave the president broad leadership over the armed forces and authorized him to choose a supreme military commander in time of war. Articles 36 and 37 entitled the president to introduce martial law or a state of emergency. On other matters, however, presidential powers were less clear-cut. The president was given discretion to appoint the chief of the General Staff, but he was obliged to solicit ministerial recommendations for other top military appointments. The document failed to specify what should be done if the president and national defense minister were at odds. A similar gap was evident in Article 61, which required the prime minister to "seek the president's opinion" before appointing the ministers of national defense, internal affairs, and foreign affairs, without establishing a means to resolve impasses that might arise. Nor did the document fully spell out the parliament's role in military affairs. Overall, the Small Constitution strengthened the president's hand in military policy but left ample room for jurisdictional disputes.

The 1995 "Law on the Post of National Defense Minister" only partially resolved the ambiguities in civil-military relations.[18] Article 7.2 of the new law stipulated that the defense minister must be a civilian, and Article 7.1 explicitly subordinated the chief of the General Staff to the minister, thus precluding further infighting of the sort that had marked Lech Walesa's five-year presidency. It also gave the defense minister direct jurisdiction over military intelligence organs (the Military Information Services, or WSI), which since 1994 had reported solely to the chief of the General Staff. On other matters, however, the law did nothing to eliminate the potential for conflict. In particular, it left to the forthcoming constitution (adopted in May 1997) to specify how the minister, the chief of the General Staff, and other senior ministerial officials should be appointed.

All these ambiguities and lacunae might not have mattered if the president and cabinet had remained on good terms. But amidst the turmoil of Polish politics in the early and mid-1990s, the lack of a full-fledged constitution became crucial to civil-military relations. It deprived civilian leaders (i.e., the principals) of the most reliable way to mediate their differences, while giving greater leeway to military officers (i.e., the agents).

Political Turbulence.   Mazowiecki's government ended in mid-December 1990, one month after Lech Walesa soundly defeated him in the initial round of Poland's first-ever presidential election. Walesa easily won the second (and final) round of the election on December 9. Mazowiecki declined Walesa's offer to continue as prime minister. A succession of short-lived governments proved unable to enact legislation and personnel changes to eliminate the remaining military vestiges of the Communist era. The first government, headed by Jan Krzysztof Bielecki, proved relatively successful in domestic economic and political reform, but it devoted less attention to military affairs. Bielecki did follow up on Mazowiecki's earlier decision and established an interministerial reform commission on national defense, chaired by the then-head of the Office of Ministerial Council, Krzysztof Zabinski. The State Defense Committee (under Walesa) and the government approved its final report, which called for the civilianization of the defense ministry, including appointment of a civilian as defense minister; the restructuring of the army; the rationalization of Poland's defense industry; and the establishment of effective parliamentary oversight.[19]

Nevertheless, implementation of military reform confronted important obstacles. The Solidarity movement as a whole was increasingly riven by disagreements and personal rivalries, which slowed the fulfillment of the Zabinski Commission's recommendations. In addition, because 65 percent of the 460 seats in the Sejm had been reserved for PZPR candidates in the 1989 elections, Communist deputies were able to keep the lower house from adopting measures supported by the government and the Senate (both of which were controlled by Solidarity). However, Walesa forced the rescheduling of parliamentary elections, moving them up from 1994 to 1991, which ended Bielecki's government.

The inconclusive results and exceptionally low voter turnout (43.2 percent) in 1991 ushered in growing political turmoil as twenty-nine political parties won seats in the Sejm. An unstable coalition government emerged under Jan Olszewski, who heeded the Zabinski Commission's recommendation by appointing the first civilian national defense minister, Jan Parys. Parys expressed interest in carrying out drastic military reforms and personnel changes, but his abrasive manner and penchant for infighting prevented that and antagonized many within the military. By the end of his four-month tenure at the ministry, Parys began making highly publicized—albeit unfounded—charges that Walesa and his allies in the military were planning a coup d'état.[20] Olszewski removed Parys, but the government was unable to survive.

The advent of Hanna Suchocka's government in summer 1992 and the reappointment of Janusz Onyszkiewicz as defense minister (a post to which he was first appointed in the brief government of Waldemar Pawlak a few weeks before Suchocka took over) restored a modicum of political stability to Poland over the next year, bringing hope that military restructuring could be pushed further. Onyszkiewicz, like his predecessors, refrained from making wholesale replacements of senior military personnel, yet he expanded civilian control over the defense ministry, introduced new reforms in military budgeting and the army's force structure, and issued two key defense documents, "The Principles of Polish Security Policy" and "The Security Policy and Defense Strategy of the Polish Republic," which were approved in November 1992.[21] Both provided a valuable framework for changes in the army that had already occurred and for additional measures implemented in late 1992 and 1993.

Nevertheless, after just one year, Suchocka's government was derailed by labor unrest and political skirmishing between Walesa and other former Solidarity leaders. A no-confidence vote in May 1993 prompted Walesa to order the dissolution of parliament and call for new elections. Solidarity explicitly broke ranks with Walesa and lost overwhelmingly in the parliamentary elections in September 1993, failing to acquire the 5 percent threshold (set in 1993) needed to obtain representation in either house of parliament.[22] A coalition of leftist parties, including the former Communists (renamed the Democratic Left Alliance, or SLD) and the Polish

Peasants' Party (PSL), gained more than enough votes to form a new government, ushering in a new phase of Poland's transition. Earlier divisions between the president and the government, particularly during Olszewski's brief tenure, had caused upheaval in military reform and civil-military relations, and those divisions were bound to intensify with the emergence of a leftist government.

The relationship between Walesa and the SLD-PSL government was uneasy, but Prime Minister Pawlak initially tried to defuse the tension by giving Walesa broad discretion to appoint ministers of national defense, internal affairs, and foreign affairs. (Under Article 61 of the Small Constitution, Pawlak himself was entitled to make those appointments in consultation with the president.) Walesa's first nominee as defense minister was Piotr Kolodziejczyk, who had served in that same capacity in Mazowiecki's and Bielecki's governments when he was still an active military officer. Regarded as a firm ally of Walesa, the new defense minister soon found himself buffeted by a political tug-of-war between Walesa and Pawlak.[23] Walesa was determined to control military affairs rather than ceding partial jurisdiction to the government.

The political turbulence came to a head in late September 1994. Walesa claimed that the chief of the General Staff, General Tadeusz Wilecki, and other senior officers had expressed a lack of confidence in Kolodziejczyk.[24] Walesa insisted on the appointment of a new defense minister. Walesa's statements were motivated primarily by a desire to revive his sagging political fortunes by solidifying his grip over military policy. To the extent that military officers intervened in what seemed to be a political dispute, they did so purely at Walesa's behest, not at their own initiative. A parliamentary investigation exonerated senior officers of any wrongdoing and strongly criticized Walesa for his attempt to replace Kolodziejczyk by questionable means. The scandal surrounding the whole "Drawsko affair" (as this incident was called) gave Pawlak an opportunity to retaliate against Walesa by firing Kolodziejczyk. Pawlak then rejected Walesa's replacement, Zbigniew Okonski, and instead appointed an old-line Communist ideologue, Longin Pastusiak. This action, at a time when Poland was trying to burnish its candidacy for NATO membership, expedited the collapse of Pawlak's government. After several more weeks of political skirmishing, Walesa finally secured Pawlak's ouster.

The next Polish government, under prime minister Jozef Oleksy, agreed to Walesa's choice of Okonski, but tensions between the right-of-center president and the SLD-PSL coalition remained acute. An argument erupted between them in mid-1995 over which should exercise direct control over the military. This dispute went unresolved as political maneuvering gathered momentum in the 1995 presidential campaign. SLD leader Aleksander Kwasniewski's narrow victory over Walesa solidified the SLD's control over both the government (and parliament) and the presidency, ending the sharp governmental-presidential divide. Even so, the furor surrounding the "Oleksy affair" in early 1996—when Prime Minister Jozef Oleksy was forced to resign amidst allegations that he had been a Soviet and Russian spy—indicated that political stability in Poland was not yet at hand.[25]

Combined with the lack of a full-fledged constitution, the recurrent political infighting in Poland forestalled the resolution of most disputes about civil-military
relations.

Popularity of the Army. Even if Poland had not experienced political uncertainty and instability after 1989, it comes as little surprise that military restructuring in Poland would have been somewhat less drastic than in neighboring East
European states. Unlike in Hungary and the Czech Republic, where the armed
forces command very little public esteem, in Poland the army has enjoyed a privileged spot in society. Even during the darkest period of martial law in the early
1980s, the Polish army retained much of its popularity (though, admittedly, this
was probably because the ZOMO, rather than ordinary soldiers, carried out most
of the arrests and other repressive measures). After the collapse of Communism,
the army was by far the most popular institution in Poland, with approval ratings
consistently over 75 percent.[26] Only the police approached the army in public ad-
miration. Other institutions, including the Catholic Church and all political and
social organizations, ranked far behind, usually with approval ratings well below
50 percent. The military and the police were the only institutions in Polish society
whose popularity increased after the late 1980s. Thus, the Polish armed forces,
though certainly forced to adjust to the post-Communist era, were not under the
same pressure to carry out massive personnel changes and were not subjected to
the same withering criticism that the Hungarian and Czech armies encountered.

INSTITUTIONAL FORMATION AND REFORMATION

Despite the many constraints on institutional change, the Polish military establishment underwent sweeping reforms that nullified the full array of external and
internal control mechanisms from the Communist era. A discussion of categories
of institutional reform highlights both the importance of what was achieved and
the obstacles to even more drastic change.

Efforts to Establish Civilian Control of the Defense Ministry

During the Communist era, defense ministries in all the Warsaw Pact countries
were staffed exclusively by military officers. One primary aim of the early reforms
in Poland, as well as in Hungary and the Czech Republic, was to establish firm
civilian control over the defense ministry. Of the three countries, however, only the
Czech Republic made far-reaching progress along these lines. Although two civilians, Janusz Onyszkiewicz and Bronisław Komorowski, were appointed deputy defense ministers in Poland in April 1990, it was not until December 1991 that a civilian, Jan Parys, was placed in charge of the ministry and a third civilian deputy
minister was appointed. Far from expediting civilianization of the ministry, however, Parys's acrimonious four-month term temporarily slowed the process.

Following a two-month lull when Renuald Szeremetiew served as acting minister, former Deputy Minister Janusz Onyszkiewicz succeeded Parys. Onyszkiewicz had resigned in February 1992 to protest certain steps taken by Parys. Seeking to repair the damage and renew the drive for greater civilian control, Onyszkiewicz signed a directive in October 1992 that separated the military command structure, headed by the chief of the General Staff, from the defense ministry's administrative apparatus.[27] This change had been proposed as early as 1990 and won the endorsement of the Zabinski Commission in 1991; but the reorganization was delayed by ongoing political turmoil.[28] By spring 1993, the plan was in place to have civilians in charge of Polish defense policy, while military officers would be responsible mainly for implementing the decisions of civilian leaders. In practice, however, the civilianization of the ministry proved slow and superficial.

The main obstacle to the intended reforms was the dearth of civilians well versed in military affairs. The leading members of Solidarity (not to mention the rank and file) had not paid much attention to defense policy before 1989. Civilian defense ministers had a limited grasp of military affairs, which prevented them from exercising tight control over the ministry. Onyszkiewicz acknowledged as much when he signed the directive in October 1992. That order sparked complaints that the General Staff had "been granted undue power to bypass the defense minister," but Onyszkiewicz's successors (most of whom knew far less about defense policy than he did) had to adopt roughly the same approach.[29] In the process, they gave back to the General Staff several ministerial functions (officer training/education, military intelligence, defense budgeting, etc.) that had been placed under civilian control in 1990. In 1995 it even appeared that the ministry's civilian leadership might allow the General Staff to acquire primary responsibility for ties with NATO, a function previously handled by the civilian-led Department of Foreign Military Affairs.[30] Not until early 1996, when the new Law on the Post of National Defense Minister took effect, were these functions transferred back to the purview of civilians. New regulations for the defense ministry promulgated in July 1996 further cemented civilian control.[31]

Even after these changes, however, civilian ministers and deputy ministers still often deferred to the General Staff. Jerzy Milewski, a very influential national security official under both Walesa and Kwasniewski, argued that deference had gone too far: "Major problems arise because politicians still tend to be firmly convinced that defense and military issues are the domain of the military and that only military officers are experts on both the development of national defense policies and the implementation of them."[32] The experience of the early to mid-1990s showed that the appointment of civilians to head the defense ministry did not necessarily translate into full civilian control.

Serious obstacles to reform also existed at lower levels, where the civilian presence was minimal at best. Although the number of civilians slowly increased, most appointees were unable to deal with complex military issues and had to rely heavily on military officers for direction. Nor were civilian experts available outside the ministry to provide unofficial oversight of military affairs.

A further complication was posed by the role of the parliament's two National Defense Commissions (one in the Sejm, one in the Senate), which attempted to stake out a fixed position overseeing the military establishment. Initially, the twenty to twenty-five civilians who served on each commission knew little about military affairs and relied almost exclusively on the defense ministry's own information. They found, however, that military officers were not always eager to cooperate.[33] Despite these obstacles, members of the two commissions did gradually acquire reasonable expertise and were increasingly willing to encroach on the secrecy and prerogatives of the military. Although the parliament's influence on defense policy remained limited in the early and mid-1990s—what influence it did enjoy stemmed primarily from its budgetary authority—some precedents for legislative oversight were established, with the promise of a greater role in the future.

The faltering pace of civilianization in the defense ministry was due not only to the paucity of qualified civilians but also to resistance (mostly informal) on the part of some military officers. Although Polish officers never questioned the desirability of civilian control over the army per se, many were reluctant to turn over certain functions to nonmilitary personnel. As one senior officer explained, this stemmed primarily from concern that civilians were not up to the task of overseeing technical military issues: "The exercise of democracy by [civilian] organs must not be allowed to incapacitate the army or undermine what stems from its very special professionalism. The right to civilian, democratic control must not be interpreted as a one-way street. Those who want to exercise control must also be prepared to shoulder responsibility."[34]

It is not surprising that such concerns emerged when Parys was in office, but it is less clear why they persisted for so long afterwards. General Stanislaw Koziej of the Polish defense ministry acknowledged that at least some of the concerns expressed by military officers were unwarranted and were due mainly to engrained professional attitudes. Although Koziej emphasized that problems could have been avoided, he and other military officers argued that a smoothly functioning system could not take root while civilian principals were in acute conflict, as was the case until late 1995.[35] In this context, many officers found that they had greater leeway to forestall or defer unwanted changes, including proposals for rapid civilianization of the ministry.

Despite these sundry problems, the norm of civilian control of the military took firm hold in Poland in the early to mid-1990s. Comprehensive opinion surveys in late 1995 revealed that only 4 percent of respondents in Poland were favorably disposed to the idea of military rule—a remarkably low percentage if compared with the army's approval rating.[36] The same outlook was reflected in official circles. No one, either inside or outside the military, even hinted at the desirability of a Pilsudski-like coup. On the rare occasions when army officers became embroiled in political disputes, their involvement came at the behest of civilian leaders. For the most part, military commanders did their best to stay out of political struggles. Moreover, civilian leaders, despite their bickering, were not about to allow military prerogatives to return to the level of the pre-1989 period. Walesa may have argued that "military people should run the military," but he never suggested that military officers should run the government.

On the one notable occasion when a senior military officer, Colonel Wieslaw Rozbicki, openly challenged civilian authority, the government evinced its commitment to punish insubordination. In June 1994, Rozbicki argued that the government had erred in signing the Conventional Forces in Europe (CFE) Treaty because it had weakened the army, and he urged the transfer of military intelligence organs (WSI) from the civilian apparatus to the General Staff on the grounds that it was "better for national security if a civilian minister does not receive full information provided by the WSI."[37] Shortly thereafter Rozbicki was fired. To the extent that civilian control of the army depends on a "credible commitment to punish" unauthorized increases in military prerogatives, the Rozbicki incident both signaled and helped guarantee the entrenchment of civilian supremacy.

Detailed investigations were also conducted into the Drawsko affair in 1994 and into reports in mid-1995 that a warrant officer in Siemiatycze had collected fifteen signatures endorsing Aleksander Kwasniewski for president. In both cases, the threat of disciplinary action and the strong criticism expressed by the Polish media helped demarcate the bounds of acceptable conduct for military personnel. The dismissal of Rozbicki had shown that outright insubordination would be severely punished, and these other episodes put senior officers on notice that questionable behavior—even if done at the behest of legitimate civilian authorities—entailed significant risks. Overall, then, civilian control of the Polish army was less precarious than often implied. Military officers had some leeway to pursue their own ends, but military prerogatives remained far fewer than in the pre-1989 period.

Renationalization, De-Communization, Personnel Changes

As in other East European states, key aspects of civil-military reform in Poland were the renationalization and de-Communization of the army and an overhaul of the senior officer corps. In 1990 the Polish armed forces reclaimed their traditional uniforms, insignia, anthems, decorations, unit names, and flags. More importantly, Poland reasserted full command of its own army and reestablished jurisdiction over units that had long been assigned to the Warsaw Pact's Joint Command. The departure of Soviet troops from Poland in 1992–1993 put the finishing touch on the renationalization of the Polish army.

Compared to countries such as Czechoslovakia, the de-Communization of the Polish armed forces occurred slowly. By autumn 1990, however, the last remnants of Communist control over the Polish army had been abolished. In their place, the Polish authorities set up a Central Education Board (initially under Komorowski) to promote the historical, civic, and religious values associated with Polish nationalism and military traditions.[38] Starting in late 1990, Poland set up exchanges with Western military academies and sought to broaden its military cooperation and "unconventional contacts" with all the major NATO states.[39]

The de-Communization was reinforced by the dissolution of the long-standing military-educational links between Poland and the Soviet Union. During the Communist era, attendance at a Soviet military academy was a prerequisite for Polish officers' career advancement. In October 1990, an officer who had never attended a Soviet military college, General Zdzislaw Stelmaszuk, was appointed chief of the Polish General Staff, symbolizing the ongoing de-Communization of the officer corps. In 1990 and 1991, the Polish government withdrew most of its military personnel who were studying in the Soviet Union, including those attending the Lenin Military-Political Academy, the main training site for military commissars. Only senior Polish officers nearing completion were allowed to conclude their studies.

Far-reaching changes in the senior officer corps accompanied the de-Communization of the Polish army. The first major personnel shake-up came in September 1989, just two weeks after Jaruzelski had consented to the formation of a government led by Solidarity.[40] When Lech Walesa succeeded Jaruzelski as president in December 1990, any lingering constraints on the removal of personnel whose loyalties were suspect evaporated (as was indicated symbolically by Jaruzelski's simultaneous relinquishment of his post as an army general). The Polish legislature included provisions in its defense bill for 1991 to expedite the dismissal of all "remaining personnel in the army who made their careers solely by being in the party [and] who are now incompetent and old."[41] The replacements of senior Polish officers did not proceed as far as in some other East European countries (notably the Czech Republic), but they were impressive nonetheless. By mid-1991, only 88 generals were still on active duty in the Polish armed forces, compared to roughly 130 at the start of 1990 and almost 200 in 1984.[42]

Changes just below the top also were extensive. Some 8,300 colonels and middle-ranking officers were dismissed in 1990 alone, and others chose to leave of their own accord. The central staff of the Ministry of Defense, numbering around 5,000 military personnel, was cut by nearly 50 percent in the early 1990s, replacing, in the process, many high-ranking officials in the ministry, the military districts, and the individual services.

Budgetary Politics

The level of military spending fell by roughly 80 percent between 1989 and 1992, reflecting a drastic shift of national priorities in the post-Communist era and dramatic budget constraints. In 1985, military expenditures accounted for 10.2 percent of Poland's gross national product (GNP), whereas in the early to mid-1990s the defense budget was barely 2 percent of GNP.[43] The precipitous decline in Polish military spending and the high cost of personnel left only about 5 to 10 percent of the budget for weapons purchases. By contrast, in the 1970s and early 1980s Poland devoted more than one-third of its much higher defense budget to weapons procurement.[44] The effects of this twofold shift were striking. In the late 1980s and early 1990s, according to official estimates, the Polish army received an annual average of only a half-dozen new fighter aircraft and thirty new T-72 tanks. By the mid-1990s, only about 20 percent of the Polish army's equipment was deemed "modern," compared with a rate of roughly 40 percent for the average NATO army.[45] At a press conference in late 1992, Onyszkiewicz denied that "excessive pessimism" was in order regarding the quality of Poland's equipment, but he acknowledged that "the weapons of the Polish army are not among the best, especially in the air force."[46]

The shortfalls in procurement were accompanied by severe constraints in other categories of military spending, notably for research and development (R&D), training, and infrastructure upkeep. In 1993, only about 0.7 percent of the defense budget went to R&D. Funds for training were just as restricted, limiting flying time for pilots and artillery rounds fired to approximately 50 percent of the NATO standard. Spending on infrastructure and housing was similarly constrained. According to official estimates, in the mid-1990s lack of funds precluded urgent repairs on more than 45 million cubic meters of premises.[47]

The extensive cuts in defense expenditures sparked protracted debate in Poland. Senior military commanders and many civilian officials, including members of parliament, argued that the spending levels of the early to mid-1990s would not permit the Polish army to keep up with the demands of modern warfare. A document released by the Polish defense ministry in mid-1994, titled "Fundamental Issues of Poland's Defense System," claimed that increases in military spending were necessary to "ensure that the army retains the ability to deter potential aggressors."[48] Some ministry representatives—civilians as well as military officers—were even blunter in their comments. In mid-1995 the second-highest civilian official, Andrzej Karkoszka, warned that budget constraints were also affecting Poland's chances of joining NATO.[49]

Sentiment in favor of increased military spending grew within the Polish parliament in the mid-1990s because of concerns about Polish military capabilities and because of the political fallout after earlier cuts. Most Polish military factories were operating at less than 25 percent of capacity, and hopes of conversion to nonmilitary production proved largely chimerical. Polish legislators hoped to revive the industry through increased funds for procurement. In mid-February 1995, the Sejm adopted a resolution calling for military spending to rise to 3 percent of GNP by the end of 1996. The resolution stipulated that the increase go to procurement of domestically manufactured equipment.

Nevertheless, Parliament's action had only a minor impact on Polish military spending. In October 1995, the Polish finance minister, Grzegorz Kolodko, warned that the Sejm's resolution could not be fulfilled.⁵⁰ Kolodko's remarks, not cleared beforehand, rankled some of his colleagues on the KOK, but his prediction was amply borne out. In real terms, the defense budget increased only modestly in 1995, reaching 2.4 percent of GNP, and in 1996 overall economic growth in Poland was so brisk (7 to 8 percent) that the proportion of GNP devoted to military spending actually declined to 2.3 percent. (The defense budget itself did not decline; the decrease came in the proportion of GNP devoted to military spending, which is what the Sejm resolution addressed.) The head of the government's Defense Affairs Committee, Aleksander Luczak, maintained that sharp cuts in the defense budget were warranted by the "transformation that has occurred in the world, which has made our borders safe."⁵¹ It is doubtful that most army commanders were comfortable with Luczak's views, but clearly his position won out. The military's prerogatives on this key issue were subordinated to civilian preferences.

Regional Relations

Poland was the first East European country to abandon the Warsaw Pact's traditional military doctrine, even though the Polish National Defense Ministry at the time was not yet under Solidarity's control. Poland's new "national defense doctrine," adopted in February 1990 and subsequently refined, differed fundamentally from the Pact's blitzkrieg-style approach. The new doctrine focused on defensive operations and explicitly ruled out massive offensive thrusts outside Polish borders. Rather than protecting against a purported "threat" from NATO, the new doctrine stipulated that the army must safeguard "all the borders" of Polish territory against any potential threat, whether from the east or the west.⁵² It thus enabled the Polish authorities to take elaborate measures to deter or, if necessary, resist incursions from the former Soviet Union. Until 1990, Polish troops were overwhelmingly concentrated in Poland's two western military districts (the Pomeranian and Silesian), leaving the country's eastern border exposed to Soviet military incursions. To help bring about a more uniform deployment in accordance with the new doctrine, the Polish government in late 1990 established a fourth military district in eastern Poland by splitting the large Warsaw military district into two. The creation of this fourth district, with staff and headquarters in Krakow, was intended to facilitate the redeployment of tens of thousands of Polish troops, including airborne assault and mountain infantry units, to locations near the eastern border with the former Soviet Union.⁵³ Polish early-warning radars and surface-to-air missile (SAM) installations also were moved eastward, and their coverage was reoriented toward the east.

As of April 1993, some 25 percent of the Polish army had been redeployed along the eastern border, and another 20 percent were supposed to be shifted there by the end of 1995. This latter target, however, was only partly met. The redeployments of ground forces proved to be "enormously expensive" (in

Kolodziejczyk's words) and were impeded by the lack of basing infrastructure in eastern Poland.[54] The transfer of air defense facilities proved more expeditious, but in this area, too, many units were "not yet fully effective" by the target date in early 1996.[55] Although the original aim was to have only 25 to 30 percent of the armed forces stationed in Poland's western military districts by the late 1990s, some slippage in that schedule was unavoidable. Even so, the general trend of eastward redeployments was firmly under way in the 1990s. The paramount aim of the redeployments and restructuring was to ensure that Polish units could cope with "any eventuality" from the former Soviet Union, whether a civil war, a flood of refugees, or even a full-fledged military incursion by Russia, Ukraine, or some other "currently unidentified aggressor."[56]

These steps took on added significance in light of revelations about illegal border crossings and the influx of well-armed Russian and Ukrainian narcotics gangs into Poland. The growing salience of these "unconventional threats" was nearly as important as traditional military considerations in bringing about the fundamental changes in Poland's force deployments.

From early 1990 on, the Polish government sought to reduce and even eliminate its dependence on Moscow for weaponry and spare parts. This quest was motivated in part by the Polish authorities' desire to mitigate the leverage that the Soviet Union had long derived from its dominant role in weapons manufacturing. Poland's efforts to diversify were also spurred on by economic considerations, especially after late 1990 when Soviet foreign transactions, including arms sales, shifted to a hard-currency basis, and the price of Soviet military goods and services rose by more than 600 percent.[57]

Initially, Polish officials tried to obtain Soviet-made weapons through other channels. They laid claim to equipment left over from the former East German army, arguing that the new German government could demonstrate its peaceful intent and good will by transferring weapons to the Polish army free of charge or at greatly reduced prices.[58] It gradually became clear that Poland would be better off moving away from Soviet-made arms and emphasizing greater compatibility with NATO's forces. The Polish government sought to purchase Western-made arms, despite obstacles posed by lingering export controls (which were not fully removed until February 1995) and acute shortages of hard currency. As early as 1990, Polish leaders expressed interest in U.S.-made military hardware, including F-16 aircraft and explored the possibility of obtaining Mirage aircraft, Exocet missiles, and other advanced weapons from France. The Polish government particularly welcomed coproduction ventures in certain high-technology areas— such as reconnaissance, digital communications, guided antitank missiles, homing radars, thermal-imaging radars, surface-to-air missiles, and fighter aircraft—that would permit a decisive shift away from the Soviet Union "in the direction of the West."[59] Despite these early overtures and the lifting of U.S. restrictions on arms exports in 1995, economic constraints made it difficult for Poland to obtain Western-made armaments.[60]

As with all the former Warsaw Pact countries, the CFE Treaty signed in November 1990 required Poland to make large cuts in its heavy weapons. Beginning in late 1992 the Polish army reduced its tanks from 2,850 to the CFE limit of 1,730, its artillery systems from 2,300 to 1,610, its armored combat vehicles from 2,377 to 2,150, and its combat aircraft from 551 to 460. These reductions affected weapons that were particularly useful for offensive operations, so the treaty limitations fit well with Poland's new "defensive" doctrine and the restructuring of the Polish army. The magnitude of the cuts sparked concern among certain military commanders, including the then-chief of the General Staff, Wilecki.[61] Their misgivings, however, as well as anxiety about the financial costs of dismantling so much equipment, had no effect on Poland's compliance with the treaty.

Overall, the troop strength of the Polish army shrank from 400,000 in 1988 to just over 300,000 by 1991 and to only about 230,000 by late 1995, in accordance with the limits set by the CFE Treaty.[62] These reductions were facilitated by the 1990 decision to shorten the period of compulsory military service, from two years to eighteen months. Polish leaders expressed interest in eventually cutting back to a force of 180,000 to 200,000 troops (based on a twelve-month period of conscription), less than half the size of the Communist-era army.[63] Because personnel costs (compensation, benefits, pensions, etc.) constituted 60 to 70 percent of military expenditures in the 1990s, a pared down military force allowed better military preparedness during budgetary austerity.

Realignment Toward NATO

As with Hungary and Czechoslovakia, Poland moved decisively in the early 1990s to realign itself with NATO. The aim of this shift was twofold: to secure a reliable military guarantee against external threats, and to promote internal political and economic stability and democratization. The first objective was seen as a crucial hedge against the uncertainties of post–Cold War Europe. Almost all Poles, both inside and outside the government, sensed that the only way to obtain concrete insurance against future threats was through full membership in NATO. Anything short of full membership, they argued, would leave the country exposed.[64]

Polish officials often cited another benefit of NATO membership—the formal reintegration of Poland into the West. By helping to nourish and sustain democratic values and institutions, NATO played an important role in bolstering democratic systems among its members.[65] Joining NATO would thus give Poland entrée to a vibrant community of democratic states. Although the military benefits of allied membership figured prominently in Polish discussions of NATO (more so than in the Czech Republic, for example), the political benefits of membership—the notion of being part of the West again—were cited at least as frequently.[66]

Indeed, well before the Soviet regime collapsed, Polish leaders were regularly lauding NATO as "the central pillar of European security," a "crucial stabilizing force in Europe," and "a necessary counterbalance to the Soviet Union."[67] The Polish government first considered applying for "associate" or "observer" status in the alliance's military (as well as political) organs as early as the summer of 1990. Although Polish leaders acknowledged that "NATO is not considering any expansion of its membership at the moment," they indicated that Poland "will not be able to protect its own security for a long time to come" and would therefore "seek the support of NATO" in any large-scale military contingency.[68] In addition, the Poles suggested that a formal network of "associate" NATO members could be created for the East European states as an interim step, a proposal that the NATO countries embraced in December 1991 with the establishment of the North Atlantic Cooperation Council (NACC).

By late 1990, Poland and other former Communist countries in central Europe had worked out "indirect" security guarantees with the Western European Union (WEU), an organization whose ten member-states all belong to NATO. The WEU formally regarded "the continuation of democracy in Poland" to be "a key factor of international security in the new strategic and political situation in Europe," which must be preserved.[69] Poland also received indirect security guarantees from the United States during Walesa's first presidential visit to North America, in March 1991.[70] The then-chief of the Polish General Staff, General Zdzislaw Stelmaszuk, obtained similar guarantees from NATO in July 1991.[71] Those guarantees were strengthened and reaffirmed on numerous other occasions in the early 1990s.

Although the threat once posed by the Soviet army dissipated with the collapse of the USSR, Poland's interest in joining NATO did not diminish. The official document on "The Principles of Polish Security Policy," adopted in November 1992, explicitly declared that "Poland's strategic objective in the 1990s" would be to gain "membership in NATO and in the WEU as NATO's European branch."[72] The document also reaffirmed Poland's staunch support for "the presence of American forces on our continent." In the 1993, 1995, and 1997 elections, all candidates for public office pledged to do their utmost to ensure Poland's swift entry into the alliance. Public support for NATO membership was consistently around 80 percent in the 1990s (with some 6 to 7 percent opposed and the rest undecided) and at times approached 90 percent.[73] Surveys among military officers turned up a similar level of 85 to 90 percent support for NATO membership.[74] On no other major issue—foreign or domestic—would this degree of consensus have been possible.

Even so, NATO itself was initially wary of Poland's bid for full allied membership because of concern about Russia's reaction. Russian leaders spoke out vehemently against the proposed expansion of NATO, and Western governments were reluctant to challenge Moscow's position for fear of undermining President Boris Yeltsin and sparking a militant, hard-line backlash.[75] NATO's stance prompted frequent complaints by Polish leaders that Russia was being given an effective veto over Polish membership.[76] Polish leaders emphasized that they did not want to "isolate Russia" or to "enlarge NATO at Russia's expense," and they endorsed close links between Russia and Poland in the military as well as other spheres. Nevertheless, Polish officials stressed that "if Russia's policy on expansion of the alliance becomes increasingly hostile," the NATO countries must "move expeditiously to bring Poland into the alliance." Any further delays, they argued, would simply permit Russia to "pursue its security interests vis-à-vis Poland by going over our heads [and] exploiting the West's apprehensions."[77]

To make Poland a more suitable candidate for NATO membership, Polish leaders sought direct military collaboration with NATO countries, both bilaterally and multilaterally. During the Gulf War in early 1991, Polish military medical units were placed under the direct command of U.S. officers. Because Polish construction and engineering firms had done extensive work in Iraq for many years, Polish officials in 1990 were able to supply detailed information about Iraqi military facilities and precise maps of Baghdad to the United States.[78] Most dramatically of all, Polish intelligence officials masterminded the escape of six key U.S. intelligence agents who had been inadvertently trapped behind Iraqi lines when the crisis broke. A senior Polish diplomat later exclaimed that this operation "proved to the Americans that we [in Poland] are a reliable partner who can carry out sensitive, delicate missions on behalf of the American government."[79]

After 1991, Polish military and intelligence cooperation with NATO countries steadily increased. Polish units served with NATO forces in various UN-sponsored peacekeeping missions; and beginning in 1993 Poland took part in joint military and naval exercises with the United States, Great Britain, France, Germany, and other NATO countries.[80] These activities became a regular feature of the Partnership for Peace (PfP), an organization that Poland joined in 1994 despite Walesa's initial suspicion that the PfP was designed mainly to brush aside Poland's bid to gain full NATO membership. Poland also established a bilateral military working group with the United States to deal with all aspects of security issues that might confront NATO. Soon thereafter, the Polish government signed an agreement with NATO to protect secret information. That agreement cleared the way, in mid-1996, for Poland to receive NATO's classified Defense Planning Questionnaire, which is normally distributed only to member-states of the alliance. NATO's aim in providing the document was to allow the Poles to "test their defense planning procedures against NATO requirements."[81]

Although Poland's de jure role in NATO by the mid-1990s was limited for the time being to membership in NACC and PfP, its de facto role was already more consequential than that of at least a few full-fledged member-states. No longer did it seem fanciful for Polish leaders to expect full NATO membership by the end of the decade. (Poland's membership was eventually approved in July 1997). An official *Study on NATO Enlargement* in September 1995 left no doubt that the alliance would eventually expand.[82] The growing prospect of NATO membership had far-reaching consequences for civil-military relations in Poland. The *Study on NATO Enlargement* laid out specific criteria that new members would be expected to meet. In particular, it emphasized that "prospective members" must "have established appropriate democratic and civilian control of their defense force," a requirement similar to provisions in the military-political "Code of Conduct" of the

Organization on Security and Cooperation in Europe (OSCE) adopted in December 1994.[83] The OSCE Code and the NATO study sparked concern among Polish officials and commentators that rough spots and controversies in civil-military relations might be deemed sufficient reason to deny Poland admission into the alliance. In light of these concerns, Polish leaders reaffirmed their intention to conform with NATO's norms and expectations. After Kwasniewski signed the Law on the Post of National Defense Minister and the Polish parliament resolved other problems, Polish leaders could claim by mid-1996 that Poland had lived up to NATO's demands.[84] The dismissal of Wilecki in early 1997 from his post as chief of the General Staff reinforced the norm and perception of civilian control.

CONCLUSIONS

The demise of Communism in Eastern Europe produced drastic changes in the Polish army, both internally and externally. Military restructuring in Poland was not as wrenching as in some other East European countries, but it did mark a fundamental break with the past. The various mechanisms of Communist control within the military were dismantled, and new institutions were established (with varying degrees of success) to make the army compatible with Poland's democratic system. Military spending was drastically reduced, and Polish forces were reconfigured and sharply cut back to comply with the CFE Treaty. Military prerogatives also declined despite the army's widespread popularity. Although ambiguities and contentious issues emerged in civil-military relations after 1989, these resulted from competition among civilian leaders, rather than attempts by military officers to don a political mantle. Despite potential opportunities, the Polish army did not seek, and was not given, a higher level of prerogatives. Overall, then, military reforms in Poland were successful in ensuring that the army would not impede the country's political and economic transformation.

The external realignment of the Polish army also helped stabilize Poland's new political order. By adopting a new military doctrine and force posture, eliminating Soviet and Warsaw Pact command structures, securing the departure of all Soviet/Russian troops, and restructuring Polish foreign intelligence, Polish leaders left no doubt that the army was no longer subordinate to Moscow. These steps were all part of a broader realignment with NATO, motivated not only by hopes of obtaining a reliable security guarantee but also by Poland's quest to become a full-fledged member of the community of democratic states. Polish officials depicted membership in NATO as a crucial step toward, and symbol of, that goal, and they consistently emphasized the nonmilitary as well as military benefits of joining the alliance.

These changes in Poland's civil-military relations after 1989—internal as well as external—created a new principal-agent dynamic. Until 1989, the main principal for the Polish army was the Soviet Union (both the CPSU Politburo and the Soviet General Staff), whereas after 1989 the main principal was the Polish government, and the Soviet Union was deprived of any role at all. This transformation and other recent developments in Poland's civil-military relations generally support the hypotheses derived previously from the institutionalist and principal-agent literature. The process of civil-military change in Poland largely confirms what rational-choice theorists would expect at a time of great institutional flux, as in Eastern Europe in the early 1990s. Contending political elites in Poland sought to encode their own preferences in newly emerging institutions. Walesa attempted to consolidate presidential control over military policy, and other civilian officials tried to assert their own roles. The lack of a full-fledged constitution and the frequent changes of government in Poland inhibited the entrenchment of new institutions, creating further incentives for rival elites to seek greater influence in civil-military relations while opportunities were still available to shape the new "rules of the game." All of this is consistent with a rational-choice framework.

Nevertheless, the Polish case also demonstrates one of the advantages of "sociological" institutionalism over a rational-choice approach. Whereas rational-choice theorists assume that actors' preferences are exogenously formed, sociological institutionalists maintain that leaders' preferences as well as their specific policies and strategies are determined by the broader sociopolitical context.[85] According to this argument, officials are "embedded" in political, social, and economic structures that help guide their institutional choices. The notion of "embeddedness" seems particularly appropriate when discussing recent developments in Poland's civil-military relations. The Polish government was able to abandon (or at least greatly modify) Soviet-imposed institutions from the Communist era, but other features of Polish life—notably, the popular esteem of the army, the underlying concerns about security and national independence, and the consensus favoring reintegration into the West (specifically NATO)—had a far-reaching effect on civil-military relations. The perceived desirability of being associated with the army—a perception not shared in the Czech Republic—caused Polish leaders to vie for political backing from the military even as they sought to establish new mechanisms and procedures of civilian control. Similarly, the overwhelming public support for a reorientation of Polish security policy ensured that all those who came to power in Warsaw, even former Communists, had to press vigorously for NATO membership.

Civil-military developments in Poland after 1989 also lend weight to one of the main points emphasized by the "historical" institutionalist school, namely, the far-reaching effects of existing institutions and norms.[86] Unlike rational-choice theorists, who argue that existing institutions merely constrain specific policies, historical institutionalists aver that institutions are crucial both in shaping actors' preferences and in determining whether those preferences are likely to be realized. A rational-choice perspective would suggest that Polish civilian leaders would quickly assert tight supervision over the national defense ministry. That hypothesis was not wholly realized. Although dozens of senior military personnel were replaced, efforts to civilianize the ministry were halting. Two civilians were appointed deputy ministers in April 1990, but the ministerial post itself did not go to a civilian until December 1991. Moreover, at lower levels of the ministry, civilianization faltered. These delays were largely rooted in the institutional framework left from the Communist era, when the Polish national defense ministry was staffed exclusively by military officers.[87] Consequently, during the transition, few civilians were qualified to take on meaningful responsibilities at the defense ministry. Civilianization of the ministry was thus hindered by decades of engrained practices and information asymmetries.

The tradition of military staffing at the defense ministry also impeded attempts to establish legislative oversight. The creation of a parliamentary defense committee marked a sharp break with the Communist era (when the parliament was largely impotent and had no role in defense policy), but the new committee's impact was relatively superficial, at least initially. Civilian legislators and their small staffs lacked the expertise to challenge the defense ministry's data and reports, and the parliament had no entities comparable to the Congressional Budget Office or the General Accounting Office to carry out in-depth audits and assessments of ministry activities. The parliament's inability to maintain detailed oversight left a crucial gap in the "police patrol" supervision of the defense ministry.[88] That gap was especially important because "fire-alarm" style monitoring was also rudimentary. With few exceptions, Polish journalists and commentators were incapable of probing into technical defense issues, and no private organizations comparable to the RAND Corporation or the Defense Budget Project were available to scrutinize the details of military policy.

The Polish case only partly bears out the expectation that military agents will have greater leeway to pursue their own ends if conflicts among civilian leaders prevent well-defined patterns of civil-military relations from congealing. The infighting among civilian principals, rather than any direct initiatives by military agents, was indeed the chief source of uncertainty in the principal-agent relationship between 1990 and 1995; but the broad consensus in Poland in favor of democracy placed sharp limits on military prerogatives. The Polish military's efforts to benefit from divisions among principals and from information asymmetries were not beyond the bounds of democratic give-and-take. Had the norm of civilian supremacy not been so widely accepted after 1989 (as part of a broader democratic consensus), the splits among civilian leaders might well have led to increased military prerogatives.

Limits on those prerogatives were perhaps best illustrated by budgetary trends. Although senior military officers repeatedly warned that spending constraints were endangering the army's capabilities and leaving Poland exposed to outside pressure, the Polish defense budget continued precipitously downward until 1994, when a small increase was finally approved. The failure of military officers to gain what they deemed to be a sufficient level of funding was a clear sign of how circumscribed military prerogatives remained throughout this period, despite the bickering among political elites.

Developments in Poland also underscore how important it is for civilian principals to display (in Shepsle's words) a "credible commitment to punish" insubordinate officers.[89] The challenge posed by Colonel Rozbicki in June 1994, at a time of great political flux in Poland, might have damaged the principal-agent relationship if civilian leaders had not responded so swiftly. The prompt dismissal of Rozbicki was a crucial signal that breaches of the relationship would not be tolerated, thus precluding further incidents. As Deputy Defense Minister Karkoszka proclaimed in August 1995, the government had shown that it was ready to "discipline any military commanders who go beyond a certain permissible limit."[90]

There are, of course, extraordinary occasions when military agents would be justified in disobeying orders. If the civilian principals are flagrantly violating domestic norms and legal restrictions, or if they demand that agents perform horrendous acts, the cause of democracy is likely to be served if the agents refuse to carry out orders. This point underscores the importance of the post-1989 consensus in Poland in favor of abolishing the army's "internal" mission (i.e., its task of violently quelling unrest). During the Communist era, the Polish military was ordered to carry out domestic repression, either alone or in support of the security forces. That function was explicitly eliminated at the outset of the post-Communist transition. Because the Polish army can now concentrate on its external missions, dilemmas about whether to obey orders will no longer arise.

In addition, the Polish case illustrates the importance of having orderly constitutional mechanisms in place to forestall or, if necessary, adjudicate disputes about civil-military relations. The failure of Poland's Constitutional Tribunal (supreme court) to develop into a strong adjudicative mechanism, especially when it was called on to resolve intragovernmental disputes, intensified the problems caused by the absence of a full-fledged constitution. The delay in adopting a new constitution may itself have contributed to the weakness of the Constitutional Tribunal, but that alone is insufficient to explain the tribunal's performance. After all, Hungary experienced similar difficulty in designing a new constitution, but that did not prevent the Hungarian Constitutional Court from emerging as a strong, authoritative body. No doubt, if a comparable adjudicative mechanism had existed in Poland, competing political elites would have been less inclined to try to manipulate the civil-military relationship to their advantage.

Contrary to expectations, changes in the perception of external threat did not have a major effect on military prerogatives in Poland. Officially, the Polish government since 1989 has refrained from identifying specific countries as threats, but unofficially Polish leaders have made clear that their only real concern over the long term is the possibility of a hard-line backlash in Moscow. Perceptions of the threat from Moscow have varied considerably since 1989—with the greatest anxiety stirred by the hard-line coup attempt in August 1991, the confrontation at the Russian parliament in October 1993, the invasion of Chechnya in December 1994, and the strong showing of extremist parties in Russia's 1993 and 1995 parliamentary elections—but at no point has this led to a higher level of military prerogatives in Poland. Military officers have not been asked (or permitted) to define any specific threats to Polish security, much less to play up those threats for their own purposes (e.g., asking for greater budgetary outlays).

Finally, the Polish case provides valuable evidence about the role that external actors can play in shoring up the norm of civilian supremacy. The Polish government's effort to forestall further bickering about civil-military relations was largely motivated by its desire to join NATO. Through the Partnership for Peace and other contacts, Polish leaders recognized that establishment of firm civilian control over the military was a prerequisite for membership. When the official *Study on NATO Enlargement* pointed this out, senior Polish officials and commentators claimed that Poland would have to improve its record, and during late 1995 and early 1996 Polish leaders encouraged parliament to adopt legislation clarifying the ambiguities in civil-military relations. The experience in Poland thus suggests that international institutions can profoundly affect state behavior. The extent of NATO's influence on civil-military relations in Poland—even before Poland had any solid prospect of being admitted into the alliance—bears out the predictions made by Jack Snyder in early 1990 that Western institutions like NATO and the European Union could be highly beneficial for democracy in the former Warsaw Pact countries.[91]

Even without NATO's influence, civil-military relations in Poland would have changed drastically after 1989. The elimination of the Soviet Union as the main principal and the demise of Communist rule were enough to change the entire principal-agent relationship. Still, the importance of NATO should not be underestimated. Although coordination problems among rival elites hindered Poland's efforts to strengthen "democratic and civilian control" of the army, the prospect of allied membership gradually helped to overcome those problems. By spurring Polish officials to push harder for democratic institutions, NATO effectively reversed the external-internal linkages of the Communist era.[92] Until 1989, the dominant external influence on Poland (i.e., the Soviet Union) required the maintenance of highly artificial structures of civil-military relations, whereas in the 1990s the chief external actor (NATO) has encouraged a pattern of civil-military relations that is conducive both to democracy and to Polish traditions.

NOTES

1. Mark Kramer, "Civil-Military Relations in the Warsaw Pact: The East European Component," *International Affairs* 61, no. 3 (Winter 1984–85), pp. 45–67.

2. Alfred Stepan, *Rethinking Military Politics: Brazil and the Southern Cone* (Princeton: Princeton University Press, 1988), p. 93.

3. Alfred Stepan, "The New Professionalism of Internal Warfare and Military Role Expansion," in Alfred Stepan, ed., *Authoritarian Brazil: Origins, Policies, and Future* (New Haven: Yale University Press, 1973), pp. 51, 52; Claude E. Welch, Jr. and Arthur K. Smith, *Military Role and Rule: Perspectives on Civil-Military Relations* (North Scituate, Mass.:

Duxbury Press, 1974); and Moshe Lissak, *Military Roles in Modernization: Civil-Military Relations in Thailand and Burma* (Beverly Hills, Calif.: Sage Publications, 1976).

4. Thomas A. Koelble, "The New Institutionalism in Political Science and Sociology," *Comparative Politics* 27, no. 2 (January 1995), pp. 231–243. For useful presentations of the rational-choice, historical, and sociological brands of institutionalism, see Kenneth Shepsle, "Studying Institutions: Some Lessons from the Rational Choice Approach," *Journal of Theoretical Politics* 1, no. 2 (1989), pp. 131–147; Walter W. Powell and Paul J. DiMaggio, eds., *The New Institutionalism in Organizational Analysis* (Chicago: University of Chicago Press, 1991); and Sven Steinmo, Kathleen Thelen, and Frank Longstreth, eds., *Structuring Politics: Historical Institutionalism in Comparative Analysis* (New York: Cambridge University Press, 1992). My hypotheses are derived indirectly, rather than directly, from the literature.

5. Oliver E. Williamson, *The Economic Institutions of Capitalism* (New York: Free Press, 1985), pp. 218–222.

6. Kathleen Bawn, "Political Control Versus Expertise: Congressional Choice and Administrative Procedures," *American Political Science Review* 89, no. 1 (March 1995), pp. 62–73.

7. In this paper, opportunistic behavior is defined as an unauthorized attempt to increase military prerogatives.

8. James M. Lindsay, "Congress, Foreign Policy, and the New Institutionalism," *International Studies Quarterly* 38 (1994), pp. 298–299.

9. Murray J. Horn and Kenneth A. Shepsle, "Commentary on 'Administrative Arrangements and the Political Control of Agencies': Administrative Process and Organizational Form as Legislative Responses to Agency Costs," *Virginia Law Review* 75, no. 2 (March 1989), p. 502.

10. These oversight mechanisms could be set up either by the executive (e.g., a National Security Council) or by the legislature (e.g., a parliamentary Defense Committee)—or most likely by both. The oversight provided by civilian officials both inside and outside the defense ministry fits into the broad category that Mathew D. McCubbins and Thomas Schwartz have called "police patrols" (as compared to "fire alarms"). See "Congressional Oversight Overlooked: Police Patrols Versus Fire Alarms," *American Journal of Political Science* 28, no. 2 (August 1984), pp. 165–179.

11. This view is likely to be shared by senior military officers, in part because they believe that conscript armies are not well suited for internal policing and in part because their institutional culture is geared toward external missions.

12. Andrew A. Michta, *Red Eagle: The Army in Polish Politics, 1944–1988* (Stanford: Hoover Institution Press, 1990).

13. Powell and DiMaggio, eds., *The New Institutionalism in Organizational Analysis*.

14. "Ustawa konstytucyjna z 17 pazdziernika 1992 r. o wzajemnych stosunkach miedzy wladza ustawodawcza i wykonawcza Rzeczypospolitej Polskiej oraz o samorzadzie terytorialnym," *Dziennik Ustaw Rzeczypospolitej Polskiej* (Warsaw), no. 84 (November 23, 1992), Item 301.

15. Compare Stephen A. Holmes, "Conceptions of Democracy in the Draft Constitutions of Post-Communist Countries," in Beverly Crawford, ed., *Markets, States, and Democracy: The Political Economy of Post-Communist Transformation* (Boulder: Westview Press, 1995), pp. 81–91; and Barry Weingast, "Constitutions as Governance Structures: The Political Foundations of Secure Markets," *Journal of Institutional and Theoretical Economics* 149, no. 1 (1993), pp. 3–32.

16. "Ustawa z dnia 21 listopadu 1967 r. o powszechnym obowiazku obrony Rzeczy-pospolitej," *Dziennik Ustaw Polskiej Rzeczypospolitej Ludowej* (Warsaw), no. 43 (December 14, 1967), Item 165.

17. The original law designated the prime minister as head of the KOK, but in November 1983 the law was amended (at Wojciech Jaruzelski's behest) to ensure that Jaruzelski could continue directing the KOK after he gave up his post as prime minister.

18. "Ustawa z dnia 14 grudnia 1995 r. o urzedzie Ministra Obrony Narodowej," *Dziennik Ustaw Rzeczypospolitej Polskiej* (Warsaw), no. 10 (January 30, 1996), Item 159.

19. *Raport Miedzyministerialnej Komisji do Spraw Reformy w Organizacji Obrony Naro-dowej* (Warsaw: Urzed Rady Ministrow, July 1991).

20. Dariusz Fikus, "Incydent wojskowy," *Rzeczpospolita* (Warsaw), April 9, 1992, p. 1; and "Prezydent w PAP: Zadalem dymisji ministra obrony," *Rzeczpospolita* (Warsaw), April 10, 1992, p. 1. A special parliamentary commission, set up to investigate the charges, found no evidence to support them.

21. "Polityka bezpieczenstwa i strategia obronna Rzeczypospolitej Polskiej," *Polska Zbrojna* (Warsaw), November 12, 1992, pp. 1–2; and "Zalozenia polskiej polityki bez-pieczenstwa," *Polska Zbrojna* (Warsaw), November 3, 1992, p. 2.

22. "Obwieszczenie Panstwowej Komisji Wyborczej z 23 wrzesnia 1993 r. o wynikach wyborow do Senatu Rzeczypospolitej Polskiej przeprowadzonych 19 wrzesnia 1993 r.," an 18-page supplement to *Rzeczpospolita* (Warsaw), September 27, 1993.

23. Published interview with Piotr Kolodziejczyk, *Wodowanie Admirala* (Warsaw: Editions Spotkania, 1995).

24. Published interview with Janusz Onyszkiewicz in "Akcja generalow byla wywolna przez Walese," *Zycie Warszawy* (Warsaw), October 6, 1994, p. 2.

25. Janusz A. Majcherek, "Przesilenie bez powiklan: Kryzys rzadowy, wywolany dymisja Jozefa Oleksego, nie przyniosl SLD zadnych strat, a opozycji zadnych korzysci," *Rzecz-pospolita* (Warsaw), February 14, 1996, p. 5.

26. Centrum Badania Opinii Spolecznej, "Zmiany opinii o instytucjach i organizacjach miedzy pazdziernikiem 1991 r. a majem 1992 r.," *Serwis Informacyjny* (Warsaw), no. 6 (June 1992), pp. 19–21.

27. "Poznawanie wojska," *Polska Zbrojna* (Warsaw), October 24–26, 1992, pp. 1–2.

28. See the interview with Onyszkiewicz, then-deputy defense minister, in "Nowy ksztalt Ministerstwa Obrony Narodowej," *Polska Zbrojna* (Warsaw), April 26–28, 1991, pp. 1–2; and Lt. Col. Andrzej Medykowski, "Trwaja, prace nad nowymi strukturami MON: Za urzedniczymi biurkami—tylko cywile," *Polska Zbrojna* (Warsaw), March 12, 1991, pp. 1–2.

29. Romuald Szeremetiew, "Terra Incognita," *Tygodnik Solidarnosc* (Warsaw), no. 1 (January 1, 1993), p. 4.

30. "NATO w rekach wojska: Stanowisk w sztabie dostatek," *Gazeta Wyborcza* (Warsaw), October 26, 1995, p. 2.

31. Robert Kowal, "Reforma MON," *Polska Zbrojna* (Warsaw), July 15, 1996, pp. 1, 3.

32. Interview in "Cywile boja sie wojska," *Polityka* (Warsaw), no. 22 (June 1, 1996), pp. 17–18.

33. Interview in *Wprost* (Poznan), July 9, 1995, p. 27.

34. Colonel Tadeusz Mitek, "Demokracja i Wojsko," *Polska Zbrojna* (Warsaw), July 4, 1995, p. 2.

35. General Stanislaw Koziej, "Formulowanie i wyrazanie potrzeb obronnych," *Rzecz-pospolita* (Warsaw), January 4, 1996, p. 7.

36. *New Democracies Barometer IV* (Vienna: Paul Lazarsfeld Society, 1996), p. 17; Richard Rose, *What Is Europe?* (New York: HarperCollins, 1996).

37. "Rozbroilismy sie sami," *Gazeta Wyborcza* (Warsaw), June 9, 1994, pp. 12–13.

38. "Nowy klimat moralny w armii: Rozmowa z Bronislawem Komorowskim—wice ministrem obrony narodowej ds. wychowawczych," *Polska Zbrojna* (Warsaw), November 23–25, 1990, pp. 1–2.

39. "Sprzet z ZSRR, wiedza z Ameryki," *Gazeta Wyborcza* (Warsaw), April 9, 1991, p. 2.

40. The personnel changes, affecting the command of military districts and the "central institutions of the National Defense Ministry," were featured prominently on Polish television on September 4, 1989, and published the following day on the front page of *Zolnierz Wolnosci.*

41. Interview with Jacek Szymanderski, deputy chairman of the Sejm's National Defense Committee, in "Co przyniesie nowa ustawa o obronnosci panstwa?" *Polska Zbrojna* (Warsaw), February 12, 1991, p. 2.

42. "Model lat 90-tych," *Polska Zbrojna* (Warsaw), November 16–18, 1990, p. 1.

43. Calculated from data in U.S. Arms Control and Disarmament Agency, *World Military Expenditures and Arms Transfers, 1995* (Washington, D.C.: U.S. Government Printing Office, April 1996), p. 90.

44. Interview with General Krzysztof Pajewski, chief of the economic and finance board on the Polish General Staff, in "Budzet na otarcie lez," *Polska Zbrojna* (Warsaw), November 13, 1995, pp. 1–2.

45. Interview with General Zdzislaw Graczyk in *Nowa Europa* (Warsaw), December 19, 1994, p. 2.

46. Tadeusz Mitek, "Konferencja prasowa ministra Janusza Onyszkiewicza," *Polska Zbrojna* (Warsaw), November 26, 1992, p. 1.

47. Interview with Krzysztof Pajewski, head of the economic and finance board on the Polish General Staff, in "Budzet na otarcie lez," p. 2.

48. Ministerstwo Obrony Narodowej, *Podstawowe problemy obronnosci Polski* (Warsaw: MON, June–August 1994), p. 4.

49. Interview in "Pociag do NATO," *Polska Zbrojna* (Warsaw), July 14–16, 1995, pp. 1–3.

50. "Kolodko szczodrobliwy," *Gazeta Wyborcza* (Warsaw), October 5, 1995, p. 1.

51. Interview with Polish deputy prime minister Aleksander Luczak, in "Rzeczywistosc i sposobnosci Polski," *Polska Zbrojna* (Warsaw), October 6–8, 1995, pp. 1–2.

52. "Doktryna obrony narodowej Rzeczypospolitej Polskiej," *Zolnierz Wolnosci* (Warsaw), February 26, 1990, p. 1.

53. Miroslaw Kozmin, "Znowu bedzie Armia 'Krakow'," *Gazeta Krakowska* (Krakow), April 11, 1991, p. 1.

54. Interview with Kolodziejczyk in "Byc daleko od polityki," *Rzeczpospolita* (Warsaw), January 26, 1994, p. 3.

55. Interview with Lt.-Gen. Jerzy Gotowala, then-commander of Polish air forces (later chief of the Polish General Staff), in *Jane's Defence Weekly* 25, no. 11 (March 13, 1996), p. 32.

56. "Doktryna obrony narodowej Rzeczypospolitej Polskiej," p. 1.

57. Interview with I. S. Belousov, chairman of the State Commission on Military-Industrial Affairs, in "Voennyi eksport v svete glasnosti," *Pravitel'stvennyi vestnik* (Moscow), no. 3 (January 1991), p. 12.

58. "Delegacja MON zakonczyla oficjalna wizyte w RFN: Wracamy z precyzyjnym planem dalszego dzialania," *Polska Zbrojna* (Warsaw), November 30–December 2, 1990, pp. 1–2.

59. Colonel Jozef Pawelec, "Stan wojska," *Polska Zbrojna* (Warsaw), October 24, 1990, pp. 1, 5.

60. Grzegorz Lubczyk, "Kosztowne 'Partnerstwo'," *Rzeczpospolita* (Warsaw), January 15–16, 1994, p. 23; Ian Anthony, "International Dimensions of Industrial Restructuring," in Ian Anthony, ed., *The Future of the Defence Industries in Central and Eastern Europe*, SIPRI Research Report no. 7 (Oxford: Oxford University Press, 1994), p. 101; and Dana Priest and Daniel Williams, "U.S. Allows Arms Sales to 10 in Ex-East Bloc: Barrier to Offensive Weaponry Is Removed," *Washington Post*, February 18, 1995, pp. A–1, A–12.

61. "Silne wojsko—stabilne panstwo: Przemowenie szefa Sztabu Generalnego WP gen. broni Tadeusza Wileckiego," *Polska Zbrojna* (Warsaw), August 16, 1995, p. 2

62. International Institute for Strategic Studies, *The Military Balance, 1995/96* (London: IISS/Oxford University Press, October 1995), pp. 75–77.

63. Colonel Tadeusz Mitek, "Restrukturyzacja oznaczala masowa redukcje," *Polska Zbrojna* (Warsaw), March 22, 1995, pp. 1–2.

64. Colonel Marian Kowalewski, *Polityka bezpieczenstwa Polski* (Warsaw: Ministerstwo obrony narodowej, January 1996), p. 7; Centrum Badania Opinii Spolecznej, "Czy Rosja nam zagraza" (N = 1,117), June 1993, June 1994, December 1994, February 1995, April 1995, July 1995, and December 1995. For somewhat higher figures, see the Demoskop survey results in Jan Skorzynski, "Orientacja: na Zachod," *Rzeczpospolita* (Warsaw), August 1, 1995, p. 6.

65. The record in this regard is imperfect—the breakdown of democracy in Greece in 1967 is an obvious exception—but it comes very close. Although numerous problems remain today in Turkey, those problems are undoubtedly less severe than they would be if Turkey were not a NATO member.

66. Andrzej Olechowski, "Lepsza historia kontynentu: Europa wedlug ministra spraw zagranicznych," *Polityka* (Warsaw), no. 50 (December 10, 1994), pp. 1, 13.

67. Interview with then-foreign minister Krzysztof Skubiszewski in "Otwieramy sie na Zachod, ale nie zamykamy na Wschodzie," *Rzeczpospolita* (Warsaw), March 26, 1991, p. 7.

68. Interview with Lech Kaczynski, presidential minister for national security, in "Wyscie na Zachod z 'szarej strefy'," *Rzeczpospolita* (Warsaw), May 23, 1991, p. 2.

69. "Misja sondazowa NATO," *Polska Zbrojna* (Warsaw), April 23, 1991, pp. 1–2.

70. "Przyjazn i nadzieja: Stosunki polsko-amerykanskie," *Rzeczpospolita* (Warsaw), March 25, 1991, pp. 1, 7.

71. "Gen. Z. Stelmaszuk zakonczyl rozmowy w NATO," *Polska Zbrojna* (Warsaw), July 15, 1991, p. 1.

72. "Zalozenia polskiej polityki bezpieczenstwa," p. 2.

73. "Pragnienia i brak zainteresowania: Poszerzenie NATO w oczach Polakow i Rosjan," *Rzeczpospolita* (Warsaw), February 26, 1996, p. 5; Centrum Badania Opinii Spolecznej (CBOS), *Polska-Rosja-NATO* (Warsaw: CBOS, January 1995), pp. 3–8; CBOS, "Partnerstwo dla Pokoju i przystapienie Polski do NATO," *Serwis Informacyjny* (Warsaw), July 1994, pp. 11–17; and CBOS, "Miejsce Polski w Europie, pozadani partnerzy gospodarczy i polityczni," *Serwis Informacyjny* (Warsaw), August 1994, pp. 28–34.

74. Data from the Polish Military Institute of Sociological Research, January 1996, as reported in Pawel Swieboda, "Poland: In NATO's Waiting Room," *Transition* 2, no. 7 (April 19, 1996), p. 54.

75. Mark Kramer, "NATO, Russia, and East European Security," in Kate Martin, ed., *Russia: A Return to Imperialism?* (New York: St. Martin's Press, 1995), pp. 120–123 passim.

76. Interview with deputy prime minister Aleksander Luczak, in "Rzeczywistosc i sposobnosci Polski," pp. 1–2.

77. Kowalewski, Polityka bezpieczenstwa Polski, pp. 14–15.

78. Witold Beres, *Gliniarz z "Tygodnika": Rozmowy z bylym ministrem spraw wewnetrznych Krzysztofem Kozlowskim* (Warsaw: BGW, 1991), esp. pp. 73–78.

79. Cited in John Pomfret, "Escape from Iraq," *Washington Post,* January 17, 1995, p. A–27.

80. Kramer, "NATO, Russia, and East European Security," pp. 105–161.

81. Wojciech Luczak, "Dowiadywac sie o tajemnicach NATO," *Sztandar* (Warsaw), July 12, 1996, p. 2.

82. North Atlantic Treaty Organization, *Study on NATO Enlargement,* Brussels, September 1995.

83. Chapters VII and VIII in Organization for Security and Cooperation in Europe, "Code of Conduct on Politico-Military Aspects of Security," DOC.FSC/1/95, adopted in Budapest, December 3, 1994. Quoted passage from NATO, *Study on NATO Enlargement,* is on p. 25.

84. Interview with Andrzej Karkoszka, Polish first deputy defense minister, in *Nowa Europa* (Warsaw), June 19, 1996, p. 26.

85. Powell and Dimaggio, eds., *The New Institutionalism in Organizational Analysis,* especially Powell's and Dimaggio's chapters.

86. See Steinmo, Thelen, and Longstreth, eds., *Structuring Politics.*

87. Many of these were Soviet officers until 1956; after 1956 the ministry was staffed by Polish officers. The point, however, is that military personnel rather than civilians were responsible for the ministry's affairs.

88. McCubbins and Schwartz, "Congressional Oversight Overlooked," pp. 165–179.

89. Shepsle, "Studying Institutions."

90. Interview in *Rzeczpospolita* (Warsaw), August 18, 1995, p. 2.

91. Jack Snyder, "Averting Anarchy in the New Europe," *International Security* 14, no. 4 (Spring 1990), pp. 5–41.

92. On external-internal linkages, see Peter B. Evans, Harold K. Jacobson, and Robert B. Putnam, eds., *Double-Edged Diplomacy: International Bargaining and Domestic Politics* (Berkeley: University of California Press, 1993).

PART THREE

Civil-Military Partnerships

In this section, we explore civil-military relationships classified as pacted relationships, or partnerships. Four countries in this project have such a relationship: Chile, Thailand, Guatemala, and Brazil. The authors examine the evolution of the civil-military relationship in these countries as it affects both the consolidation of democracy and the tenor of regional relations.

Chile's civil-military relationship is one of the most complex of those studied in this project. The military dictatorship of General Augusto Pinochet set the foundations for the transition to democracy with the creation of the 1980 Constitution, approved by a plebiscite long before the actual transition began. The transition occurred in 1989 after Pinochet lost a national referendum on continued rule, despite having received 43 percent of the vote. Civilians of the Right allied with the military to add "institutional safeguards" to the Constitution that have raised barriers to fundamental changes. Francisco Rojas and Claudio Fuentes analyze the evolution of the civil-military relationship in the democratic period, demonstrating how it allowed for both the consolidation of democracy and a decrease in regional tensions.

The Thai civil-military relationship has evolved erratically in a domestic situation of military rule and a regional context characterized by overt war. Surachart Bamrungsuk investigates the process by which Thai elites and civil society finally chose democracy, much to the surprise of the military. He also shows that the commitment of some sectors of Thai society to democracy is shallow and that even those with a deep commitment to democracy have encountered serious difficulties in making civilian control effective.

Guatemala is in the process of moving toward democracy after decades of civil war. Caesar Sereseres argues that the military began the transition in the early 1980s because it perceived that it was winning the civil war and could thus turn to the task of professionalizing its institution. The process nevertheless spanned fifteen years as the rebels proved more resilient than expected, the right-wing civilian sector expressed ambivalence about an effective transition, and the military itself suffered from disunity over the issue.

Brazil has moved from a military-dominant civil-military relationship to a partnership, which currently appears to be moving toward civilian domination. The military had overseen a twenty-year transition process but lost control of it at the end. The poor condition of legislative-executive relations, however, gave them unforeseen opportunities to continue to be influential in Brazilian political life. Thomaz Guedes da Costa investigates how this process has affected the role and prerogatives of the military in both domestic and regional politics.

■

CHAPTER EIGHT

Civil-Military Relations in Chile's Geopolitical Transition

Francisco Rojas and Claudio Fuentes

Determining a nation's grand strategy requires constructing an understanding of the route that country must travel to achieve long-term sustainability for its development.[1] For Chile, with its position in the Antarctic and its 2,000-mile coastline on the Pacific Rim, the future lies in developing ties not just within the Western Hemisphere but also with the Asian Pacific. To effectively implement its grand strategy, Chile's policymakers must build a consensus within civil society that makes possible the consolidation of its new democracy and the maintenance of its export-oriented economic policies. Those steps must be taken first if the country is to achieve its long-term development and security goals.

Neoliberal, free-market thinking, more than the end of the Cold War, has shaped Chile's national planning during the 1990s. Economic opening has produced increasingly fluid relations with partners throughout the world and has dramatically affected the Chilean view of international change, regional transformation, and the country's own democratization. Globalization has created opportunities that seem to be continuously multiplying: More than 40 percent of Chile's gross domestic product (GDP) is currently linked to the external sector. Maintaining this position in the international economy will depend on Chile's consolidation as a service economy and a "port country," a concept highlighting its multiple linkages with the Asian Pacific. These economic developments have been complemented by a strengthening of the country's diplomatic and political presence in the international arena since the return of democracy in 1990.

The market has a fundamental influence on the regional network. As neoliberal export-oriented policies deepen Chile's interdependence with South America, it has become increasingly difficult to promote policies of autarkic development or import-substitution industrialization. The market also influences the defense sector: Although greater market interdependence enhances optimism in the country and presents opportunities to forge a sense of trust between civilians and the military, it also generates new concerns over possible risks that these developments present. The market itself alters the nature of a nation's vulnerabilities. Given the decline in state involvement and the increasing role of the market, the locus of those vulnerabilities has shifted from classical notions of sovereignty toward the protection of resources and market access. Chilean international relations, focused previously on security matters, are now characterized by market concerns. Nevertheless, these changes are as yet incomplete. The view of the country's future held by Chile's principal political, social, and cultural coalitions also constitutes an essential source for the design of Chile's new grand strategy.

This chapter has three parts. First, we analyze factors that shape grand strategy, focusing on the domestic political coalitions in contemporary Chile and on traditional threat perceptions that have influenced the current defense structure. Next, we examine the evolution of Chile's civil-military relationship during the democratic transition from both a political point of view (the relationship between the armed forces and the political system) and a professional standpoint (modernization of the institution). We conclude by analyzing the external forces that play an important role in the shaping of the domestic agenda.

FACTORS SHAPING GRAND STRATEGY

Two facts have set Chile's historical trajectory. First, until recently the national planning process excluded domestic political coalitions. These coalitions express opinions rooted in a complex network of ideological, strategic, economic, and political views, and their characterization as a threat to the state transcends the artificial division of "government versus opposition." Second, since the creation of Latin America's nation-states in the nineteenth century, Chile has perceived its regional neighborhood as a locus of threat. Chile's economic opening and increasing subregional interdependence are now redefining both these "traditional" threat perceptions.

Coalitions and Grand Strategy

The design of Chile's new grand strategy depends on its preexisting domestic political conditions, which have been influenced by the international environment. The end of the Cold War was critically important, as was the civil-military relationship that developed during the transition to democracy. The competing proposals for Chile's future grand strategy reflect political alliances of an inclusive character that cut across every dimension of Chilean society, including the civil-military relationship. Within this, we see that two major political-cultural coalitions—one the "corporatist" and the other the "democratic-modernizers"—express the aspirations of a majority of Chilean society through two well-defined political projects.

The first coalition is corporatist in its vision, which springs from the legacy of the military government. This coalition's ideology is marked by its championing of "protected democracy," which materialized in the 1980 Constitution (approved during military rule). In rough electoral terms, the coalition can be characterized as the 43 percent of the vote in the 1988 plebiscite that sought to retain General Augusto Pinochet as president. In the 1993 presidential election, this opposition group shrank to 30 percent. In the new democratic era, the best safeguard for this coalition is constitutional immobilization. To achieve this, they have defended the presidentialist structure, with its highly centralized powers and functions, and they have promoted a reduced role for Congress, greater involvement of the armed forces within state institutions (for example, through the National Security Council and designated senators), and a two-party electoral system that makes possible a minority veto.

The corporatist coalition also champions a constitutionally guaranteed autonomy of the armed forces, in both institutional and budgetary matters.[2] It is distrustful of economic integration, both at the regional level and with the United States. The corporatist position presupposes that Chile's accession to a regional bloc would affect aspects of its national defense. Thus, the opening of the Chilean economy to international markets is accepted but brings with it a distrust of accords that imply complete interdependence. Many of the political conflicts over grand strategy focus on how the corporatist ideology can fit into and coexist with the democratic system. The views of a large segment of the political opposition, composed primarily of the Independent Democratic Union (Unión Demócrata Independiente, UDI) and a portion of the National Renewal Party (Renovación Nacional, RN), are representative of the corporatist coalition.[3]

The democratic-modernizers exemplify the main thrust of Chilean public opinion at the end of the twentieth century. They are represented by the Concertación por la Democracia, the coalition of political parties that won 55 percent of the vote in the 1988 plebiscite and later won two consecutive presidencies, in 1989 with Patricio Aylwin and in 1993 with Eduardo Frei Ruiz-Tagle, who received 58 percent of the vote. In regard to the deepening of the democratic institutional framework, the more liberal segment of the political opposition shares the ideology of the democratic-modernizers.

The democratic-modernizers accept the limitations set by the military government, but they do so in order to pursue the establishment of policies aimed at modifying those limitations. By working within the rules of the game as established during the authoritarian government (that is, within the framework of restricted democracy), the coalition has constructed a broad and substantive political consensus. This, in turn, has reaffirmed Chile's political stability, a key requirement for the country's further economic development.

The most important goals of the democratic-modernizers are the further democratization of the institutions inherited from the military regime and the resolution of the problem of the authoritarian enclaves (the presence of designated senators, a high degree of autonomy for the armed forces, and an electoral system designed to favor the status quo). In the socioeconomic arena, the coalition supports modernization of state structures to improve efficiency. While working to improve national planning to resolve social inequality, the coalition is also continuing Chile's integration with the centers of the developed world and with the rest of Latin America.[4] The strategy of multiple insertion into international markets has made the Latin American region a priority for Chile. But regional integration will require overcoming the colonial legacy of borders conflicts. Consequently, the search for regional peace and international security has become important in Chile's campaign for global economic and political integration.[5]

The democratic-modernizers have proposed three strategies for implementing Chile's national project. The first seeks greater domestic solidarity and integration, which will require that political activity focus on improving social equity. Political reforms are needed to democratize the country and modernize the state apparatus so that it can efficiently implement policies. Chile's development as a "port country" is another important goal, and, if achieved, it should improve growth in both the southern and northern regions of the nation, where social justice has long been ignored.[6]

A second strategy arises from the efforts to integrate Chile with the world's megamarkets and with the global security system. While Chile has entered a number of Latin American regional agreements, including MERCOSUR (Mercado Común del Sur), it has also kept open the possibility of cooperation with other blocs, such as NAFTA (North American Free Trade Agreement), the European Union (EU), and APEC (Asia-Pacific Economic Council).[7] This integrative strategy is expressed regionally in a qualitative change in Chile's relationship with Argentina since 1990, in the signing of treaties with several Latin American countries, and in its negotiations over NAFTA. Integration with the Asian Pacific will develop according to its own rhythm, but promising developments are underway.

The third strategy designed by the coalition of democratic-modernizers is in the defense realm, and it has as its central objective the transformation of civil-military relations. The goal is the creation of an effective defense community, led by civilians and emphasizing the professionalization of the armed forces. In the evolution of this strategy, the reinsertion of defense issues in the international arena plays a primary role. Progress is slow but steady. The political differences over this strategy, which have arisen during the democratic transition, have not changed its basic intent. Achievement of this strategy will require constitutional reforms.[8]

The Importance of the Regional Neighborhood

The second element that shapes the formulation of grand strategy is the maintenance of traditional threat perceptions. Chile's defense logic still has a nineteenth-century stamp. Despite the end of the Cold War, regionally based threat perceptions continue in Chile and more generally throughout South America. Regional issues shaped a strategic culture that provided a framework for the widely differing governments that have held power in Chile since the early nineteenth century. Strategic culture transcends the question of the relative importance of civilians and military personnel in the shaping of policy; the presence of one or the other can highlight certain elements, but the structural base remains the same. Four factors define and characterize threat perceptions in Chile.

Undoubtedly the most important determinant is regional history. In the early nineteenth century, Chileans founded a nation-state while neighboring countries were still in political chaos. The people of Chile believed that subregional anarchy could be confronted successfully only through a reaffirmation of the centrality of the state. Out of this sprang a second determinant, still in force today: Chile's armed forces established a conception of themselves as a state institution and a national organization, and this was accompanied by the creation of a tradition of professionalism and hierarchical organization. The Chilean military has tried to preserve this image even in the face of great domestic tensions that have arisen at specific historical junctures.

A third determinant of threat perception is the inertia produced from recurring outbreaks of regional conflict. When compared to these conflicts, the importance of the United States or other world powers in relation to Chile has seemed minimal or, at most, only somewhat significant. This inertia lies in the bureaucratic standard operating procedures that repeatedly reproduce old responses to these regional threats.

The fourth and final determinant of threat perception is the absence of institutionalized mechanisms to increase trust. To change regional threat perceptions requires safeguards that are stable over time and mutually beneficial, making possible the achievement of national goals for all involved. The opening of Latin American markets and the development of global linkages are as yet too new to produce significant changes in this area. Altering the regional dialectic will be a process that gradually affects the way politics and interstate relations are defined.

These four determinants of threat perception play a vital role in shaping civil-military relations in Chile. The debate in Chile centers on the scope and the constitutionally mandated role of the armed forces, that is, on domestic issues more than on external concerns. The location of the debate implies a consensus on a realist perception of foreign affairs, with policy options set by the basic understanding that international politics is competitive.[9]

This raises two important points about the interpretation of military capacity and doctrine. Chile has developed a strategic doctrine that privileges defensive deterrence. In a small country with limited communications, deterrence plays a key role. Chile looks at the strategic, and not merely military, balance of power. This balance takes into consideration national idiosyncrasies, especially the lack of strategic depth. Chile's military doctrine is also defensive: A potential aggressor will not be able to win control of major assets and would pay a high price in such an attempt. This military policy combines traditions privileging diplomacy and

international law, based upon a recognition of, and a respect for, treaties and accords.

Because Chile's national boundaries were set in the nineteenth century and accepted by a series of governments with distinct political orientations, the protection of national territory is perceived as a national duty for which the country's
own military capacity constitutes the basic safeguard. Regional and hemispheric
security frameworks alone are not enough to guarantee safeguards and stability.

If we establish some general measures of threat, Chile seems to be in a relatively
safe environment. For example, the country's national sovereignty is unquestioned. No foreign power has shown interest in mounting an aggression against
Chile, and its strategic relations with the United States, the predominant hemispheric power, have become significantly more cooperative in recent years. Furthermore, no political, ethnic, or religious groups advocate secession. There are
no active internal subversive groups and no international drug activity. Political
conflicts are almost nonexistent, and there is a high degree of domestic cohesion,
national unity, and loyalty to government authority. Political debate is expressed
through democratic institutions; and ethnic differences, immigration, and
poverty are channeled in nondisruptive ways. There also exists a monopoly of
force: The legality and legitimacy of the judiciary are unquestioned and law making is carried out in accord with constitutional rules; and through its control of
the armed forces and the police, the state exercises an unquestioned monopoly
over weapons.

In these terms, the regional neighborhood poses no signs of serious, concrete,
or imminent threat. However, although Chile is not particularly vulnerable, the
country's historical roots and the recent political decisions taken by neighboring
countries have created an atmosphere of great distrust. In contrast to Argentina
and Peru, which have been embroiled in significant conflicts or wars within the
last decade and a half, Chile has been at peace with its neighbors for more than a
century. Bolivia has recently claimed part of Chile's national territory, but the situation was handled through diplomatic channels. In short, Chile is not facing
conflict that threatens to escalate nor crises that required the use of force, even
targeted force. This stability in regional relations reinforces the view that deterrence has fulfilled a critical role and has made possible the century-long peace enjoyed by Chile. In regard to new risks, however, there are mixed signals. While not
confronting transnational terrorism, Chile faces growing environmental threats
from the overexploitation of ocean resources and the movement and transfer of
toxic and nuclear wastes.[10]

The lack of threat is not synonymous with a complete absence of interstate tension. Because the Latin American regional scene is characterized by instability, the
development of bilateral, regional, and hemispheric preventive mechanisms is essential.[11] Chile has been maintaining a balance that makes cooperation possible
and creates space for bilateral and multilateral conflict prevention. The resolution
of these traditional regional tensions is required for the development of a new

strategic outlook that will complement Chile's insertion in the global marketplace. Just as the newly democratic Chilean political system attempts to respond to Chile's needs and its vision of where it is going in the twenty-first century, a similar process is occurring in the defense arena. Challenges and options are conceptualized with the framework established by the historical tradition of a permanent policy of deterrence (in contrast to an offensive policy), a focused bureaucratic response, a strong emphasis on respect for international law, a high level of political, diplomatic, and military credibility, and a high level of professionalism in the civil as well as the military bureaucracy.

Civil-military dialogue in the post–Cold War era should facilitate the construction of a governing coalition that can shape grand strategy. Nevertheless, progress depends upon resolving the legacy of the authoritarian government. Especially important are the issue of the political autonomy of the armed forces and the need for interelite agreement that would empower leadership to act. Yet, contemporary institutional rules, which continue to express the authoritarian model even within the new democratic framework, create confusion and conflict.

CIVIL-MILITARY RELATIONS IN TRANSITION

Understanding the development of civil-military relations contributes to an understanding of the factors critical to the consolidation of Chile's democracy. Chile is a presumed archetype of "tutelary democracy," in which the military's level of autonomy is so great that it is no longer subordinate to the state. This is reflected in both the many legal privileges that allow the Chilean military a role in policymaking and the reduced capacity of civilian authorities to meddle in the internal politics of the armed forces. The paradigm is, of course, General Pinochet, who, after seventeen years in power and defeat in the 1988 plebescite, continues as commander in chief of the army.[12]

We dispute the view that Chile is a tutelary democracy. An analysis of the unfolding of the democratic transition reveals a series of factors that allow us to enrich the study of civil-military relations by proposing distinct analytical elements to explain the Chilean case.[13] By this analysis, we shall demonstrate that Chile is a consolidated democracy.

First, we must distinguish between the autonomy of the armed forces in its professional role and its institutional autonomy as established in Chile's 1980 Constitution. The two are in constant conflict. A high degree of autonomy exists in regard to planning and implementing defense-related activities (acquisitions, military service, international security relations, education). The involvement of the armed forces in the political system, however, requires the political support of civilian groups that share its goals. Because the legitimacy of attempting to modify the 1980 Constitution is no longer in question, the military has been obliged to build alliances to protect certain of its features that, in its view, are essential to maintaining the institutional order. For example, the armed forces fear politicization of their institution. They have successfully blocked the executive branch from gaining power to make military appointments, reassign officials, or remove commanders in chief. Because legal initiatives exist to modify these privileges, the military has defended its position publicly and has succeeded in gaining the support of the majority within the corporatist coalition.

In addition, when speaking of autonomy, one must distinguish among the different branches of the armed forces. The behavior of the army, air force, and navy differs in important ways. The army plays an active role, highlighted by the presence of General Pinochet at the head of the institution, whereas the air force and navy play only minor roles. By focusing its activities on professional concerns, the navy in particular has maintained good relations with the democratic administrations and appears to have played an auxiliary role in the two peaceful changes of command since 1989.

A final element concerns the way in which the democratic transition unfolded and how that influenced future civil-military relations. The crux of the transition was the decision by Chile's political actors to play by the institutional "rules of the game," as embodied in the 1980 Constitution. As a result, modification of those rules now requires agreement between actors affiliated with the former military government and those who are currently in power. Their failure to reach consensus could inhibit reform of key characteristics of the institutional order. The structure of the electoral system and the presence of "designated senators" provide those opposed to reforms with at least one-third representation, and because constitutional modifications require the support of two-thirds of each legislative chamber, a minority veto exists, making constitutional reforms very difficult.

Finally, among the external factors facing Chile are global changes that call into question the role of the military in the post–Cold War period. The dynamism achieved at the neighborhood and regional levels as a result of the push for economic integration also raises questions about future security concerns in the region.

The Military and Politics

Contemporary Chilean civil-military relations are the result of two principles underlying the democratic framework: the acceptance of a negotiated transition and the "pact on governability." The negotiated transition to democracy involved relinquishing the polarization of the authoritarian period. Between 1985 and 1990, government and opposition slowly ceded ground to each other, allowing their relationship to evolve peacefully.[14] This process meant, however, that the military government would not be overthrown completely nor would the democratic opposition win a clear victory. The military gave up power, but the new government authorities were forced to accept the constitutional limitations set during the Pinochet regime. This established a logic whereby any change to the political system requires negotiation among all the political actors represented in Congress.[15]

The success of the negotiated transition also depended on a pact made by the parties opposed to the military regime. For the first time in Chilean history, the Social Democrats, the Radical Party, the Party of Democracy, and the Socialist Party (as well as a dozen other small groupings that revolved around these four main political organizations) created an alliance, the Concertación, which coordinated the activities of all the opposition groups. The political leadership of these parties realized that their only option was the construction of this alliance because otherwise the nature of the electoral system and the number of competing parties would preclude winning an absolute majority.

The pact on governability developed out of the process of reforming the political system and the institutional order. The pact is basically an agreement to disagree: Competing views coexist, but there is consensus about avoiding a level of political or social tension that would render the country ungovernable. As a result, the armed forces and the right, which believe the military government was a huge success, works with the center-left government, which is critical of the regime (especially of its human-rights violations). The tension is strong, but both groups coexist without destabilizing the institutions of government.[16]

Another dimension of the pact is the institutional autonomy of the armed forces, which the Pinochet regime ensured by means of modifications made to the Constitution while it was still in power. The armed forces and parties on the Right consider the military's autonomy from civil control legitimate and extremely important. The parties of the Concertación, on the other hand, argue that autonomy undermines the military's subordination to the state, but they conditionally accept the constitutional rules supporting autonomy because, for the time being, they lack the mechanisms to change them. The continuation of Pinochet as commander in chief of the army illustrates how well the pact functions.[17]

The negotiated transition and the pact on governability condition the nature of civil-military relations in democratic Chile. During the military regime, the leadership provided the armed forces with constitutionally mandated administrative and budgetary powers, something they had lacked before 1973.[18] The new juridical and administrative framework embedded in the 1980 Constitution provides three types of safeguards for the military.

Constitutional Definition.   The Constitution assigns three roles to the armed forces: the Chilean military is the defender of national sovereignty; protector of national security; and guarantor of the institutional order. This last element, absent before 1980, allows the armed forces to participate actively in the National Security Council.

Nominations and Appointments.   There is constitutional recognition of the right of commanders in chief not be to removed from their posts during their four-year term. In other words, the president now lacks his traditional power to control the appointment of the highest military authorities. The commanders in chief who were in power at the end of the military regime (such as Pinochet, Martínez, and Stange) were allowed to hold their positions for eight more years. The president's power to retire or appoint an official to a post was also modified; now the commander in chief "suggests" to the president who should be appointed and who should be retired.

Allocation of Resources. Another constitutional law established a floor for budgetary allocations to the armed forces. It was set at the level of the 1989 budget plus an annual increment to offset inflation. The *Ley de Cobre* (Copper Law of 1958) also provides the military with 10 percent of export revenues, which guarantees a minimum budget for equipment acquisitions.

The first Concertación government, the administration of Patricio Aylwin (1990–1994), had to focus on the task of subordinating the armed forces to civilian control. By means of various presidential decisions and judicial initiatives, the government tried to reinstate presidential powers and assert its political authority over the military, but this resulted in a series of conflicts and tensions between the government and the armed forces, in particular the army.

During the first months of Aylwin's presidency, conflict centered on two key questions: human rights and the structure of the administration's relationship with the military. The president sought to channel the administration's relationship with the armed forces through the civilian Minister of Defense Patricio Rojas. But, as commander in chief, Pinochet believed himself subordinate only to the highest government authority, that is, the president of the Republic, and he made it clear that he thought of the Ministry of Defense as a mere administrative bureau. This created serious disputes between Pinochet and Rojas, and the minister was forced to emphasize the political character of defense issues while asserting his leadership. The relationship was even more tense because the content of politics at this time was being shaped by these symbolic actions.[19]

The administration's policy on human rights was focused on uncovering the truth and carrying out justice "as far as was possible."[20] A Commission on Truth and Reconciliation was formed to find out the facts about the human-rights violations and to channel cases through the judicial system. For the armed forces, this meant that human-rights violators could be prosecuted, despite the existence of the Amnesty Law promulgated by the military government. In their view, it put the military regime itself on trial. In response, the armed forces published its version of the events between 1973 and 1990. Notably, this was not a collective interpretation. Each service delivered its own report, and they show the diversity of judgment used to assess the record on human rights. The army and navy reports focused on interpreting the historical record whereas the air force looked more toward the future.[21]

A review of the crises that arose in the relationship between the democratic administrations and the armed forces reveals important aspects of the Chilean civil-military conflicts following the transition to democracy.[22] The three most impor-

TABLE 8.1   Conflict and Crisis in Civil-Military Relations, 1990–1995

	1990 enlace	*1993* boinazo	*1995* peucazo
Features	Surprise action	Surprise action	Progressive actions
Context	Conflict	Normalcy	Conflict
Cause of crisis	Valmoval scandal; Pinochet's possible resignation	Valmoval scandal	Valmoval scandal; human rights
Action taken by army	Confinement to quarters of troops	Confinement to quarters (meeting of the high command)	Interference with arrest orders; public demonstrations of army solidarity
Government response	Surprise	Surprise; actions not coordinated	Surprise; coordinated action
Support from other forces	Navy	Not discernible	Navy and air force
International repercussions	Low	Medium	High
Duration	Short (2 days)	Medium (1 week)	Long (episodic)

SOURCE: Center for Documentation, FLACSO, Chile.

tant moments for democratic government were the 1990 *ejercicio de enlace,* the 1993 *boinazo,* and the 1995 Contreras case and *peucazo* (see Table 8.1). All three conflicts between the civilian government and the armed forces were triggered in part by the Valmoval scandal. By implicating one of General Pinochet's sons, this episode threatened to prematurely terminate his term as president. Notably, these conflicts occurred primarily between the government and the army. The other branches of the armed forces usually distanced themselves or responded only when their interests were directly affected. In 1995, the navy played a role in the transfer of Gen. Manuel Contreras (rtd.), and the air force offered logistic support for the operation, and during the *ejercicio de enlace,* press reports mentioned the navy's tacit backing. But the *boinazo* apparently was engineered by the army alone and is notable for the institutional character of that branch's demands.

Two of the crises were sparked by the army's concern over the possibility of prosecution of those involved in the Valmoval scandal, an issue that directly affected General Pinochet because it involved one of his sons. Thus, in two of the three crises, the army openly showed its displeasure at having the general implicated in dubious situations that might force his departure before the end of the term mandated by the Constitution. Although not involving an actual use of force, the actions of the army threatened the democratic system, and this led to negotiations that would raise new, previously unforeseen issues.

The three crises differ in the way they developed. The *ejercicio de enlace* was marked by an element of surprise. It also involved a show of force through the confinement to quarters of army officers. Force was also a feature of the *boinazo,* as personnel in combat gear stood guard over the generals, but this action lasted longer, with the military units remaining on alert for six days until the government began negotiations. The 1995 predicament had two critical moments: on June 13, when the army mounted a surprise maneuver to take General Contreras from his home to a naval hospital in Talcahuano following the order for his arrest; and on July 22, when approximately 300 active-duty army officers in civilian dress, together with their families, gathered at the Punta Peuco prison to show solidarity with another ex-comrade in arms, Gen. Pedro Espinoza (rtd.), jailed in the Letelier case.[23] Both actions took the public by surprise, but their distinctive characteristic was the ability of the army to achieve its objective of placing certain concerns on the negotiating table.

The 1990 *ejercicio de enlace,* as well as the transfer of Contreras and the *peucazo* in summer 1995, occurred in a context of civil-military conflict. The antecedents included the discovery of clandestine graves of the "disappeared"; the Cutufa scandal, a speculative financial swindle; President Aylwin's refusal to accept certain promotions in the army's high command; the meetings at which General Pinochet's resignation was proposed; and the strained relationship between Minister of Defense Rojas and General Pinochet. The 1995 crisis was also exacerbated by the repercussions of the decision in the Letelier case. In the 1993 *boinazo,* in contrast, conflict centered only on the government initiative to amend constitutional laws governing the armed forces, something that the Aylwin administration was not actively promoting.

The Valmoval scandal and the human-rights issue are a common thread running through these three crises. In 1990, the Valmoval case began a chain reaction. When the public learned that the army had made a payment to a son of General Pinochet, the critical question became whether the general knew about the deal in advance. Before the crisis, a series of meetings took place between General Jorge Ballerino and Minister Enrique Correa, Senator Sergio Onofre Jarpa and President Aylwin, and Colonel Carlos Molina Johnson and Minister Edgardo Boeninger, in which the retirement of the general was proposed (at least partly as a way to avoid further embarrassment over the scandal). The government quickly dropped the issue of General Pinochet's retirement, which left only the question of his involvement in the Valmoval case. After the *ejercicio de enlace,* attempts were made to minimize the issue, but doubt remained about the degree of General Pinochet's involvement, and accusations were raised over whether the general had tried to transfer the blame to other military officers.

In 1993, the immediate cause of the *boinazo* was the decision by the Consejo de Defensa del Estado to send the Valmoval case to the courts, an issue which the government-controlled media made public on May 27 and 28. In the days after the military decided to remain on alert, at least nine additional points of contention emerged. The government hoped to resolve the principal problem, the Valmoval case, by sending it to an appeals court or to the military tribunal. The government also indicated it would not speed up congressional debates on the reform of constitutional laws governing the armed forces. On the human-rights issue, the Ley Aylwin (Aylwin Law) provided for a solution requiring the agreement of Congress. As far as the relationship with the media went, the newspaper *La Nación* agreed to publish the comptroller's report, as the army had requested, and state-run television postponed airing its reports on military service and in commemoration of the anniversary of the 1973 coup. Patricio Rojas stayed on as the minister of defense, but the undersecretary of war changed. A working group was established to examine the legal situation vis-à-vis ownership of military property. Sale of military equipment was authorized and a line of credit for the army's arms factory was established with CORFO, the state-run development corporation. And the minister of education in the Ley Orgánica de la Enseñaza (Constitutional Law on Education) did not prohibit the military from running their own educational institutions. In the course of the meetings, however, the government refused to discuss certain other issues, such as salaries or the proposal to build a special jail in case of a guilty verdict in the Letelier case.

In 1995, the army's foremost priority was finding a definitive solution to the human-rights issue, which indicates that the opposition and the government were both seeking a way out of their conflicts. The army had three other items on its agenda: (1) their opposition to the arrest of General Contreras; (2) a resolution of the Valmoval case; and (3) salary raises for military officers. The government, for its part, had three distinct responses. On the first issue, it maintained that the decision to jail Contreras was in the hands of the courts. With regard to the scandal, the president asked the Consejo de Defensa del Estado (National Security Council) to drop the appeal for "state reasons." On the third issue, the government had already negotiated a salary increase.

This examination of the antecedents to the three civil-military crises reveal important themes in Chile's government-military relationship under democracy. First, we see a constant tension between subordination and autonomy. The army, in particular, has defended its corporatist interests by ensuring the retention of its prerogatives, whether through General Pinochet's continuation in power; by seeking closure on the human-rights issue and the exoneration of military officers implicated in these cases; or by seeking guarantees of favorable media coverage about the military's handling of human rights. Likewise, the military continues to use every available legal means to exhibit its discontent. In contrast to the period before 1973, when pressure tactics were explicit and required the use of force *(tacnazo, tanquetazo)*, the military has been careful thus far to use forms of pressure that do not contravene the institutional order. In 1990, the military used the *ejercicio de enlace,* which was a form allowed by law; in 1993, they decreed a state of alert; and in 1995, the transfer of Contreras was justified by a series of legal dispensations made in order to prevent risks to the well-being of the ex-general.

For their part, government authorities have continued to "submit institutions to the rule of law," a tactic that has avoided a direct confrontation with the army and the possibility of a constitutional impasse. The government has left open ways out of crisis situations with the armed forces. The government recognizes that the executive lacks legal mechanisms to act effectively by means of actions that normally fall outside constitutional rules (for example, by calling for the resignations of certain military officers or convoking the National Security Council). The civil authorities behave with the same precaution as the military, with both sides sharing the goal of avoiding a situation so tense that it leaves no way out constitutionally. This approach extends the boundaries of what constitutes the institutional order and risks routinizing certain practices by the army without establishing the limits of what is permissible. In other words, the ambiguity of the law permits actions and consecrates practices that put in question the rule of law.

Finally, in politically risky situations—the role of the National Security Council, human rights, the continuation of Pinochet as commander in chief—the army requires the support of the Right to influence policy. For example, in 1995, the military knew that pressuring the government was not enough. The "compliant voices" of retired generals, designated senators, and UDI and RN congressmen helped achieve the political pact needed to overcome the crisis.

The Modernization of the Armed Forces

Our second analytical perspective is the professionalization of the armed forces. Chile has a strong tradition of military professionalism. Prior to 1973, the military held itself apart from the political debate. During the Pinochet regime the armed forces made political decisions, but they nevertheless remained outside the formal political system. A clear differentiation existed between those military personnel who worked in the government and those who continued to fulfill combat functions. Today, there is an obvious empathy between the Right and the armed forces, yet there is still no institutionalized political participation by military personnel, and the tradition of separation of the armed forces from political parties continues.[24]

Chile also has a tradition of institutional hierarchy. Throughout the military's history, the commander in chief has been at the top of the pyramid. Unlike other Latin American countries, Chile's hierarchical tradition precluded internal dissidence or power struggles and created strong institutional discipline. In negotiations, civilian authorities can be certain that the heads of the air force, the navy, or the army are representatives of their institutions. In sum, the military accepts a professional role associated with the strategic conception of defense-deterrence, which focuses on the protection of national sovereignty. Civilians, and society in general, also accept that role.

Beyond simply protecting Chile's territorial sovereignty, the military has tried to contribute to national development. Notably, at the beginning of the political transition, it was the armed forces who first produced documents examining the position of Chile's combat institutions within the new international environment.[25] The individual reports of the navy (1990), air force (1991), and army (1992) emphasized different objectives, but all sought to consolidate their role within the new institutional framework. The navy made "sea presence" and maritime security its priorities. The air force developed an extensive space program based on the creation of an agency responsible for the launching of satellites and satellite communications. And, since 1992 the army has advanced a plan "to conquer and consolidate control in Chile's interior frontiers" as a response to the need to improve state presence in marginalized and poverty-stricken zones within Chile.[26]

There are two possible explanations for this repositioning of the armed forces in society. First, the democratization of the country forced a reorientation toward strictly professional activities. The response was most immediate precisely in those branches that had played a less prominent role in the military regime. The army reacted more slowly and is the only institution that continues to have significant political and social problems because of its implication in human-rights cases. Second, the armed forces' search for answers to the changing world scene has led them to seek to create axes of orientation for its actions ("sea presence," "space program," "interior frontiers"). The creation of these concepts indicates that the military, beyond attempting to justify their existence in the face of threatened budget cuts and lack of interest on the part of civil society, have tried to influence the development of public policy concerning specific strategic concepts.

Civilians have also suggested initiatives related to the modernization of the armed forces. In 1994, the administration of Eduardo Frei (1994–2000) announced its decision to create a clear-cut defense policy designed through a public, informed process, which they hoped would strengthen long-term commitments to the state's military policies. Officials in the Ministry of Defense set four goals: citizen commitment, state responsibility, a context of peace, and efficiency within the armed forces.[27]

The first goal advances the idea of national defense as an obligation of all citizens. The second requires restructuring and coordination to give coherence, rationality, and leadership to the state's role in defense. This calls for an articulation of defense policy with sectorial development policies so that the latter can be aligned with Chile's defense considerations and so that there may be adequate interaction between both policymaking realms. The third involves the promotion of peace and stability in the region using whatever means necessary. The last goal seeks a harmonization of defense and military policies in alignment with the dynamics of the new emerging global context and Chilean national interests. Within this, it will fall primarily to the armed forces to develop its traditional function of guarding the independence of Chile.

Conceptually, defense policy is defined as the totality of the institutions and instruments destined to "successfully confront threats and/or aggressions that might affect Chile's security, sovereignty, peace, quality of life, the common good of its people, and in general the fundamental values established by the Constitution."[28] Defense policy in this framework is understood in regard to both the proper defense role for and the organization of the armed forces. Defining policy is the primordial task of government, that is, of the executive and its principal actor, the president of the Republic as well as the bureaucratic apparatus on which he depends, including the armed forces, as subordinates to him. The democratic administrations must guarantee certain conduct in the region and generate measures of trust in the international arena. But government efforts have run into three difficulties.[29] First, mistrust arising from divisive political issues between the government and the military has limited discussion of more professional issues. The Ministry of Defense's 1994 agenda included stages for public debate over the defining of defense policy, but delays resulted from problems related to the human-rights issue, the jailing of General Contreras, and the passage of laws relating to the armed forces. In short, the failure to resolve issues that arose during the transition now affects opportunities to modernize the state and its public policy, especially in regard to defense.

The government's second difficulty involves the armed forces' extensive autonomy in the determination of its own institutional policies. At the beginning of the democratic regime, the military still counted on relatively stable funding and could still carry out programs. Even now, legal obstacles prevent government officials from "meddling" in military matters and the lack of human and material resources in the Ministry of Defense makes it difficult to track and coordinate activities of the various branches. Moreover, the armed forces have always viewed the Ministry of Defense as a bureaucratic department and not as a place where long-term policies are set. Modernization will require the ministry to develop the capacity to design, direct, coordinate, and evaluate policy.

Finally, the development of defense policy is also limited by inadequate preparation on the part of civilians in the defense field. For many years, Chilean civilians did not participate in decisionmaking in defense matters. Between 1932 and 1973—a period of great democratic stability when there were few civil-military tensions—the notion took root that military matters should be handled exclusively by military personnel. Ever since the military's discredited intervention in national politics in June 1932, the political elite has viewed combat institutions as a specialized province where civilians can do little. This lack of interest in military matters on the part of the political class caused a general devaluation of the armed forces in the eyes of civilians. Many people came to believe that the mission of the armed forces is not relevant when compared to more pressing national problems, such as improving education, health, and living standards for the country's population. This neglect on the part of civil society provided the military with freedom to discuss and debate their own policies and even reformulate their mission. The international scene also had great influence over the setting of Chile's "national security doctrine." But those factors only worked to further alienate Chilean civilians from decisionmaking on defense matters.

During the Pinochet regime, academic centers in Chile carried out systematic studies on defense and civil-military relations in an attempt to understand why the military had intervened in the country's political life. These studies examined the roots of the military, systematized the history of civil-military relations, and near the end of the regime, began to propose initiatives that involved members of the armed forces. These activities helped make possible the first encounters between civilians and military personnel (but only in an academic context).[30] More was needed. During the first years of democratic government, the civilian political elite confronted the difficulty of achieving meaningful administrative changes. Budget shortfalls made it impossible to put new people in the Ministry of Defense, and a law prohibiting the removal of functionaries in the public administration blocked cutbacks of existing personnel. By 1994, when the second democratic administration announced its intention to formally define national defense policy, there was a need for personnel who could understand and analyze politico-strategic and military issues. Defining national defense policy was particularly challenging because it meant that a civil administration as part of state policy was proposing the establishment of norms, objectives, goals, and strategies for Chile's military institutions in the middle term. It was also critical because it reflected a new civilian interest in defense matters, even though that interest was ultimately blocked by the difficulties discussed previously.[31]

Thus, there appear to be two dimensions to the civil-military conflict under democracy. First is the role of the armed forces, where we see a tension between retaining its autonomy and the need to subordinate the military to civilian constitutional power. The legal framework favoring military autonomy, which has influenced democratic leaders and has forced both sides to accept a mutually unsatisfactory situation, has exacerbated the tension, as has the political support for the status quo demonstrated by parties of the Right and the designated senators. Because part of the political elite accepts military autonomy under democracy, the government's ability to transform the legal framework is severely limited. There is no political consensus on the role that the armed forces should play, and the failure to set limits to the military's autonomy creates ongoing civil-military tension.

The second dimension is the military's *professional* autonomy, that is, the capacity of the armed forces to develop its own policies. The lack of civilian leadership in defense matters and the military's development of its own institutional policies creates strain. Historical conditions have led to a conception of the specificity of the role of defense and explicit cultivation of that concept in the armed forces. Moreover, the relationship is strongly influenced by the mistrust that evolved during the transition, the legal framework favorable to the armed forces, the limited role of the Ministry of Defense in the determination and implementation of defense policy, and finally, the lack of civilian expertise in the field of defense and military matters.

External Determinants

The Chilean political transition (1988–1995) must be placed in the context of larger processes of global transformation of the international system.[32] It coincided with important transformations in the international arena (the fall of the Berlin Wall, the dissolution of the Soviet Union, and the democratization of most of Latin America). This poses new questions about the future of Chile's military. These questions do not revolve around the emergence of a peaceful international environment and the reduction in the use of force as much as they do around the role of force in a context of greater international interdependence and higher levels of globalization.[33]

In the Chilean case, a favorable subregional environment has helped diminish threats of conflict. Chilean foreign policy has attempted to resolve the ongoing border disputes with Argentina and Peru, to stimulate subregional economic cooperation, and to make treaties to resolve controversies peacefully. As a result, the armed forces face four overarching questions. First, what is the military's vision in regard to the new international environment? Second, what is the appropriate role and mission for the armed forces in this new context? Third, what is the position of the United States in the region? And, fourth, what is the process of subregional integration and its impact on threat perceptions?

On the first question, the Chilean population holds at least two views about the new international environment.[34] There exists a realist assessment of international relations, and given the enduring uncertainties around the globe, that assessment calls for a restricted involvement for Chile in the world arena. At the other extreme is a positivist view that emphasizes opportunities for cooperation and interdependence and seeks to have Chile use both specific and general initiatives to place itself in the international system. On the second question, many Chileans believe that the primary function of the armed forces is the defense of Chile's sovereignty. Thus, public opinion is cautious concerning the military's involvement in international security (for example, peace missions or participation in international armed forces), and it generally rejects participation in issues foreign to the defense function (such as drug trafficking or the environment).

On the third question, the Chilean armed forces mistrust U.S. policy on Latin American security because U.S. leaders have failed to differentiate specific subregional problems. Many Chileans believe that the United States seeks hegemony in its relationships with each Latin American country. A corollary to this is the conviction that the United States is pursuing a reduction of the armed forces throughout Latin America as a step in converting them into police in the fight against drugs. Such a plan ignores the specific conditions found within each country as well as the regional perceptions of threat that exist between individual Latin American countries. A cooperative but separate relationship with the United States seems desirable, and from an economic point of view, it would benefit Chile to participate in NAFTA, which would not necessarily require submission to the policies of its northern neighbor.

Finally, there is the question of regional integration and threat perception. Regional integration, although desirable, must bring with it sufficient safeguards because a process of this nature does not necessarily mean an end to threat. To the contrary, threat perceptions tend to increase as neighboring countries come to share more concerns. From another point of view, integration is seen as a dynamic, multifaceted process that affects traditional threat perceptions and calls into question current security frameworks based on power equilibrium. Greater ties will fortify cooperation, and the moment will arrive when it will be desirable to have a stable, consolidated, and peaceful relationship rather than one based on the perception of threat.

CONCLUSION

Today Chile has a historic opportunity to stabilize and continue its development. But it needs a strategy that "organizes resources of both national power, under new political, social, and cultural conditions, and security, nationally and internationally."[35] The historic importance of the regional neighborhood must be taken into consideration in shaping a new strategic vision. For Chile, the corporatist coalition and the democratic-modernizers must both play a role. Achieving minimal agreement between these groups is a basic step necessary for creating the stability required for Chile's continued development.

The need for consensus is particularly evident in the area of security. The development of strategy must appraise the role of the Chilean military in a context that recognizes Chile's relationship to the rest of the world. If national strategy includes commercial and political opening to neighboring countries, then defense matters will necessarily be part of the debate. To the extent that regional interdependence reduces threat perception, Chile's leadership must create an environment that prevents the armed forces from overstating the threats they perceive. Nevertheless, complex interdependence will surely bring about new risks, and these will have to be evaluated and measured so as not to create asymmetries in the integration processes currently underway. Integration, which up until now has been economic and political, affects the vision of traditional geopolitics, and this calls for new ways to assess threat.

The debate over the role of the armed forces is certainly not finished in Chile. Two contradictory views still exist: One side believes that the armed forces are the guarantors of the institutional order and as such should enjoy special privilege, which General Pinochet has called "relative independence."[36] Another group believes that the armed forces, subordinated to the state, should limit its role to fulfilling its constitutional mission to protect Chile's sovereignty.[37]

Chile must reach a consensus on the role appropriate for the armed forces under democracy, establishing along the way limits on military intervention in the institutional order. One way to achieve this would be to work for transformation of the current constitutional rules and laws affecting the armed forces. A less traumatic option, and one that is less certain, would be to routinize the current institutional order and, by means of repeated practice, gradually establish boundaries for what is acceptable.

Chile's overall development—political, social, and economic—depends on a resolution of current problems, and among the most important is defining the part that the military will play in Chile's civil society, government institutions, and national strategy.

NOTES

Translated by Patricia Rosas.
SOURCE: Center for Documentation, FLASCO, Chile.

1. We define grand strategy as the harmonization of diverse policies that makes possible a sense of equity and that allows for the planning of overall national development, providing it with long-term sustainability. On this subject, see Paul Kennedy, ed., *Grand Strategies in War and Peace* (New Haven: Yale University Press, 1991); Augusto Varas, *Chile: Política de defensa y gran estrategia,* International and Military Relations Section, Facultad Latinoamericana de Ciencias Sociales (FLACSO) Working Paper Series, Chile, 1994.

2. The armed forces received a fixed minimum budgetary allocation, which was set at the 1989 level with an annual percentage increase to offset inflation. The Ley de Cobre (Copper Law) also gave 10 percent of CODELCO's profits from foreign sales to the military. The state would have to cover the difference if the minimum was not met. Francisco Rojas A., *Gasto militar en América Latina: Procesos de decisiones y actores claves* (CINDE/FLACSO, 1994).

3. Since 1993, factionalization within the RN has become more apparent. Andrés Allamand, the party president, is a leader with liberal tendencies, whereas the more conservative sector includes a group of senators who during 1995 explicitly rejected agreements reached by the political commission working on the reform of the constitution.

4. See the 1989 and 1993 platforms of the Concertación for a further elaboration of these principles.

5. See Carlos Figueroa, "Una diplomacia para del desarrollo," paper prepared for the Ministry of Foreign Relations, Chamber of Deputies, April 5, 1994; and "Bases programáticas del Segundo Gobierno de la Concertación, *Un gobierno para los nuevos tiempos* (Santiago: Concertación de Partidos por la Democracia, 1993), mimeo.

6. See Francisco Rojas A., *La Reinserción International de Chile* (1991); *De la Reinserción a los Acuerdos* (1992); *Consolidando una insercion multiple en el sistema internacional* (1993); and *Construyendo un nuevo perfil externo: Democracia, modernización, pluralismo* (1994), each published by FLACSO-Chile.

7. Chile joined APEC in 1994, and it signed the MERCOSUR and EU treaties during 1996.

8. Edmundo Pérez Yoma, "Inauguración del año académico de las academias de guerra," *Fuerzas Armadas y Sociedad* (FLACSO-Chile), no. 1 (1996).

9. Claudio Fuentes, "El mundo desde Chile," *Fuerzas Armadas y Sociedad,* no. 4 (October–December 1994):21–32.

10. Francisco Rojas and Carlos Martin, "Entre las viejas and las nuevas percepciones de amenaza: El caso del medio ambiente," *Nuevas Amenazas a la Seguridad* (CESPAL, IDESCI, Buenos Aires, 1995).

11. *Paz y seguridad en las Américas,* Políticas de Seguridad Hemisférica Cooperativa: Recomendaciones de Políticas (FLACSO/Woodrow Wilson Center), no. 1 (March 1995).

12. Brian Loveman, "Protected Democracies and Military Guardianship: Political Transitions in Latin America, 1978–1993," *Journal of Interamerican Studies* 36, no. 2 (Summer 1994):105–189.

13. Augusto Varas, *La autonomía militar en América Latina* (Caracas: Editorial Nueva Sociedad, 1988).

14. Paul W. Drake and Ivan Jaksic, *The Struggle for Democracy in Chile* (Lincoln: University of Nebraska Press, 1991).

15. Manuel Antonio Garretón, "Coaliciones políticas y proceso de democratización: El caso chileno," *FLACSO Documentos de Trabajo 22* (1992); and *Hacia una nueva era política* (Santiago: Fondo de Cultura Económica, 1995), esp. chapter 5.

16. For a general overview of the human-rights question during the democratic transition, see José Zalaquett, "Derechos humanos y limitaciones políticas en las transiciones democráticas del Cono Sur," *Colección de Estudios CIEPLAN* 33 (1991):147–186.

17. Before taking power in 1990, President Aylwin repeatedly said that General Pinochet should relinquish his position as commander of the army, but Aylwin acknowledged that he would accept the continuation of Pinochet in that post because the constitution mandated it.

18. Gonzalo García y Esteban Montes, *Subordinación democrática de los militares* (Santiago: Centro de Estudios de la Democracia, 1994).

19. For example, General Pinochet did not attend the inauguration of the regular session of Congress, which at the time was viewed by some politicians as a gesture of rebellion. See *El Mercurio,* August 24, 1990.

20. Garretón "Coaliciones políticas y proceso de democratización," chapter 7.

21. Claudio Fuentes, *El discourse militar en la transición Chilena: Mesianismo, autonomia, y conviviencia en democracia.* Nueva Series FLACSO (1996, in press). On the army's view of its role, see *Presentación del Ejército de Chile ante la Comisión Nacional Verdad y Reconciliación,* vol. 1 (Santiago: Ejército de Chile, 1990).

22. The review of the crises was drawn from newspaper accounts written during the time conflicts occurred. For an analysis of the situation from a journalist's point of view, see Rafael Otano, *Crónica de la transición* (Santiago: Editorial Planeta, 1995).

23. Orlando Letelier, Allende's foreign minister ambassador to the United States, was assassinated by a car bomb in Washington, D.C., in 1976. It was not until after the end of the military regime that the perpetrators were brought to justice.

24. Arturo Valenzuela, "The Military in Power: The Consolidation of One-Man Rule," in Drake and Jaksic, *The Struggle for Democracy in Chile;* Augusto Varas, *Los militares en el poder* (Santiago: Pehuén Editores, 1987).

25. Augusto Varas y Claudio Fuentes, *Defensa Nacional, Chile 1990–1994: Modernización y desarrollo* (Santiago: FLACSO Book Series, 1994).

26. Memorial del Ejército [Official Records of the Army], issue dedicated to *"Conquista y consolidación de las fronteras interiores: Una tarea del ejército,"* no. 445, Santiago 1994. For the army, the most relevant documents include Augusto Pinochet, "Ejército, trayectoria y futuro," August 21, 1992; and "Ejército de Chile: Posibles elementos a considerar en su proyeccion future," August 19, 1993.

27. Eduardo Frei, Mensaje Presidencial al Congreso Nacional, May 21, 1994; Edmundo Pérez Yoma, "Inauguración del año académico de las Fuerzas Armadas," *Fuerzas Armadas y Sociedad,* no. 2 (FLACSO-Chile, 1995). and Edmundo Pérez Yoma, "Inauguración del año académico de las academias de guerra," *Fuerzas Armadas y Sociedad,* no. 1 (FLACSO-Chile, 1996).

28. Yoma, "Inauguración del año académico de las academias de guerra."

29. Claudio Fuentes, "Política de defensa en Chile: Desafíos para su construcción," *Revista Ser en el 2000,* no. 7 (Buenos Aires, 1995).

30. Augusto Varas, *Sociologia de la instituciones en Chile,* (FLACSO Area de Relaciones Internacionales y Militares, 1994). See also the special issue of *Fuerzas Armadas y Sociedad* (FLACSO-Chile), no. 1 (1995).

31. The army was the first institution to offer an M.A. in Military Science, mencion politica de Defensa, for interested civilians in 1992. Later, the Minister of Defense opened the way for joint studies with the participation of civilian academics at the National Academy of Policy and Strategic Studies, ANEPE. In 1995, the same minister started a loan program for courses at the postgraduate level.

32. Paul W. Drake, "Los factores internacionales en la coyuntura democrática," paper prepared for the conference on "Chilean Democratization in Comparative Perspective," (FLACSO, Santiago, July 1993).

33. See Augusto Varas, *La seguridad hemisférica cooperativa de post-guerra fría* (Area de Relaciones Internacaionales y Militares, FLACSO-Chile, 1994).

34. In this chapter, we concentrate on two predominant visions about the international area, even though a much broader spectrum with greater shadings exists. On this topic, see Claudio Fuentes, "El mundo desde Chile," *Fuerzas Armadas y Sociedad,* no. 4 (1994).

35. Augusto Varas, *Chile: Política de defensa y gran estrategia,* p. 27

36. General Augusto Pinochet, *Exposición del comandante en jefe del Ejército sobre el proyecto de reformas a la Ley Orgánica Constitucional de las FF.AA. ante la Comisión de Defensa de la Cámara* (January 1993). Also Sergio Fernández, "Estado moderno y fuerza militar: Perspectiva jurídica e institucionalidad chilena," prepared for the conference on the Modern State and the Army: A National Perspective, The Army War Academy (October 1992).

37. For a synthesis of the discussion of the role of the armed forces under democracy in the Chilean case, see Francisco Rojas, "Los militares y la democracia: El caso chileno," prepared for the project on *Civil-Military Relations Compared Across Small Democracies* (Fundación Arias, August 1996). A work that questions the thesis of relative independence is Patricio Aylwin, "Consideraciones al proyecto de ley que modifica las leyes orgánicas constitucionales de las Fuerzas Armadas y de Carabineros de Chile," Ministry of the Secretary General of the Government, April 26, 1993.

■

CHAPTER NINE

Changing Patterns of Civil-Military Relations and Thailand's Regional Outlook

Surachart Bamrungsuk

The Thai military faces new challenges with the end of the Cold War. Thailand's external security environment has been transformed by the withdrawal of Vietnamese forces from Cambodia in 1990. The long-standing internal battle with the Communist Party has been resolved in the military's favor. Moreover, the transformation of Thailand's political ideology and institutions have wrought fundamental changes in civil-military relations. This chapter explores how the evolution of domestic and international politics has redefined Thai civil-military relations. In turn, it discusses the implications of changes in civil-military relations on Thailand's goals and behavior in the regional context.

The chapter is organized in two parts. The first section is a historical review of the role of the military in Thai politics. It explains how changes in the ideological context and constitutive rules that govern Thai politics have forced a reorientation of the position of the Thai military in society. The second section discusses how civil-military relations affect the definition of economic and security goals. Here the focus is primarily on the post-1992 period and how the process of democratization and the concomitant development of civil society have affected Thailand's interests in the region.

THE EVOLUTION OF POLITICAL IDEOLOGY
AND CONSTITUTIVE RULES: THAI CIVIL-MILITARY
RELATIONS IN TRANSITION

Since the 1932 revolution, which marks Thailand's liberation from absolutism and the initiation of the era of constitutional monarchy, Thai politics has been regulated by episodes of overt intervention and behind the scenes string-pulling by the Thai military.[1] At the same time, the gradual development of civil society has altered societal notions of the appropriate relationship between society and the military. With the growth of democracy and civil society in the post–Cold War period, ideology can be broadly understood to have evolved from a militarist perspective—in which the armed forces act as the guardian of the state and the representative of popular will—to an orientation that is more liberal individualist. The transformation of the constitutive rules of Thai politics mirrors the ideological evolution as the strengthening of civilian institutions has begun to reduce military dominance in the political arena.

The ideological and institutional parameters of Thai politics interacted with the particular way in which the Cold War played itself out in Indochina to produce a Thai military strategy oriented toward defeating the internal threat posed by the Communist Party and protecting the country from possible Vietnamese expansion, characterized most vividly by Vietnam's invasion of Cambodia. These threats both reflected and perpetuated the hegemonic position of the military in domestic politics. During the Cold War, consequently, military intervention in politics was justified on the basis of the threat to national security. The military's duty to defend the country during the Communist war period privileged it relative to civilian organizations. Moreover, the broad definition of national security justified a rapid expansion of the military's roles in society, especially in the political arena.

Political Transition: 1973–1976

Like the politics of many Third World countries in the postcolonial period, Thai politics can be divided into episodes of political struggle between civilian and military leaders. Accordingly, one of the major turning points in civil-military relations in the modern era occurred in October 1973 when the student movement, in cooperation with other forces in society, successfully overthrew the military government.[2] With the ousting of the military regime and the mobilization of civilian groups in society, Thai politics entered "an era of democratic blossom." However, Thailand's experiment with democracy was cut short in October 1976, when escalating conflict between the left and right culminated in right-wing groups killing over 100 students and arresting 3,000 more on the Thamasat University campus. On the evening of the massacre, the military seized power, and the country entered a new phase of authoritarianism.[3]

With the support of the King Bhumipol and the military, a new government was formed under the prime ministership of Thanin Kraivichien—a former Supreme Court judge. Fiercely anti-Communist, the Thanin regime imposed strict press censorship and carried out anti-Communist purges of the civil service and universities. These measures, in turn, catalyzed the growth of a student-led Communist resistance movement and led to the declaration of martial law in an effort to subdue the resistance groups. The regime's repressive measures alienated many groups in society—the press, labor, students, politicians, sectors of big business, the bureaucracy, and also the military.

The Thanin government's repressive measures, which actually increased support among the general populace for the Communist insurgents, worried the military. The military perceived the growth of communism as an internal threat to the regime—one which they sought to counter by removing the Thanin government in an October 1977 coup. Reflective of the ideological current of the period, the military rejected the reintroduction of democracy out of fear it would precipitate a weakening of the state. Instead, the military assumed open control of the government.[4] It received support for its actions against the Thanin regime both internationally and domestically. The leader of the new regime, General Kriangsak Chamanand, was viewed favorably not only by Washington but also by Peking.[5] The general was also greeted warmly by a wide cross-section of society—labor, students, liberals, many politicians, and the press—because of his efforts to resolve the conflicts and tensions that had developed after the October 6, 1976 coup.

The new military government was markedly more liberal than its predecessors, allowing limited press freedom and offering amnesty to political dissidents. A new constitution was promulgated in December 1978 and a general election was held on schedule in April 1979.[6] Yet it is a mistake to view the ensuing liberalization as a disengagement of the military from politics; "this was not a hasty retreat" for the military.[7]Rather, this "transition through transaction" was initiated in 1977 in response to a high level of threat—a threat to the country's national survival and to the military institution.[8]Members of the armed forces decided that the best strategy to win its battle against the Communists was to return to open politics. In a fashion similar to Spain and Brazil, the military maintained its prerogatives in the post-transition regime. The constitutive rules of politics, in particular, perpetuated the central role of the military in politics. Military officers occupied the office of the prime minister and held many ministerial portfolios. The constitution was designed to provide the military with veto power in important areas in the House of Representatives, including votes of no confidence, the budget, and national security, while the appointed Senate became the "power base" for the military. As such, the period came to be known as the Half-Democracy Era, as the military ruled without widespread internal or external resistance.[9]

Nevertheless, by early 1980 support for the Kriangsak government waned. Demonstrations were organized in protest of the price increases implemented by the regime in response to the second oil crisis. As a result, General Kriangsak re-

signed in March 1980 and General Prem Tinsoulanon became the next prime
minister.

Liberalization and Military Rule in the 1980s

Although a military leader, General Prem gave civilian politicians a greater role in
his regime. In contrast to Kriangsak, he appointed mostly civilians to his cabinet
and elicited the support of major political parties in the House. The relatively open
political environment proved to be fertile ground for the development of civil society. Yet, the transformation was gradual and, paradoxically enough, occurred in
conjunction with the institutionalization of the military's role in society. Concomitant with liberalization came a codification of the military's role in guarding the
state against threats to its security stemming from domestic insurgency. At the same
time, the military assumed a greater role in economic development, embodied in
the new professionalism doctrine—the Prime Minister's Office Order Nos. 66/2523
and 65/2525.[10] Through the promulgation of such measures, the military's role in
development became an explicit component of doctrine.

At the same time, changes in the military's strategy in its battle against communism bolstered the growth of incipient democracy in the Prem period. In the past,
the armed forces believed that authoritarianism was the most effective means to
fight the Communists; democracy was equated with a weakening of the state. In the
1980s, the Thai military began to accept "the principle of democracy as a guideline"
and to argue that "the important factor in the struggle to win over communism and
destroy all forms of dictatorship is the development of democracy."[11]

Economic factors also bolstered the case for democratization. The authoritarian government had produced instability and, as a result, discouraged foreign investment. In fact, the decline of foreign investment during Thanin's authoritarian
regime was one of the justifications for the 1977 coup.[12] Military intervention was
viewed as detrimental to economic growth; for example, rumors about conflict
between the military and government destabilized the stock market. It was increasingly perceived that economic success required a stable, resilient, and democratic government.

The turn toward democracy represented a shift in the military's strategy for
fighting the internal threat posed by the Communists, protecting its institutional
interests, and promoting economic growth. At the same time, it contributed to
the gradual evolution of political ideology and constitutive rules in Thai politics,
and hence it marks a turning point in the decades-long redefinition of civil-military relations. Yet the military's apparent warming to democracy—as a manifesta-
tion of the military's strategic, not simply normative, calculations—did not alone
alter the military's perception of itself as caretaker of the country. Rather a series
of factors interacted to produce the changes in the civil-military configuration
that began to take hold in the 1980s.[13]

The end of the military's internal battle with the Communists was, for example,
essential to the transformation. International events, including the Vietnam War

and subsequent Vietnamese invasion of Cambodia, had created fragmentation in the Communist Party, as internal conflicts emerged over the party's interests in the war. This, in combination with the military's adoption of a new doctrine, led to the defeat of the Communists. In 1983, the Prem government announced its victory over the Communists and the end to what the military perceived as a long-standing internal threat to the regime.[14] Concomitant with this were changes in the normative view of democracy in broader Thai society. Democracy was increasingly viewed as essential to the establishment of a "civilized polity," whereas authoritarianism represented "political underdevelopment" of the country. Besides, democracy was generally accepted as a principal ideology in the society.

Perhaps the biggest indicator of the Thai political transition was the failure of two military coups in the 1980s. Although these events reveal that the Thai military remained a salient political actor during the liberalization period, the military's failure to gain support from outside constituencies or from the king indicates the extent to which the ideological and legal foundation of Thai politics was changing. Because the king occupies a special position in Thai politics, his unwillingness to support the coup makers was a major turning point. As formal head of state, the king enjoys a supreme legitimacy in the eyes of the Thai population as the reserve of truth and equity. As such, the king performs an important role in the political process. He has intervened in periods of severe crisis—in 1973 against the military crackdown, in 1981 in favor of the Prem government, and most recently in 1992—but not without the complicity of some faction in the armed forces, which each time supported his initiatives. Thus, although the 1981 coup constituted the biggest deployment of force in Thai political history, the royal decision to stay with the government totally destroyed the legitimacy of the coup makers and the coup failed.[15] In 1985, there was another coup attempt with a similar outcome.[16]

At the same time, the extent to which democratic processes had taken hold was illustrated when General Prem, after eight years in power, turned down the prime ministership following the 1988 election. This allowed Thailand to have its first elected prime minister in many years: Chartchai Choonawan, a former military leader and head of the Chart-thai Party (the Thai Nation Party). This appeared to mark the end of the Half-Democracy Era. The constitutive rules of politics had evolved from a situation in which the military enjoyed complete dominance in the institutions of governance to significant civilian participation in politics.

Civil-Military Relations in the Post–Cold War Period

Events in the post–Cold War period contributed to the evolution of Thai civil-military relations. The end of the Communist Party and the withdrawal of Vietnamese forces from the area beginning in 1980 reduced the external threats the country faced. General Prem's conservative economic policy resulted in double-digit growth (13.2 percent in 1988, 12.2 percent in 1989).[17] Economic growth and political liberalization fostered the expansion of interest group activity.

Nevertheless the government still faced obstacles in its effort to assert civilian control over the military. When the prime minister's policy advisor responded to attacks by General Chaovalit Yongchaiyuth, Supreme Commander and Army Chief, on corruption in the government by suggesting that critics of the government should "clean their own house," his comments prompted the military to call for the advisor's resignation.[18]Ultimately, the government prevailed in the confrontation and the expression of opposition was limited to large parades of officers demonstrating in support of the general. For the armed forces, these confrontations were manifestations of the government's attempt to establish political control over the army institution and to reduce the military's influence on politics.

Weakness in civilian institutions complicated the effort to establish mechanisms of civilian control. Accusations against the cabinet of catering to private interests discredited them. At the same time, the Thai military remained strong throughout the period of democratization. The Thai army was not defeated either by interstate war or by an internal war; it was not forced to retreat to the barracks. Thus, the consolidation of democracy depended heavily on the performance of elected government as a guard against military intervention in politics.

Ultimately, it was the civilian government's efforts to assert control over the military that led to a final confrontation between the civilian government and the military institution. In response to a report that the government planned to dismiss General Sunthorn Kongsompong, the supreme commander, and General Suchinda Kraprayoon, chief of the army, and appoint instead a rival of the military leadership to the top post in the Ministry of Defense, the armed forces organized a coup against the Chartchai regime. The first elected prime minister since 1976 and his cabinet were toppled on February 23, 1991.[19] It was the first successful coup since 1977.[20]

Yet, although it appeared to be a continuation of Thailand's long chain of interventions, the coup was qualitatively different than previous ones.[21] A fundamental shift in the legitimacy and efficacy of military rule had taken place. Moreover, the armed forces seemed to recognize that the transition to democracy had yielded profound changes in civil society; most importantly, military leaders appeared to acknowledge the implications of such changes for the capacity of the armed forces to rule without support from civil society. Thus, political parties were not banned, curfew and press censorship were not imposed, and the military promised to return to elected politics in one year. The coup leaders held a meeting with bankers and labor leaders to explain their reasons for undertaking the coup. Moreover, because the military was not confident enough to set up a military regime even as a caretaker government,[22] the postcoup government was organized around civilian bureaucrats and businessmen.

Nevertheless, while promising a return to parliamentary politics, the generals carefully manipulated the drafting of the new constitution. Thus, while the coup had been in part welcomed as a relief to the rampant corruption that characterized Chartchai's government, popular support began to wane when these initiatives were interpreted as an attempt to reverse the democratization process and to enhance the military's position in politics. When the 1992 election saw the victory of the military's hand-picked candidate, General Suchinda, as prime minister, the stage was set for a massive uprising against the military government.

The May 1992 Uprising

By May 1992 large groups of "well-dressed, middle-class" men (primarily businessmen and private-sector workers) were actively participating in rallies against the generals. An ad hoc committee—the Federation for Democracy—was formed by the democratic opposition. The group called for Suchinda's resignation and for the promulgation of constitutional amendments mandating that the prime minister be elected to office. Ultimately, as opposition mounted, the military resorted to force to suppress the opposition. Only the intervention of the king put an end to the violence.[23]

The uprising caused a major political defeat for the armed forces. Pictures of the brutality of the Thai military were transmitted worldwide. The process of democratization had taken root, prompting a redefinition of the military's role in society. Although the army retained its duty to protect the nation, in the postcrisis political climate this no longer meant that the army was superior to other institutions in Thai society or that it exercised the unconditional right to intervene in civilian politics when it deemed necessary.

Changes in the ideological climate prompted by the military's behavior in the crisis coincided with modifications in basic institutions of governance. The Thai constitution was amended; it now required that the prime minister be an elected member of parliament. The power of the appointed Senate was also reduced. Absent any civilian support, the military-supported government was forced to resign and a general election was scheduled for September 1992. By March 1996, in its institutional power base, the upper house, the military held only 48 of 260 seats (104 seats fewer than it held in 1992).[24] Moreover, many high-ranking officers from the three services were not reappointed. Since the appointment of senators is the prerogative of the government, the sharp reduction in military representation in the upper house represents the extent to which the government has been able to draw on nonmilitary constituencies for political support.

Moreover, since the uprising, the legal power of the military has been significantly reduced. The government has moved decisively to revise all major laws that grant extraconstitutional powers to the military in crisis situations. For example, the government revised the Government Administration in a Crisis Situation Act of 1952 and the Martial Law Act of 1954 and abolished the Internal Security Act of 1976, so that the use of armed forces in riot control now requires authorization by the cabinet. As a result, the Capital Peace-Keeping Command, key to controlling security in the capital since 1976, was dissolved.[25]

Nevertheless, despite the success of these institutional and legal challenges to the military's position, the establishment of civilian dominance is far from complete. One of the major barriers to such efforts has been the absence of effective parliamentary committees and government expertise necessary for regulating military affairs. As a result, the government and public must depend on the military for advice. The success of efforts to effect further institutional changes in this direction will play a large role in the ongoing evolution of civil-military relations. Thus far, there has been a failure to design an explicit strategy to control the military, beyond mandating the election of a civilian prime minister. Even after the 1992 uprising, there was no serious debate about what mechanisms were necessary to assert democratic control over the military. Debate was limited to a government investigation of the role of the armed forces in the uprising and the removal of key officers responsible for the military's actions.[26]

In summary, the pre-1992 period in civil-military relations is characterized by an evolution in civil-military relations, in David Mares's terminology, from a situation of military dominance to a "pact among equals" and since 1992 to an even greater assertion of civilian control. The military's preeminent role in the polity from the 1950s to the 1980s is indicated both by the ideological and constitutive rules that regulated Thai politics. The ideology was one in which the military viewed itself as caretaker of the country, while civilian governance was viewed with suspicion if not contempt. Constitutive rules also reflected and promoted military influence, as military dominance in the governing apparatus greatly circumscribed the influence of civilian groups.

Yet, especially in the 1980s, changes in ideology and constitutive rules coincided with a redefinition of the civil-military configuration. With the eclipse of the Communist threat, the strengthening of civil society, and perhaps most importantly, changes in how the interests of the military as institution might best be served, the legitimacy of democratic governance was enhanced. This was reflected in changes in the institutional environment, as in the late 1980s the military transferred power to an elected prime minister. These changes were codified by constitutional and legal changes in the post-1992 period. In short, the evolution in political ideology and institutional practices has increasingly supported the assertion of civilian influence in domestic politics. As such, the May uprising marks a turning point in Thai civil-military relations. Nonetheless, further evolution in the ideological and institutional context is essential to the consolidation of civilian control over the military.

IMPLICATIONS OF CIVIL-MILITARY RELATIONS FOR THAILAND'S REGIONAL ORIENTATION

How have the ideological and institutional changes that underlay the reconfiguration of civil-military relations affected the definition of economic and security goals and objectives and the design of strategies to accomplish them? The following section explores a number of areas in which changes in civil-military relations may affect Thailand's foreign economic and security policy.

Civil-Military Relations and the Guardianship of Democracy

One of the core arguments of this chapter is that changes in the domestic and international context have prompted a redefinition of the military's role in society. Concomitant with its reevaluation of the role it can and should play in Thai politics, the military must arrive at new conceptions of what constitutes international and domestic "threats."

The resolution of the Vietnamese invasion of Cambodia and the defeat of the Thai Communists, in conjunction with changes in domestic politics, have altered the context in which the military must define its goals and strategies. The military in the post–Cold War has no major enemy to fight. The Communist Party of Thailand does not exist anymore. The relationship between Thailand and Vietnam has been normalized. Moreover, due to the ideological and institutional evolution of Thai politics, the military no longer retains the authority to define its goals as broadly as it once did. Changes in the international and domestic political context mean that the military can no longer define its goals expansively under the rubric of protecting the country's national security.

Nevertheless, although the uprising helped to clarify the perceived limits to the military's rights and privileges, the challenge of redefining the relationship between the Thai military and civil society remains. So how has the military redefined its goals and objectives? The military once viewed itself as being in opposition to democracy; now it defines itself in relation to democracy. Hence, new military leaders, such as Air Chief Marshal Voranat Apicharee, have frequently stated, "professional soldiers do not stage coups."[27] Instead the military appears to accept that "Thailand has to amend its political system to be more democratic"[28] and that its national objective is "to maintain a democratic system."[29] According to a book issued by Supreme Command, *Democracy in Thailand:* "The military has stated its position clearly that it will not get involved with politics . . . . It will always protect democracy which has the king as the head of a state as well as safeguard national independence and sovereignty."[30]

Interestingly enough, one of the ways that this is translated into policy is through the professionalization of the military, which has declared that "the adjustment of the armed forces is to make the soldiers more professional."[31] Its leaders assert that the primary objective of the army is "to make the soldiers democratic." The armed forces exist as a "state instrument."[32] Noninvolvement in politics has became a guiding principle of the Thai officer corps.

It is important to note that although such statements reflect the constraints posed by the development of democratic government, they also reflect a definition of which policies and objectives are truly in the interests of the armed forces. The military's prestige was undermined by its participation in the uprising: "The people do not have faith in the army."[33] But beyond the domestic resistance the military faces to its intervention in politics, there is growing realization that supporting a return to authoritarianism will elicit international condemnation.[34] It appears that the Thai military as an institution has made the "Dahlian calculus": hence, "the more the costs of suppression exceed the costs of toleration, the greater the chance for a competitive regime."[35] Military leaders and their civilian counterparts, at least for the present, appear to have decided that they will take their chances with an elected regime.

The Military's Role in Development

Development is an area in which the military continues to play a crucial role. During the Communist war period, the military's role in development aimed at winning the "hearts and minds" of people in rural areas. It was an instrument to eradicate what was perceived as the root cause of Communist support—poor living conditions. In fact, every constitution since 1974 has mentioned the military's role in development. For instance, Chapter 5, "Directive Principles of State Policies," Section 61 of the 1991 constitution states that "the armed forces shall be employed for maintaining the security of the State and for national development."[36] Since the end of the war against the Communists, the military has been involved in the following development projects:

- Green the Northeast Project (in the Northeast),
- Doi Tung Development Project (in the North),
- Panang Basin Development Project (in the South),
- New Hope Project (in the five southernmost provinces), and
- Royal Development Projects.[37]

Economic development continues to be perceived as essential to Thailand's national security to the extent that it constitutes the foundation for political stability. In other words, economic instability is viewed as a threat to the political fabric of Thai society; development remains a core pillar of Thailand's grand strategy. Moreover, it remains a central component of the military's definition of its goals and responsibilities—a position supported by the king. In the king's words, "combat" and "development" have to be carried out simultaneously.[38] Moreover, "the soldier's primary mission is to defend the Nation and safeguard national sovereignty and independence with military power. In addition, soldiers have another duty which is equally important, that is, performing relief and development work that will bring prosperity and happiness to the country and the people."[39]

With the conclusion of the Communist war, the military's role in development programs is one way in which it has defined its relationship to society. The military has effectively made the case that soldiers have a duty to improve the living conditions of the populace.[40] The military has to "participate in solving economic and social problems with the aim of reducing inequality in opportunity and incomes, and lessening social conflict."[41] The rationale underlying the military's involvement in development is the presumption that when living conditions improve, national security is strengthened:[42]

[Development] roles will be increased in the future because the Royal Thai Armed Forces has available the units and resources that are able to support these activities. The Armed Forces can provide support to national development in many ways . . . . In addition, the Royal Thai Armed Forces has units which are directly involved in development, such as the Corps of Engineers, Development Division, and the National Security Command. If sufficient budget is allocated, these units will be able to contribute greatly to national development.[43]

In the future, the military's "role in improving the well-being of the people"[44] will probably be expanded to include activities in environmental protection, antidrug trafficking, protection of natural resources, and disaster relief.[45]

Implications for Thailand's Regional Security Policy

Although too early to predict, there appears to be evidence that the changes in Thai civil-military relations will affect the country's international goals and strategies. This may be due partly to the different calculations civilian political leaders and military leaders make in weighing the costs and benefits of different policies. One recent event serves as an example.

Thai-Burmese relations since 1985 have been positive. Thailand adopted a policy of "constructive engagement" to provide the Burmese regime with a channel of communication and opportunity for opening the country to the international community. As a result, the Thai government strongly recognized the Burmese military government—the SLORC—despite international condemnation of it. At the same time, Thai policymakers anticipated that good relations with the SLORC would reduce tension along the Thai-Burmese border. Disregarding the military's advice, the cabinet of the Chuan Leekpai government, which came to power after the September 1992 election, allowed eight Nobel Peace laureates to visit Thailand. The objective of the visit was to increase pressure on the Burmese military government to release Aung San Suu Kyi, a Burmese democratic leader and 1991 Nobel Peace laureate. The visit was opposed by the chief of the army, General Wimol Wongvanich because he feared it would antagonize the Burmese military and provoke conflict on volatile border issues.[46] From the military's perspective, the border problem was significant, thus warranting extreme caution to avoid alienating the Burmese military regime.[47]

Strengthening the security relationship with China also remains a priority. Although there was security cooperation between Thailand and China against Vietnam during the civil war in Cambodia, Thailand still worries about the Chinese role in the region.[48] The military believes that conflict with China is not in the Thai national interest. One of the major concerns is Chinese military activity in Burma.[49] They fear that the conflict with China may lead to another insurgency.

The military's sensitivity to Thai-Chinese relations is evident in its concern about the Chinese reaction to a visit to Thailand by the Dalai Lama, the Tibetan leader. In that incident, the military placed greater weight on the security issues at

stake in sponsoring the visit than did the civilian government. Nevertheless, although the military voiced its concerns, the army accepted the cabinet's decision
without threatening intervention.

The Banharn Silpaarcha government has, in fact, taken a number of initiatives
to reinforce positive relations with China. For example, the government sent General Chaovalit, after he was appointed minister of defense, to China. It then sent
Prime Minister Banharn Silpaarcha in March 1996 in a follow-up visit. Recently,
there was a visit in return by Army General Zhang Wannian, vice chairman of the
Chinese Communist Party's military committee. During his visit to Bangkok, he
announced a grant of $3 million in military aid to the Thai armed forces. This is
the first time that the Chinese have officially offered military aid to Thailand.[50]
Technically it is not a large sum, and the Thai armed forces do not need foreign
military aid, except in the form of a supplementary fund to repair the weapons
that Thailand has bought from China.[51] Nevertheless, politically, military aid is a
sign of the countries' close relationship. It is also an indication that China remains
an important factor in Thailand's security policy, especially in the post–Cold War
era.

Thus, despite provocations in the past, such as the conflict over the Nobel laureates' visit, the relations between Thailand and both Burma and China have been
positive. Sometimes there are different perceptions in the policymaking process
between civilians and the military. But the basic belief remains the same; that is,
good relations with China and Burma will enhance Thailand's national security.

The Military's Role in National Defense

Changes in civil-military relations may affect not only the assessment of Thailand's goals and objectives, but how the military prepares to meet them. The core
issue that has been opened for debate with the changes in civil-military relations
is the future role of the armed forces in national defense. Central to the debate is
how much and what type of resources should be allocated to the military. Although there is no immediate threat to Thai security in the post–Cold War era,
the military continues to press for the implementation of a comprehensive force-
modernization program encompassing four areas: (1) command, control, and
communication; (2) training and personnel development; (3) weapon systems
and logistics; and (4) social welfare in the armed forces.[52]

Nevertheless, despite the military's lobbying efforts, there were no major arms
purchases under the Chuan government between 1993 and 1995. Furthermore,
the government tried to limit military expenditure by restricting growth in the
1995 FY military budget to 7.5 percent and in 1996 to 7 percent of its 1994 level.
(Table 9.1 compares the military budget to the national budget from 1986 to
1995.) The military opposed this plan because it would undermine efforts to acquire new weapon systems, including one hundred M-60 A3 main battle tanks
and new assault rifles for the army, two submarines for the navy, and one

TABLE 9.1   Comparison Between National Budget and Ministry of Defense Budget, 1986–1995

Fiscal Year	National Budget (million baht)	Increase (%)	M o D Budget (million baht)	Increase (%)	% National Budget
1986	218,000	2.35	39,266.220	–0.28	18.01
1987	227,500	4.36	39,165.222	–0.26	17.22
1988	243,500	7.03	41,150.309	5.87	16.90
1989	285,500	17.25	44,427.228	7.86	15.56
1990	335,000	17.33	52,634.635	18.47	15.71
1991	387,500	15.67	60,575.222	15.09	15.63
1992	460,400	18.81	69,272.982	14.36	15.05
1993	560,000	21.63	78,625.342	13.50	14.04
1994	625,000	11.61	85,423.917	8.65	13.67
1995	715,000	14.40	91,638.768	7.28	12.82

SOURCE: Ministry of Defense, *The Defense of Thailand, 1996* (Bangkok: Ministry of Defense, 1996).

squadron of F-18 jets for the air force. If the government had consented to these proposals, the total military budget would have been more than 100 billion baht (about US$4 billion) for the 1996 FY.[53] Ultimately, resolution of these issues was delayed when the Chuan government was forced to resign due to its mismanagement of a land-reform program.

The new coalition government established after the 1995 election was softer on the arms procurement issue. The Banharn government sought "good relations" with the military and abandoned the 7 percent benchmark. Moreover, General Chaovalit, former head of the army, was appointed minister of defense. Soon thereafter the general issued a plan calling for the acquisition of 100,000 assault rifles and 1,000 machine guns for the army; 16 F-18 jets for the air force; 2 mine sweepers, integrated logistic support equipment for a new helicopter carrier, and 2 submarines for the navy; and a military satellite for the Ministry of Defense. The total arms budget for 1996 was estimated at 50.7 billion baht (about US$2 billion).[54]

Ultimately, it will be up to the cabinet to approve these proposals. The government has not yet made a decision on whether to approve the satellite program or the procurement of the submarines. When and how such decisions are made will have profound implications for the strategies the military pursues and for Thailand's overall military status in the region. The latter issue, in turn, potentially has much broader ramifications for Thailand's relationship with its neighbors in the region.

Civil-Military Relations and Foreign Economic Policy

In general, Thailand's foreign economic policy is not a major concern for the officer corps. Nevertheless, changes in the civil-military context have coincided with experimentation in Thailand's strategy toward Southeast Asia. During General

Chaovalit's term as army chief, he proposed the idea of "Suwan-naphum" ("the Golden Peninsula," which refers to the area of mainland Southeast Asia). Although the strategy was not successful,[55] it clearly represented a reorientation of Thai security policy in that the military hoped to use diplomatic and trade relations, rather than military means, to forge a more favorable security environment. The strategy was intended to provide a means for the accommodation of Communist and non-Communist countries in Southeast Asia; it was anticipated that economic relations would soften ideological differences. It also aimed to integrate the socialist economies of Indochinese states, especially Laos and Cambodia, into the Thai economy. In short, Bangkok hoped to increase its trade and investment in Indochina in order to secure its position in the region.

Interestingly enough, the controversy surrounding the adoption of the policy is indicative of the changing pattern of civil-military relations in Thailand. The Golden Peninsula proposal was a source of friction between General Chaovalit and Prime Minister Chartchai. At the time, they were engaged in a competition over who would be "peacemaker" between Thailand and Indochina. Thus while General Chaovalit was formulating the Golden Peninsula concept, Chartchai proposed the idea of "Changing the Battlefield to a Market Place." In fact, prior to the end of the civil war in Cambodia, the military leaders sought to directly participate in foreign affairs. In the end, however, civilians were able to consolidate their position in the policymaking arena. As a prime minister, Chartchai, for example, enjoyed a superior position in supporting his political maneuvers. Consequently, military leaders since General Chaovalit have not displayed an active interest in foreign economic policy.

Beyond the direct influence of the military in policymaking, the concomitant diminution of military influence and enhancement of civilian groups in the governing apparatus may have an indirect effect on Thailand's foreign economic policy priorities. Changes in the domestic context, such as the emerging role of business groups, may prompt a reconfiguration of economic goals in the international arena. High rates of economic growth have bolstered the direct participation of business in politics. In the past, these groups primarily have played a behind the scenes role in financing political candidates. But in the 1992 election, businessmen actively participated in parliamentary elections. The partisan composition of the upper house reflects the emerging role of business groups in Thai politics; there has also been increased representation of businessmen in cabinets. In the Chartchai cabinet, 73 percent (33 out of 45) of the ministers were businessmen (1988–1991). In the same period, 68 percent of the representatives in the lower house were businessmen (243 out of 357).[56] The growth of the business sector in general is indicated by the share of industry and service sectors in the gross domestic product (GDP). The share of industry in 1990 GDP was 37.2 percent and the service sector was 50.0 percent relative to 30.8 percent and 46.0 percent in 1980.[57] Thailand has also experienced stable growth in per capita GDP, which grew from $360 in 1975, to $810 in 1985, to $1840 in 1992.[58] In general, the success of the Thai economy has bolstered the influence of the business sector. In short, "through their numbers, their personal links with government and technocracy, their influence over media, their capacity for organization, their command of the means of expression, [business] groups wielded potential political influence out of proportion to their size."[59]

Although, again, it is probably premature to draw conclusions about how the increasing influence of business groups will affect Thailand's foreign economic policy it does appear that they are in competition with the military for influence in policymaking and resources. Many campaigns, for example, in the post-1992 crisis period were launched by business groups against the military and military-related activities. There were also campaigns to withdraw deposits from the Thai Military Bank. Signatures were collected for petitions demanding that military figures be removed from boards of directors of public enterprises.[60] Three major economic organizations, the Board of Trade, the Thai Bankers Association, and the Federation of Thai Industries, played significant roles in these activities.[61]

CONCLUSION

Clearly, the military's power in Thai politics in the post–Cold War era has been shrinking, and many changes preclude a return to the "golden days of the generals." The age of democratic revolution is running against the concept of military rule. Military leaders repeatedly say, "The soldiers will not get involved in politics." Yet for Thailand, we cannot be optimistic that the military has retreated to the barracks never to return again. Three obstacles remain for the consolidation of democracy.

First, as the 1992 crisis confirmed, Thai civil society is not fully developed or organized. Neither political parties nor parliament can be relied on to resist authoritarianism and promote democracy. In terms of their continuity and financing, parties are increasingly strong. But parliamentary institutions are still fragile, and they are more an elite instrument than a true channel of representation for the interest of the people. It is fair to say that many Thais do not have much respect for politicians, who are seen as selfish and corrupt.

Second, the country's economic development is moving faster than its political development. The urban middle classes as well as business groups are expected to contribute to democratic progress and be the primary promoters of democracy.[62] However, we cannot take for granted that these classes are fully committed to democratic development. For instance, should the Thai economy in the future suffer a dramatic collapse, how will these classes view the role of the military? They may want the military to play a role in maintaining national security. The 1992 uprising provided little guidance because we do not know whether these groups truly were the champions of democracy or whether they opposed the military primarily because the military had failed to keep up with the progress made by the business community.

At the same time, the 1992 uprising proved that the military cannot run the country in the age of globalization. A military coup or intervention in the past might have been accepted as a means to "stabilize" economic development. But today it would "destabilize" economic growth. Rumors about political conflict between the military and a government would bring down the stock market and might also cause investment to leave the country. Therefore, a coup will not be supported unless Thailand faces a serious threat or major domestic chaos that might have significant impact on, in military terms, "national independence and sovereignty." Although such a situation is unlikely in the foreseeable future, democracy cannot be consolidated unless business accepts democracy as a goal in and of itself.

The problem of how to control the military democratically constitutes the third obstacle to Thai democratic consolidation. From the Cold War to the post–Cold War era, the role of the military shifted from dominant partner to one of power sharing. On the other hand, the Thai parliament has not yet taken steps to empower itself to be an informed and authoritative actor concerning military affairs. Both houses have an "Armed Forces Committee," but neither is institutionalized nor do they have expertise in military and security affairs. Given the lack of technical competence, military affairs are not properly debated in the legislative branch. The Thai parliament has not yet played a powerful role in helping to establish democratic civil-military relations.

In addition, Thai civil society has failed to incorporate information and analysis of military and security affairs into its political discourse and action. Political society has a duty to help create a model of democratic professionalism that would reduce military autonomy and prerogatives. This duty requires an increase in the technical capacities of civil society concerning military and security affairs. Society's weakness in this area impedes the transition toward a new model of democratic civil-military relations in Thailand.

Because the capacity of the democratic government to exercise its control of the military remains limited, the generals have retained control of military affairs. This makes democratic consolidation over military issues more difficult, while making it easier for those who advocate military intervention to organize a coup coalition. In order to avoid another direct intervention, the democratic leadership of Thailand must play a role in creating a model of democratic soldiers and a democratic doctrine of national defense.

The Thai people cannot take it for granted that military intervention will not occur in the post–Cold War period. Although since the 1992 uprising there have been positive factors contributing to a democratic professional military, the political legacies of the military still remain as major obstacles to the task of consolidating democracy. For these reasons, a democratic strategy toward the military will be a necessary condition of democratic consolidation. As Alfred Stepan warns us,

> A passive executive who abdicates responsibility would probably mean that any initial effort in the newly democratic regime to "reprofessionalize" the military would be militarily led. A purely negative executive who devotes all his efforts to eliminating

military prerogatives but neglects to play a leadership role in attempting to formulate and implement an alternative model of civil-military relations, would probably be locked in dangerous conflicts with the military.[63]

NOTES

I would like to thank Risa Brooks, Ph.D. candidate, Department of Political Science, University of California, San Diego, for her assistance in the revision of this chapter.

SOURCE: Ministry of Defense, *The Defense of Thailand, 1996* (Bangkok: Ministry of Defense, 1996).

1. David A. Wilson, "The Military in Thai Politics," in Robert O. Tilman, ed., *Man, State, and Society in Contemporary Southeast Asia* (New York: Praeger, 1969), pp. 326–339; and Barbara L. LePoer, *Thailand: A Country Study* (Washington, D.C.: Library of Congress, 1989).

2. Far Eastern Economic Review (FEER), *Asia 1974 Yearbook* (Hong Kong: Far Eastern Economic Review, 1974), pp. 308–313. (Hereafter it will be cited as FEER, *Asia Yearbook*).

3. FEER, *Asia 1977 Yearbook*, pp. 313–318; see also David Morell and Chai-anan Samudavanija, *Political Conflict in Thailand: Reform, Reaction, Revolution* (Cambridge, Mass.: Oelgeschlanger, Gunn and Hain, 1981).

4. Chalermkiat Piew-nuan, *Political Thoughts of the Thai Officer Corps, 1976–1992* (Bangkok: Manager Publishing House, 1992), pp. 61–95 (in Thai).

5. FEER, *Asia 1978 Yearbook*, p. 323.

6. FEER, *Asia 1978 Yearbook*, pp. 321–323; and *Asia 1979 Yearbook*, pp. 307–310.

7. Guillermo O'Donnell, "Transition to Democracy: Some Navigation Instruments," in Robert A. Pastor, ed., *Democracy in the Americas: Stopping the Pendulum* (New York: Holmes and Meier, 1989), p. 63.

8. On the concept of "transition through transaction," see Donald Share and Scott Mainwaring, "Transition Through Transaction: Democratization in Brazil and Spain," in Wayne A. Selcher, ed., *Political Liberalization in Brazil: Dynamics, Dilemmas, and Future Prospects* (Boulder: Westview, 1986), p. 175. On the Thai case, see Surachart Bamrungsuk, "The Military and Democratization: Transition Through Transaction in Thailand, 1977–1988," paper presented at the 43rd Annual Meeting, Association for Asian Studies, New Orleans, April 12, 1991.

9. Chai-anan Samudvanija, *The Young Turks and Democratic Soldiers: The Analysis of the Military Role in Thai Politics* (Bangkok: Bannakit, 1982), p. 105 (in Thai).

10. For English versions, see appendices in Surachart Bamrungsuk, *Thailand's Security Policy Since the Invasion of Kampuchea*, Essays on Strategy and Diplomacy, no. 10 (Claremont, Calif.: Keck Center for International Strategic Studies, Claremont McKenna College, 1988), pp. 18–26.

11. The Prime Minister's Office Order no. 65/2525.

12. Announcement of the Revolutionary Group, October 20, 1977.

13. Surachart Bamrungsuk, *Report on Public Opinion Concerning the Vietnamese Attack of June 1980* (Bangkok: Chulalongkorn University's Social Research Institute, 1980) (in Thai).

14. Counter-Revolutionary Warfare Committee, Department of Joint and Combined Operations, U.S. Army Command and General Staff College, *A Case Study of Thailand's Counterinsurgency Operations, 1965–1982*, no date.

15. *Prem the Statesman* (Bangkok: The General Prem Tinsoulanon Foundation, 1995), pp. 167–180.

16. *Prem the Statesman,* pp. 558–562.

17. See economic reports on Thailand in FEER, *Asia 1989 Yearbook, Asia 1990 Yearbook, Asia 1991 Yearbook.*

18. FEER, *Asia 1990 Yearbook,* p. 235.

19. FEER, *Asia 1992 Yearbook,* pp. 205–208.

20. Surachart Bamrungsuk, "Political Transition and Democratic Consolidation," *Communique,* no. 11, May 1991, no page number.

21. Surachart Bamrungsuk, *United States Foreign Policy and Thai Military Rule, 1947–1977* (Bangkok: Editions Duang Kamol, 1988).

22. FEER, *Asia 1992 Yearbook,* pp. 205–208.

23. See FEER, *Asia 1993 Yearbook,* pp. 213–215; and Bangkok Post, *Catalyst for Change: Uprising in May* (Bangkok: Bangkok Post, 1992).

24. See the list of new senators in *Matichon Daily Newspaper,* March 23, 1996, p. 2.

25. The Royal Thai Army, *The Army in Forty Years* (Bangkok: O.S. Printing House, 1995), p. 234 (in Thai).

26. The Government of Thailand's Investigation Committee, *An Investigative Report on the Military Role from May 17–20, 1992* (confidential, n.d.) (in Thai).

27. "The Soldiers in Line," in *Matichon Weekly Magazine* 15, no. 750, January 6, 1995, p. 14 (in Thai).

28. Ministry of Defense, *The Defense of Thailand 1994* (Bangkok: Strategic Research Institute, National Defense Institute, 1994), p. 22.

29. Ibid., p. 21.

30. The Supreme Command, *Democracy in Thailand* (Bangkok: The Supreme Command, no date), p. 35.

31. The Royal Thai Army, *The Army in Forty Years,* p. 235.

32. Ibid., p. 236.

33. Statement of General Wimol Wongvanich at the meeting of civil affairs officers, October 16, 1992.

34. The Royal Thai Army, *The Army in Forty Years,* p. 235.

35. Robert Dahl, *Polyarchy: Participation and Opposition* (New Haven: Yale University Press, 1991), p. 15.

36. See the text of the 1991 constitution in the *Government Gazette* 108, Part 216, Special Issue, December 9, 1991 (in Thai).

37. The Royal Thai Army, *The Army in Forty Years,* pp. 192–194.

38. The Supreme Command, *Democracy in Thailand,* p. 33.

39. Ministry of Defense, *The Defense of Thailand 1996* (Bangkok: Strategic Research Institute, National Defense Institute, 1996), p. 33.

40. See the statements of General Suchida Kraprayoon, General Issarapong Noonpakdee, General Wimol Vongvanich in The Royal Thai Army, *The Army in Forty Years.*

41. Ministry of Defense, *The Defense of Thailand 1996,* p. 33.

42. The Supreme Command, *Democracy in Thailand,* pp. 28–31.

43. Ministry of Defense, *The Defense of Thailand 1994,* p. 68.

44. The Supreme Command, *Democracy in Thailand,* p. 32.

45. Ministry of Defense, *The Defense of Thailand 1996,* pp. 35–41.

46. "Peace Mission: Everybody Wins," and "Peace Mission May Have Soured Government-Military Ties," *Bangkok Post,* February 21, 1993, p. 17 and p. 20.

47. Surachart Bamrungsuk, "Constructive or Destructive Engagement? Thailand's Policy Toward Burma," paper presented at the conference on Burma after SLORC, Association for Asian Studies Annual Meeting, Boston, March 24, 1994.

48. See chapter on "Sino-Thai Security Cooperation: From Friend to Foe," in Surachart Bamrungsuk, *The Year 2000: Military Strategy in the Post–Cold War Era* (Bangkok: Matichon Publishers, 1994), pp. 111–118 (in Thai).

49. See chapter on "Sino-Burmese Relations: Its Strategic Implication on Thailand," in Surachart, *The Year 2000,* pp. 159–176.

50. It is interesting to note that there is no report on the Chinese military aid to Thailand in the Thai newspapers. See the report by the AFP and the Associated Press on April 18, 1996.

51. The Thai defense budget in the 1996 FY has increased to 100 billion Baht ($4 billion). In the 1977 FY, the defense budget is about 108 billion Baht (over $4 billion). The budgetary adjustment was approved by the cabinet on April 2, 1996. The new defense budget of the 1997 FY has been increased from 107.65 billion Baht to 108.71 billion Baht ($4.3 billion). See details on the new government budget in *Matichon Daily Newspaper,* April 22, 1996, p. 2 (in Thai).

52. "Four Modernization Policy: New Step of the Army," in The Royal Thai Army, *Army in Forty Years,* pp. 235–239.

53. "The Armed Forces' Budget of 96," in *Matichon Daily Newspaper,* September 18, 1995 (in Thai).

54. "Hot Arms: 50,000 million Baht in Chaovalit's Hands," *Matichon Weekly Magazine,* October 29, 1995, p. 2 (in Thai).

55. FEER, *Asia 1990 Yearbook,* pp. 236–237.

56. Pasuk Phongpaichit and Chris Baker, *Thailand: Economy and Politics* (New York: Oxford University Press, 1995), pp. 338–339.

57. Figures calculated from the World Bank, *World Table 1994* (Baltimore: John Hopkins University Press, 1994), pp. 648–649.

58. World Bank, *Social Indicators of Development 1994* (Baltimore: John Hopkins University Press, 1994), pp. 340–341.

59. Phongpaichit and Baker, *Thailand,* p. 409.

60. Kowit Sanandang, "Business and Military Can't Be Bedfellows," in Bangkok Post, *Catalyst for Change,* p. 78.

61. Peter Ungphakorn, "Business Vows It Must Not Happen Again," in Bangkok Post, *Catalyst for Change,* p. 75.

62. Lipset believes that democracy arises due to its functional fit with industrial economy. "Economic Development and Democracy," in Seymour Martin Lipset, *Political Man: The Social Bases of Politics* (New York: Anchor Books, 1963), pp. 27–63.

63. Alfred Stepan, *Rethinking Military Politics: Brazil and the Southern Cone* (Princeton: Princeton University Press, 1988), p. 139.

■

CHAPTER TEN

The Interplay of Internal War and Democratization in Guatemala Since 1982

Caesar D. Sereseres

Guatemala held first-round presidential elections on November 12, 1995, followed by a final round in January 1996. It was the third presidential election since March 23, 1982, when a coup by young officers denied General Aníbal Angel Guevara, the winning candidate of the March 6, 1982 elections, the presidency. The November 12 elections were also held one day short of the thirty-fifth anniversary of the "13 de noviembre" failed military coup against president Miguel Ydígoras Fuentes. That 1960 coup attempt laid the foundation for the only guerrilla insurgency in Latin America established and led by noncommunist military officers. During the 1960s, Guatemala was the only Central American country to confront an insurgency, but it was one of four that fought a counterinsurgency war during the 1980s. By the mid-1990s, the Guatemalan war was the only one still underway in the region.[1]

The Central American wars of the 1980s were an international issue that involved, directly or indirectly, every country in the region. Armies doubled or tripled in size. Guerrilla movements became large, complex, internationalized organizations. The United States, the Soviet Union, Cuba, East Germany, Israel, Taiwan, Argentina, Mexico, Venezuela, and others became deeply involved in the region's wars. The U.S.-backed contra war in Nicaragua split and polarized the region. The wars came at a high price: They cost the lives of hundreds of thousands; left over one million citizens of the region in exile, in refugee camps, or as illegal migrants to the United States; halted regional integration (including the Central American Common Market) and cooperation; and brought economic growth to a standstill and, in some cases, pushed socioeconomic indicators back to the levels of the early 1950s.

This chapter discusses the interrelationships between the army's counterinsurgency strategies and democratization, regional cooperation, and the peace process since 1982. In doing so, the chapter also assesses the institutional role and the evolution of the Guatemalan armed forces since the 1960s. That assessment points to the thirty-year war against Marxist-Leninist-oriented guerrillas and radical changes in the counterinsurgency strategies as the major influences on the character of the Guatemalan army.

Five principal points are made in this chapter. First, the process of Guatemalan democratization since 1982 was initially guided by military leaders (and a few civilian allies) and became a tacit partnership between civilians and the military by the late 1980s. Second, between 1982 and 1995, the Guatemalan armed forces were a dominant national institution in the democratization process. Third, by January 1991, at the end of the five-year Christian Democratic presidency of Vinicio Cerezo and after the election of Jorge Serrano of the Movement of Solidarity Action (MAS), Guatemala reflected a distinct political environment. Guerrillas continued to fight in the far-northern regions of the country, while the Guatemalan military continued to be politically influential as an institution. Political violence, killings, kidnappings, and intimidation did not disappear. Guatemala's political culture, however, matured and the number and diversity of political actors grew substantially after the "dark days" of the 1980s. Following the Esquipulas II Agreement (also known as the Arias Peace Plan) of August 1987 and with the support of the international community, research institutes and policy forums appeared in Guatemala. Universities enhanced their research programs and began to compete in the presentation of forums on questions such as the peace process, the role of the military, indigenous concerns, and economic reform. Weekly and monthly news journals resurfaced, and television and major newspapers increased news coverage, political forums, and more critical assessments of government and private sector performance. As the peace process progressed and as Guatemalan grassroots organizations resurfaced in the urban and rural areas of the country, the number of nongovernmental organizations (NGOs) increased because governments and international institutions preferred to fund NGOs rather than directly funding the Guatemalan government.

Fourth, the Coordinating Committee of Agricultural, Commercial, Industrial, and Financial Associations (CACIF), the powerful organization of Guatemala's trade associations and chambers, began its own internal debate about the peace process, economic reform, and the role of the military. CACIF leaders (in alliance with military officers of the army general staff) would play an instrumental role in the ouster of President Serrano in the aftermath of the attempted Fujimori-like *autogolpe* of May 25, 1993.

Finally, the arrival of the United Nations Observer Mission (MINUGUA) to Guatemala in early 1994 provided an additional dimension to the opening of the political system and to a semblance of political and judicial accountability in Guatemala. The mission provided some three hundred human rights monitors

located throughout the country, and they have enjoyed more access to people, institutions, and localities than any other international or national organization in
recent Guatemalan history. MINUGUA periodically makes public reports concerning human rights in Guatemala, which have included violent cases involving
the National Police, the armed forces, and the paramilitary groups known as *pa-
trulleros*. Nevertheless, the peace process and the responses by the Guatemalan
government and the international community to the socioeconomic problems resulting from three decades of war have brought civil society and the military institution closer together than at any time since the post-1944 revolutionary period.

The causal link between democratization, democratic elections, civilian governance and authority over the military institution, and constructive civil-military
relations in Guatemala, as well as regional political and economic cooperation, is
not easy to determine. The Guatemalan national process fed off regional dynamics and opportunities: Regional progress on peace negotiations, political cooperation, rejuvenation of regional economic integration processes (a rebirth of the
Central American Common Market), and the success of the Central American
Parliament depended upon the distinct national dynamics of each country as well
as the sustained support and resources of international actors—especially the
United States, the European Community, and the United Nations.

Each of the Central American wars had to wind down in order for regional cooperation to proceed. Presidential and congressional politics in Washington helped to
end one war by stopping support for the Nicaraguan Resistance against the Sandin-
ista regime in Managua. In El Salvador, the war concluded as a result of the end of
the Cold War, strong United Nations mediation, and the defeat of the Sandinistas
(FSLN) in the February 1990 elections in Nicaragua. In Guatemala, exhaustion and
lack of international allies and supporters led to a cooling of tensions.

The conclusion of these wars facilitated cooperation. Regional forums and institutions stimulated national dialogue and the strengthening of civilian leadership and institutions. Cooperation first came at the level of the Central American
presidents who held an unprecedented number of "summits" throughout the
1980s and early 1990s. The Contadora Group formally began the Central American peace process in the early 1980s. Today, the Central American foreign ministers are attempting to codify and institutionalize regional peace and cooperation
through the Central American Security Commission treaty, signed in December
1995 in Honduras. In between, an assortment of groups, meetings, and summits
led to the eventual signing of treaties and agreements—including Esquipulas I
and II, the Tesoro Beach Agreement, and the Tela Accords.[2]

For Guatemala, these regional peace efforts provided the setting (if not the
cover) for democratization, for changing the civil-military relationship, for re-
shaping the character of the Guatemalan state, for subtly pushing for decentralization and the emergence of local community organizations and power, and for
the expansion and diversification of Guatemalan political leadership and institutions. Initially, it was the Guatemalan armed forces that provided the vision of a

need for (1) a national sociopolitical-military strategy for dealing with the Unión Revolucionaria Nacional de Guatemala (URNG) insurgency, (2) a regional strategy to confront political and security issues affecting Guatemala, and (3) an international strategy to engage major global actors—including the United States, the Europeans, the United Nations, and the plethora of NGOs that had become part of Guatemalan society.

At first, these three initiatives were largely a response to the highly effective "foreign policy" achievements of the URNG. By the early 1990s, the Guatemalan military along with civilian leaders and institutions recognized that events and conditions in Guatemala would be heavily influenced by regional dynamics and the rapidly changing context of global politics (including the dramatic collapse of the Soviet Union, U.S. military intervention in Panama and the destruction of the Panama Defense Forces, and the quick U.S. military victory in the Persian Gulf).

Between the 1982 coup and the 1995 peace negotiations, the Guatemalan armed forces were at the forefront of political change, institution building, and regional cooperation. Although such behavior often was for self-serving institutional or security reasons, more and more these endeavors, especially when allied with civilian leaders and institutions, have aimed at building a new, secure Guatemalan society, free of insurgency but with a place for the military into the twenty-first century.

DOMESTIC AND INTERNATIONAL SOURCES OF GUATEMALAN DEMOCRATIZATION

Since the 1940s, Guatemala has undergone extreme shifts in government, accompanied by organized violence, more intense and destructive in each succeeding decade. By 1944, the "October Revolution" ended the thirteen-year presidency of General Jorge Ubico. The junta that followed represented an odd coalition of students, professionals, and military officers. When he took office in March 1945, Juan José Arévalo began the "decade of revolution." Arévalo had the distinction of being the first Guatemalan president in the twentieth century to be elected, serve his term, and step down peaceably. Under Arévalo, and later Colonel Jacobo Arbenz, Guatemalan society began the difficult process of institutional and cultural democratization. For the first time, organized political and labor movements took root, and legislation was passed promoting education, health, social security, and labor reform.

When Arbenz, Arévalo's minister of defense, assumed the presidency in 1951, his administration moved quickly on such issues as agrarian reform, rural labor unions, and land expropriations. These and other domestic policies, and a foreign policy that seemed closely allied with the Cold War enemies of the United States, provoked considerable opposition from traditional business, agricultural, and urban commerce interests. By early 1954, an alliance of groups in Guatemala and Washington combined to topple President Arbenz. The instrument was a "liberation army"—a largely nonexistent, ill-equipped, and poorly trained paramilitary force—supported by the U.S. government, which invaded Guatemala with the full operational support of the Central Intelligence Agency. It made every effort to avoid contact with the Guatemalan army; to some extent, the army also avoided contact with invaders. Thus, the success of the U.S. intervention was determined in Guatemala City—among members of the Arbenz regime, senior army officers, and officials in the U.S. Embassy—not on the battlefield of northeastern Guatemala.[3]

The 1954 intervention by the United States and the politics and psychology of the "liberation" began a history of military politics, fragile civil-military relations, and a thirty-five-year Cold War context for Guatemalan society. The 1944 "revolution" liberated the Guatemalan armed forces from the yoke of a civilian dictator and allowed it to develop into a professional institution of the state. The 1954 "liberation" politicized it and cast it into a Cold War mold. However, 1954 is also known for the "2nd of August" rebellion, which was staged by young cadets from the military academy. The rebellion against the liberation army launched a subtle, tacit antagonism between the military institution and the Guatemalan political right, which had associated itself with a foreign power—the United States. The cadets, along with many officers, viewed "the liberation army" as an affront to the dignity and institutionality of the Guatemalan armed forces.[4]

From 1954 until 1982, Guatemalan politics was tumultuous. Carlos Castillo Armas, the colonel who became president as a result of the 1954 intervention, was assassinated in 1957, General Ydigoras, in his seventies, won election in 1958 and survived a coup attempt in November 1960 by junior and mid-grade officers, who were displeased with his decision to allow the U.S. government to use a Guatemalan military base to train Cubans for the invasion of Cuba, and because the general had threatened war against Mexico after Guatemalan shrimp boats were attacked by Mexican forces.

In March 1963, the military, represented by the high command, acted as an institution to remove Ydigoras on the grounds of incompetence. Colonel Enrique Peralta Azurdia, the leader of the coup, declined the presidency but assumed the position of chief of state. Peralta had first been Ydigoras's minister of agriculture and then minister of defense after the failed 1960 military revolt. During the three years of military government, Guatemala's anticommunist posture was reaffirmed, the central government bureaucracy was reorganized, new labor and electoral laws were written, and a new constitution and military organic law were written in preparation for the 1966 presidential elections. The military government's goal was to put Guatemala's political house in order prior to returning to civilian governance.

Between 1963 and 1966, the military government took a somewhat passive stance toward the two guerrilla groups that had evolved out of the 1960 military revolt. The Fuerzas Armadas Rebeldes (FAR), led by Lt. Luis Turcios Lima, operated in the northeastern region of Zacapa and Izabal provinces; the Movimiento

Revolucionario 13 de Noviembre (MR-13), led by Lt. Marco Antonio Yon Sosa, operated in the region of southern Petén province. Both leaders had been active participants in the 1960 coup attempt. The military government, focusing more on reorganizing the structure of government and constitutional setting of nation politics, gave low priority to fighting these groups. As a result, the task of destroying the guerrillas would be left to the elected civilian president.

In 1966, following a brief interlude of "stability," the military government held elections. A civilian and former university dean, Julio Castro Méndez Montenegro, candidate of the Partido Revolucionario (PR), was elected president. Because the PR traced its roots to the 1944 revolution, the presidency of Méndez Montenegro was called the *tercer gobierno de la revolución*—the third government of the revolution. He unleashed the army in major counterinsurgency operations in Zacapa, Izabal, and Petén to rid Guatemala's northeast of the guerrilla threat. By 1969, the army had defeated the guerrillas in the mountains of the northeast, and in 1970 the guerrillas lost the urban war in Guatemala City. As a result of the counterinsurgency operations, the army grew in size and expanded its presence in most of the major urbanized departments of the nation.

Between 1970 and 1982, Guatemala underwent a period of apparent political stability that masked a gradual disintegration of the state and society. A series of elected presidents, each of whom had served his predecessor as minister of defense, governed the country.[5] These military officers had fought the guerrillas in the northeastern provinces, and their faith in the counterinsurgency methods successfully used in that campaign shaped their political style and programs. The "operational code" of these presidents and their advisors was "What worked militarily in the Zacapa counterinsurgency campaign would work for the nation politically." By 1980, however, it was clear that the strategy had failed. The methods that had worked for Méndez Montenegro in northeastern Guatemala had been aimed at a small cadre of guerrillas with a weak, narrow political base and no international support links.

The militarized response of the Lucas government (1978–1982) to the Ejército Guerrillero de los Pobres (EGP), the Organización del Pueblo en Armas (ORPA), and the Fuerzas Armadas Revolucionarias (FAR) only produced more armed guerrillas and more territorial advances by the three guerrilla groups. The guerrillas of the 1980s had learned from the failures of their colleagues of the 1960s. By 1981 the guerrillas were clearly winning the war on the battlefield and in the international arena of diplomacy, alliances, and politics.[6]

The civilian-oriented regime of Méndez Montenegro was only an interlude. In July 1970, Guatemala began twelve years of military guardianship. President Carlos Arana, commander of the Zacapa counterinsurgency campaign and president from 1970 to 1974, was succeeded by his minister of defense, General Kjell Laugerud. Although General Efraín Rios Montt had easily won the election as the presidential candidate of the Christian Democrats, Laugerud assumed the presidency through blatant fraud. In turn, President Laugerud's minister of defense, General Romero

Lucas García, succeeded him following the March 1978 election. In March 1982, the presidential election was won by General Aníbal Angel Guevara—the former minister of defense. Had the "young captains' coup" of March 23 not succeeded, General Guevara would have become president of Guatemala in July 1982.

The March 23 coup was the beginning of the end of a political order that had arisen from the convolutions of the October revolution and the 1954 liberation. It set Guatemala on a long, torturous road toward an institutionalized democracy, viable and sustained civilian rule, a professionalized and nonpartisan military, and the conclusion of thirty years of insurgency. Between the 1982 "captains' coup" and the January 1996 election of Álvaro Arzu Iroygen, Guatemala experienced

- the rapid rise and fall of General Rios Montt as chief of state;
- the military defeat of the URNG insurgency;
- the casting of a new constitution—replacing the constitution that emerged from the 1963–1966 military government of Col. Peralta Azurdia—and the reform of the constitution after the failed *autogolpe* by President Serrano in May 1993;
- three elected civilian presidents (Vinicio Cerezo, Jorge Serrano, and Álvaro Arzu) and one appointed civilian president (Ramiro de Leon Carpio—Guatemala's human rights ombudsman at the time) to replace Serrano;
- two failed military-civilian coup attempts against Cerezo and one failed *autogolpe* attempt by President Serrano;
- an invigorated peace process with the coming to the presidency of Ramiro de Leon and the rise to senior positions of a distinct generation of military officers supportive of the peace process; and
- the dismissal or imposed retirement between 1990 and 1996 of no fewer than ten ministers of defense and army chiefs-of-staff by three presidents.

Unlike the October revolution and the 1954 liberation, following the 1982 coup, the military institution along with civilian allies and civilian partners designed a grand strategy. Its aims included the military defeat of the URNG insurgency; a return to civilian rule and the institutionalization of democracy; the reform and reorganization of the state; military reforms to modernize in preparation for Guatemala's new postwar society and for the twenty-first-century mission of the armed forces; and a formally negotiated peace between the government and the URNG, which would end the war politically. Major battlefield successes were not sufficient to terminate the war. What was lacking was a political settlement produced through direct negotiations between the Guatemalan government and the URNG guerrilla leadership. The guerrillas and their supporters required a formal agreement on their political legitimacy and on desired constitutional, governmental, military, and socioeconomic reforms. Without such reforms, national reconciliation in postwar Guatemala would be impossible.

The military high command, despite numerous changes in leadership and distinct styles and personalities of the presidents, has pursued this grand strategy. From the beginning, the military realized that it alone could not resolve Guatemala's security, political, and socioeconomic problems; the military knew that civilians had to take the lead in regional and international matters. The high command and general staff recognized both the opportunities and the threats posed by interacting with regional and international processes, institutions, and actors. However, by 1985, when the military governments of Rios Montt and Mejía Victores had successfully destroyed the infrastructure and main bases of the URNG guerrilla groups, the civil-military alliance, seeking to overcome Guatemala's isolation and black image, viewed regional and international cooperation not as a threat but as essential to their political and democratization strategy.[7] Years of political violence, kidnappings and disappearances of prominent political, social, religious, and community leaders, thousands of refugees and exiles, and a successful diplomatic and propaganda campaign by the URNG had made Guatemala a pariah state in the international community. Thus, the concern over Guatemala's isolation and international image became the core motivation and justification for the young officers who carried out the March 1982 coup.

By late 1995, Guatemala had seen demonstrable changes in civil-military relations, the institutional growth of democratization, civilian authority over the military, progress in the peace process, and a nurturing of the desire—strongly supported by the military—for a major voice and role in regional cooperation and integration. The November 1995 elections provide a remarkable snapshot of the changes in the Guatemalan polity during the previous fifteen years.

The traditional and dominant political parties between 1966 and 1982 had been the Movimiento de Liberación Nacional (MLN), the PR, the Partido Institucional Democrático (PLD), and the Democracia Christiana Guatemalteca (DCG). The MLN traced its roots to the 1954 liberation movement and was clearly the torchbearer of international anticommunism in Guatemala. The PR, founded in 1957, traced its roots to the 1944 revolution and the governments of Arévalo and Arbenz. It moved drastically to the right along the ideological spectrum, until it participated in a political alliance that supported the candidacy of General Romero Lucas García in 1978. The DCG, established in the 1960s, was influenced and supported by the European Christian Democrats. The DCG represented the permanent opposition until its candidate was elected president in 1985. The PLD was a Peralta military government creation modeled after Mexico's PRI!

Only one of these parties could rally an electoral base—the Christian Democrats. But, their 12 percent of the total valid vote was won only in alliance with two other parties (the Unión del Centro Nacional [UCN] and Partido Social Demócrata [PSD]). All the traditional "right-wing" parties of the past thirty years had faded. Five army generals (two former ministers of defense, two former chiefs of staff, and one former air force chief, who had also served as minister of government) ran for the presidency. These five individuals collectively received less than

3 percent of the total valid vote. In contrast, in the 1974, 1978, and 1982 presidential elections, candidates who were former ministers of defense regularly received between 40 and 60 percent of the total votes cast.

The Democratic Front of the New Guatemala (FDNG) was a "leftist" alliance that absorbed the PR (which ceased to exist) and also incorporated human rights groups, rural and urban mass organizations and unions, such as the Committee of Peasants United (CUC), and indigenous movements, such as the Council of Ethnic Communities (CERJ). The URNG publicly endorsed and supported the FDNG candidates during the 1995 elections. In the presidential race, the FDNG received 7 percent of the total vote. In addition, elected to the Guatemalan congress were such FDNG candidates as Nineth Montenegro (leader of the human rights group GAM), Amilcar Méndez (leader of the indigenous human rights group CERJ), and Rosalina Tuyuc (leader of the war-widows organization CONAVIGUA). All were internationally recognized critics of the Guatemalan armed forces and to a lesser extent of the civilian governments since the mid-1980s.

The opening of the political order, constitutional and electoral reform, support for civilian rule and constitutional institutionality, the success of the peace process, and the military reforms underway have not come about as the result of civilian imposition over a defeated and dishonored military (as in Argentina) nor the result of an international peace treaty (as in El Salvador). The changes that have taken place occurred either at the initiative of the military or with the encouragement and support of the military. Civilians have done most of the work, whether it be legal, constitutional, or technical. To do so, they have taken advantage of the space and cooperation available in the aftermath of the March 1982 coup and the military defeat of the URNG in 1985.

The strategy of political liberalization initiated by the army and its civilian allies after the 1982 coup represented a watershed in Guatemalan politics. During the period of military government under Generals Rios Montt and Oscar Mejía Victores, civilians participated as personal advisors to the presidency or to the Ministry of Defense. Fernando Andrade, minister of foreign relations during the Mejía administration, played a central role in the formulation of the military government's international and liberalization strategies. Jorge Serrano, president of the Council of State, was a driving force behind new legislation and constitutional reforms carried out between 1982 and 1985. Civilian influence was evident in all the major government institutions and reform processes. Three factors led to this participation: (1) friendships between senior military officers and civilians; (2) the need for technical and professional assistance found only in civil society, and (3) the political and psychological necessity to bring civilians into the reform process and make them parties to constitutional and institutional changes.

Constitutional reforms, along with major changes in the army's organic law, the creation of the first independent electoral tribunal in Guatemalan history, and the funding and security provided by the presidency and the Ministry of Defense to political parties were unprecedented. Treasury funds revitalized parties or, in the case of the UCN, created new ones. Bodyguards were supplied to protect individuals and party facilities, gun permits issued for party officials and their bodyguards to carry weapons, and senior military and civilian officials of the government signaled through public posturing their welcoming (and thus legitimizing) the existence and activities of these political parties after ten years of intense warfare and bloodshed. The Christian Democratic victory of Vinicio Cerezo in 1985, the two failed coups encouraged and supported by civilians, the failed Serrano *autogolpe,* and the Arzu electoral victory over the party of Rios Montt suggest that the door to political liberalization and democratization opened significantly following the 1982 coup.[8]

MILITARY POLITICS, DEMOCRATIZATION, AND REGIONAL COOPERATION

Between 1982 and 1995, the Guatemalan armed forces carried out a strategy (more often than not in a manner of "muddling through") that has had as its objectives (1) the military defeat of the URNG insurgency; (2) the development and sustaining of a process of political liberalization and democratization; (3) the strengthening of the state institution as a stabilizing factor in society; (4) the reform, modernization, and professionalization of the armed forces; (5) the establishment of a civil-military "model" in which civilian authority is recognized and the military institution is recognized as an essential element of the state; and (6) the political termination of the insurgency through a formal, internationally recognized peace accord.[9]

If there is a "reigning model" of civil military relations in Guatemala, it would be that of mutual respect and nonintervention in the respective "internal affairs" of civilians and military alike. The military as an institution has no major stake in the direction and pace of economic liberalization. There are extensive personal debates within the officer corps and in forums offered by Centro ESTNA and the Centro de Estudios Militares (CEM) concerning the benefits and costs of moving in the direction of full Central American economic integration or a unified Central America associated with the North American Free Trade Agreement (NAFTA). There is not a strongly voiced position by the military on such issues as the Central American Common Market or NAFTA.

While on the whole, at least in public forums, military officials have expressed support for the liberalization of the nation's economy, they also point to the new security threats posed by open borders, a global economy, and by what appears to be part of the future: a borderless Guatemalan society. Indeed, with the fading away of the internationalized "left" in Guatemala, the military may be the last defenders of state sovereignty. The movement of undocumented immigrants into Guatemala; the flow of contraband goods; the drug trade; damage to the environment and the exclusive economic zone; threats to the national patrimony and historic sites; and the rise of international crime organizations all suggest to the military that free and open societies (political, economic, and social) bring with them new security concerns.

The effort to raise the tax base in Guatemala is one area in which the military has periodically led the fight or been called upon to strongly support the presidency. Proportionally, Guatemala has the lowest tax base and the smallest public sector of all Latin American countries—with the exception of (pre-U.S. intervention) Haiti. The inability of the state to tax its population—especially the wealthy—has been one of the most politically sensitive issues in Guatemala. Because Guatemala has one of the most skewed land and income distribution patterns in Latin America, the only other issue that generates as much political frenzy is that of land reform and expropriation.

Economic policies have not been a central concern of the military. Unless it was a question of taxes or land, the military as an institution has pushed no major policy nor openly supported major changes in economic policies. Between 1976 and 1985, the military as an institution depended heavily on "raiding" the Ministry of Finance or called upon the president to draw from his *confidenciales,* funds to pay for major weapons and equipment purchases or to make up shortfalls in budgets for the war against the insurgency. More recently, the army leadership has unofficially downsized the number of military officers and active-duty personnel, reduced operations in the areas of conflict, and halted major purchases of equipment.

There are approximately two thousand officers in the Guatemalan army. During the past ten years, every effort has been made to safeguard the welfare of the military family: subsidized housing in military colonies, a military hospital and clinics, a "military" bank (the Banco del Ejército, which operates under national banking laws and is accountable to the Guatemalan Central Bank), the Instituto de Prevision Militar (IPM), and a viable pension system for officers and specialists. The establishment of a military social security system, which has been essential to sustaining the military's professionalism, minimizing personal ties to economic interests, and maintaining the viability of the officer corps and their families as part of the vulnerable Guatemalan middle class, was a legacy of the military government of Peralta Azurdia.

The army institution has few economic interests to protect. It runs a munitions factory, a boot factory, and a uniform factory. The Military Officers Club earns income from a multilevel parking lot in the capital, the IPM runs clinics for profit, and the IPM (through the Military Bank) holds majority interests in an insurance company and a warehouse complex. The Ministry of Defense controls (and profits from) the importation of explosives, handguns, and ammunition and offers security to major business establishments through the Extraordinary Mobile Military Police. There are no significant business enterprises owned or operated by the military, and the business community has expressed little concern over the military's few income-earning activities. All income from these activities either goes into the operational budget of the armed forces or into the pension or social security funds, or toward the recreational needs of the active and retired officers and specialist ranks and their families. Funds for education and scholarships come either from the D-III (Operations) of the General Staff, the Ministry of Defense, or the scholarships offered by the United States, Mexico, Venezuela, and several other Latin American countries, and such countries as Taiwan, Spain, Italy, and France.[10]

The Guatemalan army, largely preoccupied with an internal war since the early 1960s, has shown little aggressive behavior toward its neighbors. With the exception of President Ydigoras's threat in the late 1950s to go to war with Mexico and the territorial dispute with Great Britain (over the status of Belize), the Guatemalan army has few enemies beyond its borders. When Guatemala officially recognized Belize as an independent nation during the presidency of Jorge Serrano, criticism came primarily from the old, traditional right and from entrenched, constitutional lawyers who had won fame and income by defending Guatemala's historic right to acquire Belize. The military as an institution offered no comment. Privately, senior officers were happy to take Belize off their "security threat" plate—there were enough other security issues requiring their attention and resources. Furthermore, the thought of taking on the British on the Belizean battlefield was not that appealing—the implications of the Falklands war were not lost on the Guatemalan army.[11]

The Guatemalan military has historically paid only lip service to the idea of regional military cooperation. The concept of a Central American defense cooperation pact has always been seen as a "gringo" idea. With a few exceptions, during the height of the Central American wars, the military provided minimal operational support to neighboring military institutions engaged in wars against leftist guerrillas. Both the Honduran and Guatemalan armed forces were often more concerned with the balance of military power shifting in favor of El Salvador as a result of the enormous amounts of U.S. military assistance and political support to defeat the FMLN. On its own, the Guatemalan military eventually developed significant military cooperation and intelligence-exchange procedures with the Mexican army (in dealing with Guatemalan guerrillas and refugees residing on Mexican territory near the border) and with the British along the Belizean border (dealing with drug, contraband, and wood smugglers—and to a lesser extent Guatemalan guerrillas operating in Belize).

Domestically, the military focused on the need to defeat the URNG militarily and to help guide the establishment of a viable political system that would not only lead to democratization but would also be protective of the military as an institution. The objective of the army's leadership was to gain the needed recognition that the Guatemalan armed forces is a legitimate and necessary element of the Guatemalan state and society. Internationally and regionally, beginning with the ouster of Rios Montt in mid-1983, the military government (led by Foreign Minister Fernando Andrade) set out to establish a proactive foreign policy unique to the needs of Guatemala. One of the aims of the March 1982 coup was to break the international isolation of both Guatemala and its military. Andrade's foreign policy sought Guatemala's acceptance as a regional diplomatic actor. The strategy, and its designer, were both highly successful.

Since the mid-1980s, the military itself has taken an active role in foreign affairs. It has developed its own cadre of military and civilian professionals to travel, represent, and analyze international politics. Military officers often accompany presidential and foreign ministry officials to international conferences and as members of official delegations engaging in talks and negotiations with other governments and international organizations. By the mid-1990s, the "diplomatic" wing of the Guatemalan armed forces had grown in terms of its skills and successes. These "military diplomats" had also created animosities and jealousies among officers and civilians in the Foreign Ministry. Visibility, extensive travel to Europe and the United States, and playing a high stakes game with the future of the officer corps and military institution made them targets of criticism—especially the majors and lieutenant colonels involved in the army's peace diplomacy.

For over ten years, Central American countries engaged in repeated presidential summits aimed at developing treaties and accords to bring peace, all of which resulted in documents upon documents providing data and options to the respective governments. Most of these efforts included representation from Guatemala—on most occasions including representation from the Ministry of Defense. The military had little enthusiasm for these peace processes because they called for (1) placing limits on specific weapons and the number of personnel at a time when the Guatemalan army was at war; (2) negotiating with the guerrilla adversary while the battlefield outcome had not yet been decided; and (3) intervention by international actors into the domestic affairs of Guatemala. It was only with the presidency of Vinicio Cerezo, beginning in 1986, that Guatemala became a proactive player in the Central American peace process.

Much of this activism took the form of open competition between President Cerezo and President Oscar Arias of Costa Rica. Then-Minister of Defense Hector Gramajo was a participant and a proponent of Guatemala's more energetic involvement in these processes, and thus the military did not stand in the way of these efforts. Cerezo and Gramajo both saw the importance of helping to shape the Central American peace in order to legitimize Guatemala and rehabilitate its black image as an "outlaw" state under the military presidents. Involvement in the peace processes would also protect, if not enhance, Guatemala's domestic political situation. On August 7, 1987, at Esquipulas II, Arias got his comprehensive peace accord and Cerezo got the location of the summit (Esquipulas is in the Guatemalan department of Chiquimula) and the Central American Parliament (the forum for much of the region's cooperation and integration efforts in the mid-1990s).

The military was supportive of the accord—especially since its signing had no immediate impact on Guatemala. Its focus was the war in Nicaragua and the desire to end the U.S. support for the contras. Esquipulas II had little to do with

Guatemala's core politico-military problems, but it made Guatemala look good because it was supporting peace and democracy elsewhere in the region.

One of the few times when the Guatemalan military publicly declared its opposition to a regional endeavor was in the Central American Security Commission (CASC) in the early 1990s. Since the late 1980s, efforts had been made to inventory military hardware, budgets, manpower, installations, and capabilities. The Guatemalan delegations (civilian and military) attended the sessions but seldom provided requested data. The Guatemalan position was that it was still fighting a war and was not going to compromise its operational capabilities against the guerrillas (who had not yet agreed to negotiations) in order to satisfy some regional desire to calculate regional military power relationships in Central America.

With little fanfare or publicity, however, the Guatemalan government signed the Central American Democratic Security Treaty in December 1995 in Honduras. The Guatemalan armed forces took no position nor did it offer detailed comments about the implications of such a comprehensive agreement. Instead, the focus remained on the government-URNG peace negotiations.

CONCLUSIONS

The armed forces have been a determining institutional factor in the politics and life of Guatemalan society since the 1944 October Revolution. The armed forces helped give birth to a genuine social revolution. That social revolution freed the military to seek out its own level of professional development and institutionalization. Both were cut short of their natural evolution by the Cold War and the 1954 liberation and U.S. government intervention. The army has endured, survived, and adapted to foreign intervention, a dozen coups, two insurgencies lasting a total of thirty-four years, two military governments, three governments headed by retired military officers, international isolation and condemnation, and now a difficult peace process that will extract a price from the institution and its officer corps.

Guatemalan society has also endured its military institution. The war has produced between sixty and eighty thousand deaths; thousands of disappearances; hundreds of thousands of refugees and exiles; and thousands of displaced inhabitants. The budgetary needs of the army have not been overwhelmingly unbearable. But, given the fact that the Guatemalan state's tax base is one of the smallest in Latin America, the financial burden is relatively high. During the violence of the 1970s and 1980s, Guatemala lost a generation of leaders from across the political spectrum and from all socioeconomic strata. This social cost cannot be calculated. Political polarization, political extremism, and political violence were the mainstay of Guatemalan society. These conditions helped to fuel the undemocratic nature of Guatemala, including creating a distance and hostility between the military and the civilian population and an image of a society on the edge of the apocalypse.[12]

The Guatemalan militaries of 1944, 1954, 1963, 1982, and now 1996 were each slightly different—institutionally, psychologically, politically, and in their vision of Guatemala's future. The domestic, regional, and international environments have changed—often radically. In order to adapt and survive, the military leadership has consciously sought to keep up with political dynamics and institutional needs. Thus, the form of involvement and influence changes. Most importantly, the vision of the army and its role in society has changed remarkably fast—especially during the peace negotiations of the past five years.

The concept of security has drastically evolved since 1982. Regional security matters have come to the forefront of military thinking and doctrine. The Cold War is no longer relevant to the Guatemalan military preparing for institutional challenges (professionalization and education, global security issues, force modernization, regional cooperation, and revised doctrines and missions) of the next decade. It is a military institution more disposed toward regional cooperation than conflict. The Mexican border is being worked out with ever more cooperative Mexican military and security officials. Belize is no longer an issue for the military. The military seeks a broader role in rural development, international peacekeeping operations, and nontraditional security areas—environment, resource management, immigration, contraband, international crime.

While supporting, largely out of self-interest, the process of democratization and civilian rule, the withdrawal of the military from various internal security responsibilities may be problematic for "law and order" in Guatemala for the remainder of the decade. In fact, the process of democratic consolidation faces challenges from outside the military. Unprecedented levels of migration to the capital; higher and higher levels of common crime and violence; underemployment and unemployment; a weak national police force unable to take over operations at the level previously maintained by the military and paramilitary forces; and a largely nonfunctioning judicial system clearly point to a "security vacuum" that can easily undermine the process of democratization.

The "new" military mission of the Guatemalan army is not yet clear nor cast in stone. Much, ironically, depends on the civilians in the presidency and the congress. What do they want the military to do? Provide development and social projects in isolated rural areas where the state does not have a strong presence? Provide for enhanced "law and order" when and where the civilian police cannot function? Protect the forests, the exclusive economic ocean zone, the national treasures and historic sites, fight international crime, represent Guatemala in international peacekeeping operations? What does the military want to do? Much of the new mission will not be formalized until after the peace accords have been implemented.

As of late 1996, the Guatemalan army was making no effort to restrain the further liberalization of the political or economic system. While there are exceptions, the officer corps has come to accept the necessity to end the war. Since 1991–1992, senior army commanders have come to understand that the most appropriate means by which to protect the institutional integrity of the Guatemalan armed forces in a postwar society is to actively participate in the peace process. Seeking to act as a "political guardian" by placing limits on political participation or economic reforms would not be in the interest of the institution in a postwar Guatemala.

Furthermore, the Guatemalan army will support increased regional cooperation on economic, social, and political matters. The army has no interest in fighting Belize (meaning the British) on behalf of the Guatemalan right or the "constitutional nationalists" lawyers. The army continues to support the development of a strong presidency supported by independent, well-financed, and professionally staffed secretariats—including a new secretariat for national security affairs and intelligence. The army strongly supports the current process of decentralization of the government ministries, of regional and municipal development councils, and the concept of local community power.

The Guatemalan military has been a principal architect of the political liberation, democratization, and regional cooperation strategies of governments since 1982. The army was at first the driving force, later a partner, and now the strong (often silent) supporter of the presidency and a stabilizing political order. The army leadership has sought to build and support a constitutional order that not only provides for national security and stability but also for the institutional survival of the armed forces as a modern, professional, and legitimate sector of the Guatemalan state.

NOTES

1. For a discussion of the current situation in Guatemala in the aftermath of the January 1996 second-round election victory of Álvaro Arzu, see Rachel M. McCleary, "Guatemala: Expectations for Peace," *Current History* (February 1996):88–92.

2. A concise history of the Central American peace process is provided by Jack Child, *The Central American Peace Process, 1983–1991* (Boulder: Lynne Rienner Publishers, 1992).

3. Piero Gleijeses examines U.S. government involvement in Guatemala during this period. See his *Shattered Hope: The Guatemalan Revolution and the United States, 1944–1954* (Princeton: Princeton University Press, 1991).

4. Brian Jenkins, Caesar Sereseres, and Luigi Einaudi, *U.S. Military Aid and Guatemalan Politics*, California Arms Control and Foreign Policy Seminar, Pasadena, California Institute of Technology, 1974; interviews with Army officers who were involved in the August 2 rebellion. Marta Cehelsky, "Guatemala's Frustrated Revolution: The Liberation of 1954," master's thesis, Columbia University, New York, 1967, describes the U.S. intervention, the creation of the "liberation movement," and the battle between the liberation army and the cadets.

5. The fight against Marxist-Leninist-oriented guerrillas from the mid-1960s through the early 1980s cost the lives of combatants and innocents alike. Victims of political violence included the political leadership of political parties across the ideological spectrum. As presidential prospects of the major parties were either murdered, forced into exile or

opposition to the government, or intimidated into early "retirement" from electoral politics, political parties turned to candidates who could ensure their personal security and a strong possibility of electoral victory. Military officers, especially ministers of defense, provided any coalition of political parties with the elements of victory and security. See Caesar D. Sereseres, "The Guatemalan Legacy: Radical Challengers and Military Politics," in *Report on Guatemala,* SAIS Papers in International Affairs, no. 7.

6. For a comparison of the two guerrilla generations, see Caesar D. Sereseres, "Lessons from Central America's Revolutionary Wars," in Robert E. Harkavy and Stephanie G. Neuman, eds., *The Lessons of Recent Wars in the Third World* (Lexington, Mass.: D.C. Heath, 1985).

7. A detailed assessment of the senior military leadership strategy is found in Francisco Fernando Beltranena Falla, *Guatemala: Pretorianismo y Democracia Estratégica* (Guatemala: Instituto de Estudios Políticos, Universidad Francisco Marroquin, 1992).

8. The old political party and electoral systems are described in Francisco Villagran Kramer, *Biografía política de Guatemala: Los pactos políticos de 1944–1970* (Guatemala: FLACSO, 1993).

9. General Hector Alejandro Gramajo Morales, a major architect and implementor of the army's counterinsurgency and political liberalization strategy, has written about his experiences in *De la Guerra . . . A la Guerra: La difícil transición política en Guatemala* (Guatemala: Fondo de Cultura Editorial, 1995).

10. Sources for these data are interviews over the past several years with the Minister of Defense, Chief of Staff, and members of the General Staff. In addition, I have spoken, off the record, with the Defense Attaché and the U.S. Military Group Commander of the U.S. Embassy in Guatemala.

11. Discussions with senior Guatemalan military officers, civilian "experts" on the subject of Belize, Guatemalan academic researchers, and U.S. Embassy officials.

12. Fighting in the villages of rural Guatemala, where the war would be lost or won, involved everyone. There was no escape from the guerrillas or from the army. See David Stoll, *Between Two Armies in the Ixil Towns of Guatemala* (New York: Columbia University Press, 1993).

■

CHAPTER ELEVEN

Democratization and International Integration: The Role of the Armed Forces in Brazil's Grand Strategy

Thomaz Guedes da Costa

The evolution of Brazilian regional relations and domestic politics in recent years exhibits a dialectical quality. On the one hand, structural events shape the internal politics of the country, while, on the other hand, the process of democratization has altered the scope of options available to Brazil in its relationship with its neighbors. In this context, the principal argument advanced here is that Brazilian regional relations, the dependent variable of the study, are influenced by a set of diverse factors. These factors, which include structural as well as national-level political and bureaucratic forces, create a network of new and complex issues that Brazil must contend with in an era of turbulent change in the international system.

With the aim of elucidating these new relationships, this chapter examines (1) the background of Brazil's transformation, both in the international system and the domestic regime, and the outlines of Brazil's emerging grand strategy; (2) the establishment of a new paradigm of relations between the armed forces and political authority as reflected in the internal process of decisionmaking and the ideological climate; and (3) implications of these changes for regional relations in both the economic and security arenas.

GLOBAL AND DOMESTIC CHANGES

Since the Constitution of 1988 inaugurated the New Republic, Brazil has witnessed an era of substantial political and economic adjustment. These internal changes, in the context of an evolving international environment, provide the basis for the formulation of a new grand strategy of global engagement.

The Brazilian domestic environment has been transformed by both the establishment of full democracy and the stabilization of the economy. Incremental reform of the Constitution and the resulting laws have produced a new framework of economic regulation consistent with neoliberal precepts. At the same time, Brazil's old rules of political competition have been replaced by a more liberal regime, in which market forces and interest-group demands operate in a more participatory political marketplace. Related to these changes, conflict among social groups has become more impartial and transparent as the National Congress has emerged as the principal forum for interaction. The effort to control inflation under the Real Plan, in combination with increased exposure to competitive international markets, has provoked turmoil in the productive sector, both in the public sphere and between private entrepreneurs and workers. Yet despite the challenges posed by the process of reform and the effort to contain public spending and liberalize the economy, the initial successes of the administration of Fernando Henrique Cardoso engender optimism.

Along with internal adjustment, Brazil has been experiencing the effects of globalization of its economy and the pressures of regional integration.[1] The new economic model requires that Brazil undertake internal reforms so that the country can meet the requirements of international regimes governing commerce, investment, international capital, and technology flows. These changes have contributed to the ongoing transformation of the Brazilian economy. Hence, while capital movements and commercial flows increase the complexity of domestic adjustments and require new regulations, they also present novel opportunities for reconstructing the Brazilian productive system. Regionally, the staged phase-in of the Mercado Común del Sur (MERCOSUR) agreements has created important opportunities for domestic and international negotiation over key economic issues.[2] Since January 1, 1995, the members of MERCOSUR have implemented a common external tariff to serve as the basis of a customs union. As these reforms progress, Brazilian grand strategy will increasingly reflect the effort to build a "common market" under the auspices of MERCOSUR; the possibility of expanding the regional idea to encompass a South American Free Trade Zone and a Hemispheric Free Trade Zone will also be explored.

The complex situation produced by the dialectical process of internal and external adjustment provides the context for a transformation of Brazilian grand strategy. As such the current era marks a departure from Brazil's previous economic and security goals and strategies. In the Old Republic, Brazil's strategy consisted of a close association with the United States on the South American front (anchored to the effort to insulate Brazil from conflicts of interest with European powers), the promotion of peaceful and favorable resolutions of border disputes with the country's neighbors, and the use of external commercial ties to enhance national wealth. From the Revolution of 1930 and the period of Tenentism (when colonels had great influence within the military) through the termination of protection for chemicals in the 1980s, Brazil pursued a strategy of autonomy in order to enhance national power and promote national development. With the opening of the national economy and regional economic integration, initiated in the Collor administration in 1990, leaders are seeking to articulate a new grand strategy capable of providing unity and direction as Brazil moves into the twenty-first century.[3]

The outlines of a new grand strategy are emerging in this context of transition, in both the global system and the domestic regime, in which new structures shaping the political game coexist with elements of the old regime. Among the principal objectives advanced by the Cardoso administration, the following stand out: the opening of the country to international markets; the liberalization of capital, technology, product, and service flows; the privatization of the means of production formerly under state control; adherence to international regimes; emphasis on cooperative economic coordination with MERCOSUR in resolving pending issues, such as the intellectual property law that also affects Brazil's relations with the United States; expansion of economic exchange with the countries of the European Union and Japan; the exploration of new strategic partnerships with the People's Republic of China, Russia, and India; and the desire to improve the general global competitive position of the country.[4]

A NEW PARADIGM IN CIVIL-MILITARY RELATIONS

The modifications Brazil is experiencing, both internationally and domestically, occur in the context of the evolution of civil-military relations. This section examines these changes in an effort to assess how they have contributed and continue to contribute to the redefinition of Brazil's regional relations.

Following the inauguration of the Cardoso administration, a new configuration in the relations between the armed forces and the remaining sectors of the state and society was consolidated. Perhaps most notable is the pervasive decline in the military's political activity.[5] It is my contention that there is a manifest reduction in military participation in national politics, as expressed through both statements and actions. "We took the lead and we got burned. So, let the civilian politicians take over." This is the general sentiment, but its acceptance among the rank and file is difficult to demonstrate.[6] Nevertheless, the absence of explicit pronouncements regarding current national issues such as constitutional revision, in both active-duty units and the reserves, suggests that there has been a reduction in the military's organized political participation.

In order to understand what appears to be a change in civil-military relations, it is necessary to look to the ideological climate in which these changes have occurred. This civil-military configuration is a product of a new ideological alignment constructed between the dominant ideology in the military and among the national political leaders. As such, the interpretation that the role of military institutions is receding to the background in policy debates, maintaining a discrete presence, passive or silent on national issues, could lead to an interpretation of political impotence. But such discrete behavior could well be expected if the military ideology were in harmony with that dominant in Brazilian politics today, and especially with that which was ratified in the 1994 presidential elections. It is probably too early to tell whether this relative equanimity in civil-military relations stems from the emergence of a more liberal political culture in Brazil or whether it represents a simple harmony of interests.

Regardless of its origin or its label, perhaps the best evidence of this ideological alignment is the absence of substantive debates among the military questioning the constitutional reforms affecting the economic model that accompanied the nationalist-developmentalist grand strategy. The end of state control in various areas, most importantly the energy sector, the easing of regulations regarding the productive activity of foreign capital, and the negotiations on the internal and external public debt have all been accepted with tranquillity in the barracks. The military has stayed away from the critical issues of privatization of oil, transportation, and telecommunications sectors, as well as the reduction of trade barriers and the creation of MERCOSUR.

Nevertheless, although the military does not play an active role in politics in these areas, the armed forces retain a prominent position in the regime. Although changes in the ideological climate and constitutive rules have reoriented the military's relationship to society in many arenas, the military is perceived as embodying a reserve of morality and maintaining a role as a servant of the state. This represents a great contradiction in Brazilian democracy: The military is still widely perceived as a reserve of competence and honesty, especially in the management of policy issues, including the maintenance of "law and order" where "civilians" are less well suited to the tasks at hand.[7] For example, the army has been called in to manage the local offices of the government's land reforms after outbreaks of violence and charges of corruption discredited the civilian officials. The role of the military in national politics is also evident in the president's occasional appointment of military officials to key political posts. The extent to which such attitudes and actions represent an important qualification in the growth of civilian authority remains to be seen.

The following section provides an overview of how and to what extent Brazil's current civil-military configuration has prompted a redefinition of the military's role in key policy areas. The discussion speaks to the perennial debate regarding military autonomy within the state[8] and to the potentially larger question of the nature of the status of civil-military relations in Brazil. In an effort to assess the military's "autonomy," the analysis focuses on the military's prerogatives in the area of human rights and justice, the budget, military careers, and organization of defense—points of friction among and within the military branches, and between the military and other political forces.

Human Rights and Justice

One area previously dominated by the armed forces, which illustrates the growing assertion of political authority, is the legal control of military institutions associated with administering justice. Changes in the country's legal framework reflect this dynamic. For example, there has been some revision of legal codes in order to address violations of human and political rights under the former military regime. In August 1995, President Cardoso's proposal to indemnify the families of those who disappeared or were killed was approved by Congress. In order to establish the official list of approximately 170 persons recognized as victims of the military regime, a Special Commission on Political Disappearances was formed, which included representatives from government, the armed forces, and nongovernmental organizations. No cases after August 15, 1979, would be considered because that was the day the Amnesty Law was passed, establishing institutional guidelines for investigating individual responsibility of persons involved in torture and political crimes during the Brazilian military regime.[9] This revision of the code has revived past events despite the validity of the Amnesty Law. The most recent is the reopening of the investigations of the Riocenter explosion on April 30, 1981, and of other events that occurred after 1979.[10]

Civilian control is also progressing without provoking national controversy in some areas of the military justice system. Routine interventions by the judicial branch in the armed forces occurs without restriction when investigating accusations of common crimes and human rights violations by military personnel.[11]

The same does not hold, however, with respect to the Military Police. In this case, the impartiality of the military justice system in the treatment of crimes committed by military police is of widespread concern. The Military Police, under the control of the state governments, is composed of organizations that undertake policing duties when called upon. There is some ambiguity in the definition of the police's role in terms of its official powers and in the context of the organizational culture of these policing bodies. As police, they should act within the strict limits of the law. As military organizations, the emphasis placed on preparation for violent combat when fighting crime often translates into arbitrariness and aggression toward citizens.

In the case of crimes committed by military personnel in fulfillment of their duties, the process of investigation and deliberation occurs within the military justice system. The fact that military officials make up the majority of these tribunals raises doubts about the impartiality of the system. Consequently, within the debates over constitutional revision, there is strong pressure to reduce the autonomy of the military justice system.

Budget

Budgetary controls over military expenditure have been maintained in "civilian" hands for quite some time, leading to a significant reduction in investment and spending. On the side of budget forecasts for investment, whether annual or multiyear, the Planning and Budget Ministry often makes arbitrary cuts in order to bring military spending in line with available funds. On the side of expenditure, the disbursements of the National Treasury for the armed forces are also restricted, which on occasion creates impediments to the timeliness of payments. For example, in 1993, the Itamar Franco administration agreed to allocate US$800 million to the army. But no funds were released.[12] Thus far in 1996, the army has an outstanding debt of US$120 million with suppliers, but the treasury secretary will not release funds for payment.

Another form of political control of the armed forces can be seen in the multiyear budget forecasts. In the 1995 forecast, the armed forces were given a lower priority than other federal government entities. For the line item "modernization of the armed forces and maintenance of operations," estimated costs and investments are US$5.6 billion, excluding personnel and administration of US$4.9 billion, in a total federal administration budget for the next four years of US$460 billion.[13]

Another modification in the budgetary decisionmaking process regards transferring the locus of power to Congress, which has gained the power of initiative and veto over the Budget Law since 1988. If during the military government the executive had autonomy in determining military expenditure, now, as in all other sectors, these expenditures are politically contested and modified in the Congress before approval. In the annual routine of budget making and the design of the Multiyear Budget Plan, intense negotiations with Congress are now necessary, since that body controls most of the deliberations. This struggle between the branches is seen even in the constitutional amendment that permits the president, and not Congress, to authorize the cost and the dispatching of up to 4000 men to foreign soil in fulfillment of peacekeeping missions.[14]

One consequence of the growing emphasis on technical and budgetary questions in the administration of military affairs is the growing distance among the service branches. The navy, the army, and the air force have become more independent from each other, and hence there is more diversity in their political views. Young officers do not support the political debate that some retired officers still want to carry on in military clubs. Such trends may, in turn, strengthen the effort to further distinguish the military and political spheres.

Compensation

One area that has been subject to careful negotiation is the issue of salaries and compensation in the military. Due to budgetary restrictions, military salary benefits and perquisites have remained unaltered, both for active and inactive personnel. Up to 1988, a separate statute governing military careers was in place, which guaranteed salary increases and retirement benefits distinct from those for civilians. Arguing that military careers are substantially different from others, the military lobby is proposing a distinct set of criteria and benefits for the members of the armed forces. If such a scheme is approved, discriminatory salary adjustments will be effected and a separate retirement system established.[15] For example, a new law to be put into effect establishes a separate social security system for the armed services, one that is better than that of civilian federal employees.

Organization

Finally, from an operational point of view, changes are appearing in the organization of the armed forces for national defense. Until the inauguration of the Cardoso administration there had not been any direct interference by political authorities in the military's traditional control over the planning of military preparation and employment. In the area of defense, Brazil was characterized by the absence of an approved defense policy, the lack of a military doctrine for joint operations, and an operational independence between the air force, marines and army.

The first signs of change can now be observed. First, on assuming office, Fernando Cardoso decreed a legal adjustment that allowed generals who had entered the reserves to continue to serve in the Joint Chiefs of Staff of the Armed Forces. Thus, he appointed the new head of the Joint Chiefs of Staff to study the creation of a defense ministry. This report, still preliminary and yet to be released publicly, will perhaps permit some reflection regarding the different doctrines of the separate forces and an agreement for reducing the rivalries regarding questions of joint operations. The pressure for participation in peacekeeping missions and support in the combat of narcotics trafficking provide objective conditions for greater discrimination of priorities in preparation and perfection of joint operations.

REGIONAL POLICY

These international and domestic changes provide a new context for Brazil's regional policies. Perhaps the most outstanding feature of Brazil's outlook is the aspiration to mold the country into a consequential actor on the international scene. This is reflected in the country's desire to participate in the international political game, globally and in its various regional arenas, and in cultural images of the greatness of the country. As such, Brazilian grand strategy does not reflect the automatic subordination to the hegemonic power, the passive acceptance of international regimes, or a willingness to sacrifice future options in exchange for short-term benefits. These attitudes are seen in the continuing development of Brazil's national capacity combined with respect for international rules.

Economic Policy and Regional Integration

Brazilian grand strategy reflects the commitment to regional integration under the auspices of MERCOSUR and the efforts at rapprochement with the other nations of South America and the western coast of Africa.[16] Brazil's efforts toward economic cooperation and integration have fostered a climate of tranquillity with its neighbors and provided opportunities for mutual benefits. The president's secretary of strategic issues, Ambassador Ronaldo Mota Sardenberg, argues as follows:

> Today regional integration appears to signify, at the minimum, a necessary stop on the path to globalization and, at the maximum, the actual manner in which global

engagement is structured. Brazil and Argentina, together with Paraguay and Uruguay chose to form a partnership, MERCOSUR, which on the one hand modifies some rights of sovereignty, and we are witnessing this in the economic realm, but, on the other hand, furnishes a necessary shield for the fierceness of the global competitive game. The regionalism we plan to practice, open and not exclusive, should, in the future, embrace all of South America, and it will provide us with a sufficiently robust economic base such that we can begin to act dynamically and decisively to create our own profile in the global market. I emphasize that integration with the Latin American countries is, in Brazil, a constitutional precept.[17]

Although the MERCOSUR agreement is the most relevant and developed, the Brazilian strategic plan is in no way restricted to this course, as some may believe.

Brazil has chosen to embark on a gradual process of integration, accepting risks and opportunities and emphasizing the promise of mutual benefits. In the few years of mutual ties, the development of the MERCOSUR regional integration has led to great success. But it also obliges the Brazilian government to harmonize decisions of domestic and foreign policy with regionally assumed commitments. The country, with the responsibility of a mature actor, accepts the paradox of interdependence: the more regional integration is sought, the more it will condition the national political process. It can be easily affirmed that, from a material point of view, Brazil would not be seriously affected if it were to break ties with MERCOSUR. But the uncertain consequences of such a move imply significant political risks and the abandonment of important cumulative benefits.

President Cardoso himself emphasizes the influence of this regional commitment and its impact on the country's concept of security: "The international order that has emerged in recent years, and Brazil's relations with its neighbors— maturing and consolidating at an accelerated pace with the implementation of MERCOSUR—reduce the probability that conventional external regional conflicts involving our country will manifest."[18]

The necessity of greater cooperation in determining the fate of the Amazon Basin and the economic development of the area has, in fact, led Brazil to explore new opportunities for exchange with countries of the region. The idea of opening the Pacific coast to a flow of Brazilian goods, involving the integration of border areas, has stimulated an exchange of proposals. Corridors of integration and export axes are fundamental concepts in Brazilian government planning. The rapprochement, both with Peru as well as with Venezuela, has already resulted in joint economic and environmental protection projects with significant long-term impact on regional relations.

Although this integration process establishes a situation of tranquillity along the border, it does not however produce conditions for an intense military cooperation or the coordination of defense policy. A few hypotheses regarding this limitation can be suggested.

First, there is a strategic asymmetry that minimized, up to this point, the value of an integrated defense policy. From the Brazilian point of view, the areas of the

Amazon and the South Atlantic Zone of Peace and Cooperation overshadow general proposals for close defense cooperation and military operational integration in the Plata Basin. In addition, as problems of illegal trafficking and population movement in the border areas of the Amazon increase and peacekeeping missions on the west coast of Africa continue, the general structure of Brazilian military deployments will move from the south to the north. Second, Argentina's dissatisfaction regarding the current political status of the Malvinas Islands and the preference for close military relations with the United States reduce Brazil's willingness to enter into a partnership with Buenos Aires for joint planning exercises. Finally, within the political reforms taking place in Brazil and Argentina, the pressures and motivations to use international military cooperation as a means to legitimate the function of the armed forces are different. Consequently, the processes of economic integration and defense cooperation each proceed at their own pace, without reciprocal commitments.[19]

These qualifications aside, from the Brazilian political leaders' point of view, the emphasis on international cooperation has led to revisions in the defense planning and procurement process and inspired an increased emphasis on peacekeeping missions and the employment of the armed forces in combating illegal border activities.

Defense Policy

Changes in the defense planning process have occurred in the context of a changing international and domestic environment.[20] Structurally, perceptions of international relations in the core countries of the international system bolster a climate of tranquillity and movement toward new military missions. Alterations in Brazil's constitution and economic policy have produced new institutional arrangements that affect military autonomy and the preparedness of the armed forces.

Concomitant with the operational redefinition of the armed forces toward a new role in the prevention of illicit activities and in international peacekeeping missions (see the following section), the new Brazilian democracy has redefined relations between the armed forces and political authorities. These new features, occurring in the context of an ideological congruence, generally, support the notion that civilian political control is supreme and military institutions are subordinated to the priorities of the democratic regime.

Related data help evaluate this hypothesis. The Brazilian defense industry has been dismantled. The important industrial and marketing experience that characterized the "Brazil Great Power" period aimed at reducing dependence on foreign suppliers has been all but abandoned. For example, since 1993 Engesa, the major producer of armored combat vehicles, has been bankrupt, with a debt approaching US$700 million. Another firm, EMBRAER, was privatized with heavy participation from international capital. Moreover, the missile manufacturer, Avibras, re-oriented its manufacturing operations toward civilian products.[21]

Those projects that remain viable today are circumscribed by substantial budgetary and political controls. With regard to naval construction, there are continual delays in the release of the Timbira and Tapajos submarines due to lack of funds. Moreover, the nuclear submarine program has been suspended temporarily in favor of the development of conventional systems of propulsion.[22] In the remaining sectors, particularly aeronautics, production programs have been maintained in order to support assembly operations.

Moreover, Brazilian military equipment is seriously outdated. In spite of authorizations for international loans for purchasing anti-aircraft systems for six frigates and for Igla anti-aircraft missiles for the army, arms systems are very limited and do not present a threat to any regional balance of power.[23] This situation, if unfavorable for minimum professional preparedness of the Brazilian armed forces, tends to reinforce an air of tranquillity in conventional strategic relations. To the extent that a reconfiguration in the balance of civilian and military concerns in the regime has created this climate, it has served to promote a less competitive regional environment.

Peacekeeping Forces

From 1945 until 1996, Brazilian thinking and policymaking regarding collective security have oscillated between an idealist discourse, proclaiming the merits of such a system, and limited efforts to secure the realization of such a regime. In practice, for a variety of historical reasons, Brazil has sent contingents of observers and troops in support of multilateral organizations engaged in observation and peacekeeping missions.[24] Since 1990, the tenor of the Brazilian contribution to collective security has been to reinforce the existing efforts and contribute to them within the limits of the country's foreign policy.

Thus, while Brazil dispatches civilian and military observers to foreign lands in response to the solicitations of multilateral organizations, the contributions reflect Brazil's zone of regional projection. With regard to a commitment for troop presence, the sub-Saharan African front is preferred. In this way Brazilian troops participate in the multilateral force for peacekeeping in Mozambique and Angola and in the strengthening of the international security of countries like Namibia and Cape Verde.[25]

A related subsidiary point is the fact that Brazil's international military presence has not been the subject of internal debate, whether as part of the consideration of foreign policy or in specific discussions of the role of the armed forces. Peacekeeping activities are viewed as part of the international role of the country. Yet the perpetual engagement of Brazil's forces in such endeavors demands more systematic preparation of the forces deployed as well as greater coordination between Brazilian troops and their foreign partners. The greater the magnitude of Brazil's involvement, the greater the need for appropriate planning and discussion in order to guarantee operational effectiveness and the security of Brazilian soldiers.

Illicit Transborder Activities

The other dimension of Brazil's operational use of the armed forces arises from the country's efforts to combat illicit transborder activities. In this context, the goal is to define a limited use of the armed forces without undermining or displacing the role of the police forces. This was a political decision made by President Cardoso that entailed a careful consideration of the risks. As he pointed out recently:

> We cannot have the same peace of mind [with regard to our relations with our neighbors] in that concerning the new and concrete threats to national security, represented by grave illicit transborder activities that not only challenge our sovereignty at the borders, in our air space and in the rivers of the Amazon basin, but also present a serious risk of rending the Brazilian social fabric. Among these stand out international narcotics trafficking and arms smuggling carried out by organized crime. These problems merit consideration by all those who, like us, administer the defense of the country and society, and who, therefore, must maintain Brazilian sovereignty intact and preserve our social structure, two objectives of defense policy and a continual presidential policy goal.[26]

This represents a significant change in policy. In President Cardoso's address to the ministers, bureau chiefs, and military officials in Rio de Janeiro in November 1995, there were no references to the question of planning in general nor of the fight against illicit border activities in particular. Nevertheless, a few months later there were indications of a change in the directives regarding the use of the armed forces in the combat of illicit activities, which have had repercussions for the country's foreign policy and its relations with its neighbors.

New directives for training the armed forces in the control of border areas and in operational and logistical support of the military organization have emerged from this change in policy.[27] With respect to control, the principal project is the establishment of a system of reconnaissance in the Amazon, Sistema de Vigilancia da Amazonia (SIVAM), with investment estimated at US$1.6 billion.[28] This system will constitute one component of a larger program of regional protection oriented to the control of the flow of people, vehicles, and merchandise; to the generation of information for environmental protection; and to the establishment of a state presence in remote regions.

In the context of Brazil's international policy, this posture represents a national response to pressures emanating from the U.S. military policy for the region, which demands that the South American armed forces take a stronger policing role in the combat of narcotics trafficking. For Brazil's part, this policy of limited engagement establishes preventative and prohibitive measures against illicit activities and seeks to preserve sovereignty by guarding against the "overflow" of repressive actions against crime in neighboring countries. Various efforts are being developed for coordination among neighboring countries. Of special note is the recent security agreement in the tripartite border region of Argentina, Brazil, and Paraguay, with the intent to exchange information and to prevent illegal activities and possible terrorist acts.[29]

For the military, which from this point forward should balance the operational gains (principally budgetary) with the political risks (primarily corruption) of the support of the police in the combat of illicit activities, the unequivocal subordination to the directives issued by political authorities reflects the new era of relations between "civilians" and "the military."

CONCLUSION

Brazil is currently experiencing both a process of external adjustment to the structure of global power relations and internal adjustment to the forces of democratization. The abandonment of the nationalist-developmentalist model and the formulation of a new grand strategy, economic integration under the auspices of MERCOSUR, and cooperation with other South American and African states represent the search for common interests among countries with diverse values. Hence, the themes of Brazil's defense policy have a constructive tone, no longer focused on potential conflict, but based on the resolution of common problems.

Brazil's participation in international peacekeeping missions and its efforts to combat illicit transborder activities are key strategic problems facing the current administration. They provide the framework for the use of the armed forces in the coming years, in conjunction with the traditional goal of conventional modernization. Brazil's incentives for the adoption of new policies to address security concerns derive as much from the new possibilities and promises of traditional and emerging collective security arrangements as from an awareness of the costs of passivity in the face of unconventional conflicts such as organized crime.

Nevertheless, the preparation, organization, and use of the armed forces in Brazil in the post-1988 democratic regime depend on the changes occurring in the national political game. The redistribution of power in national politics has prompted an infusion of new players into the decisionmaking processes that define the political goals of the armed forces as well as the allocation of scarce resources. Although the armed forces have lost a certain amount of decisionmaking autonomy, they have gained greater political legitimacy in pursuing their interests.

With regard to regional relations, the current climate of Brazilian politics is one that welcomes the association between economic advances and greater coordination in defense matters. Yet, even with these changes, an air of conservatism and caution prevails. Moreover, Brazilian strategy remains diverse and complex. Thus, while recent negotiations yield new facts and new perspectives in regard to the Rio Plata as well as the Amazonian and African regions, much is still uncertain. In addition, the coordination of national defense measures in the context of MERCOSUR will encounter natural limitations, due both to the complexity of the situation as well as to the diversity of individual countries' interests.

NOTES

1. It is important to note that Brazil lags behind among Newly Industrialized Countries in adjusting for the effects of globalization. A recent study shows that it contributes less than 1 percent of world trade, with an annual rate of increase in participation of 6.7 percent, below the world's average of 8 percent. "PIB dos emergentes superara o dos ricos," *Gazeta Mercantil,* April 8, 1997, p. A–14.

2. On Brazil's policies toward MERCOSUR, see Sergio Florencio and Ernesto Araujo, *Mercosul Hoje* (São Paulo: Alfa Omega, 1995); Conselho Brasileiro de Relaçoes Internacionais, *Mercosul: Desafios a Vencer* (São Paulo: CBRI, 1994); on political positions, see "Brazil and Its Neighbors: Necessary Partnerships," remarks by Ambassador Ivan Canabrava, London, March 11, 1996, mimeo from the Ministry of Foreign Affairs.

3. For a description of these periods, see Amado Luiz Cervo and Clodoaldo Bueno, *Historia da Politica Externa do Brasil* (São Paulo: Editora Atica, 1992), pp. 135–386; E. Bradford Burns, *A History of Brazil,* 3d. ed. (New York: Columbia University Press, 1993), pp. 259–485.

4. For a summary of these views, see the discussion of Fernando Henrique Cardoso, "FHC analisa consequencias da globalizacão," *Folha de São Paulo,* February 21, 1996, pp. 1–6.

5. On the subject of the presence of Brazilian armed forces in domestic politics, see João Batista Magalhaes, *A Evolução Militar do Brasil* (Rio de Janeiro: Biblioteca do Exercito, 1958); Alfred Stepan, *The Military in Politics: Changing Patterns in Brazil* (Princeton: Princeton University Press, 1971); Edmundo Campos Coelho, *Em Busca da Identidade: O Exercito e a Politica na Sociedade Brasileira* (Rio de Janeiro: Forense Universitaria, 1974); Eurico de Lima Figueiredo, *Os Militares e a Democracia: Analise Estrutural da Ideologia do Presidente Castello Branco* (Rio de Janeiro: Graal, 1980); Glaucio Ary Dillon Soares, Maria Celina D'Araujo, and Celso Castro, eds., *A Volta aos Quarteis: A Memoria Militar sobre a Abertura* (Rio de Janeiro: Relume Dumara, 1995); Eliezer Rizzo de Oliveira, *De Geisel a Collor, Forcas Armadas, Transição e Democracia* (Campinas: Papirus, 1994).

6. Reference to such attitudes are in interviews presented in Soares, D'Araujo, and Castro, *A Volta aos Quarteis.*

7. For example, in the text of Law 69, approved by Congress in 1991, it is quite clear that, in addition to its role in national defense, the military is charged with the maintenance of law and order. The 1988 Constitution and the Complementary Law of 1991 preserved three basic functions for the Brazilian Armed Forces: (1) defense of the country, (2) protector of the constitution and of law and order, and (3) subsidiary functions in support of the population and the development of Brazil, without compromising their constitutional role. For a discussion of constitutional issues, see Miguel Reale, "A Seguranca Nacional nas Constituicoes Brasileiras: Seu Significado Atual," *Politica e Estrategia* 7, no. 1 (January–March 1989):53–60.

8. On military autonomy, see Stepan, *The Military in Politics;* and Brian Loveman, *The Constitution of Tyranny* (Pittsburgh: University of Pittsburgh Press, 1993).

9. Law no. 6.683, August 28, 1979, which established a broad, general, unrestricted, and reciprocal amnesty, reinforced by art. 4 of Constitutional Amendment no. 26, November 27, 1985.

10. Comissão de Direitos Humanos da Camara dos Deputados, "Camara decide reabrir caso Riocentro" *Correio Brasilense,* March 27, 1996, p. 7.

11. For example, see "Cabo sofre tortura e acusa superiores" *Jornal do Brasil,* March 7, 1996, p. 5, which describes the good relations between the armed forces and the civilian justice system.

12. "Exercito ainda espera verbas do presidente," *Correio Brasiliense,* October 19, 1995, p. 7.

13. *Plano Pluranual 1996–1999, Sumario Executivo* (Brasília: Ministerio do Planejamento e Orçamento, 1995, mimeograph), appendix.

14. The dispatching of 1100 troops to Angola was delayed due to the difficulty in the disbursement of US$130 million. In the multiyear allocations for 1996–1999, US$200 million is proposed to send 1200 troops abroad annually.

15. The majority of the criticisms on the military's retirement system focus on excessive privileges. With the death of military pensioners, their wives and adult dependent daughters maintain rights to the pension. With regard to expenses, the direct contributions of the military do little to defray the costs. As noted by Jose Carlos Jacob de Carvalho of the Social Security Ministry in 1994, the military contributions equaled US$100 million, while expenses for inactive personnel reached US$2 billion. For each active duty military, there are 1.2 who are inactive. Josias de Souza, "Aposentadoria Militar," *Folha de São Paulo,* November 24, 1995, p. 2.

16. President Fernando Henrique Cardoso, *Discurso do Presidente Fernando Henrique Cardoso por Ocasião da Despedida do Navio-Escola "Brasil,"* March 5, 1996, p. 2, mimeo.

17. Ambassador Ronaldo Mota Sardenberg, "Algumas Questoes Estrategicas Contemporaneas," March 1996, p. 5, mimeo.

18. See Cardoso, *Discurso,* note 16.

19. Regarding these separate processes, see the commentary in General Martin Balza, "La Seguridad entre los paises del Mercosur," *SER 2000* (Argentina) 8 (October 1995):25–27; Thomaz Guedes da Costa, "Condiciones para la integracion de politicas de defensa," *SER 2000* (Argentina) 7 (March 1995):8–9; Centro de Estudos Estrategicos, *Mercosul: Seguranca Regional e Defesa Nacional do Brasil,* Documento no. 4, June 1993; Gen. Gleuber Vieira, "La variable estrategica en el processo de constitutiucion del Mercosul," *SER 2000* (Argentina) 5 (March 1994):10–11.

20. On this change and the adoption of the political variable "defense policy" now taking shape in Brazil, see Thomaz Guedes da Costa, "Politica de Defesa: Uma discussão conceitual e o caso do Brasil," *Revista Brasileira de Politica Internacional* 31, no. 1 (1994):106–120. With regard to the recent press debates, see Geraldo Lesbat Cavagnari, "Uma nova politica de defesa," *Estado de São Paulo,* February 22, 1994, p. 2; Antonio Carlos Pereira, "As Alternativas do Comando," *Estado de São Paulo,* February 6, 1996, p. A–4; Domicio Proenca e Clovis Brigagão, "Velhos Tigres de Papel e o Ministerio de Defesa," *Globo,* February 22, 1996; Ambassador Ronaldo Motta, "Inserçãoestrategica e defesa nacional," *Estado de São Paulo,* March 7, 1996, p. 2; Jorge Zaverucha and Timothy J. Power, "FHC e o Ministerio da Defesa," *Jornal do Brasil,* November 9, 1994, p. 11.

21. A collection that updates and analyzes the state of the Brazilian arms industry more fully can be found in Domicio Proenca, Jr., ed., *Uma Avaliacão da Industria Belica Brasileira* (Rio de Janeiro: Grupo de Estudos Estrategicos/ Forum de Ciencia e Cultura, UFRJ, 1993).

22. A $280 million loan from Germany has been authorized. "Marinha suspende projeto por falta de recursos," *Folha de São Paulo,* September 18, 1995, p. A–4.

23. One hundred missiles have been bought. "Brasil encomenda misseis Igla," *Gazeta Mercantil,* June 8, 1995, p. A–9.

24. On the participation of Brazil in peacekeeping missions, see Thomaz Guedes da Costa, "La Securité Collective Pensée et Politique du Bresil," *Relations Internationales* (Switzerland, forthcoming); Brig. Manoel Carlos Pereira, "Participaçãoem forcas de Paz: A Experiencia Brasileira," paper prepared for the 2nd Encontro Nacional de Estudos Estrategicos, São Paulo, August 15, 1995.

25. *Nomar* (Ministerio da Marinha), 17, no. 610 (December 1993):6.

26. Cardoso, *Discurso*, note 16.

27. The first reports of this new policy indicate that the armed forces have already begun interdiction operations; see "FAB intercepta tres avioes suspeitos," *Folha de São Paulo*, March 30, 1996, p. A-7.

28. Brig. Sergio Xavier Ferola, "A Industria Nacional no SIVAM: Breve Analise," *Folha de São Paulo*, January 23, 1996, p. 13.

29. Agreement of February 7, 1996.

CHAPTER TWELVE

———————— ■ ————————

Conclusion: Civil-Military Relations, Democracy, and Regional Security in Comparative Perspective

David R. Mares

Do our case studies support the claim that the dynamics of the civil-military relationship fundamentally affect the consolidation of democracy and the construction of cooperative regional relations? To answer that we must place each of the twelve countries studied along a continuum that measures whether a country's civil-military relationship is civilian-dominated, pacted, or military-dominated. In the Introduction, I hypothesized that an analysis of two basic political elements can help locate each country along that continuum: its political culture and the nation's constitutive rules guiding political participation and the role of the military. Having used these two factors to determine a pattern in civil-military relationships across the twelve countries, we can take the additional step of correlating the category of relationship with the evidence concerning a country's ability to consolidate democracy and its degree of security and economic cooperation vis-à-vis its regional neighbors.

THE CIVIL-MILITARY RELATIONSHIP

The civil-military relationships in six of our case studies are classified by chapter authors as civilian dominant: Argentina, Venezuela, Thailand, Poland, and the Czech and Slovak Republics (see Table 12.1). Yet, only Argentina, Poland, and the Czech Republic have a liberal political culture and constitutive rules stipulating inclusive political participation. These three countries represent the extreme end

TABLE 12.1   Summary of Civil-Military Relationships in Twelve Countries, 1996

Country	Political Culture	Constitutive Rules[a]	Civil-Military Relations
Argentina	liberal	inclusive/subordinate	civilian-dominant
Brazil	liberal-corporatist	inclusive/partner (reserve)	pacted
Chile	liberal-corporatist	inclusive/partner	pacted
Venezuela	corporatist-liberal	inclusive/reserve	civilian-dominant
Guatemala	corporatist-militarist	inclusive/partner	pacted
Indonesia	patrimonial-militarist-corporatist	exclusive/partner	pacted
Thailand	patrimonial-liberal	inclusive/reserve	incipient civilian-dominant
India	liberal-corporatist	inclusive/reserve	pacted
Pakistan	patrimonial-militarist	inclusive/partner	pacted
Poland	liberal	inclusive/subordinate	civilian-dominant
Czech Republic	liberal	inclusive/subordinate	civilian-dominant
Slovak Republic	corporatist-liberal-militarist	inclusive/subordinate (reserve)	civilian-dominant

[a]First entry refers to rules for civilian participation; second entry refers to the role of the military.

of the civilian-dominant section of the civil-military continuum (see Figure 12.1). Thus, civilian-dominated civil-military relationships characterize all cases of liberal and inclusive polities (see the chapters by David Pion-Berlin, Mark Kramer, and Thomas S. Szayna).

The experiences of Venezuela, Thailand, and the Slovak Republic suggest that civilian domination of the military does not require a liberal political culture or a liberal definition of the role for the military. Gisela Gómez Sucre and María Dolores Cornett argue that, despite civilian dominance, Venezuela's political culture can be characterized as corporatist in both its societal and military dimensions; only among Venezuela's political elite do liberal tenets of unquestioned civilian control reign. Despite its inclusive rules of political participation, the Venezuelan military exercises moral and administrative leadership. In February 1992, civilians expected the military, as part of its duty to safeguard democracy, to overthrow an unpopular president by extraconstitutional means and to call for new elections. Thus, Venezuela's strong corporatist foundation places it close to the dividing line between civilian dominance and a pacted relationship.

240

FIGURE 12.1   Continuum of civil-military relations, 1996 and selected comparison years

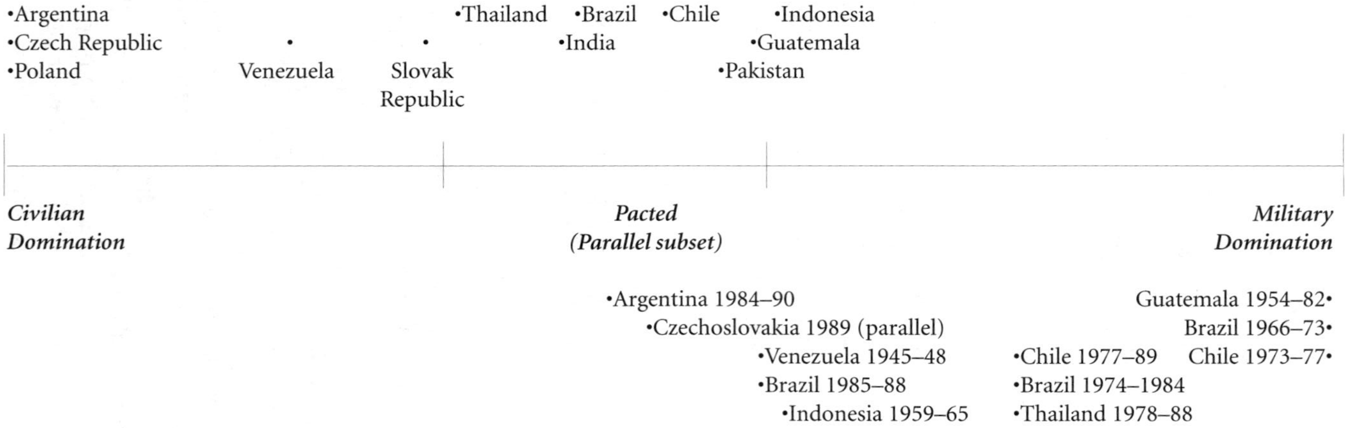

•Argentina
•Czech Republic
•Poland

•Venezuela

•
Slovak
Republic

•Thailand   •Brazil   •Chile   •Indonesia
              •India   •Guatemala
                                •Pakistan

Civilian
Domination

Pacted
(Parallel subset)

•Argentina 1984–90
•Czechoslovakia 1989 (parallel)
   •Venezuela 1945–48
      •Brazil 1985–88
         •Indonesia 1959–65

Military
Domination

Guatemala 1954–82•
Brazil 1966–73•
•Chile 1977–89   Chile 1973–77•
•Brazil 1974–1984
•Thailand 1978–88

Since the mid-1970s, Thai civil-military relations have moved away from military domination. Although the country has been civilian dominated since 1992, the key role of the king indicates a strong strain of neopatrimonialism in Thai political culture. At the same time, the constitutive rules governing the military do not demand clear subordination. This is particularly clear in the military's role in economic development, which is recognized as inherently legitimate because of its national-defense component. Additionally, the lack of civilian expertise in military affairs weakens civilian ability to subordinate the military on budgetary and other matters relating to defense. Surachart Bamrungsuk suggests that the Thai business elite and middle classes want to hold the military in reserve, a card to play in case democracy should prove too populist or radical. Thailand, although still falling within the civilian-dominated segment of the continuum, verges on a pacted relationship.

Szayna demonstrates Slovakia's clear civilian-dominant relationship, but he attributes this more to civilian rejection of the communist past and to the professional interests of the military than to liberalism. Liberalism not only is losing out to corporatism in Slovakia, but the country is also confronting an undercurrent of militarism in the civilian-led construction of a new national identity. Unlike Venezuela or Thailand, the Slovak military, created virtually from scratch after the breakup of Czechoslovakia, suffers institutional weakness from its lack of historical tradition. Thus, the Slovak Republic, while still within the civilian-dominant segment of the continuum, lies close to the border with the pacted segment (see Figure 12.1).

The six remaining countries—India, Brazil, Chile, Guatemala, Indonesia, and Pakistan—have pacted civil-military relationships. These countries exhibit great variance in their political cultures and constitutive rules, as well as in regard to the terms of agreement between civilians and the military. Although none has a fully liberal political culture, in India, Brazil, and Chile liberalism has competed with other political philosophies that would grant groups of specific actors a special place in the nation's social and political life. In those three countries, the military bargained for a pacted relationship in which it serves as a partner upon whom civilians rely in extraordinary circumstances to save the political system from collapse.

Rebecca Schiff's analysis of concordance among India's political elite, society, and military suggests that the military's role may endow the political system with added strength. Although liberalism has influenced India's inclusive constitutive rules, its political culture has caste and functional-interest representation reminiscent of corporatism.[1] On our continuum, India and Venezuela are about equidistant, with India falling on the pacted side and Venezuela falling on the civilian-dominant side (see Figure 12.1).

Thomaz Guedes da Costa's analysis of Brazil suggests that the military, once active in politics, is increasingly a partner held in reserve by civil society. In Chile, as Francisco Rojas and Claudio Fuentes demonstrate, the auxiliary role of the military reassures the political right that playing by the rules of the democratic game will not lead to an attack on its economic and political assets, as occurred during the Popular Unity government (1970–1973).

The remaining cases—Guatemala, Indonesia, and Pakistan—congregate very near the military-dominant side of the continuum while still falling within the pacted segment. These three polities have had scant exposure to liberalism and their political cultures contain a tradition of militarism. In the case of Guatemala, Caesar Sereseres argues that the military, now believing that democracy is the most appropriate option, has attempted to guide civil society into political stability. Despite its historical leadership role, today the Guatemalan military's conception of its place in the polity is more corporatist. For the first time, new constitutive rules are inclusive, in that they offer indigenous communities and former guerrillas a place in the political process. The military sees itself as the originator as well as guarantor of democratic consolidation.

As J. Soedjati Djiwandono notes, Indonesia's civil-military relationship has evolved erratically over time. Following independence, a parliamentary democracy provided for civilian control over the military. But the country was too diverse politically and socially, and democracy collapsed. Sukarno attempted to implement a populist authoritarian regime, building on corporatist and neopatrimonial elements in Indonesian political culture. In his scheme, the military was a representative, not a subordinate, of civil society. He relied on the armed forces to help implement his vision for development of the nation. During the early years of the Soeharto regime, an extreme version of the corporatist and militarist worldview of *Dwifungsi* led to military collaboration with General Soeharto in developing a polity based on corporatist representation, enforced consensus, and neopatrimonial leadership. As Soeharto consolidated his control, he supplemented his base of support with civilian interest groups, thereby shifting Indonesia's civil-military relationship from military domination toward a pact.

As Schiff makes clear, Pakistan and India shared a colonial legacy of liberalism. Pakistan's constitutive rules included parliamentary democracy and civilian control of the military. A hybrid political culture incorporated these liberal elements but also used militarism to construct a national identity. Ultimately, the political leadership lacked the capacity to effectively articulate and mediate competing civilian interests, resulting in the collapse of the civilian-dominated relationship in 1958. In 1971, the country split in two when the civil war between East and West Pakistan became internationalized in a third India-Pakistan war. Although the Pakistani military did not intend to subvert civilian control, in a classic irony, it was drawn into politics in part to safeguard its professional interests.[2] Since 1988, a civil-military pact has underpinned a shaky democratic process.[3]

None of our twelve cases can be identified as either clearly military dominant or characterized by parallel spheres of action. This situation is partly a function of the time period analyzed (as selected comparative cases in Figure 12.1 indicate). Argentina, Chile, Brazil, and Thailand shifted from military domination to pacted relationships only in the 1980s, and Argentina and Thailand subsequently moved into civilian-dominated relationships. Guatemala and Pakistan are easing away from military domination, but, as President Soeharto's control begins to slip, Indonesia may fall back into military domination.

The absence among our cases of instances of parallel spheres of action may represent the difficulty of sustaining a balanced division of labor over time. For example, economic performance affected the domestic political order in both Chile and Indonesia making it difficult for the military to allow civilians complete control of their own sphere of activity. In Czechoslovakia, the parallel relationship was premised upon a continuation of the NATO-Warsaw Pact standoff, so that when the Warsaw Pact dissolved, the military's control over defense policy dissipated.

The tremendous variation in civil-military relations in our twelve cases indicates that there is no simple formula for the appropriate mixture of political culture and constitutive rules that will establish a given relationship. Instead, specific details of the bargains made between civilians and the military appear to determine the nature of the relationship. It seems that only a dominant liberal political culture has a predictable impact on civil-military relations.

Two conclusions are apparent: First, a civilian-dominant civil-military relationship is not characterized by a single type of political culture or constitutive rule. Second, civil-military relationships are fluid, with a tendency in recent years to move away from military domination (see Table 12.1 and Figure 12.1). Indonesia is the only exception among our cases, because its pacted relationship is moving toward military domination.

THE CIVIL-MILITARY RELATIONSHIP AND DEMOCRACY

In the Introduction, I hypothesized that three factors could lead to a failure to consolidate democracy: the inability of political institutions to produce compromise among competing political groups; civilians willing to utilize extraconstitutional means to bring about change or defend the status quo; and a military willing to play an active role in political battles. We will now consider whether the category of civil-military relationship is empirically associated with the consolidation of democracy. Do these twelve case studies support the claim that civilian domination of the military is a necessary, though not sufficient, requirement for the consolidation of democracy? In other words, civilian-dominated democracies may fail to consolidate democracy, but for reasons having nothing to do with the nature of the civil-military relationship, whereas no consolidated democracy should also be a case of a pacted or military-dominant relationship.

We should also expect that inclusionary political systems with civilian-dominated civil-military relations and a liberal political culture will be likely to consolidate democracy. But inclusionary polities with corporatist political cultures could be supportive of democracy if civilians do not push their policy disagreements to the point of destabilizing the polity. In addition, since a professional military will be reluctant to identify threats from internal sources, it may use the legitimacy of its role in a corporatist political culture to help keep civilians from undermining the democratic process by identifying domestic opposition groups as threats.

Three civilian-dominated relationships occur in countries with stable consolidated democracies: Argentina, Poland, and the Czech Republic. During its democratic transition, Argentina suffered greatly from political maneuvering by factions of the military that sought either to overthrow democracy or to consolidate a pacted civil-military relationship.[4] President Menem met the challenge by decimating the military, in terms of both personnel and budget. Having experienced twelve years of peaceful alternation of parties in power and successful modifications to its constitution, Argentine democracy has clearly reached the consolidation stage.

In Poland, the military's failure to structure the transition to democracy began a process of civilian domination of the civil-military relationship. Kramer argues that the stability of democratic government and effective civilian control over the military were difficult to establish because of civilian competition and the lack of clear rules governing the distribution of responsibilities. Although Poles hold the military in high regard, civilians have effectively established control. The initially frequent changes of government followed constitutional provisions and even the electoral defeat of Walesa did not provoke a crisis.

The strong antimilitarist beliefs of Czech citizens seem to have effectively eliminated any military threat to democracy. As Szayna demonstrates, the Czech Republic purged the military of its communist-era leadership, and the process of rebuilding has dramatically restructured the armed forces in favor of democratic (versus communist) civilian control. After the fall of communism, Czechoslovak civil-military relations followed a parallel spheres of action model, with civilians controlling internal politics and the military dominating defense policy. But the disintegration of the Warsaw Pact, the division of the country into the Czech and Slovak Republics, and the area's liberal political culture quickly terminated that model.

Venezuela and Thailand both have civilian-dominant relationships, but their consolidated democracies are under pressure. In Venezuela, many citizens, while supporting the concept of civilian domination, believe it is the military's prerogative to intercede in a crisis (and then, of course, to return to the barracks). This attitude helped sanction the first military coup attempt of 1992. Venezuela's politicians and generals, not its civilian population, crushed the revolt and reaffirmed that democracy would provide the means for handling the emergency. The resiliency of Venezuelan democracy was proven in November 1992 by the mass repudiation of a second coup attempt, which was undertaken by generals who were disinclined to return the government to civilian control and who opposed peaceful reincorporation into democratic society of the organizers of the first coup attempt.

Thailand's most recent transition to democracy began only in 1992. Today its democracy is far more inclusive and open than at the beginning of the transition. The military sees democracy as being in its professional interests, but disturbingly, it also perceives itself as a defender of democracy.[5] Bamrungsuk argues that democratic consolidation depends on both civilian expertise in military affairs and a change in the political values of major civilian actors. In the case of Thailand, civilian control of the military may be a fundamental requirement for democratic consolidation. Bamrungsuk makes another important point: The business sector could cause the downfall of a government by withdrawing their investments. For these actors, tension exists between the value of exercising individual rights and the aggravation of abiding by unfavorable policies developed within the democratic structure. Because this instrumental view of democracy still prevails among important actors, Thai democracy is not yet consolidated.

Democratic consolidation in India is increasingly problematic, not because of a lack of civilian control over the military but because of civil strife. The concordance between civilians and the military noted by Schiff places India in the pacted category. Although the military has been willing to follow civilian leadership—even to the extent of supporting Indira Gandhi's emergency suspension of democracy in 1975—the terms of their inclusion into Indian society has been negotiated rather than imposed under the banner of civilian control. The relationship has been marked by its stability, as it has weathered military defeat at the hands of the Chinese in 1962 and growing ethnic separatism and intolerance in the 1990s. Even today, the current dysfunction of India's democratic institutions has not been laid at the feet of the military.

Brazil has made important progress in consolidating democracy over the past decade. Direct presidential elections were instituted ahead of the military's scheduled transition plan, and elections are extremely competitive at the state and national levels. The military provided cabinet officers and support for the president in disputes between the executive and legislative branches early in the democratic consolidation process and performed police functions by patrolling the streets in major cities more recently. This involvement in areas outside of territorial defense missions, however, has been at the request of civilian authorities and with the support of broad sectors of the population.

Costa's analysis suggests that democracy has been consolidating even as civil-military relations were operating on a pacted relationship, but that the relationship may be moving in the direction of a more liberal model of civilian domination. If so, we may find the consolidation of democracy leading to a change in the civil-military relationship, rather than vice versa.

Chile is one of the most controversial cases for the discussion of democratic consolidation. The military dictatorship designed the 1980 constitution, yet the transition to democracy occurred under two powerful constraints: in the 1988 plebiscite, 43 percent of those voting supported General Pinochet's bid for another ten-year presidential term and the center-right political parties supported legislation designed to make constitutional reform difficult after the return of democracy. Through this legislation, the right, a large minority, sought protection of its political and economic interests, which they feared would be diminished as the left sought political and social justice in the new regime.

In the case of Chile, the question is whether consolidation of democracy requires the ability of the majority to overturn these safeguards for minority interests. The answer is not self-evident because one could argue that any voting rule beyond simple majority rule constrains the majority. Chile's designated senators would have been disempowered had the center-left coalition won more seats to give them more votes in the chamber.[6] The winning democratic coalition negotiated fifty-four changes to the 1980 constitution. But the inability of the left to convince the right and the military of its commitment to a constitutional democracy, respectful of minority and property rights, meant that many of the center-left proposals failed. All the same, the Chilean political process moves forward, with more elections, with the retirement of General Pinochet fast approaching and with an opportunity for the democratic government to help appoint designated senators who would facilitate constitutional reform. In short, the center-left government has demonstrated its willingness to abide by constitutional procedures, and the elections are recognized as legitimate by the opposition. Eight years and two presidential elections after the transition, democracy has consolidated in Chile.

Guatemala and Indonesia are the volume's two cases that have yet to reach a stage of democratic consolidation. Guatemala began its transition in the 1980s as relatively free and open elections produced competitive politics, but civil-rights violations and continued guerrilla activity were a barrier that is only now being overcome, following the peace agreements of 1996. Whether the pacted civil-military relationship will facilitate, hinder, or be irrelevant to democratic consolidation in Guatemala is unclear, but the situation is hopeful.[7]

Indonesia has not met the minimal institutional criteria for democracy.[8] The violent suppression of government protests in 1996 against the selection of the leader of the "opposition" party underscores the undemocratic character of the Soeharto regime. The question for us is whether the pacted relationship among civilians and the military is antithetical to democracy. Djiwandono agrees with Schiff: Civilian domination of the military is a normative and historical product of the European and U.S. experience rather than a prerequisite for democracy. The Chilean and Brazilian cases provide additional empirical support for that claim. Yet the militaries of those countries have a far less radical claim to intervene in domestic politics than does the Indonesian military. So while the first obstacle to democratization in Indonesia is clearly Soeharto's insistence on a noncompetitive polity, the military's conceptualization of *Dwifungsi* may require modification that makes the armed forces a partner rather than "first among equals" in Soeharto's governing coalition.

In conclusion, civilian dominance does not assure consolidation of democracy, but neither does its absence preclude consolidation (see Table 12.2). Only at two extremes does the type of relationship correlate directly with democratic consolidation. Civilian dominance seems to always lead to consolidation in liberal polities. At the other extreme, military-dominated relationships cannot, by definition,

TABLE 12.2   The Civil-Military Relationship and Progress on the Consolidation of Democracy, 1996

Country	Civil-Military Relationship	Democratic Consolidation
Argentina	Civilian-dominant	Yes
Brazil	Pacted (in transition to civilian-dominant?)	Yes
Chile	Pacted	Yes
Venezuela	Civilian-dominant	Yes
Thailand	Civilian-dominant (process recently begun)	Problematic (weak civilian control)
India	Pacted (concordance)	Yes (weakening civil institutions)
Pakistan	Pacted	Problematic (due to civilian leadership)
Poland	Civilian-dominant	Yes
Czech Republic	Civilian-dominant	Yes
Slovak Republic	Civilian-dominant	Problematic (due to civilian leadership)
		Democratic Transition
Guatemala	Pacted	Problematic but likely
Indonesia	Pacted	Not yet in transition

exist in a democracy since military leaders are the most influential in government yet are not competitively elected to office. In the middle range of pacted civil-military relationships, the politics in the relationship will determine the extent of democratic consolidation.

THE CIVIL-MILITARY RELATIONSHIP AND REGIONAL SECURITY RELATIONS

As noted in the Introduction, regional security can be built upon cooperative or competitive interstate relations. If regional peace is built upon the balancing of power, defense expenditures will be higher and the underlying level of tension in the region greater than if peace is built on cooperation. There are two keys to cooperative regional relations: A professional military does not have a major role in the identification of threat, and the constitutive rules of domestic politics must be inclusive. The implication is that civilian-dominated and inclusive polities, as well as polities that combine pacted or parallel civil-military relations with nonprofessional militaries and inclusive politics, pursue confidence-building measures and economic cooperation with their neighbors. Power-balancing is sought by polities with pacted or parallel civil-military relationships and professional militaries, by polities with military-dominated relationships and by exclusive democracies.

If these hypotheses are correct, we should expect the regional policies of Argentina, Poland, the Czech and Slovak Republics, Thailand, and Venezuela to emphasize cooperation, whereas the regional policies of Brazil, Chile, Guatemala, India, Pakistan, and Indonesia should be more competitive than cooperative. (See Figure 12.2.)

As Pion-Berlin notes, "Democratic Argentina has promoted a policy of regional engagement." This policy includes a 180-degree reversal of Argentina's historically antagonistic relationship with the United States, which is now marked by intense cooperation, even to the point of supporting U.S. intervention in Haiti. Argentina's relations with Brazil have also changed dramatically: Institutionalized cooperation resolved their nuclear competition; and the two militaries together with those of Uruguay and Paraguay implemented formal exchanges that have enhanced trust among them. With respect to Chile, Argentina's defense strategies have ameliorated border disagreements and facilitated confidence-building measures in the military arena. Yet Argentina's security relations with Chile retain an element of distrust and competition. The Argentine Ministry of Defense (headed by a civilian) fears that Chile's continuing military deterrence strategies will make Argentina increasingly vulnerable.

Poland and the Czech Republic overwhelmingly emphasize integration with western Europe via the European Union and NATO as part of their security strategies. They see NATO as an important guarantor of security vis-à-vis unforeseen instabilities coming from the east, Russia in particular. The fragility of civilian control over the military in postcommunist Russia has led Poles and Czechs to take a competitive posture that seeks NATO expansion eastward despite Russian protests. Poles and Czechs are also concerned with the nationalist sentiments among important segments of the Russian population. Thus, again we find that competitive regional relations can arise whether or not the military plays an important role in formulating regional policy.

The regional security situation of the Slovak Republic is perhaps the most complex of our twelve cases. Hungary's potential threat to the Slovak Republic is recognized only tacitly because the Slovaks want good relations with the West (some even want to join NATO) and Hungary is closely allied with western Europe. Consequently, as Szayna notes, the Slovak military views Russia as an important ally in the event of a clash with Hungary. Slovaks essentially want to cooperate with both western Europe and Russia. Although instability in civilian politics provides the military with a degree of autonomy in this otherwise civilian-dominated relationship, the competitive elements in the Slovak policy toward Hungary are the result of ethnic conflict, not of military influence.

FIGURE 12.2   Level of cooperation in regional policies (selected dyads), 1996

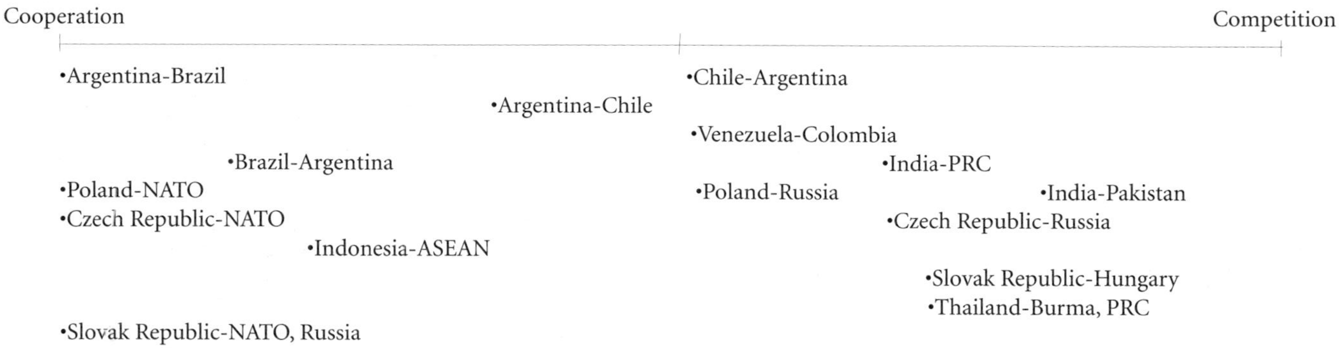

Cooperation   Competition

•Argentina-Brazil

        •Brazil-Argentina

•Poland-NATO
•Czech Republic-NATO

              •Indonesia-ASEAN

•Slovak Republic-NATO, Russia

                      •Argentina-Chile

                              •Chile-Argentina

                                      •Venezuela-Colombia

                                              •India-PRC

                                      •Poland-Russia

                                              •India-Pakistan

                                              •Czech Republic-Russia

                                                      •Slovak Republic-Hungary
                                                      •Thailand-Burma, PRC

Thailand, along with Indonesia and India, participated in the first ASEAN Regional Forum meetings to discuss defense policies and increase transparency.[9] Thailand complements these multilateral confidence-building measures with bilateral arrangements. Bamrungsuk notes that civilians are willing to use economic relations to apply slight pressure on Burma and China to modify their policies on political liberalization and on Tibet. The Thai military, on the other hand, views those issues as essentially domestic political problems, and it would prefer not to offend its two neighbors with whom it has important disagreements over borders and guerrilla movements in Burma and Cambodia. Because the civil-military relationship has moved toward civilian domination, the military is unable to block these aspects of regional policy.

The Thai government has not ignored the competitive side of regional relations. Thailand has been concerned about possible Indian-Chinese competition in the eastern Indian Ocean, and it has invested in surface ships, antisubmarine warfare, and antiship capabilities.[10] Bamrungsuk suggests that this may be a case in which civilian reliance on military analysts for security matters increases the military's impact on defense policy. Foreign civilian analysts examining the region, however, also find a security context which calls for caution because of, among other factors, border disagreements, a new perception of self-reliance after the Cold War, and the proliferation of weapons with inherently offensive capabilities, as affluent regional states modernize their arsenals.[11] Thai regional policies, therefore, are a mix of cooperative relations with fellow ASEAN countries and competitive balancing with Burma and China.

There are important cooperative elements in Venezuelan regional policy: It was a founding member of the Contadora Initiative, which sought to negotiate an end to the Central American wars of the 1980s; it also settled a major dispute with Brazil, and the two countries now cooperate in patrolling the Amazon.[12] Nevertheless, Venezuela disputes thirty-four points along its Colombian border and has rejected Colombian overtures toward arbitration. Colombia buffets Venezuela with illegal migration, contraband (including drugs), and guerrilla incursions. In 1986, Venezuela mobilized its armed forces after a Colombian naval vessel refused to leave disputed waters. In 1995, Venezuelan President Rafael Caldera flew over disputed islands in a military plane. That year, Venezuela's newspapers also played up fears that border incidents could escalate into war. That created a willingness among Venezuelan civilians to incorporate competitive, balance-of-power elements into their relations with Colombia.

Brazil's regional policies, as Costa presents them, represent a complex but cautious strategy to take advantage of new opportunities. Brazil focuses particularly upon the Amazon Basin and has sought increased cooperation with Peru and Venezuela as one way of ensuring that the Basin meets national needs without too many international constraints. Brazil's economic size and strategic depth relative to its neighbors has allowed it to feel secure while keeping military expenditures very low (on the order of 1 percent of GNP). Security relations with Argentina improved after the 1988 decision to avoid a nuclear arms race. Nevertheless, as Costa notes, Brazil's security relations with Argentina are not as cooperative as in the economic realm.

Chile's regional relations are complicated: It has outstanding disputes with Bolivia; it suffers ongoing distrust of Peru (exacerbated by the 1995 Peruvian war with Ecuador); but it enjoys new levels of cooperation with Argentina. Chile's cooperative policies include participating in negotiations over border disputes with Argentina and engaging in confidence-building measures with the Argentine and Peruvian militaries. But Chile's domestic civilian and military consensus that the country requires a credible deterrent means that Chile's regional policies retain a strong element of competition. This has led some commentators, including former U.S. President Jimmy Carter, to accuse Chile of provoking a regional arms race.[13]

The Guatemalan military perceived a double threat in the 1980s from the regional negotiations over the Central American wars. First, discussion of regional disarmament challenged Guatemala's ability to maintain a strong military to fight its ongoing internal war. Second, as Sereseres notes, U.S. aid to El Salvador for its fight against guerrillas threatened to shift the regional balance of power. The Guatemalan state waited until it won on the domestic battlefield before becoming involved in disarmament discussions, and even now little progress has been made because of internal and regional disagreement over acceptable armament levels.[14] Because it saw guerrillas as Guatemala's chief threat, the military has cooperated with Mexico and the British in Belize on security issues. Tensions were still strong enough that Belize sought first British, then Central American security guarantees.[15] Sereseres notes that once Guatemala's internal war ended, the Guatemalan military privately welcomed the government's recognition of Belizean independence so that they could remove that country from their security agenda. Nevertheless, for the next six years no steps were taken to delimit the border and the territorial issues remained competitive.[16]

Schiff argues that India's domestic concordance allows it to maintain a credible military posture. This characterization means that India's regional policies toward its two important neighbors, Pakistan and the People's Republic of China (PRC), are characterized by power balancing. Both these countries have pacted civil-military relations, and exclusive constitutive rules guide the PRC. Since India itself has a pacted civil-military relationship, we would expect a competitive relationship between India and Pakistan. Of course, given the severity of ethnic and religious conflict, as well as the size of the territories in dispute, even a civilian-dominated polity would be hard-pressed to eschew competitive regional relations. Indeed, India almost went to war with Pakistan over Kashmir in 1987 and 1990,[17] and it is concerned about Chinese activities in the Indian Ocean, especially in light of China's close naval relations with Burma.[18]

Indonesia's regional policies are mainly focused on economic relations in the context of ASEAN, although it does dispute some islands with Malaysia and disagrees with Vietnam over the demarcation of the continental shelf in the South China Sea. In the 1960s, Indonesia flexed its military might in the region, threatening Malaysia and seizing West Irian from the Dutch. Under Soeharto, however, regional security policy is mainly focused on building cooperative relations in the context of ASEAN, of which it was a leading proponent.[19] Security cooperation is not the result of harmony: In the 1970s there were disagreements within ASEAN because of Indonesia's support for Vietnam in the Indochina wars, Indonesia's seizure of East Timor in 1975, and disputes with Malaysia concerning some islands. Yet Indonesia has not adopted balance-of-power strategies to defend its interests. Indonesia has fallen behind in the regional arms competition; its defense spending fell by half in the decade between 1981 and 1991.[20] The Indonesian military's focus on domestic matters is probably at the root of its weak regional policies. Still, reluctant to fall too far behind, the Indonesian government recently purchased forty jet fighters from Britain and nine F-16s from the United States.[21] All the same, the nation's regional posture remains predominantly cooperative.

In summary, the relationship between the characteristics of civil-military relations and regional security policies is strong but not perfect (see Table 12.3). Four of the six countries with civilian-dominant relationships, professional militaries, and inclusive politics have extremely cooperative relations, and thus they support the hypothesis concerning cooperative security relations: Argentina (with the exception of its relationship with Chile), Poland (vis-à-vis NATO), Czech Republic (also vis-à-vis NATO), and Thailand (vis-à-vis ASEAN). But the hypothesis is not supported by the cases of Poland and the Czech Republic (vis-à-vis Russia); Venezuela (vis-à-vis Colombia); the Slovak Republic (vis-à-vis Hungary); and Indonesia (vis-à-vis Malaysia in the early 1960s).

The explanation for their security relationship cannot be that any two countries whose civil-military relationships are of an opposing or different character will be suspicious of each other. Although that reasoning may work in the Argentine-Chilean and Thai-Chinese cases, the Venezuelan-Colombian, Slovak Republic-Hungarian, and Polish-Russian/Czech-Russian dyads all have civilian-dominated, inclusive polities with professional militaries. In the case of Indonesia in the early 1960s, despite its pacted civil-military relationship, a nonprofessional military, and inclusionary politics, its relationship with Malaysia was very competitive. After Soeharto seized power the institutional rules for political participation became exclusive. In accordance with our hypothesis, we should have seen the relationship with Malaysia remain competitive. Instead, policies toward Malaysia became more cooperative.

The hypotheses concerning competitive security policies were supported by the contemporary experience of Chile, India, Pakistan, and Guatemala, as well as Czechoslovakia in 1990. During the years of military dominance in Chile, Brazil, Guatemala, and Thailand, these countries were also characterized by competition more than by cooperation. Yet today Indonesia and Brazil both have more cooperative policies than the hypotheses predicted, given that Indonesia has a pacted

TABLE 12.3 The Civil-Military Relationship and Regional Relations (1996 and selected comparison years)

Characteristics of the Civil-Military Relationship	Regional Policy	Hypothesized Tendency Examples	Counter Examples
Civilian dominant with professional military and inclusionary politics	*Cooperative*	Argentina, Poland, Czech Republic, Thailand	Venezuela-Colombia, Slovak Republic-Hungary, Poland-Russia Czech Republic-Russia
Civilian dominant with nonprofessional military and inclusionary politics	*Cooperative*		
Civilian dominant with professional military and exclusionary politics	Competitive		
Civilian dominant with nonprofessional military and exclusionary politics	Competitive		
Pacted with professional military and inclusionary politics	Competitive	Chile, India, Guatemala 1997	Brazil-Argentina
Pacted with professional military and exclusionary politics	Competitive	Guatemala 1982–96	
Pacted with nonprofessional military and inclusionary politics	*Cooperative*		Indonesia-Malaysia 1960s
Pacted with nonprofessional military and exclusionary politics	Competitive		Indonesia
Parallel with professional military and inclusionary politics	Competitive	Pakistan Czechoslovakia 1990	
Parallel with professional military and exclusionary politics	Competitive		
Parallel with nonprofessional military and inclusionary politics	*Cooperative*		
Parallel with nonprofessional military and exclusionary politics	Competitive		
Military dominant with professional military	Competitive	Chile 1973–77, Brazil 1966–73	
Military dominant with nonprofessional military	Competitive	Guatemala 1954–82, Thailand 1978–88	

relationship, with a nonprofessional military and exclusive institutional rules, while Brazil has a pacted relationship with a professional military and inclusive rules (see Table 12.3).

In addition, the prediction that Chile's regional policy will be competitive may be borne out, but for the wrong reasons. The hypothesis expected a competitive regional security policy because Chile has a professional military (who therefore preferred to focus on a neighbor as the security threat) and a pacted relationship (which allowed the military's view of threat to influence regional security policies). But civilian consensus on the need to maintain a credible military deterrent suggests that even if Chile had a civilian-dominant civil-military relationship, its regional policies would have a similar mixture of cooperative and competitive elements.

These exceptions to both cooperation and competition in regional relations suggest that the hypotheses need to be modified. First, there appear to be multiple paths to cooperative regional relations beyond those initially hypothesized. Why, for example, does the professional Brazilian military not view Argentina as an important security threat? The answer is not difficult: Argentina's military establishment collapsed in the 1980s and was largely dismantled by the mid-1990s. Hence, one can make an argument that the preponderance of power on the Brazilian side has freed up resources for the Brazilian military to concentrate its attention elsewhere. Thus, we need to factor into organizational-interest calculations of the military the credibility of a neighbor's threat. This is a minor adjustment.

A second modification concerns civilian determinants of threat. The Venezuelan, Slovak, Polish, Czech, and Indonesian exceptions raise more serious concerns. In the first four cases, the countries failed to implement cooperative policies, contrary to expectations. In the case of contemporary Indonesia, the country failed to exhibit the competitive stance predicted by the hypothesis. The puzzle points toward civilian interests, rather than those of the military. Sukarno sought to consolidate domestic power in the early 1960s partly through an anticolonial diplomatic strategy. As a result, Indonesia adopted a confrontational policy toward Malaysia, accusing it of being a British "neocolonial project."[22] Soeharto, in contrast, sought to consolidate domestic power by promoting Indonesia's economic growth, and he turned toward more cooperative policies. In the four contemporary cases of less cooperative security relations, civilians, not the military, determine regional policy. Since their institutional rules for politics are inclusive, the attitudes of these countries suggest that some important determinants of civilian perceptions of threat remain to be discovered in future research.

THE CIVIL-MILITARY RELATIONSHIP
AND REGIONAL ECONOMIC RELATIONS

In the Introduction, I hypothesized that the regional economic cooperation that occurred in the 1990s would be based on economic liberalization rather than state-managed integration. I also hypothesized that the type of civil-military rela-

TABLE 12.4   Civil-Military Relationships and Tendencies of Regional Economic
Relations, 1996

Country	Civil-Military Relations	Tendency
Argentina	Civilian-dominant	Cooperative-regional
Brazil	Pacted	Cooperative-regional
Chile	Pacted	Cooperative-global
Venezuela	Civilian-dominant	Cooperative-regional
Guatemala	Pacted	Cooperative-regional
Indonesia	Pacted	Cooperative-global
Thailand	Civilian-dominant	Cooperative-global
India	Pacted	Cooperative-global
Pakistan	Pacted	Competitive/state-managed
Poland	Civilian-dominant	Cooperative
Czech Republic	Civilian-dominant	Cooperative
Slovak Republic	Civilian-dominant	Cooperative

tions would not determine a country's support of economic liberalization. Finally, I hypothesized that if a professional military took the lead in pursuing economic liberalization, it would be oriented globally more than regionally, given the professional military's perception of neighbors as the main threat to the security of the nation.

We can see from Table 12.4 that there is no pattern between type of civil-military relations and the character of economic relations in today's world. Whatever the civil-military relationship, the regional economic policies of all of our cases, with the exception of Pakistan, have moved toward cooperation. Pakistan is the outlier because the economy has not yet been liberalized. Instead it is being plundered by civilian corruption and the military budget.[23]

It must be kept in mind that economic cooperation does not have the same characteristics everywhere. Some countries have sought gradual economic integration with their neighbors, whereas others have thrown open their doors to the world economy as a whole. Four Latin American countries—Brazil, Argentina, Guatemala, and Venezuela—all began economic opening through tentative steps at the regional level by means of MERCOSUR, the Central American Common Market, and the Venezuelan-Colombian economic integration process begun in 1989.[24] ASEAN began as a regional scheme but has grown to encompass much broader economic partnerships, such as APEC (Asia Pacific Economic Council, which includes Canada, the United States, Mexico, and Chile among other countries). Chile, India,[25] Poland, and the Czech and Slovak Republics, in contrast, threw their markets wide open to the world economy. Poland and the Czech Republic, however, would like to join the European Union, which represents a step toward a regional rather than a global emphasis. Nevertheless, the regional-global distinction still does not break down by type of civil-military relations.

In only one case, Chile, was the economic liberalization process promoted by a professional military. The Chilean effort, as I hypothesized, was directed toward the world economy. Although not sufficient to confirm the hypothesis, this one case invites further research on the impact of a professional military on the characteristics of economic liberalization.

CONCLUSION: THE CIVIL-MILITARY RELATIONSHIP AS AN INTERVENING, NOT DETERMINANT VARIABLE

We began this study with the expectation that institutions mattered, but that a government's domestic and international behavior could not be explained simply by reference to its civil-military relationship. This intuition was rooted in a belief that politics matters. What each side in the relationship wants to accomplish with its influence is a fundamental determinant of policy. Because civilians are not always disposed toward cooperation and because the military does not blindly follow the maxim that force is the best response to all situations, the type of civil-military relationship cannot be the chief determinant of a nation's policy.

The civil-military relationship is an important causal variable. It determines whose interests will dominate government policy, although it does not determine what that interest will be. The case studies in this volume demonstrated that civilian control is neither necessary nor sufficient for democratic consolidation and regional cooperation.

It may be disappointing to some policymakers and analysts that the type of civil-military relationship does not provide a shorthand for understanding democracy and regional cooperation. It is, nevertheless, reassuring in a diverse and complex world that there exist multiple paths to democracy and peace. Since politics matters, people have a fairly wide latitude to reach these goals.

NOTES

1. Jyotirindra Das Gupta, "India: Democratic Becoming and Combined Development," in Larry Diamond, Juan J. Linz, and Seymour Martin Lipset, eds., *Politics in Developing Countries* (Boulder: Lynne Rienner, 1990), pp. 219–269.

2. Cf. Alfred Stepan, *The Military in Politics* (Princeton: Princeton University Press, 1971).

3. For information on the evolution of Pakistan's redemocratization, Ahmed Rashid, "Pakistan: Trouble Ahead, Trouble Behind," *Current History* (April 1996):158–64.

4. Deborah L. Norden, *Military Rebellion in Argentina: Between Coups and Consolidation* (Lincoln: University of Nebraska Press, 1996).

5. Loveman makes a persuasive case that militaries, when they perceive themselves as guardians of democracy, become embroiled in contentious politics. Although this may perhaps be a normal part of the democratic process, the hierarchically oriented military officers interpret the contentiousness as a sign that the system is on the verge of collapse. Brian Loveman, *The Constitution of Tyranny* (Pittsburgh: University of Pittsburgh Press, 1993).

6. Ricardo Lagos, "Como vamos a triunfar, preparemonos todos para recontruir a Chile," *Cauce* 27 (November 1989):5–9, as cited on p. 139 in Rhoda Rabkin, "The Aylwin Government and Tutelary Democracy: A Concept in Search of a Case? " *Journal of Inter-American Economic and World Affairs,* 34, no. 4 (Winter 1992/93):119–194.

7. Rachel M. McCleary, "Guatemala: Expectations for Peace," *Current History* (February 1996):88–92.

8. A portion of legislative representatives are appointed by the government, and all candidates for the legislature are subject to government approval. Additionally, the Indonesian president must be elected by unanimous consent.

9. "Defense Ties Flourish at Asian Security Forum," *Asia Times,* October 31, 1996, p. 3; "Thailand, Burma Agree No Arms on Moei River," *Bangkok Post,* November 6, 1996, p. 5; and "Myanmar Joins with Thailand for Gas Sales," *Asia Times,* October 29, 1996, p. 1.

10. Desmond Ball, "Arms and Affluence: Military Acquisitions in the Asia-Pacific Region" *International Security* 18, no. 3 (Winter 1993/94).

11. Ball, "Arms and Affluence" notes twelve stimulants to the regional arms dynamics (see pp. 81–95).

12. In 1991, the Venezuelan Air Force shot down a Brazilian plane in disputed territory, leading to a rupture in relations that lasted until 1993. *El Nacional* (Caracas), April 14, 1994, p. A10; *Diario* (Caracas), April 15, 1994, p. 31 and April 16, 1994, p. 25.

13. "Carter Concerned over Arms Sales to Chile as He Continues Latin American Tour in Argentina," *Chile Information Press* (*CHIPNews,* Santiago), January 22, 1997; see also "Chile Acquires Mirage Jets, *CHIPNews,* March 20, 1995.

14. "Constant Border Disputes Represent Latent Danger for Central American Integration Initiatives," *EcoCentral* 1:18 (October 17, 1996) (Latin American Data Base, Latin American Institute, University of New Mexico).

15. David Reid, "Belize: Country Wants a Central American Security Blanket," *InterPress Service,* January 21, 1994.

16. "Guatemala and Belize Plan to Renew Territorial Negotiations," *EcoCentral,* February 27, 1997.

17. Devin T. Hagerty, "Nuclear Deterrence in South Asia: The 1990 Indo-Pakistani Crisis," *International Security* 20, no. 3 (Winter 1995–1996):79–114.

18. Ball, "Arms and Affluence," pp. 78–112.

19. Allen C. Choate, "Political Pluralism and Regional Cooperation: The Case of ASEAN," paper presented at the Annual Meeting of the American Political Science Association, New York, September 1994.

20. Ball, "Arms and Affluence," p. 82.

21. *Asia Times,* October 29, 1996, p. 8.

22. Harold Crouch, *Government and Society in Malaysia* (Ithaca: Cornell University Press, 1996), p. 134.

23. Rashid, "Pakistan: Trouble Ahead, Trouble Behind," pp. 158–64.

24. Alberto Urdaneta and Ramon Leon, *Relaciones Fronterizas entre Venezuela y Colombia* (Caracas: CENDES, 1991).

25. Shalendra D. Sharma, "India's Economic Liberalization: The Elephant Comes of Age," *Current History* (December 1996):414–418.

---------------------- ■ ----------------------

About the Editor
and Contributors

Surachart Bamrungsuk is assistant professor of political science, Chulalongkorn University, Thailand, and a Ph.D. candidate of the Department of Political Science, Columbia University, New York. He is also a lecturer at various military institutions in the Thai armed forces. Bamrungsuk is the author of *United States Foreign Policy and Thai Military Rule, 1947–1977.*

María Dolores Cornett is a member of the faculty at the Instituto de Altos Estudios de la Defensa Nacional de Venezuela and is Research Adviser at the Escuela Superior de la Guardia Nacional. She has an M.S. in Security and Defense Studies from the Instituto de Altos Estudios de la Defensa Nacional, as well as a degree in Education from the Universidad Central de Venezuela. She has also undertaken postgraduate studies in Administration and Planning of Higher Education at the Universidad Simon Rodriguez and in Contemporary History of the Americas at the Universidad Catolica Andres Bello. Cornett has organized numerous international and national seminars on international security issues and participated in short courses at the U.S. Air Force Special Operations School in Hurlburt Field, Florida, and the Naval Post Graduate School in Monterey, California. She has been an adviser to the U.S. armed forces on relations with Colombia, covering the issues of borders, subversion, migration, and drugs.

Thomaz Guedes da Costa received his doctorate from Columbia University, New York. He is a researcher with Brazil's National Council for Scientific Development (CNPq). Currently, he is the Coordinator for Studies at the Center for Strategic Studies (CEE/SAE) and a research associate in the International Relations Department, University of Brasília. He has published both in Brazil and abroad on strategic planning, national defense, and international security.

Claudio Fuentes is a research professor at the Facultad Latinoamericana de Ciencias Sociales, FLACSO-Chile, and past editor of the journal *Fuerzas Armadas y Sociedad*. He is currently a doctoral student at the University of North Carolina, Chapel Hill and has a degree in History from the Universidad Catolica de Chile. Fuentes's research interests include international security, civil-military relations and the consolidation of democracy in Latin America. He is coauthor of the book *Defensa Nacional: Chile 1990–1994* and has published numerous articles in Latin American journals as well as FLACSO working papers, including "El discurso militar en la transicion"; "Chile-Argentina: El proceso de construir confianza." He is a past recipient of a European Union fellowship to study the European integration process.

Gisela Gómez Sucre is Academic Adviser at the Instituto de Altos Estudios de la Defensa Nacional de Venezuela. She has an M.S. degree in Political Science from the Universidad

Simón Bolívar de Venezuela and an M.S. in Security and Defense Studies from the Instituto de Altos Estudios de la Defensa Nacional. Gómez Sucre has held positions in the Venezuelan public administration and served as Adjunct Professor for the United States Air Force special courses for Latin American officers covering various aspects of civil-military relations.

Mark Kramer is a senior associate at the Davis Center for Russian Studies, Harvard University, and the director of the Harvard Project on Cold War Studies. Professor Kramer has taught at Harvard, Yale, and Brown Universities and is a member of the Harvard-MIT Political Economy Group. He is the author of the forthcoming book *Crisis in Czechoslovakia, 1968: The Prague Spring and the Soviet Invasion,* which draws heavily on new archival materials from East-Central Europe and the former Soviet Union. He recently completed another book, *Soldier and State in Poland: Civil-Military Relations and Institutional Change After Communism,* which will be published in mid-1998. He is finishing another book, *From Dominance to Hegemony to Collapse: Soviet Policy in East-Central Europe, 1945–1991,* and is editing a book on *The Collapse of the Soviet Union.*

David R. Mares (Ph.D. Harvard) is Professor in the Political Science Department and Adjunct Professor in the School of International Relations/Pacific Studies at the University of California, San Diego. Mares has taught in Mexico, Chile, and Ecuador and was a consultant to the Government of Mexico. He is author of *Penetrating the International Market* (Columbia University Press, 1987; Spanish translation El Colegio de Mexico, 1991) and has published numerous articles and chapters in the areas of international security, international political economy, and comparative foreign policy, including "Deterrence Bargaining in the Ecuador-Peru Enduring Rivalry" in the journal *Security Studies.* His new book, *Violent Peace: Lessons from Latin America for Managing Interstate Conflict* will be published by Columbia University Press.

David Pion-Berlin is associate professor of political science, University of California, Riverside. He received his doctorate from the Graduate School of International Studies, University of Denver. He is a specialist on U.S. foreign policy toward Latin America and Latin American military political thought. Pion-Berlin is the author of *The Ideology of State Terror* and *Through Corridors of Power: Institutions and Civil-Military Relations in Argentina* and articles that have appeared in *Comparative Politics* and *Journal of Latin American Studies.*

Francisco Rojas, Master in Political Sciences, is a specialist in international relations and international security and the Director of FLACSO-Chile and Co-Director of the program Peace and Security in the Americas. He is Professor at the Instituto de Estudios Internacionales of the Universidad de Chile and at the University of Stanford in Santiago and has also been Visiting Professor of the Latin American and Caribbean Center at Florida International University of Miami. He has also been an adviser and consultant for different international organizations and regional governments. He is Director of the review *Fuerzas Armadas y Sociedad.* Rojas is a member of the Editorial Commission of the review *Estudios Internacionales of Guatemala* and the *Journal of Interamerican Studies and World Affairs.* He is author and editor of several books and his last publications include *Balance Estratégico y Medidas de Confianza Mutua* (FLACSO/Wilson Center/P&SA, 1996); *Medidas de Confianza Mutua: Verificación* (FLACSO/Wilson Center/P&SA/FOCAL/1996); *Gasto Militar en América Latina: Procesos de Decisiones y Actores Claves* (CINDE/FLACSO, 1994); *El Cono Sur y las Transformaciones Globales,* with William C. Smith (FLACSO/North-South Center/CLADDE, 1994).

Rebecca L. Schiff currently works as a corporate adviser and has her own company, Corporate Concordance. Before establishing her company, she worked as a visiting lecturer in political science at the University of Michigan. She has elaborated her theory of concordance by applying it to business settings. Schiff completed her Ph.D. at the University of Chicago. Publications include "Civil-Military Relations Reconsidered: A Theory of Concordance" and "Concordance Theory: A Response to Recent Criticism," which appeared respectively in the fall 1995 and winter 1996 issues of *Armed Forces and Society*. In the business field, Schiff has published "The Concordance Approach to Team-Building: Achieving Agreement on Values and Objectives in a Competitive Business World," in ASQC's 51st Annual Quality Congress Proceedings, May 1997.

Caesar D. Sereseres is Associate Dean, School of Social Sciences, University of California, Irvine and Associate Professor of Political Science in the Department of Politics and Society. He received his Ph.D. from the University of California, Riverside. Professor Sereseres has been a consultant to the RAND Corporation on national security issues and served as a staff member in the Office of Policy Planning, Bureau of Inter-American Affairs, Department of State. He has written extensively on the internal wars and civil-military relations of the Central American region. Sereseres's articles include "United States Military Assistance and the Guatemalan Armed Forces," "The Highlands War in Guatemala," "Lessons from Central America's Revolutionary Wars, 1972–1984, "Guatemalan Paramilitary Forces, Internal Security, and Politics," and "U.S. Policy for Central America."

J. Soedjati Djiwandono is Director of International Studies, Center for Strategic and International Studies in Jakarta and a political columnist for the *Jakarta Post*. He has written extensively on Indonesian domestic and international affairs. Among his publications are the edited books *ASEAN: An Emerging Regional Security Community?*; *Soldiers and Stability in Southeast Asia* (with Yong Mun Cheonq); *ASEAN and China: An Evolving Relationship* (with Joyce K. Kallgren and Noordin Supiee); and *ASEAN in Regional and Global Context* (with Karl D. Jackson and Sukhumbhand Paribatra).

Thomas S. Szayna is a national security analyst in the International Studies Group at RAND in Santa Monica, California. His research has concentrated on global conflict issues in the post–Cold War era, peacekeeping and interventions in intrastate strife, and military reform in the former communist states. His recent publications include RAND monographs, "East European Military Reform After the Cold War," "Intervention in Intrastate Conflict: Implications for the Army in the Post–Cold War Era," and "Ethnic Conflict in Central Europe and the Balkans: A Framework and U.S. Policy Options." He has also published articles on aspects of European politics and defense issues that have appeared in Study Papers of the Joint Economic Committee of the Congress of the United States and in policy and academic journals.

Index

ABRI. *See* Armed Forces of the Republic of Indonesia

Acción Democrática (AD), 60, 62

AD. *See* Acción Democrática

Afghanistan, 14

Africa, 232

Agrarian/industrial coalition, 10

Alfonsín, Raúl, 88, 93, 95, 98(n26), 99(n38)

Ali Jinnah, Mohammed, 38

Ali Khan, Liaquat, 38

Allamand, Andrés, 184(n3)

Andrade, Fernando, 214, 217

Andrejcak, Imrich, 113, 124

APEC. *See* Asia Pacific Economic Council

Arana, Carlos, 211

Arbenz, Jacobo, 209

Arévalo, Juan José, 209

Argentina
    civil-military relations in, 7, 77, 79–80, 238–239, 242–243
    and democracy, 2, 244
    economic liberalization, 255
    foreign policy, 84–97
    military dictatorship policy, 80–84
    political culture, 3, 5
    and regional relations, 182, 231, 234, 248, 250–251, 252

Arias, Oscar, 218

Armas, Carlos Castillo, 210

Armed Forces of the Republic of Indonesia (ABRI), 48–57

Arzu, Álvaro, 212

ASEAN, 250, 252, 255

Asia Pacific Economic Council (APEC), 168, 184(n7), 255

Association of Slovak Soldiers (ASV), 113

Association of Workers of Slovakia (ZRS), 122, 123

ASV. *See* Association of Slovak Soldiers

Athens, 12

Auel, Heriberto, 98(n26)

Aung San Suu Kyi, 197

Austria, 114, 120

Aylwin, Patricio, 90, 167, 174, 176, 185(n17)

Azurdia, Peralta, 216

Balance of power issues, regional, 15, 16, 248

Ballerino, Jorge, 176

Balza, Martín, 92–93

Bamrungsuk, Surachart, 163, 241, 244–245, 250

Bangladesh, 41

Banharn Silpaarcha, 198, 199

Barcelona, Eduardo, 99(n47)

Baudys, Anton, 118

Bavaria, 118

Beagle Channel, 89

Belize, 217, 220, 221, 251

Benes decrees, 103

Bharatiya Janata Party (BJP), 42

Bielecki, Jan Krzysztof, 139

BJP. *See* Bharatiya Janata Party

Boeninger, Edgardo, 176

Boinazo, 175–177

Bolivia, 87, 170, 251

Border issues
    and Argentina, 80–82, 89–90
    and Brazil, 224, 233–234
    and Guatemala, 220
    and regional security, 250, 251
    and Thailand, 197
    and Venezuela, 69–70

Brazil
    and Argentina, 81–82, 86, 90–93, 99(n38), 248, 254
    civil-military relations in, 7, 164, 225–229, 234, 241, 242–243

and democracy, 2, 223–225, 245
economic liberalization and, 255
political culture, 5
regional relations/integration and,
229–234, 248, 250–251, 252–254
and Venezuela, 250, 257(n12)
Brezhnev doctrine, 104
Burma, 197, 198, 250
Business sector, 200–201, 207, 241, 245

CACIF. See Coordinating Committee
of Agricultural, Commercial,
Industrial, and Financial
Associations
Caldera, Rafael, 68, 250
Cambodia, 200
Camilión, Oscar, 86
Caputo, Dante, 88, 89
Cardoso, Fernando Henrique, 224, 227,
229, 230, 233
Carter, Jimmy, 87, 251
CASC. See Central American Security
Commission
Cavallo, Domingo, 94–95
CEFTA. See Central European Free Trade
Area
Central American Common Market, 208,
215, 255
Central American Democratic Security
Treaty, 219
Central American Security Commission
(CASC), 208, 219
Central American wars, 206, 208, 218, 250,
251
Central Education Board (Poland), 146
Central Europe, 3. See also specific Central
European countries
Central European Free Trade Area
(CEFTA), 117, 122, 127
Central Intelligence Agency, U.S., 210
Cerezo, Vinicio, 207, 212, 215, 218
CERJ. See Council of Ethnic Communities
CFE. See Conventional Forces in Europe
Treaty
Chaovalit Yongchaiyuth, 192, 198, 199,
200
Chartchai Choonawan, 191, 192, 200

Chile
and Argentina, 81, 86, 88–90, 248
civil-military relations in, 7, 8, 163,
171–181, 175(table), 183, 241–242,
242–243
and democracy, 2, 245–246
economic liberalization and, 255, 256
foreign policy/international relations,
168–171, 181–183, 248, 251
grand strategy and, 165–166
politics, 166–168, 183
Christian Democrats
Czech Republic, 116, 121, 122
Guatemala, 207
Christian Socialist Party (COPEI), 60, 62
Christian-social Union, 118
Chuan Leekpai, 197
Citizenry
in concordance theory, 32, 33–34
in Venezuela, 60–61, 65–66, 68
See also Political culture
Civic Forum, 108
Civilian institutions, 37, 56
Civilian interests
and threat perceptions, 9–12, 11(table),
254
and threat perceptions in Venezuela,
65–66
Civilians of the Right (Chile), 163
Civil-military relations
in Argentina, 79–97
in Brazil, 225–229, 231, 235(n7)
in Chile, 168, 169–184, 175(table)
civilian-dominant, 77–78, 238–241
and consolidation of democracy, 17–18,
25, 243–247, 247(table), 256, 256(n5)
in Czechoslovakia, 106–107, 110–114,
115
in Czech Republic, 118–119, 128–129
determinants of, 3–6, 4(table)
in Guatemala, 208, 210, 215, 219–221
Indonesian, 45, 48–57
pacted, 7–8, 163–164, 241–242
in Poland, 134–136, 136–137, 142–148,
152–153, 153–157, 158(n10)
and politics of threat identification,
9–16

and regional relations, 1–2, 19–21,
20(table), 247–256, 249(fig.),
253(table), 255(table)
in Slovakia, 123–127, 129
in Thailand, 187–203
theory and, 27–34, 132, 134–136
types of, 6–9, 9(table), 238–243,
239(table), 240(fig.)
in Venezuela, 59, 60, 63–65, 70–72,
74(n19), 75(n45)
CMEA. *See* Council for Mutual Economic
Assistance
Cohen, Stephen, 33, 38
Cold War, 188
Colombia, 70, 250
Commission on Truth and Reconciliation,
174
Committee of Peasants United (CUC), 214
Communism
and Czechoslovakia, 103–104, 105, 107
and Poland, 133–134, 162(n87)
and Thailand, 188, 189, 191
Communist Party (Czechoslovakia), 112
Concertación por la Democracia, 167, 173
Concordance theory, 27–29, 31–34, 34–35,
42–43
and India, 35–38
and Pakistan, 38–41
Conference on Security and Cooperation
in Europe (CSCE), 109–110
Conflict/unrest
and Argentine border disputes, 80–82
and Brazil, 224
and Chile, 169, 174–178, 175(table), 181
civil war in Pakistan, 41
and Guatemala, 206, 211, 221(n5),
222(n12)
Indian domestic, 35, 37
role of civil-military relations in, 1–2
in Thailand, 188, 189, 193
and Venezuela, 67–68, 69–70
Congress Party (India), 36, 42
Constitutional Tribunal (Poland), 156
Constitutive rules
Brazil, 226, 235(n7)
Chile, 163, 167–168, 170, 171, 172,
173–174, 178, 183

China, 251
Czech/Slovak republics, 108–109, 116
in determining civil-military relations,
2–3, 5–6, 8–9, 9(table), 238–243
Guatemala, 212, 214
Indonesia, 50, 252
Poland, 137–139, 154, 156, 159(n17)
regional security and, 247
Thailand, 188, 189, 193, 194
Venezuela, 62–65, 67, 73(n11)
Contadora Group, 208, 250
Contreras, Manuel, 175, 176, 177
Conventional Forces in Europe (CFE)
Treaty, 145, 150
Coordinating Committee of Agricultural,
Commercial, Industrial, and
Financial Associations (CACIF), 207
COPEI. *See* Christian Socialist Party
Cornett, María Dolores, 25, 239
Corporatism
in Chile, 167, 183
and civil-military relations, 239, 241, 242
Correa, Enrique, 176
Corruption/abuse of power, 47, 51–52
Costa, Thomaz Guedes da, 164, 241, 245,
250
Costa Rica, 218
Council for Mutual Economic Assistance
(CMEA), 103
Council of Ethnic Communities (CERJ),
214
Crime, 120, 149, 220, 233–234
CSCE. *See* Conference on Security and
Cooperation in Europe
CSFR. *See* Czech and Slovak Federal
Republic; Czechoslovak Socialist
Federal Republic
Cuba, 14
CUC. *See* Committee of Peasants United
Culture. *See* Political culture
Czech and Slovak Federal Republic
(CSFR), 108
Czechoslovakia
civil-military relations in, 243
prior to 1989, 102–107
transition and, 101, 107–115, 128,
130(n6)

Czechoslovak Socialist Federal Republic
    (CSFR), 104
Czech Republic
    civil-military relations in, 7, 77,
        118–119, 128–129, 142, 238–239
    and democracy, 244
    domestic politics, 115–116
    economic liberalization and, 5, 255
    foreign policy/regional integration, 114,
        116–118, 120–121, 248, 252, 254
    image of military in, 104–105, 106, 118,
        119
    and Slovakia, 127
Czech Socialist Republic, 104

Dalai Lama, 197–198
DCG. See Democracia Christiana
    Guatemalteca
de Carvalho, Jose Carlos Jacob, 236(n15)
Decisionmaking, 33
De-communization, 146
Defense/foreign policy
    Argentine, 79–80, 82, 83, 84, 85–97,
        98(n26)
    Brazilian, 229, 230–232, 233, 234
    Chilean, 168, 169–171, 179–181,
        182–183
    civil-military relations in, 256
    Czechoslovakia, 109–110, 114–115
    Czech Republic, 115, 116–118, 120–121
    Guatemalan, 217–219, 220
    Polish, 148–153
    Slovakian, 122–123, 127–128
    Thai, 197–198, 250
Defense industry, 33, 231
de Leon Carpio, Ramiro, 212
Democracia Christiana Guatemalteca
    (DCG), 213
Democracy, 2
    and Argentina, 93
    and Brazil, 224–225
    and Chile, 167–168, 171, 179
    and civil-military partnerships, 163–164
    civil-military relations in consolidation
        of, 1, 17–18, 21(n1), 24(n51), 25,
        243–247, 247(table), 256, 256(n5)
    and Guatemala, 207–221

and Indonesia, 45–48, 53–57, 257(n8)
and NATO, 161(n65)
and Poland, 150, 153
and Thailand, 190, 191, 195–196,
    201–203
in Venezuela, 60–61, 62–63
Democracy in Thailand, 195
Democratic Front of the New Guatemala
    (FDNG), 214
Democratic Left Alliance (SLD), 140, 141
Democratic-modernizers, 167–168, 183
Dictatorships, 7, 60
DiPalma, Giuseppe, 24(n51)
Diplomacy
    and Argentina, 89–90, 91, 96
    and Chile, 169–170
    and Guatemala, 208, 212, 218
    and Thailand, 200
Discrimination, 39–41, 102, 113
di Tella, Guido, 90, 93
Djiwandono, J. Soedjati, 25, 242, 246
Dobrovsky, Lubos, 112
Doctrine of national security (NSD), 83,
    98(n11)
Domestic policy, 82–83
Dominant-subordinate relationship, 6–7,
    134
Drawsko affair, 141
Dwifungsi, 45, 48–57, 242

EC. See European Community
Economic policy, 226
    Argentina, 91–92, 94
    Brazil, 224–225, 229–230
    Chile, 165–166, 168
    Czechoslovakia, 109
    Guatemala, 215–216
    Thailand, 190, 191, 196–197, 199–201,
        202
    Venezuela, 62–63, 66, 67–68
    See also Liberalization; Regional
        agreements
Economy
    and Slovakia, 109, 130(n6)
    in Thailand, 200–201
    and Venezuela, 60–61
Education, 71, 107, 146, 186(n31)

EGP. *See* Ejército Guerrillero de los Pobres
Ejercicio de enlace, 175–176
Ejército Guerrillero de los Pobres (EGP), 211
El Salvador, 208
Environment, 170
Escudé, Carlos, 88
Espinoza, Pedro, 176
Esquipulas II Agreement, 207, 208, 218–219
Ethnic conflict
    and Czechoslovakia, 102–104, 108, 112–113
    and India, 251
    modernization as accentuating, 101
    and Slovakia, 120, 127, 248
EU. *See* European Union
European Community (EC), 208, 209
European Union (EU), 248, 255
    and Brazil, 225
    and Chile, 168
    and Czechoslovakia, 109
    and Czech Republic, 116

FAR. *See* Fuerzas Armadas Rebeldes
FDNG. *See* Democratic Front of the New Guatemala
FEDECAMARAS (Venezuela), 67, 68
Federation for Democracy (Thailand), 193
Feit, Edward, 38, 40
Foreign investment, 118
Foreign policy. *See* Defense/foreign policy
Foz de Iguazú Declaration, 91
Free Legion, 112
Frei Ruiz-Tagle, Eduardo, 167, 179
Fuentes, Claudio, 163, 241–242
Fuerzas Armadas Rebeldes (FAR), 210, 211

Gajdos, Jozef, 125
Galtieri, General, 86
Gandhi, Indira, 245
Gandhi, Mahatma, 38
Geertz, Clifford, 43(n8)
Geopolítica, 82
Geopolitics, 13, 80–82, 84. *See also* Regional relations

Germany
    and Czechoslovakia, 103, 105, 106–107
    and Czech Republic, 114, 117, 118, 120
Globalization
    and Brazil, 224, 225, 229–231, 235(n1)
    effect on Chile, 165
    and Thailand, 202
    and type of civil-military relations, 255–256
Golkar (Functional Group), 47
Gómez Sucre, Gisela, 239
Gomulka, Wladyslaw, 133
Gramajo, Hector, 218
Grand strategy, 1, 184(n1)
    and Brazil, 224–225, 229
    and Chile, 165–166
Graterol, Moisés Orozco, 70
Great Britain, 217, 251
Greece, 161(n65)
Guatemala
    civil-military relations in, 7, 163–164, 241, 242, 243
    and democracy, 2, 206–221, 246
    economic liberalization and, 255
    and regional relations, 248, 251
Guevara, Aníbal Angel, 206, 212
Gulf War (1991), 86, 94–95, 152

Havel, Vaclav, 108, 111, 115, 130(n6)
Hemispheric strategies, 94
Historical institutionalism, 154–155
Historical sociology, 1–2
Holan, Vilem, 118
Human/civil rights, 5–6
    and Argentina, 87
    and Brazil, 227
    and Chile, 174, 176, 177, 178
    and Guatemala, 208
    and Indonesia, 47–48
Hungarian minorities, 123
Hungary
    constitution, 156
    and Czechoslovakia, 103, 106–107, 110
    and Czech Republic, 114
    1956 revolution, 14–15

perceptions of military in, 106
and Slovakia, 113, 115, 123, 127, 128, 248
HZDS. *See* Movement for a Democratic Slovakia

IAEDEN. *See* Instituto de Altos Estudios de la Defensa Nacional
IFOR operation, 117, 123
Independent Democratic Union (UDI), 167
India
and Brazil, 225
civil-military relations in, 25, 28–29, 35–38, 241, 242
and democracy, 2, 245
economic liberalization and, 255
martial races theory and, 40–41
and regional relations, 41–42, 248, 250, 251
Indonesia
civil-military relations in, 7, 25, 45, 48–57, 241, 242, 243
and democracy, 2, 45–48, 246, 257(n8)
political culture, 5
and regional relations, 248, 250, 251–252, 252–254
Indonesian Democratic Party (PDI), 47
Indonesian National Army (TNI), 49, 57(n5)
Industrial/agrarian coalition, 11–12
Industrial/agrarian/labor coalition, 12
Industrial/labor coalition, 10–11
and Slovakia, 114–115, 127
Information asymmetries, 134–135
Instability, political
and Chile, 167
and Guatemala, 219
and Poland, 140–142, 155
and Slovakia, 126–127, 127–128, 129
and Thailand, 196
See also Conflict/unrest
Institutional analysis, 28, 30
Instituto de Altos Estudios de la Defensa Nacional (IAEDEN), 65, 72
Instituto de Prevision Militar (IPM), 216
Interest-group politics, 2

International relations
and Brazil, 229–234
and Chile, 166, 182–183
and Guatemala, 213
and Thailand, 197–198, 199–201
See also Regional relations
IPM. *See* Instituto de Prevision Militar
Itaipú, 82
IUPFAN. *See* Polytechnic Institute of the armed forces

Japan, 225
Jarpa, Sergio Onofre, 176
Jaruzelski, Wojciech, 137, 138, 146, 159(n17)
Johnson, Carlos Molina, 176
Judiciary system, 24(n50)
Brazil, 226–227
Chile, 170
Guatemala, 220
Indonesia, 47, 48

Kanis, Pavol, 125
Karkoszka, Andrzej, 147, 156
Khan, Ayub, 39
King Bhumipol (Thailand), 189, 191, 193, 196
Kiszczak, Czeslaw, 137
Kitschelt, Herbert, 108–109
Klaus, Vaclav, 116
Kolodko, Grzegorz, 147–148
Kolodziejczyk, Piotr, 141
Komorowski, Bronislaw, 142
Koziej, Stanislaw, 144
Kramer, Mark, 78, 244
Kriangsak Chamanand, 189–190
Kwasniewski, Aleksander, 141, 153

Laguna del Desierto, 90
Laos, 200
Larrazabal, Wolfgang, 64
La Tablada, 85
Laugerud, Kjell, 211
Law on the Post of National Defense Minister (Poland), 139, 143
Law on Universal Military Duty (Poland), 138

Leadership, political
in concordance theory, 31–32
and Indonesian *Dwifungsi,* 55–56
in Pakistan, 38
in Venezuela, 69
Letelier, Orlando, 176, 185(n23)
Ley de Cobre, 174, 184(n2)
Liberalization, 3
and Brazil, 229–230
and Czechoslovakia, 108–109
and Czech Republic, 117
and Guatemala, 213–215, 220–221
and regional relations, 19–21
and Slovakia, 114–115, 121, 122
and type of civil-military relations, 7, 8,
254–256, 255(table)
See also Democracy; Economic policy;
Transition
Loveman, Brian, 256(n5)
Lucas García, Romero, 211–212, 213
Luczak, Aleksander, 148

Mainwaring, Scott, 17
Malaysia, 251–252, 254
Malvinas War, 79, 84, 86–87, 98(n20)
Mares, David, 129, 132
MAS. *See* Movement of Solidarity Action
Mayer, Hernan Patiño, 100(n52)
Mazowiecki, Tadeusz, 137, 139
McCubbins, Mathew D., 158(n10)
Meciar, Vladimir, 121, 124, 125, 126
Media, 177, 207
Mejía Victores, Oscar, 214
Méndez, Amilcar, 214
Méndez Montenegro, Julio Castro, 211
Menem, Carlos, 88, 90, 93, 94–95, 244
Mercado Común del Sur (MERCOSUR),
91–92, 168, 184(n7), 255
and Brazil, 224, 225, 229, 230, 234
MERCOSUR. *See* Mercado Común del
Sur
Mexico, 217, 220, 251
Milewski, Jerzy, 143
Militarism, 3–5
and Indonesia, 52–53
and types of civil-military relations, 7,
8–9, 241

Military
in Brazil, 228–229, 236(n15)
in Chile, 172, 178–181, 183–184
in concordance theory, 31, 34
and crisis in Venezuela, 68–70
and Czech Republic, 104–106, 110, 115,
118, 119, 120–121
in Guatemala, 206–207, 216–217, 218
in India, 37–38
in Pakistan, 40–41
in Poland, 133–134, 137–142, 142–151,
153–157, 160(n40)
and political transition in
Czechoslovakia, 111–114
roles of, 133, 158(n7)
Slovak, 123, 125–126, 127–128
in Thailand, 198–199, 199(table)
See also Civil-military relations; Officer
corps; Recruitment, military;
Resources, military
Military interests
and threat perceptions, 12–16,
15(table)
and threat perceptions in Venezuela, 66
Military intervention
concordance *versus* separation theory in
predicting, 27–34, 41–42
and Pakistan, 38–39
Military Police, Brazil, 227
MINUGUA. *See* United Nations Observer
Mission
MLN. *See* Movimiento de Liberación
Modernization, military. *See*
Professionalization/modernization,
military
Montenegro, Nineth, 214
Moravcik, Jozef, 121, 125
Movement for a Democratic Slovakia
(HZDS), 121, 122, 124, 125
Movement of Solidarity Action (MAS),
207
Movimiento de Liberación (MLN), 213
Movimiento Revolucionario 13 de
Noviembre (MR-13), 210–211
MR-13. *See* Movimiento Revolucionario 13
de Noviembre
Muslim Scholars' Association (NU), 47

NACC. *See* North Atlantic Cooperation
    Council
NAFTA. *See* North American Free Trade
    Agreement
Nasution, Abdul Haris, 49
National Defense Commissions (Poland),
    144
Nationalism
    and Czech/Slovak states, 102, 108,
        112–113, 114–115, 118, 121
    and Russia, 248
National Renewal Party (RN), 167, 184(n3)
National security. *See* Threat perception
National Security Council (Chile), 173,
    176, 177, 178
NATO. *See* North American Treaty
    Organization
Nehru, Jawaharlal, 38
Neopatrimonialism, 5, 9
NGOs. *See* Nongovernmental
    organizations
Nicaragua, 87, 206, 208
Nongovernmental organizations (NGOs),
    207, 209
North American Free Trade Agreement
    (NAFTA), 168, 182, 215
North American Treaty Organization
    (NATO)
    and Czechoslovakia, 110
    and Czech Republic, 116, 117, 119,
        120–121
    military roles and acceptance into, 136
    and Poland, 133, 137, 143, 150–153, 157
    and regional security, 248
    and Slovakia, 122, 123, 125, 128
North Atlantic Cooperation Council
    (NACC), 151
NPT. *See* Nuclear Non-Proliferation Treaty
NSD. *See* Doctrine of national security
NU. *See* Muslim Scholars' Association
Nuclear Non-Proliferation Treaty (NPT),
    41
Nuclear weapons, 41–42, 90–91, 99(n38)

O'Donnell, Guillermo, 17
OECD. *See* Organization for Economic
    Cooperation and Development

Officer corps
    concordance theory and composition of,
        32–33
    and Czechoslovakia, 106, 107, 111–112,
        113
    and Czech Republic, 118–119, 120
    Guatemalan, 216, 220–221
    Indian, 35–36
    Pakistani, 39–40
    Polish, 144, 146, 158(n11)
    and Slovakia, 124
    Thai, 195
    Venezuelan, 64
Okonski, Zbigniew, 141
Oleksy, Jozef, 141
Olszewski, Jan, 140
Onyszkiewicz, Janusz, 140, 142, 143, 147
Organic-corporatist political culture, 3, 9
Organización del Pueblo en Armas
    (ORPA), 211
Organizational theory, 2, 13–16
Organization for Economic Cooperation
    and Development (OECD), 117
Organization on Security and Cooperation
    in Europe (OSCE), 153
ORPA. *See* Organización del Pueblo en
    Armas
OSCE. *See* Organization on Security and
    Cooperation in Europe

Pakistan
    civil-military relations in, 25, 28, 29,
        38–41, 241, 242, 243
    economic liberalization and, 255
    and regional relations, 248, 251
Paraguay, 91, 234, 248
Parallel-spheres-of-action relationship, 8
Partido Institucional Democrático (PLD),
    213
Partido Revolucionario (PR), 211, 213
Partido Social Demócrata (PSD), 213
Partnership for Peace (PfP), 117, 123, 128,
    152, 157
Party of Democracy, 173
Party of the Democratic Left (SDL), 121
Parys, Jan, 140, 142
Pastusiak, Longin, 141

Pawlak, 141
PDI. *See* Indonesian Democratic Party
People's Republic of China (PRC), 41–42,
    197–198, 225, 250, 251
Peralta Azurdia, Enrique, 210
Pérez, Carlos Andrés, 67, 68
Pérez Jiménez, Marcos, 60
Peru, 92, 182, 230, 250, 251
Peucazo, 175–176, 177
PfP. *See* Partnership for Peace
Pilsudski, Jozef, 133
Pinochet, Augusto, 7, 163, 167, 171, 172,
    173, 174, 175, 176, 185(nn 17, 19), 245
Pion-Berlin, David, 77, 248
PLD. *See* Partido Institucional
    Democrático
Poland
    civil-military relations in, 7, 77–78,
        133–136, 142–148, 153–157, 238–239
    and Czechoslovakia, 103, 110
    and Czech Republic, 114, 117–118, 120
    economic liberalization and, 255
    regional relations/foreign policy,
        148–153, 248, 252, 254
    and Slovakia, 127
    transition and, 136–137, 137–142
Polish Peasants' Party (PSL), 140–141
Polish United Workers' Party (PZPR), 136,
    137, 138
Political culture, 43(n7)
    and Argentina, 84–85
    and Brazil, 225–226
    and Chile, 166, 182
    in consolidating democracy, 18
    and Czech image of military, 104–105,
        110, 129
    and Guatemala, 207
    Indonesian, 48, 54
    and Poland, 142, 144, 154, 155
    and separation *versus* concordance
        theory, 30, 32
    and Thailand, 188, 194, 202
    and transition in Czechoslovakia,
        108–109
    and types of civil-military relations, 2,
        3–5, 4(table), 7, 8–9, 9(table), 238–243
    Venezuelan, 60–61

Political parties
    in Chile, 167, 173
    Czechoslovakian, 108
    and Czech Republic, 116
    Guatemalan, 213–215, 221(n5)
    Polish, 140–141
    Slovakian, 121–122
    Thai, 190, 201
    Venezuelan, 62–63, 65–66
Politics
    Brazil, 223
    Chile, 166–168, 173, 178, 183
    Czechoslovakia, 108–109
    Czech Republic, 116, 118
    Guatemala, 210, 213–214
    Slovakia, 121–122, 131(n15)
    Thailand, 188, 200–201
    See also Constitutive rules;
        Liberalization; Transition
Polytechnic Institute of the armed forces
    (IUPFAN), 65
PR. *See* Partido Revolucionario
PRC. *See* People's Republic of China
Prem Tinsoulanon, 190, 191
Presidential power, Indonesia, 47, 48
Principal-agent theory, 132, 134–136,
    153–154
Proceso de Reorganización Nacional
    (Argentina), 79, 80–84
Professionalization/modernization,
    military, 55
    Argentine, 86–87, 98(n20)
    and Chile, 168, 178–181
    and Czech Republic, 119
    and democratic consolidation,
        17–18
    and ethnic conflict, 101
    Guatemalan, 215
    Polish, 147
    in separation theory, 29–30
    Thai, 195, 202
    Venezuelan, 66, 70–71, 72
PSD. *See* Partido Social Demócrata
PSL. *See* Polish Peasants' Party
Public Against Violence, 108
PZPR. *See* Polish United Workers'
    Party

Radical Party (Chile), 173
Rational-choice theory, 154
Reagan, Ronald, 87, 93
Recruitment, military
    and concordance theory, 30, 33–34
    in India, 36, 41
    in Pakistan, 40
Regional agreements, 19–21, 255
    and Brazil, 224, 230
    and Chile, 168, 184(n7)
    and Guatemala, 215
    MERCOSUR, 91–92
    See also specific agreements
Regional relations
    and Argentina, 80–82, 88–93, 96
    and Brazil, 223, 224, 229–234
    and Chile, 168–171, 182–183
    cooperation in, 22(n2), 248–254
    and Czechoslovakia, 106–107, 110,
        114–115
    and Czech Republic, 116–118,
        120–121
    and Guatemala, 208–209, 213, 217–219,
        220, 221
    and Poland, 148–150
    and Slovakia, 127–128
    and South Asia, 41–42
    and Thailand, 197–198, 199–201
    types of civil-military relations and,
        1–2, 19–21, 20(table), 129,
        247–254, 249(fig.), 253(table),
        255(table)
    and Venezuela, 61–62, 69–70
Renationalization, 145–146
Repression, domestic
    and Argentine dictatorship, 82–83, 87
    and Guatemala, 207
    and Indonesia, 246
    and Poland, 156
    and Thailand, 189
Resources, military, 14, 15, 16, 33
    Argentine, 80
    and Brazil, 227–228
    and Chile, 174, 184(n2)
    and Czech/Slovak states, 114, 119, 124,
        125–126, 128
    and Guatemala, 216

and Poland, 146–148, 150, 155
and Thailand, 198–199, 199(table),
    205(n51)
Rios Montt, Efraín, 211, 212, 213, 214
RN. See National Renewal Party
Rojas, Francisco, 163, 241–242
Rojas, Patricio, 174, 176, 177
Rozbicki, Wieslaw, 145, 156
Russell, Roberto, 82
Russia, 248
    and Brazil, 225
    and Czech Republic, 114, 120
    and Poland, 149, 151–152, 156–157
    and Slovakia, 122–123, 126, 127, 128

Sardenberg, Ronaldo Mota, 229
Sarney, José, 99(n38)
Schiff, Rebecca, 17, 25, 241, 242, 245
Schwartz, Thomas, 158(n10)
SDL. See Party of the Democratic Left
Separation theory, 27–31
Sereseres, Caesar, 163, 242, 251
Serrano, Jorge, 207, 212, 214
Sistema de Vigilancia da Amazonia
    (SIVAM), 233
Sitek, Jan, 125
SIVAM. See Sistema de Vigilancia da
    Amazonia
Siwicki, Florian, 137
SLD. See Democratic Left Alliance
Slovak National Party (SNS), 112–113, 121,
    122, 124, 125
Slovak Republic
    civil-military relations in, 77, 123–127,
        129, 238, 239, 241
    and Czech Republic, 116, 120
    domestic politics, 121–122
    economic liberalization and, 255
    foreign policy/regional relations,
        114–115, 122–123, 127–128, 248, 252,
        254
    political culture, 5, 105–106
Slovak Socialist Republic, 104
Slovak state, 103
Small Constitution (Poland), 138–139
Smith, Louis, 30
SNS. See Slovak National Party

Snyder, Jack, 157
Social coalition analysis, 9–12
Social Democrats (Chile), 173
Socialist Party (Chile), 173
Sociological institutionalism, 154
Soeharto, President (Indonesia), 7, 46–47, 49, 50, 52–53, 242, 243, 246, 252, 254
Solidarity, 136, 140, 143
South Asia, 41–42
Soviet Union
  and Czechoslovakia, 104, 105, 111, 115
  and Czech Republic, 114
Soviet Union, former, 148, 149
Sri Lanka, 41
Stelmaszuk, Zdzislaw, 146, 151
Stepan, Alfred, 18, 22(11), 23(n19), 202–203
Study on NATO Enlargement, 152–153, 157
Suchinda Kraprayoon, 192, 193
Suchocka, Hanna, 140
Sucre, Gisela Gómez, 25
Sukarno, President (Indonesia), 46, 49, 242, 254
Sunthorn Kongsompong, 192
Szayna, Thomas S., 77, 241, 244, 248
Szeremetiew, Renuald, 143

Tela Accords, 208
Tesoro Beach Agreement, 208
Thailand
  civil-military relations in, 7, 141, 163, 187–203, 238, 239, 242–243
  and democracy, 2, 244–245
  political culture, 5
  and regional relations, 248, 250, 252
Thanin Kraivichien, 189
Threat perception
  Argentina and, 80–97
  and Chile, 166, 168–171, 182–183
  and civilian interests, 9–12, 11(table)
  and Czechoslovakia, 107, 110, 111
  and Czech Republic, 114, 117, 120, 129
  democracy and, 244
  and Guatemala, 215–216
  and military interests, 12–16, 15(table), 136, 247–254
  and Poland, 148–149, 150, 151, 156–157

and Slovakia, 113, 115, 123, 128, 129
and Thailand, 188, 189, 195, 196
and typology of civil-military relations, 6–9
and Venezuela, 65–66
Tibet, 197–198
TNI. *See* Indonesian National Army
Transition
  and Brazil, 223–225
  and Chile, 172–173, 174–178
  and civil-military partnerships, 163–164
  and Czechoslovakia, 101, 107–109, 111–114
  and Poland, 136–137
  and principal-agent relationships, 135
  and Thailand, 188–194
  See also Liberalization
Treaty of Asunción, 91
Treaty of Peace and Friendship, 89
Turcios Lima, Luis, 210
Turkey, 161(n65)
Tuyuc, Rosalina, 214

Ubico, Jorge, 209
UCN. *See* Unión del Centro Nacional
UDI. *See* Independent Democratic Union
Ukraine, 114, 120, 127, 149
Unión del Centro Nacional (UCN), 213, 215
Unión República Democrática (URD), 62
Unión Revolucionaria Nacional de Guatemala (URNG), 209, 212, 213, 214
United Nations
  and Guatemala, 208, 209
  peacekeeping missions, 95, 117, 123, 128, 152, 232, 234, 236(n14)
United Nations Administration in Eastern Slavonia (UNTAES), 123
United Nations Observer Mission (MINUGUA), 207–208
United States
  and Argentina, 87, 93–95, 248
  and Brazil, 224, 233
  and Chile, 182
  and Czechoslovakia, 110
  and Czech Republic, 117

and Guatemala, 208, 209–210
and Poland, 151, 152
as standard in separation theory, 29–30
and threat perception, 12
and Venezuela, 62
UNTAES. *See* United Nations
Administration in Eastern Slavonia
URD. *See* Unión República Democrática
URNG. *See* Unión Revolucionaria
Nacional de Guatemala
Uruguay, 91, 248

Vacek, Milan, 111, 112
Vaclavik, Milan, 111
Valenzuela, J. Samuel, 17
Valmoval scandal, 175, 176
Venezuela
civilian/military interests, 65–66
civil-military relations in, 7, 8, 25, 59,
70–72, 238, 239
constitutive rules/democracy, 62–65, 244
economic liberalization and, 255
political crisis in, 67–70, 75(n38)
political culture, 3, 60–61
regional relations, 61–62, 92, 230, 248,
250, 252, 254, 257(n12)
Venezuelan Workers' Confederation, 67,
68
Victores, Mejía, 213
Vietnam, 14, 195, 252

Vietnam War, 190–191
Villalonga, Julio, 99(n47)
Viola, Roberto, 86
Visegrad group, 110, 116
Voranat Apicharee, 195

Walesa, Lech, 139, 140, 141, 145, 146, 151,
154
Warsaw Pact, 103, 105, 107, 111
Weapons
and Brazil, 232, 236(n23)
and Indonesia, 252
and Poland, 147, 149–150
and Thailand, 198–199, 250
See also Nuclear weapons
Western European Union (WEU), 151
WEU. *See* Western European Union
Wilecki, Tadeusz, 141, 150, 153
Wimol Wongvanich, 197
World War II, 105, 106

Ydigoras Fuentes, Miguel, 206, 210
Yon Sosa, Marco Antonio, 211
Yugoslavia, 123

Zabala, Carlos M., 100(n53)
Zabinski, Krzysztof, 139
Zhang Wannian, 198
ZRS. *See* Association of Workers of
Slovakia